P9-DDR-931

85421
Hampstead Public Library

6/10

WITHDRAWN

HAMPSTEAD PUBLIC LIBRARY

ALSO BY JOAN BISKUPIC

*Sandra Day O'Connor: How the First Woman on the Supreme Court
Became Its Most Influential Justice*

AMERICAN ORIGINAL

AMERICAN ORIGINAL

The Life and Constitution of
Supreme Court Justice Antonin Scalia

———◆———

JOAN BISKUPIC

HAMPSTEAD PUBLIC LIBRARY
9 MARY E CLARK DRIVE
HAMPSTEAD, NH 03841

SARAH CRICHTON BOOKS

FARRAR, STRAUS AND GIROUX

NEW YORK

Sarah Crichton Books
Farrar, Straus and Giroux
18 West 18th Street, New York 10011

Copyright © 2009 by Joan Biskupic
All rights reserved
Distributed in Canada by D&M Publishers, Inc.
Printed in the United States of America
First edition, 2009

Library of Congress Cataloging-in-Publication Data
Biskupic, Joan.
    American original : the life and constitution of Supreme Court Justice Antonin
Scalia / Joan Biskupic.— 1st ed.
        p.   cm.
    Includes bibliographical references and index.
    ISBN 978-0-374-20289-7 (hardcover : alk. paper)
    1. Scalia, Antonin.   2. Judges—United States—Biography.   3. Constitutional law—
United States.   I. Title.

KF8745.S33 B57 2009
347.73'2634—dc22
[B]

                                                                    2009015636

Designed by Jonathan D. Lippincott

www.fsgbooks.com

3   5   7   9   10   8   6   4   2

For Clay and Elizabeth

B4T 28.00 6113

Lawyers, I suppose, were children once.
                    —Charles Lamb, "The Old Benchers of the Inner Temple"

We have not just learned about life, we have learned about people. People at their worst. By and large, human fault and human perfidy are what the cases are about. We have seen the careless, the avaricious, the criminal, the profligate, the foolhardy, parade across the pages of the case reports. We have seen evil punished and virtue rewarded. But we have also seen prudent evil flourish and foolish virtue fail. We have seen partners become antagonists, brothers and sisters become contesting claimants, lovers become enemies. It does tend, as Charles Lamb suggested, to shatter the illusions of childhood rather quickly. Hence the image of the lawyer as the skeptical realist. Expect to find here no more a dreamer than a poet . . . Billy Budd, Pollyanna, and Mr. Micawber could never have been lawyers.
                    —Antonin Scalia, speech to law school graduates, 1984

CONTENTS

AMERICAN ORIGINAL

PROLOGUE

———————•·◦·•———————

On a raised dais at Washington's luxurious Mayflower Hotel, the Supreme Court justice Antonin Scalia is in high performance mode. His comic timing is precise. Laughter and applause ripple on cue from the five hundred lawyers packed into the ballroom. Gone in an eyeblink is most of his scheduled hour. The moderator announces that there will be one final question.

"Make it easy," Scalia jokes, standing at the lectern, in especially fine spirits on this blustery November afternoon. "You can make it like Senator Strom Thurmond's first question to me when I was up for my confirmation." The South Carolina Republican had presided over the Senate Judiciary Committee hearings for Scalia in 1986, when he was nominated by President Reagan for elevation from a federal appeals court. Thurmond had opened with a question that played right into Scalia's view that judges were wrongly going beyond the letter of the law to solve society's larger problems, whether they related to school busing, prison crowding, or environmental catastrophes. These were conflicts Scalia believed should be left in the domain of elected lawmakers.

" 'Now, Judge Scalia,' " Scalia says, mimicking the slow patois of Senator Thurmond, " 'what do you think of judicial activism?' "

Scalia turns sideways at the lectern and puts his hands together as if at the plate and ready to swing a baseball bat. The sleeves of his dark suit yank up, flashing his thick white shirt cuffs.

"I'm ready for that pitch," he says.

The Scalia illuminated by camera lights at this closing session of the

2008 annual conference of the Federalist Society is heavier than the
man America first saw at the witness table in 1986 on nationwide television. His jowls are thicker, his waist wider. His dark black hair has
thinned. Yet his eyes are lit, as always. Into his seventies, Scalia still exudes
energy and passion. His gestures are operatic. He points his fingers and
waves his arms for emphasis. His audiences at these public occasions, irrespective of whether they are conservative or liberal, continue to be large
and are nearly always captivated. When Scalia enters a room, cameras still
flash. This afternoon at the conservative legal society's convention his
audience is standing room only and hanging on his every word and
gesture.

With his biting humor, Scalia has been advancing the legal theory
known as "originalism"—insisting that judges should render constitutional decisions based on the eighteenth-century understanding of the
text. "It's a fight worth making," he says in remarks that are part battle cry,
part assertion of victory.

"I used to be able to say, with a good deal of truth, that you could fire
a cannon loaded with grapeshot into the faculty lounge of any law school
in the country and not strike an originalist," Scalia says, referring to those
of the view that the Constitution has a "constant" meaning, one that does
not change to fit the needs of a changing society. "That no longer is true.
Originalism—which once was orthodoxy—at least now has been returned
to the status of respectability."

He says that until contemporary times—"the last fifty years or so"—
judges interpreted the Constitution to mean what it meant when it was
adopted.[1] Whether the originalist view remained "orthodoxy" into the
twentieth century is debatable, but it was barely in evidence by the late
1950s as such judges as Chief Justice Earl Warren interpreted the Constitution to contain broad principles that could be applied to modern circumstances. These judges did not feel constrained by the framers'
understanding of what they had forbidden or allowed.

Gripping the sides of the lectern with his large, square hands, Scalia
has been recounting how his view of a "static" Constitution has been far-
ing better among federal judges these days.[2] He refers with satisfaction to
a recent landmark of his own Supreme Court that declared that the Second Amendment protects an individual's right to bear arms. The ruling
the previous June, written by Scalia, overturned decades of decisions by

lower court judges who had held that the Second Amendment applied only to state militias, such as state national guards. It was the first time the Supreme Court found that any law violated the Second Amendment, and it was a significant reversal of settled lower court law.[3] Especially striking was Scalia's authorship of the opinion. His no-compromise style had made him a hero on law school campuses but usually cost him votes among the justices. On the incendiary subject of gun rights, however, he was able to gain and keep the majority, helped by the youthful new chief justice, John Roberts, and the newest associate justice, Samuel Alito. The case, requiring interpretation of the Second Amendment's text and history, was the perfect match for Scalia's focus on the original intention of the men who drafted and ratified the Constitution.

"Maybe the original meaning of the Constitution is back," Scalia tells the Federalist Society. "We're not all back there yet, but maybe we're on the way."

A quarter century into his judicial odyssey, Scalia may be at the apex of his influence. Roberts and Alito, who had both worked in the Reagan administration, have long admired Scalia and the way he wages the good conservative fight. On the Court since 2005 and 2006, respectively, they have been voting with Scalia more than did William Rehnquist, the previous chief justice, and Sandra Day O'Connor, Alito's predecessor, whose moderate, consensus-seeking approach constantly thwarted Scalia.

Liberals such as Justices John Paul Stevens and Ruth Bader Ginsburg regard Scalia's ideas as perilous. They fear that if they were ever fully accepted by the nation's judges, the emphasis on individual rights established in the last half century—for the poor, the disenfranchised—would be lost.

Today in the chandeliered ballroom, however, Scalia is among the faithful, with his own. In 1982, when the Federalist Society was founded by students at Yale University and the University of Chicago to counter the liberalism of academia, Scalia was present. He was teaching at Chicago and became the faculty adviser to the founding students there. He helped the group raise money and attract prominent speakers. As the Federalist Society began to flourish, gaining wealth and adding members, Scalia was an A-list invitee for annual conferences. Now the society boasts up to forty thousand members and a record of influence, with three Republican presidents and their life-tenured appointments to federal courts.[4]

Two years before this occasion at the Mayflower, the Federalist Society celebrated Scalia at a black-tie dinner for his twenty years on the Supreme Court. "Over the last twenty years, Justice Scalia has done for the Court what President Reagan did for the presidency and the country," declared the Northwestern University law professor Steven Calabresi, one of the founding students at Yale. "He has by the force and clarity of his opinions become a defining figure in American constitutional law of the last two decades."[5]

Scalia had marched up to the stage, joined by his wife, Maureen, and all nine of their children. They smiled brightly, all grown-ups, yet jostling one another good-naturedly like children who had just emerged from a long trip in the family van.

"I really do much better at responding to criticism than at responding to praise," the man of the hour had said. "If you accept it as though it's really due, you're being conceited. If you reject it, you are being supposedly insincere or at least ungrateful. My favorite response has been one Lyndon Johnson used . . . 'I wish my parents could have been here. My father would have been proud and my mother would have believed it.' "

Scalia grew up an only child, the son of Salvatore Eugene Scalia and the former Catherine Panaro. Remarkably, he was also the only offspring of his generation from the entire Scalia and Panaro families. None of his mother's six siblings had a child. Neither did his father's only sibling, a sister. So "Nino," as he was called, became the center of attention for two tight-knit, striving Italian immigrant families. His father had come to America knowing little English, had earned a Ph.D. at Columbia University, and had spent three decades teaching Romance languages at Brooklyn College. The son did not let him down. He was valedictorian at New York's Xavier High School, first in his class at Georgetown University, and a magna cum laude graduate of Harvard Law School. A man of pride and ambition, Scalia advanced quickly through jobs in the Nixon and Ford administrations before ending up at the University of Chicago and then on the federal appeals court in Washington, D.C.

Onstage that night in 2006, Scalia saluted the next generation of his family. He motioned to his nine children—one, a priest wearing his collar, another, an army officer in uniform—and his wife, Maureen, the Radcliffe coed whom he had met while at Harvard and married in 1960. The justice called her "the product of the best decision I ever made, the mother of the nine children you see, the woman responsible for raising them with very little assistance from me . . . And there's not a dullard in the bunch!"

That was his moment in 2006. Now, in 2008, the jurist who is a combination of Felix Frankfurter and Luciano Pavarotti, entering the third act of his judicial career, is enjoying an encore. The Federalist Society is celebrating him as it does nearly every year in some way; this late Saturday afternoon there's less glitter than at the society's famously sumptuous dinners but no less gusto. Scalia's visage, bigger than life, is projected on a large screen to his right as he speaks at the Mayflower Hotel lectern.

The moderator, Leonard Leo, the executive vice president of the Federalist Society and an old Scalia friend, has been reading questions for the justice that have been penciled on small white cards and handed up from the audience. Someone asks whether the originalism approach has any theoretical flaws. Scalia pauses at first, seemingly struggling to find any shortcomings. Then, in response, he says that it is difficult for today's judges to know how the Constitution's drafters would respond to contemporary phenomena such as the Internet. He cautions that originalism is not perfect, yet adds, "But whatever our problems are, they pale next to the problems of the idea of the 'Living Constitution.' "

Another questioner notes that Scalia has called himself "a faint-hearted originalist." Oh, that was so long ago, the justice responds, referring to a 1989 law review article he wrote.[6] Scalia explains that he had used "faint-hearted" because he did not see how he, or any other judge, could vote to uphold, say, ear notching of criminals, as was allowed in the eighteenth century. If he were a true originalist, Scalia says, he would have to find ear notching today perfectly constitutional despite the Eighth Amendment ban on cruel and unusual punishment. Then he quips to the Federalist Society home crowd that maybe he could be a complete originalist these days: "I've gotten older and crankier." The audience laughs heartily.

A law student sends up a question asking what a Federalist Society member should do "in the face of militant or intolerant law professors or peers." Although the conservative legal group has developed legions of members across campuses, in law firms, and at government institutions, liberalism still dominates in law schools.

Equally significant, national politics has shifted dramatically away from conservatism. Just three weeks before the conference, on November 4, 2008, Barack Obama was elected president of the United States. This was a milestone, foremost because Obama became the first African American president, but also because his election was widely seen as the end of an era of conservatism.

In spite of that, this Federalist Society occasion is not solemn or melancholy. It is a celebration of the judicial victories that still can be claimed. Supreme Court justices reside in their own realm. At the taproot of the American legal system, the conservative legacy of three Republican presidents is still dominant, and Scalia is its central figure. It could be years before President Obama's judicial appointees are able to change the tenor of the law.[7]

Scalia also knows how to make headway against prevailing winds. He boasts that "one of my charms is that I tell people what they don't like to hear." Comfortable with tension and relishing debate, his rhetorical style is combative. But he does not enter every fight. He rebuffs criticism that his decisions are inconsistent or driven by a desire to achieve conservative goals. "I often come to decisions I don't like," he insists. He mentions that as a policy matter, he has endorsed deregulation of markets, but as a judge, he has voted to uphold regulation when federal law required it. Scalia often reminds audiences that he voted to strike down laws banning flag burning as political protest, although personally, "I don't like scruffy, bearded, sandal-wearing people who go around burning the United States flag."[8]

In response to the question about how to fight a disapproving professor, Scalia, a Roman Catholic, first jokes, "My mother used to say, 'Offer it up!' " Then he tells the audience: "Most of the professors I know . . . would welcome someone from the other side—who can serve as a foil—because they think they can beat you. That's why they publish my dissents in their casebooks!

"The harder question is, 'What do I do when it comes to writing the exam? Do I give him the answer he taught me to be the right answer?' " Scalia pauses for effect. "Yeah," he said. As his audience chortles, Scalia adds that it is best to save real protest for another day. "Wily as a serpent," he advises with a sly smile.

Now Scalia takes that final question, the one he is waiting to knock out of the park.

Reading from a white card, Leonard Leo asks Scalia how he reconciles his differing opinions in two well-known disputes, the 1995 *United States v. Lopez* and 2005 *Gonzales v. Raich* cases. Scalia voted in 1995 to overturn a federal law that regulated guns near schools because it trampled on state authority. Ten years later, he voted to uphold a federal drug law that voided a California policy allowing marijuana use for medical purposes, over dissenting justices' protests that the federal policy infringed on the states. The 2005 case had been brought by two seriously ill women who had cultivated marijuana under California's Compassionate Use Act. For the three years since, legal analysts had been buzzing over whether Scalia abandoned his abhorrence of federal intervention simply because he opposed the legalization of marijuana.

At the Court in 2005, Justice O'Connor had declared the two Scalia positions—forbidding the federal government to displace state choices about handgun regulation but letting it override state choices about drug laws—"irreconcilable." Justice Clarence Thomas, Scalia's usual soul mate on the law, had been equally critical of the notion that Congress could interfere with a carefully restricted marijuana law providing relief to the seriously ill. He had scoffed, "The federal government may now regulate quilting bees, clothes drives, and potluck suppers throughout the 50 states."[9]

The question on the little white card goes to the heart of Scalia's legacy: Is his brand of originalism simply a way to achieve conservative results? Does he talk a good game until his method fails to get him what he wants as a policy matter?

This afternoon Scalia is not going to engage such inquiry. "Oh no," he says, grimacing. "Get another question."

It has the ring of "Get over it!" That is Scalia's stock answer when someone in an audience wants him to address *Bush v. Gore,* the decision that stopped the presidential ballot recounts in Florida and gave George W. Bush the White House over Vice President Al Gore in 2000. The decision remained a political thorn in the side of the nation through Bush's two terms and, particularly for Scalia's critics, offered evidence of his willingness to abandon principle when it does not get him the outcome he desires.

At the Mayflower, the audience laughs when he says get another question. It is a friendly laugh. To them, there is nothing wrong with his ducking a hardball.

Leonard Leo sets aside the offending card and asks Scalia, "What's your favorite opera?"

Oh, says Scalia, there are so many works, all so different. He throws out some personal favorites: Strauss's comic opera *Der Rosenkavalier*, Puccini's tragic *Madama Butterfly*, Verdi's popular *La Traviata*. Then Scalia adds, "And I like country music, too."

As people leap to their feet and clap, he waves big and strides off.

HAMPSTEAD PUBLIC LIBRARY

ONE

A PLACE IN THE AMERICAN STORY

———————

The future Supreme Court justice entered the world at Mercer Hospital in Trenton, New Jersey, on a Wednesday during Lent, March 11, 1936. A ferocious rainstorm that day swelled the Delaware River over its banks and washed out railroad beds and highways.[1] Fervently anticipated, Antonin came seven years into the marriage of Salvatore Eugene Scalia and the former Catherine Panaro. He would be their only child.

Antonin's mother's parents, Pasquale and Maria Panaro, had come to America from Italy and married in New York City in 1904 before moving down to Trenton. Catherine, the eldest of their children, was born in 1905.[2] She was a serious and pretty girl who kept her dark hair pinned off her face. Born two years after Catherine was Grace, who was mentally handicapped. The doctors told Maria that Grace would survive only a few years, but she lived more than six decades, always in the family home. The other children followed, two boys, three more girls: Vincent, Eva, Rose, Anthony, and finally Lenora. The last child, forever known as "the Babe," was born in 1923 and was just twelve years old when her nephew Antonin came on the scene.

The Panaros' three-story row house at 334 North Broad Street in downtown Trenton was built in 1890 and soon stood in the shadow of the Battle Monument, erected three years later. The 150-foot-tall granite pillar paid tribute to George Washington and the soldiers who crossed the Delaware and defeated the British in the Battle of Trenton on the morning of December 26, 1776. High atop the monument was a bronze statue of the great commander and future first president. An elevator in the pillar ascended to an observatory deck, where the Panaros could look out to a downtown humming with department stores, movie palaces, and churches for the Irish, Italians, Poles, and other immigrants who had poured into the city. Even during the Depression, Trenton industries stayed busy. Smokestacks across the skyline marked plants producing vulcanized rubber for tires and steel cables for suspension bridges.[3] Dozens of Trenton plants specialized in ceramics and pottery, mainly sinks and tubs but also custom-decorated dinnerware. The Delaware River, dredged to a depth of twenty feet, opened New Jersey's capital city to seagoing ships and helped fulfill its boastful slogan: "Trenton Makes, the World Takes."

Over the years, the Panaro home doubled as a storefront tailor shop, dry cleaner, and saloon. Upstairs were two floors of living quarters: a parlor, dining room, and kitchen; three bedrooms; and a bathroom with a large bathtub on legs. There was steam heat and hardwood flooring. In the front room was a piano that Maria and her daughters played. "We always had music in the house," said Lenora, whose own name was chosen by her opera-loving father as a tribute to a character in Verdi's *Il Trovatore*.

Pasquale was an animated, effervescent figure who on New Year's Eve would be the first to lean out the upstairs window to clang pots and, in his thickly accented English, wish everyone "Happy New Year!" He worked as a tailor, making fine suits for the men in town until the Depression hit. Then he picked up an assortment of jobs, sometimes traveling to New York City for work. He mixed with other immigrants and became a leader in L'Ordine Figli d'Italia, the Order of the Sons of Italy, the community network for newly arrived Italians. He spent time with the ladies, too. When most of his children were grown, Pasquale left Maria and took up with a woman in New York City.[4]

Maria, a short, sturdy woman who loved hats and carried herself with poise despite the family weight on her shoulders, oversaw the clamorous home on North Broad Street with the help of her diligent children. Even as they became adults and took on various lines of work, many continued to live with their mother. Catherine, Antonin's mother, became an elementary school teacher, and Eva, too, taught school. Vincent was a lawyer who eventually ran for local political office, and Anthony dealt in real estate. Rose became a secretary, and Lenora, the Babe, eventually became a teacher as well. Grace, who could speak only a few words, was the responsibility of all.

The Panaros were hardy in the face of rocky economic times and the shock of the patriarch's departure. When one of their storefront businesses failed, they tried another. Maria eventually began acquiring other properties and showed herself to be a shrewd businesswoman. All the Panaro children attended Mass at St. Mary's Cathedral on Sundays, and even after some had married and moved on, all gathered at the family home for a traditional dinner after Mass.

In the early years of Antonin's life, in the late 1930s, his father, Salvatore Eugene Scalia, was in a wholly different orbit. He was as restrained as the Panaros were energetic. As they socialized about town, his head was in a book.

Salvatore Eugene was seventeen when he came through Ellis Island in December 1920. With his father, Antonino; his mother, Maria; and his younger sister, Carmela, he had left the village of Sommatino on the island of Sicily, sailing out of the Port of Palermo on the *Duca d'Aosta*, a 476-foot-long steam vessel carrying 1,800 passengers.

Like his father, Salvatore Eugene was a small man, just five feet five inches and weighing 125 pounds.[5] When father Antonino and son Salvatore petitioned for naturalization in 1923, and then in 1926 became U.S. citizens, they signed a declaration common to the era: "I am not an anarchist; I am not a polygamist nor a believer in the practice of polygamy . . . It is my bona fide intention to renounce forever all allegiance and fidelity to foreign sovereigns, particularly to King Victor Emmanuel III of Italy . . ."[6] As was the pattern of many new arrivals to America, the Scalias moved to Trenton because they had friends among the Sicilians who had already come to the New Jersey capital. Antonino, who had been a laborer in the sulfur mines of Sicily, held a series of factory jobs; his wife, Maria, sewed clothes in a plant.[7] Like many immigrants, they surrounded themselves with others from their home country and found little reason to learn more than a few words of English.

For the gifted son of the family, life was different. Salvatore Eugene, or Sam, as he was labeled at Ellis Island, ventured out creatively and intellectually. He quickly learned English. It became family lore that he would not even try out his new language in public until he had mastered it.[8] He had a fine voice and enrolled himself at the Eastman School of Music in far-off Rochester, New York. His stay, however, was brief. He tried running an

Italian American newspaper in Scranton, Pennsylvania. That, too, did not last long. Eventually Salvatore, who was more of an intellectual than an adventurer, concentrated on becoming a college professor. Antonin said later he suspected that his father, a perfectionist, may have realized that he was not going to excel in his earlier pursuits.[9] Salvatore Eugene earned a bachelor's degree at Rutgers University in 1931 and a master's at Columbia University in 1932, and he began working on a doctorate in Romance languages at Columbia.[10] He commuted between New York City and Trenton to be with Catherine, whom he married on August 19, 1929. At the time of their marriage, he was twenty-five years old, Catherine twenty-three. For at least a year they lived with his parents in Trenton while he worked as a clerk and continued his studies, and she taught elementary school.[11]

In 1934, still with no child on the scene, Salvatore Eugene, working as a humanities research assistant at Columbia University, won a prestigious Italian American fellowship from Columbia to travel to the University of Rome and the University of Florence.[12] It was in the summer of 1935, when Salvatore and Catherine were in Florence, that their only child—long hoped for—was conceived.

Two of Catherine's sisters and her two brothers would marry, but Antonin would be the only child of his generation from both sides of his family. After his March 1936 birth, the young family moved in with the Panaro aunts and uncles in their bustling row house in the heart of Trenton, then, for a little more breathing space, took a room two doors down Broad Street. In the lingering Depression, both parents worked, and Antonin was often left in the care of one Panaro or another. Maybe it was all the shuffling around, or maybe it was the clash of the boisterous Panaro and reserved Scalia clans, or maybe it was something else, but Antonin would not look back on the city of his birth with sweetness. "I hated Trenton," he would flatly declare decades later.[13]

The task of caring for the child often fell to Lenora, then a teenager and hardly eager for the chore of taking Nino to romp at the grassy Battle Monument grounds.

"Take the baby in the carriage and go around the park there," Maria, the matriarch, would order.

"He would cry and cry," Lenora recalled. "I had to run with the carriage to shut him up."[14] Yet Lenora, who painted herself as the young rebel of the Panaro family, also recalled delight in her nephew's antics. As a toddler, he climbed on the cannon at the Battle Monument grounds. He imitated the poses of soldiers. Captured in a family photograph, Antonin, wearing short pants and sporting curls, positioned himself with a sculptured soldier. Brow creased and eyes intent on something in the distance, the boy clutches the soldier's rifle with his two small hands.

Continuing their transient early years, Salvatore Eugene, Catherine, and little Nino moved in with a friend of Salvatore Eugene's named Frank Borgia, a foreign-language teacher at Trenton High School. Borgia lived across town and in a nicer residential area. "I remember first going to school from that house," the justice said years later, vividly recalling "crying like hell" at being shepherded out to wait for the bus.[15]

Around this time, his father was hired as an instructor in the Romance languages department at Brooklyn College, a tight cluster of buildings in the heart of Flatbush. The college was relatively new when the elder Scalia started in 1939. First established in downtown Brooklyn in 1930, the college benefited from the initiative of its inaugural president, William Boylan, and New York's newly elected mayor, Fiorello La Guardia. The mayor pushed for a $1.6 million city appropriation to buy forty acres of land and construct the first five buildings of a real campus. The Flatbush college grounds opened in 1937.[16] Salvatore Eugene's first decade there was spent as an instructor. After he earned his Ph.D., in 1950, he became an assistant professor.

A small but muscular man in neatly pressed suits, he impressed students and colleagues with his self-possession and sense of decorum. "In the thirty years that he taught, I can remember his having been absent only once. There must have been a compelling reason," recalled Joseph DeSimone, a fellow professor in the Romance languages department. "I remember, too, that during a general transit strike, when nothing was running in New York, he somehow got to Brooklyn from his suburb of Trenton and walked all the way from Atlantic Avenue to the college. It must have taken him three or four hours."[17] DeSimone also referred to his colleague as personally "severe" and professionally demanding. The grown son Antonin years later agreed. "Yes, he was severe," he said, shaking his head. "He was demanding."[18]

Salvatore Eugene taught Italian, French, and Spanish. His master's thesis had focused on the nineteenth-century Italian poet Giosuè Carducci, the first Italian to be awarded the Nobel Prize in literature, and for his doctorate, he concentrated on Luigi Capuana, a turn-of-the-nineteenth-century novelist and critic. But it was Dante who would become Salvatore Eugene's enduring specialty.

Salvatore Eugene's climb in academia came at a time when Italians were not welcomed by many Americans. They were among the last of the Europeans to arrive in the United States in the early twentieth century, and once in America, most clung to family and did not take easily to the ways of their new country. As Jerre Mangione and Ben Morreale wrote in *La Storia: Five Centuries of the Italian American Experience*, "The great Italian migration began at a time when America was beset by bank failures, stock market crashes, panic and mass unemployment." Such factors contributed to the reality that "the great majority of the lives of the Italians were not success stories. They lived in poverty while working at whatever jobs were available, even when working conditions were dangerous or unhealthy."[19]

With World War I fresh in people's minds and the Fascist Benito Mussolini in power, Italians were viewed with suspicion and stereotyped. Antonin's aunt Eva used to recount to the family the bias she encountered when looking for teaching jobs, not only because of her ethnicity but also because of her Catholicism. The New York governor Alfred Smith, the Democratic nominee for president in 1928 and the first Roman Catholic nominated by a major party, lost badly to the Republican Herbert Hoover partly because critics said Smith stood for "rum, Romanism, and rebellion."

Then there were words like "dago" and "wop." Anti-Italian fervor could be ugly. It also could be deadly. For Italians, the plight of the anarchists Nicola Sacco and Bartolomeo Vanzetti, who were tried for murder and executed by Massachusetts in 1927, was emblematic of their shaky foothold in America. The guilt or innocence of the men became secondary to the controversy over the fairness of the trial conducted by a prejudiced judge and an aggressive prosecutor who played to the prevailing hostilities.[20]

Any discrimination young Antonin might have faced in these years was cushioned by the insular nature of his parents' families. At the same time, the tight yet differing realms of his Trenton childhood might have contributed to the conflicts noted in Antonin's personality as an adult.

There was the vibrant, restless Panaro side, influenced by man-about-town Pasquale. From that clan, the boy picked up a knack for levity and the good timing of a storyteller, along with a sense of showmanship and the gestures of comical exaggeration. He also found his first legal and political model in Vince, the lawyer uncle who became a state assembly-man, Mercer County prosecutor, and mayor of Ewing Township.

On the other side was the reticent, scholarly father who taught Antonin to value the words of a text and appreciate cast-iron rules akin to those found in Dante's orderly universe of sin and suffering. His father's diligence and strict code of integrity impressed the boy. "Brains are like muscles—you can hire them by the hour," his father told him. "The only thing that's not for sale is character."[21]

Those dueling family forces produced a man who was at home with tension and confrontation—and readily generated it. As he grew older, his rhetorical style would become positively combative. He would use the Sicilian gesture of flicking his fingers under a raised chin—meaning "I couldn't care less," "You want to fight about it?" or worse—to someone who challenged him. "I don't like preaching to the choir," he would say about his rhetorical style. He would brag about easily falling into the role of "antihero" and revel at telling people "what they don't want to hear."[22] He would exemplify the writer Luigi Barzini's rendering of his fellow Italians' tendencies: "The vigorous passions of a turbulent and restless people are always ready to flare up unexpectedly like hot coals under the ashes."[23] The anger of the man who would be justice was often expressed in a biting humor. Just as he was defined by family, tradition, and heritage, he embodied the Italian sense of spectacle, too. Years later, wearing a standard black robe in the muted confines of the United States Supreme Court, he would exude color and zest—along with fury and restiveness.

When Antonin was six, he and his parents moved from Trenton to a small redbrick row house in the New York borough of Queens and for the first time lived at their own address. Their home at 48-22 O'Connell Court was on a narrow street in the Elmhurst neighborhood. A block and a half away was Newtown High School, an imposing structure built in a Renaissance Flemish style with a distinctive turret that loomed over the neighborhood. The Scalia two-story home had a small patch of front yard, too tiny for any real sports play. But the alleylike O'Connell Court attracted virtually no traffic, so it was easy to get a game of baseball or kick the can going. Antonin played stickball with tennis-size pink rubber Spaldings. He followed the Yankees, marveling at the slugger Joe DiMaggio and the shortstop Phil Rizzuto.[24]

Antonin's grandparents on the Scalia side had moved up to Queens first, to be near their daughter, Carmela, who had married a fellow Italian, Frank Pane, and begun a series of grocery and other retail ventures in New York.[25] As the family exchanged the tight world of Trenton row houses for the dense neighborhood of Queens, Antonin could walk just about everywhere, and he continued to experience the insularity of the family fold. Because Carmela and Frank had no children, they, too, doted on the boy.

Salvatore Eugene and Catherine focused on their only child's schooling. "They made him an education project," Justice Scalia's eldest son, Eugene, said.[26] Like her husband, Catherine had been a serious student. Her high school classmates had predicted she would have a future writing theme essays.[27] But whatever playfulness Catherine had enjoyed in the Panaro household was suppressed by her husband. Salvatore Eugene simply did not go in for joking or teasing, and he frowned on those who made it their practice.

The Scalia home was filled with books that helped foster an intellectualism that put Antonin a step ahead of the other striving sons of immigrants in the Irish-Italian neighborhood. Salvatore Eugene, a man of highbrow passions, was drawn to opera and amassed a great collection of Italian lyrics and sheet music. He eschewed sports and any conventional recreation. Much of his spare time at home was devoted to academic work. "I remember my father writing his doctorate downstairs in the basement," the justice recalled as he looked back on O'Connell Court.[28]

Antonin's parents pushed him to prove himself. Both parents valued education as the path to achievement. They also exuded a sense of propriety. With Salvatore Eugene, it was innate. He was compact, reserved, and could not abide any silliness. Catherine made more of a conscious effort to join the right clubs and act in the proper manner as she remained the dutiful eldest of the Panaro brood. She "devoted her life to making sure I did the right things, hung out with the right people, joined the right organizations," the son said years later. "By 'right,' I mean associated with young people that would not get me into trouble but rather would make me a better person . . . She made it her job to know who I was hanging out with. We had them over to my house and she was a den mother for the Cub Scouts, that sort of thing."[29]

Catherine constantly admonished her son to keep in line. "You're not everybody else," she would say. "Your family has standards and it doesn't matter what the standards of [others] are." She dressed in a practical manner around the house yet pulled out all the stops (gloves, stylish hat) to look her ladylike best when she went into town. "She had a million hats," her son recalled.

Antonin, slightly stocky, with thick black hair, attended Public School 13 in Elmhurst. He received weekly "release time" to go to Catholic education classes on Wednesday afternoons.[30] In later years the justice would cite his boyhood in Queens as determinative. He would refer to his neighborhood as his "little platoon," in the vein of the English essayist Edmund Burke, who wrote, "To be attached to the subdivision, to love the little platoon we belong to in society is the first principle (the germ as it were) of public affections."[31]

During the summers, while his father was preoccupied with his studies and teaching, Antonin would go out to Long Island to a vacation bungalow owned by his aunt Carmela. His grandfather Antonino would be there, too, sometimes hunting rabbits, sometimes playing cards and betting his grandson for pennies. In a picture from one of these summers, Antonin stands proudly with a long-barrel shotgun in his right hand, two dead rabbits in his left. His crew cut has grown out, and his pants are scruffy from the chase. His smiling face reflects a sense of achievement and the adult approval that greeted him.

He never learned Italian, so talking with his grandparents did not come easily. "We didn't have a lot of conversations," he said. "My father didn't speak Italian at home. Had he spoken Italian at home, he would have spoken Sicilian, which is vastly different from high Italian. Every educated Italian has two languages. One is his local language, and the other is the high Italian." The latter, of course, would have been more suitable for the young student to learn than the variant that would have been naturally spoken in the home. Years later the justice would regret passing up Italian lessons. "It is the shame of my life . . . I regret that I disappointed my father in that regard."[32]

Catherine ensured that the cord back to Trenton did not fray. She took

Antonin on regular trips to see his aunts and uncles. Aunt Lenora recalled that as her nephew grew, he did everything early and fast. His aunt Eva said at one point, "He would ask me such questions! He'd ask about the universe, about everything happening around. He floored me many times."[33]

But as much as they were charmed by the precocious Antonin, they were also a battery of surrogate parents needing to be impressed and pleased. "They were typical Italian aunts who wanted to make sure that their nephew did not get too smart for his own good," said Scalia's long-time friend Arthur Gajarsa, who became a judge on the U.S. Court of Appeals for the Federal Circuit. "His sense of humor was probably developed very keenly at home, being an only child, dealing with adults. He had to fend off many requests to do things: 'Lift your chin up.' 'Make sure you don't slurp your food.' From that perspective, I think he had more than one mother."[34]

Years later Lenora would recall her nephew from her own perspective and remember him as giving his mother a hard time. "He was bull-headed," Lenora said. "When he wanted to do something, and his parents [did not want him to do it], you had to give him a very, very good argument about why he could not do it . . . You couldn't say to him, 'Because I said so.' We call it in Italian a *capo tosta*. He had a hard head. You couldn't dissuade him. He knew what he wanted—even when he was little."[35]

The Scalia household was small and intense. The three of them—father, mother, child—were strong-minded and demanding in their own ways. If Antonin brought home a grade of A, the father asked why it was not an "A plus." Scalia's eldest son, Eugene (named for his grandfather), said that Salvatore Eugene's attitude was, "That's fine, Nino, but maybe next time you could do this better."[36] The justice himself said years later that he thought he had, as a youth, disappointed his father. "I wasn't all that I could have been," he said.[37] Others who knew Salvatore Eugene agreed: nothing the son did was quite enough for the father charting his own course in a new country.

Antonin earned high grades in elementary school, yet he stumbled at the end of eighth grade. He wanted to go to the Jesuit-run Regis High School on the Upper East Side of Manhattan, but he failed the entrance exam. A strong college prep school, Regis offered full scholarships to all of its qualifying students. In a conversation nearly sixty years later, Scalia could not recall being sick or otherwise experiencing some condition that would have caused him to fail. Yet he remembered one of the missed questions, a simple one: "It [involved] a comparative and superlative of 'good,' 'better,' 'best.' I screwed up." He did not recall a harsh reaction from his father about the bad score. In fact, his father uncharacteristically told him it might end up for the better to be at a place that had students with a range of abilities and were not all "brains."[38]

Antonin recouped by winning a scholarship to Xavier High School, an all-boys Jesuit institution on Sixteenth Street in lower Manhattan. Xavier was different because every student participated in junior ROTC. Students wore belted blue uniforms marked with their ranks on the sleeve. The boys saluted the headmaster and everyone else in a position of authority. Faculty wore robes: the Jesuits their black religious cassocks, lay teachers blue Oxford gowns.[39]

Four years there established Antonin's academic prowess, entrenched his regard for Catholicism, and reinforced his rule-oriented nature. With their rhetorical training and intellectual emphasis, the Jesuits shaped him as one of their own. Classes at Xavier began with prayer. "Above all, our students must live in an atmosphere impregnated with the great truths of religion," the school catalog said at the time. "Not that formal religious instruction is to occupy the major portion of his time, but that his scholastic and all other activities are rooted in and quieted by religious principles."[40] Antonin studied Latin and Greek and the great rhetoricians such as Cicero. He learned to fire a rifle and to march in formation. He discovered his ability as an orator and a thespian and, as a senior, won the lead in *Macbeth*.

During his years there, 1949–53, Xavier was in its glory. Founded in 1847, the school had celebrated a centennial in 1947 that drew commendations from Pope Pius XII and President Harry Truman. Francis Cardinal Spellman, the prominent anti-Communist crusader and long-tenured New York archbishop, presided over the anniversary events. Adjoining the school complex during Antonin's time was the Xavier Institute of Industrial Relations.[41] It educated workers of various trades and helped them organize unions. One colorful Jesuit, John M. Corridan, the so-called Waterfront Priest, helped longshoremen and became a model for the priest played by Karl Malden in the 1954 film *On the Waterfront*.[42]

After the school day, Antonin attended military drills at a nearby

armory. He carried his rifle home on the subway. He reveled in the
military-style atmosphere and was keenly disappointed when Xavier
abandoned the junior ROTC program in the early 1970s, when antiwar
sentiment was widespread. The justice complained about it years later.

Among the other sons of immigrants, Antonin stood out. During all
four of his years at Xavier, he wore gold honor cords on his blue uniform,
signifying his high grades. As he began his senior year, he was the subject
of a glowing article in the school newspaper: "For the past three years he
has compiled one of the most enviable records at Xavier. To date 19 First
Honor awards, one for each marking period, have been won by him."[43]
The story noted that he had been on a popular New York City television
show, *Mind Your Manners.* The student paper said, "[H]e displayed to the
best his fine traits of character. His keen sensible answers, well seasoned
with a bit of humor, stole the show again and again."[44]

The Xavier High School newspaper profile also emphasized Scalia's
religious devotion, calling him a leader in the Catholic life, even "an exem-
plary Catholic." It was telling that at a school run by Jesuits and attended
by Catholics in pre–Vatican II days, Antonin was conspicuous in his religious devotion. As he neared graduation, he thought about going next
into the seminary and becoming a priest. "How would a Catholic boy not
think about it?" he said years later. "That was certainly one of the things I
searched my soul about." He decided the priesthood would not be the life
for him. "I did not hear the call," he said. To a degree, his decision also
arose from the reality that joining the priesthood would have meant the
end of his family line: "I was an only child. That was part of it."[45]

As a high school student, Antonin rejected liberalism and the rhetoric
of political compromise. He followed the 1952 presidential campaign of
the Republican Dwight D. Eisenhower against the Democrat Adlai Stevenson. "Dwight Eisenhower used to insist, with demonstrably successful
effect," he later wrote, "that he was 'a conservative in economic affairs, but
a liberal in human affairs.' I am sure he meant it to connote nothing more
profound than that he represented the best of both Republican and Democratic tradition. But still, that seemed to me a peculiar way to put it—
contrasting economic affairs with human affairs as though economics
is a science developed for the benefit of dogs or trees; something that
has nothing to do with human beings, with their welfare, aspirations, or
freedoms."[46]

During the Eisenhower–Stevenson campaign, Antonin participated in a forum sponsored by *The New York Times* that again landed him on local television. Three teenage girls took the role of Democrats, and three boys, including Scalia, were Republicans in the panel discussion of the topic "Will a Democratic Victory Secure Our Future?" "The girls tried to keep the talk on the domestic scene," the *Times* reported of the event, "but the boys persisted in their attacks on Democratic foreign policy, which they said had lost much of the world to communism in spite of the expenditure of a great deal of money. They said the present prosperity was due to 'a war economy,' but the girls did not accept that argument, declaring 'the average man' had benefited greatly under the Democrats."[47]

Averell Harriman, then director of the U.S. Mutual Security Agency, was a guest on the show and sided with the girls. One can imagine the young Scalia's ire that the show to which he was invited happened to have a Democrat as its celebrity guest. But he also may have been gleeful at giving the Democrats—including Harriman—a run for their money. Scalia would later recall that watching Harriman in that session made him realize for the first time that a person of national stature and good reputation could be, at least in his particular young eyes, a dolt. Larger national debates awaited the future justice, as did a firmer attitude that some adversaries were not worthy of his talents. He would become known for not suffering anyone he took for a fool.

After he graduated first in his class at Xavier and was valedictorian, Antonin won a coveted Naval ROTC scholarship. He wanted to use it at Princeton, an Ivy League school that had long been his goal. But after completing the application and interview process, he was rejected. Even into the 1950s, and more so than Harvard and Yale, Princeton had the atmosphere of a private club. It drew its students from America's privileged classes.[48] "I was an Italian boy from Queens, not quite the Princeton type," Scalia said decades later. The Princeton episode would not be the last time he felt resentment—ethnic or otherwise—when events turned against him. He later said of the eventual course of his life, "One door closes, another door opens."[49]

In the 1950s the Jesuits wanted to keep their brightest within the fold anyway and steered them to the Jesuit-run Fordham University, Boston College, and Georgetown University. Scalia went for his second choice of college, Georgetown University in Washington, D.C. Around this time his parents moved back to suburban Trenton to be closer to Catherine's mother, Maria Panaro. They built a house on property that Maria owned in Ewing Township, and they lived a few yards from her home.

Salvatore Eugene Scalia continued to do serious scholarly work (he translated the correspondence between the influential Sicilian physician Filippo Mazzei and Thomas Jefferson), and he commuted to Brooklyn College until his retirement, in 1969. He made a bid to be chairman of the languages department but was rejected. Decades later, his son admitted that the father felt bitter about having been turned down. He resorted to concentrated physical work. With the remains from a stone quarry on the grounds of his suburban house, he built terraces throughout the Panaro property. The task preoccupied him from early morning to late at night.[50] "He loved to build those," the son recalled. "It was his only form of exercise. He did not play any sports. I don't think he would like a sport. It was wasting time. This was productive."[51]

Salvatore Eugene's Brooklyn College colleague DeSimone had a similar recollection: "He delighted in keeping his little property in Jersey looking always spick and span. I was amazed to hear him tell how he would transplant, single-handed, small trees to different locations to suit his sense of harmony."[52]

The stone terraces he built lasted. More than a half century later they could still be seen, laced in and out of the old dirt grounds, holding steady amid dead and dying trees. Even when Salvatore Eugene was gone, the little stair steps, constructed at a time when he could go no higher in his profession, held tight.

While at Georgetown University, the hard-charging son again proved his academic aptitude. Antonin majored in history and remained active in debate and drama clubs. He was president of the Mask and Bauble theater club in his sophomore year and played the fiddler and a member of the jury in *The Devil and Daniel Webster*, Stephen Vincent Benét's adaptation of the Faust tale, about a man who sells his soul to the devil. Georgetown also reinforced Antonin's Catholic beliefs and conservatism. These were the Cold War years, and Georgetown students aligned themselves with the anti-Communist cause. At the end of Antonin's freshman year, in May 1954, the senior class voted the Wisconsin senator Joseph McCarthy, then at the height of his anti-Communist crusade, as their top choice as Outstanding American. President Eisenhower took second place.[53]

For his junior year, Antonin enrolled in Georgetown's inaugural program at the University of Fribourg in Switzerland. It was a yearlong academic and sightseeing feast that included a trip to Italy—Antonin's first to the family's home country. The focus of study was history, economics, and literature. On breaks, students were allowed to explore Paris, Madrid, London, and other European cities.[54] The following year, Antonin graduated first in his class at Georgetown.

He capped his history major with a comprehensive set of oral exams that made an impression on him and focused his religious commitment. "I went before a panel of three professors who quizzed you," he recalled. "The chairman of the panel [was] a lovely man, a wonderful man, and he's giving me these questions. And I'm knocking them out of the ballpark, and I'm feeling really good. Then he says, 'Very good, Mr. Scalia. I have one last question: If you look back over all the history that you've studied here over the last four years, if you had to pick one event that you thought was the most significant, what would it be?'

"And I'm thinking, there's no wrong answer to this . . . I don't remember what I even answered, maybe the Battle of Waterloo, maybe the Battle of the Solomon Islands . . . And he shook his head sadly and said, 'No, Mr. Scalia. The Incarnation, Mr. Scalia.' " (The Incarnation refers to God becoming man in the form of Jesus Christ.) Of that moment of his education he later said, "It was the last lesson I learned at Georgetown: not to separate your religious life from your intellectual life. They're not separate."[55] This revelation would indeed define the justice's life and his place among American leaders in the law.

As Georgetown valedictorian in 1957, the young Scalia urged his fellow graduates—whom he termed "leaders of a real, a true, a Catholic intellectualism"—not to stifle their spirit and not to get caught up in cares of "wealth or fame or specialized careers." He opened his June 9, 1957, speech with florid prose: "The flaming sun has set beneath the green hills to the West, and returned to the bosom of the fertile earth which gave him birth . . . We stand on such a mountain peak tonight. Many years have we spent climbing up the rugged slope of training. Tomorrow we begin the descent into the valley men call life." Then he said to his fellow graduates, "If we will not lead, who will? Eliminate the great number of men who have never heard the voices of the past, who know nothing of the heritage of human wisdom, who begin their hunt alone and totally unaided . . . Eliminate again the men who have not heard the Word of Christ whispered to the soul . . . If we will not be leaders of a real, a true, a Catholic intellectual life, no one will!"[56]

The speech was excessive but revealing. His education, his Catholicism, and his first-in-the-class honor all led him to feel superior. This became the scaffolding of the public Antonin Scalia: smart, confident, righteous.

Scalia was admitted to Harvard Law School, confirmation for his father and the world at large of the success of this first-generation Italian American. At the center of the law school complex was Langdell Hall, which held the largest law library in the nation. The building named for Christopher Columbus Langdell, the first dean of the law school, contained an unrivaled collection of books and a large reading room. Along with other students attired in customary jacket and tie, Scalia pored over volumes as he sat at the eighteen-foot-long reading tables. Legal quotations engraved along the top of the walls inspired him: LEX EST SUMMA RATIO INSITA IN NATURA, "Law is the highest reason implanted in nature,"[57] and PROPER LEGEM TUAM SUSTINUI TE DOMINE, "Because of Thy Law have I abided Thee, O Lord."[58] Another quotation that may have had special meaning for the son of a translator and the student who would become a textualist was SCIRE LEGES NON HOC EST VERBA EARNUM TENERE SED VIM AC POTESTATEM, "To know the law is not merely to understand the words, but as well their force and effect."[59]

Scalia's pursuit of the law was both intellectual and practical. It played to his oratorical strength and his fixation on rules.

Among the students Scalia befriended at Harvard Law School were the future Massachusetts governor Michael Dukakis, who was in Scalia's small study section; Paul Sarbanes, a future Maryland U.S. senator; and Richard Arnold, who would become a federal appeals court judge two years before Scalia would reach the federal bench. Arnold, of Texarkana, Texas, shared with Scalia an orthodox Christianity and classical education. "Both of those qualities continued to characterize Richard (and me, I suppose) in later years—though he one-upped me on the classical (or perhaps the theological) by learning Hebrew later in life," Scalia would write.[60]

The political and social concerns of the day were evident in the speakers invited to the campus by the law school. The former first lady Eleanor Roosevelt addressed conditions in the Soviet Union. The South Carolina senator Strom Thurmond, a 1948 States' Rights Democratic Party (Dixie-crat) candidate for president, denounced the then-pending civil rights bill. Allen Ginsberg read his poetry and wept.[61]

Scalia cleaved to familiar guideposts. He joined the St. Thomas More Society, a fellowship of Catholic students. In his second year, a major lecture by Professor Herbert Wechsler offered the conservative Scalia a counterpoint to the prevailing liberal view of the law and probably influenced the direction of his thinking. Wechsler, then a professor at Columbia University, presented his views as part of the Holmes Lecture series, which according to Scalia's classmate Frank Michelman were "truly festival events for which everyone turned out."[62]

The dominant legal approach in the late 1950s endorsed judges' involvement in society's problems, epitomized by the 1954 *Brown v. Board of Education* decision. Wechsler articulated an alternative in the form of "neutral principles" and insisted that "value" choices should be left to the legislative and executive branches. Wechsler argued that judges should use their power in moderation and not act as "a naked power organ" seeking a particular societal result. He challenged the constitutional underpinnings of the 1954 landmark decision against segregation. He said he personally disapproved of racial segregation, but he criticized the Court's stance that separate schools were unconstitutional because of segregation's evil effects on black students. He questioned what "basis in neutral principles" the Court had to force integration. "The main constituent of the judicial process is precisely that it must be genuinely principled, resting on analysis and reasons quite transcending the immediate result that is achieved," Wechsler said in the provocative lecture covered by daily newspapers and reprinted in the *Harvard Law Review*, where Scalia and Michelman shared the joint duties of note editors.[63]

"It was stunning," Michelman recalled years later. "Professor Wechsler had stood before us declaring himself unable to explain the legitimacy of *Brown*. He had done so by way of illustrating the . . . central claim of his lecture, regarding what he called 'neutral principles' and their bearing on adjudicative legitimacy. The aptness of the illustration was later to be very sharply questioned, but no one can doubt its having been good for memorability. From personal knowledge I can say the illustration was well chosen to leave the neutral-principles thesis deeply imprinted in the minds and memories of those in attendance."[64]

Michelman speculated that the daring Wechsler speech had made a lasting impression on the justice-to-be. Scalia said he did not remember attending, but he did not argue with the idea that the "neutral principles" notion shaped his thinking and, ultimately, his method of judicial decision making. Scalia's approach to the law was so distinct that it was natural for people to look back and try to trace its intellectual origins. His upbringing and early schooling contributed to his approach, certainly. But it was difficult not to believe that someone of Wechsler's stature, arguing against the structure of the landmark *Brown v. Board of Education*, also played a part in the young Scalia's thinking.

Scalia and Michelman shared a spartanly furnished office, facing each other across the width of two desks. "The law review was all consuming," Scalia recalled of the late nights editing submissions. "I was just panicky that I would flunk the exams, because I wasn't studying much." Yet the satisfaction of being part of the prestigious intellectual review offset his anxiety: "It was a grind, but it was enormously exhilarating. You were thrown in with the brightest kids, academically, in the school. Just talking with them about cases—it was exciting."

Michelman, who would become a law clerk to Justice William J. Brennan, Jr., and then return to Harvard as a law professor, said he did not recall Scalia showing any nervousness about getting the job done. Nor did he recall sharp debate between them about the law or basic principles of judging. "He taught me what cannoli was," Michelman said. "I came in one evening and he had a brown bag. He pulled out a delicious-looking pastry. I asked him what it was. He said, 'Michelman, you don't know what a cannoli is?' " Michelman did not remember getting a share of that one. "No. I think I had to go get my own."

He recalled Scalia as convivial. He said he never would have predicted that his classmate would prove to be "such a gifted and colorful prose stylist, whose opinions would grab attention, in part, for their occasional bouts of vituperation. I did not see that coming."[65]

Scalia's worries about flunking exams were for naught. He graduated magna cum laude. Amid the stately stone buildings and ancient trees of Cambridge, his credentials were sealed. He was now part of the legal elite. It was a particularly sweet achievement for a first-generation Italian American Catholic. His father's Columbia University doctorate had set a goal that the boy—now a man—had matched with a Harvard LL.B.

With his academic record and law review position, Scalia was attractive to national firms. He had spent a summer at Foley and Lardner in Milwaukee between his second and third years of law school. "They paid the highest [salaries for summer associates] in the country," Scalia explained years later. "Also, I wanted to get a look at the Midwest."[66] But after graduation he did not want to return to that cold Wisconsin city, which he considered "too far off the beaten path." He was seriously considering a Philadelphia firm, but when he met James Lynn, who was recruiting for the Cleveland-based Jones, Day, Cockley and Reavis, Scalia changed his mind.

Lynn had gone to college at Case Western Reserve University in Cleveland and then graduated from Harvard Law School in 1951.[67] He had read through the Harvard student biographies as he rode the plane to Boston. "He leaped out at me," recounted Lynn. "When I got there, I asked a professor, 'What about this fellow Scalia?' And he said, 'No, no, he's going somewhere else.' " Lynn decided to make a pitch anyway and waited at Gannett House for Scalia. Dating to the 1830s and named for the Reverend Caleb Gannett, Gannett House was the oldest surviving building on Harvard's campus. For law students, it was the place to hang out, toss a ball around, and chew the fat after finishing in the library stacks. "I'd spent all day there," recalled Lynn. "Finally he walks in. We talk awhile."[68]

Scalia struck Lynn as unusually smart and engaging. And Scalia liked what he heard about Jones, Day. Around midnight Lynn said, "It's getting late. You hungry?" They walked over to the Hayes-Bickford cafeteria on Harvard Square and ordered bacon and eggs. Lynn continued to drop the names of former Supreme Court law clerks who had gone beyond the Hudson River for Cleveland's Jones, Day, and he played up the firm's involvement in national cases. Its reputation had been enhanced in the 1950s by its representation of the steel industry against President Truman's order seeking control of steel mills during the Korean War. The firm won the 1952 Supreme Court decision that Truman had exerted unconstitutional control over the steel industry. On the walk back to Gannett House, Scalia told Lynn, "All right, I'll come out to Cleveland" for a visit. Scalia said years later, "Jim Lynn could talk anyone into anything."[69]

When Scalia visited Cleveland, Lynn threw a dinner party for the prospective new associate with other men from the firm and their wives. Afterward, standing at the fireplace in the living room, Lynn later recalled, the conversation turned to "blue laws," under which local governments prohibited commerce, especially liquor sales, on Sunday to encourage religious and moral devotion. On this cold evening in 1959, Lynn's associates from the firm argued vigorously against the prohibitions. Scalia was for perpetuating the laws, which dated to the mid-1800s. "They really put it to him," Lynn said, "and he handled it absolutely beautifully." One can imagine the young Scalia being invigorated by the argument. He agreed to join the firm.

At Harvard, Scalia met Maureen McCarthy on a blind date, set up by a Jewish friend, Robert Joost, who thought the two Catholics in Cambridge would naturally like each other. Maureen was the daughter of a physician in Braintree, Massachusetts. (That suburb was, through a historical coincidence, the site of the payroll robbery and murders that Sacco and Vanzetti were accused of, and that exacerbated antagonism against Italian Americans.) Maureen, a former high school valedictorian and English major at Radcliffe, had short, wavy, light brown hair and a demure countenance, but she also had an intense embrace of the politics of the day that would match her date's.

In her first years at Radcliffe, Maureen had helped found the Radcliffe Young Democrats. Yet by the end of the 1950s and her senior year, she had become disillusioned with the Democratic Party, believing that it was turning toward too much social welfare. "This was not how I was raised," she recalled. "It was that you work hard and make your way."[70] Her father, John McCarthy, had grown up in a first-generation Irish household and worked long hours as a physician. Her mother, Mary Fitzgerald, had a similar upbringing. As a young woman, Mary had wanted to go to college and become a teacher, but the Fitzgerald family needed her, her three brothers, and her sister to work immediately after high school for money to support the family.

Now with her own family, Mary's ability to send her daughter Maureen to Radcliffe was a special point of pride.[71] "For my parents, a proper women's Catholic college would not have been the only choice for me," Maureen said. "I don't think I could have survived there. I'm just too confrontational." Unlike the young man who was her blind date, Maureen had grown up in a suburban town with very few Catholics and had faced discrimination because of her religion. She remembered neighborhood children not being able to play with her because she was Catholic.

In her junior year, Maureen's father died suddenly of heart failure. He had been her champion—brilliant, energetic, and always ready to challenge his high-achieving daughter. Amid the grief of the family, Maureen recalled, the one certainty was that she would finish at Radcliffe. Her mother wanted that for her, and her father would have, too.

Maureen agreed to the blind date with Scalia but did not want to waste much time with it. She told him at the outset that she had to return early to her residence, Holmes Hall. The couple went first to a *Harvard Law Review* party and then to dinner. Maureen ended up falling for him, struck by Scalia's liveliness, sense of humor, and engagement with the issues of the day. Midway through the evening, when he said, "It's too bad you have to go home soon," Maureen excused herself and pretended to have made arrangements to stay out later.[72]

In 1960, after their respective graduations and their wedding, the couple traveled across Europe on a Sheldon Fellowship Scalia had won.[73] They began in England, drove to Scotland, then went on to Germany, Poland, Czechoslovakia, Austria, Italy, and France. They got around in a Peugeot, bought with money from Salvatore Eugene and Catherine Scalia.

The pair turned out to be a perfect fit for each other. Maureen had graduated on the cusp of the liberation movement that sent droves of women into the workforce, but she was planted in the earlier era of women who chose motherhood over careers. Like her new husband, she was the product of deeply held religious beliefs. "We were both devout Catholics," Scalia recalled. "That was perhaps the most important thing that we had in common. And being a devout Catholic means you have children when God gives them to you, and you raise them." Scalia knew he was lucky to have made such a match. "How often can you get a Radcliffe graduate to settle down and devote her life to raising nine kids?" he said years later.[74] For her part, Maureen was to say she never regretted not using her Radcliffe degree for work outside of the home.

Molded by his Italian roots, yet fully assimilated, the young man with the intellectual father and classical training embraced the world of rules. He found it ballast in the rough seas of changing social values. Legal work offered Scalia, he would later say, an identity tied to precision and reverence for the text.

He would also acknowledge how the law bred a degree of cynicism. Again, that fit Scalia, who, as he grew, had developed an increasingly sarcastic tongue. At one point, when he was explaining the life of a lawyer, he referred to the hopeful characters of the authors Herman Melville, Eleanor H. Porter, and Charles Dickens and said, "Billy Budd, Pollyanna, and Mr. Micawber could never have been lawyers." Scalia could not identify with them. The erudite jurist would instead invoke for his literary point of reference a familiar line from a Charles Lamb essay, "The Old Benchers of the Inner Temple," in which Lamb laments the passing of old things, like sundials and marble fountains, that had magical meaning to him as a child: "They are gone, and the spring choked up. The fashion, they tell me, is gone by, and these things are esteemed childish. Why not then gratify children, by letting them stand? Lawyers, I suppose, were children, once."[75]

Scalia would repeat that memorable last line, perhaps revealing a sense of loss from his childhood. His grandfather had left the family. His father was a demanding taskmaster who was devoted to his own academic studies. The boy's trips to the Battle Monument were short-lived as the family moved from one place to another. "He didn't have a home," his aunt Lenora observed decades later, in part to explain his loathing of Trenton.

The recollections of childhood and the wistfulness of the "Old Benchers" essay echo in what the University of Virginia Law School professor John C. Jeffries, Jr., in later years termed "the animating vision" behind Justice Scalia's approach to the law. "Perhaps unusually among Supreme Court justices," Jeffries aptly wrote, "Scalia is informed by an awareness of the fragility of human achievement, by a sharp distrust of easy promises about a better world, and by a keen appreciation of what we have to lose."[76] Scalia was shaped by the Sicilian immigrant experience and its attendant striving. His singular place in the family, alone among the adults, and the deficits of his early years would be just as determinative in shaping the arc of the future justice's life and his view of the law.

TWO

IN THE TURBULENCE OF WATERGATE

———◆◆◆———

Antonin Scalia was formally installed as an assistant attorney general of the United States in August 1974, only a few days after Richard Nixon's resignation. The machinery of the executive branch had broken down, and the staff was demoralized. Former Nixon aides were scrambling to locate Oval Office tape recordings and documents that had been demanded by Watergate investigators. The staff of the new president, Gerald Ford, issued orders to stop any shredding or burning of papers to try to make sure potential evidence was not destroyed. Soon after Ford assumed office, on August 9, his people had been required to intervene to stop a caravan of military trucks from hauling off files that Nixon had wanted flown to his residence in San Clemente, California.[1]

The times were not auspicious. An American president had resigned for the first time in history. Nixon still faced possible criminal charges related to the White House's involvement in the June 17, 1972, break-in of the Democratic headquarters at the Watergate. The turmoil in the executive branch, where Scalia had found a home, was nowhere near over. For months Nixon's administration had been under siege by Congress, special prosecutors and grand juries, the Justice Department, and the FBI. *The Washington Post* and other newspapers carried daily revelations of a cover-up. Staffers throughout the executive branch were bailing out. "The atmosphere here in Washington is frightening," Deputy Attorney General Laurence Silberman wrote his son a few months before indictments of President Nixon's top aides were issued in the spring of 1974. "People high in the administration and high on the White House staff seem to be frantically looking around to get out."[2]

Still, the ambitious thirty-eight-year-old Scalia yearned to move into a position of more responsibility and visibility in the executive branch. He was comfortable in conflict-rife and rapidly shifting situations. In fact, he seemed to thrive in tense times. During the prior seven years, he had quit a prestigious law firm job just as he was about to be considered for a partnership; shifted to a stint as a law professor at the University of Virginia in Charlottesville; packed up and moved to Washington to be part of Nixon's newly established White House Office of Telecommunications Policy; transferred to a position as chairman of the Administrative Conference of the United States, a small independent agency that tried to improve the management of the bureaucracy; and then begun looking for another job in Nixon's administration. By the spring of 1974 he had given up and was about to move Maureen and their seven children back to Charlottesville. Then, just as the Nixon administration was collapsing, it appeared the assistant attorney general job might come through for him. He told Maureen, "Don't unpack the boxes."[3]

The fast-talking, cigarette-waving Scalia was landing a job that engaged his talents. More important for the future man of the law, it was a job that would fundamentally shape his regard for the executive branch of government. It would also bring him into the orbit of men who would be at the center of Republican politics for decades. There were Richard Cheney and Donald Rumsfeld, Nixon aides who went on to become top assistants to Ford. Nixon's longtime speechwriter Patrick Buchanan, at the forefront of cultural conservatism and holding definite ideas about the limited role of judges in society, was also on the scene as a senior adviser to Nixon, then Ford. It was here that Scalia would solidify his view that the executive had broad powers in important areas, by default of sorts, where the Constitution did not say otherwise.

He was taking a job as an assistant attorney general to run the Office of Legal Counsel, an esteemed division of the Justice Department that provided legal opinions on executive branch power. Scalia was undaunted by the fall of the president for whom he had worked since 1971.[4] For nearly two years Nixon had been dogged by investigators attempting to pin him and his closest aides with responsibility for covering up the Watergate break-in. Nixon, in turn, had pressured Justice Department officials to deter investigators and to steer them away from his friends.

Just as Scalia had been trying to win the assistant attorney general job in the Office of Legal Counsel, congressional committees and the special prosecutor Leon Jaworski neared the climax of their investigations. A grand jury on March 1, 1974, indicted the former Nixon chief of staff H. R. (Bob) Haldeman, the former assistant to the president for domestic affairs John Ehrlichman, and the former attorney general John Mitchell, who had also been the chairman of Nixon's 1972 reelection campaign.[5] In 1973, Alexander Butterfield, a Haldeman assistant, had revealed that Oval Office conversations had been taped, and Jaworski and the House Judiciary Committee now sought to enforce subpoenas for the tapes.[6]

Nixon was boxed in. The panic in his administration was widespread. The revelation of an eighteen-minute gap in a key tape regarding the cover-up had led GOP loyalists such as Laurence Silberman to believe Nixon should go. "The President ought to resign now," he had written to his son at boarding school. "I think the Rose Mary Woods—18 minute tape business is a fatal blow to The President."[7] Silberman had been undersecretary at the Department of Labor before leaving the administration at the beginning of Nixon's second term to go into private law practice. But he had returned in February 1974, this time as deputy attorney general, in the aftermath of the "Saturday Night Massacre."

That episode, which serendipitously ended up benefiting Scalia, occurred on the evening of Saturday, October 20, 1973, as Nixon ordered the firing of the first Watergate special prosecutor, Archibald Cox, and, as a direct result, caused the resignations of Attorney General Elliot Richardson and Deputy Attorney General William Ruckelshaus. Nixon believed he had the power to discharge Cox, who was threatening to seek a contempt citation against Nixon for refusing to hand over the tape recordings Nixon considered privileged. The president asked Richardson to fire Cox. Richardson would not and resigned instead. The president asked Ruckelshaus to dismiss Cox, but he resigned, too. Robert Bork, then U.S. solicitor general, stepped forward to be acting head of the Justice Department and did the job.[8]

With time plainly running out for Nixon, the president chose the U.S. senator William Saxbe, a Republican from Ohio, to be attorney general, and the Senate readily confirmed one of its own. Saxbe then tapped Silberman to be his deputy attorney general, and Silberman, in turn, played the central role in hiring Scalia.

Born in York, Pennsylvania, and reared in New Jersey, Laurence Silberman had earned a bachelor's degree from Dartmouth and a law degree at Harvard, graduating one year after Scalia. Silberman was a tall man with a ramrod bearing. His thinning hair made him appear older than his thirty-eight years. A hard driver and loyal Republican, Silberman thought Watergate was making weaklings of some administration aides. In the spring of 1974 he came to believe that the assistant attorney general at the Office of Legal Counsel, Robert Dixon, was on the verge of a mental breakdown. "He was a mess, quivering, virtually paralyzed," Silberman recalled. "He was afraid of shadows and couldn't give answers to questions. I pretty quickly decided he had to go."[9] Dixon had a law degree and a doctorate in political science. He had taught law, and the turmoil of Watergate made him ready to return to academic life.[10]

"I was pretty confident that if I recruited someone [to succeed Dixon], Saxbe would go along," Silberman recalled. "I wanted someone who was smart but also someone who had courage. In the aftermath of Watergate, there were a number of people who were afraid of being accused of doing the wrong thing."[11]

Scalia was not like that. In fact, he exuded a strong sense of confidence and the belief that if he did it, it was right. He also was no stranger to the executive branch. Before his position as chairman of the Administrative Conference, Scalia had been general counsel in Nixon's Office of Telecommunications Policy.[12] Under Director Clay T. "Tom" Whitehead, that office helped spur development of the cable industry through an open domestic satellite system. The office also became a partner in Nixon's attack on the Corporation for Public Broadcasting and other news media the administration deemed too left-wing.[13]

As general counsel, Scalia considered how the White House might be able to rein in the LBJ-created, publicly funded Corporation for Public Broadcasting, which Scalia and others at the telecommunications office believed too supportive of "liberal causes." Scalia acknowledged that they could not simply slash the funds of a popular entity that was home to *Sesame Street*, had broadcast *The Forsyte Saga*, and offered high school equivalency programs. "The best possibility for White House influence is through the Presidential appointees to the Board of Directors," Scalia wrote at one point in his series of memos in 1972. And he suggested that a good way to diminish the influence "of the liberal Establishment of the Northeast" was to increase federal funds to local stations, which he believed better reflected the views of different communities.[14]

As he became immersed in the substance of the law, Scalia was always aware of who was well connected and who was moving up. Whitehead was a player beyond the telecommunications office. When Scalia was trying to win the assistant attorney general spot, Whitehead happened to be engaged in secret meetings as part of a Ford transition group. Behind closed doors, the group was preparing for what seemed more inevitable by the day: Ford's becoming president. The team, led by Philip Buchen, an old college friend of Ford's who would become his White House counsel, was made up mostly of Washington old-timers and the thirty-five-year-old Whitehead, distrusted by the media but in the confidence of Buchen.[15]

Deputy Attorney General Silberman turned to his aide Jonathan Rose for names of possible successors to Assistant Attorney General Dixon. One of the energetic young loyalists who had joined the administration during Nixon's first term, Rose was the son of H. Chapman Rose, a former undersecretary of the treasury in the Eisenhower administration who had been a law clerk to Justice Oliver Wendell Holmes, Jr. Chappie Rose, as he was called, had become a partner in the Cleveland law firm of Jones, Day, Cockley and Reavis and was still there while Scalia was a young associate.[16]

Scalia had remained with Jones, Day for six years in the 1960s. Then, about a year before he could have become a partner, he resigned to take an assistant professorship at the University of Virginia. The teaching position enabled Scalia to relocate his family—his wife and then five children—to the idyllic Charlottesville campus. But to some at the Cleveland law firm, Scalia's move was bewildering. He was on the brink of earning a substantial salary and securing his legal career. Why would he quit just as he was about to become partner? "Because I was about to become partner!" Scalia retorted decades later. "I had intended to go into teaching. Then, the first thing I knew, nearly seven years had passed."[17] Scalia had long set a goal of becoming a professor, the work of his father. In 1967, with the partnership obligation looming and a close Jones, Day colleague leaving to teach, Scalia was prompted to find his own academic job.

"The only schools that expressed interest in me were Cornell and Virginia. I almost went to Cornell," Scalia recalled. "I had told Maureen we were going to Cornell and—she's never forgiven me for this—she went out and bought all the kids big, heavy winter stuff."[18] Scalia said he could not exactly remember why he abruptly changed his mind about working in upstate New York, but he believed he switched partly because of an encouraging conversation with the University of Virginia Law School dean Hardy Dillard and the beautiful Charlottesville setting. Scalia taught mainly first-year classes, such as contracts.

Years later Erwin Griswold, a former U.S. solicitor general and dean of Harvard Law School, said he was so baffled by Scalia's departure from Jones, Day, where Griswold had become a partner, that he looked into the situation. "[W]hy did Scalia leave the firm after six years? Was it because it had been intimated to him that he probably was not going to become a partner? I asked a couple of my present partners who were members of the firm at the time, and they said, on the contrary, he was doing very well. He was very highly regarded . . . [H]e deliberately made the choice himself to move to teaching."[19]

Scalia was perpetually restless. After four years at the University of Virginia he switched jobs again. That was the first move prompted by Jonathan Rose. Working for the assistant to the president Peter Flanigan, Rose had put forward Scalia's name in 1971 to be general counsel of the new Office of Telecommunications Policy. "We were looking then for people who would be philosophically compatible with the administration and sufficiently creative to be helpful," Rose recalled of the situation that led to Scalia's leave of absence from the University of Virginia to join the Nixon administration. Scalia, who was thirty-five years old, said later of the opportunity at the cutting-edge technological office, "I was a pretty young man. I was going to be general counsel of a brand-new agency. I suspected I would do it for a couple of years—that's all."

Instead, the thrill of the executive branch, even in the turbulence of Watergate, seized Scalia. Now, in late spring 1974, as Jon Rose helped Silberman find someone to run the Office of Legal Counsel, Rose was among those feeling anxious about Watergate. "We were in a situation that nobody could be prepared for. Once it [the Watergate scandal] blew, it was very hard for anyone to get out without people assuming you were part of it . . . You needed someone in that [assistant attorney general] job who could command the respect of staff lawyers."[20]

Rose—very much the product of the old boys' network of the nation's capital—believed Scalia could handle the stress. He set him up with Silberman in May 1974.[21] "I don't think I ever met anyone who I was considering for a government job who I liked so immediately," Silberman later said of his first encounter with Scalia. "It was his intellectual ability, his sense of humor, his family story. I immediately thought the world of him."[22] Rose was relieved that the two bullheaded men got along: "It was one of those things that could either have been a triumph or a disaster," he said, "because they are both very high-powered, self-confident people. If they happened to get off on the wrong foot, it could have been one of those things where someone says, 'Jesus, why did you do that to me?'"[23]

Cleared by Saxbe and awaiting routine Senate confirmation, Scalia prepared to join the Justice Department as the special prosecutor Jaworski was accelerating his efforts to obtain the White House tape recordings of President Nixon's conversations. Jaworski appealed directly to the Supreme Court to enforce his subpoena, and on July 8 the Court heard oral arguments in the case.[24]

Adding to the atmosphere of national upheaval in the summer of 1974, the retired chief justice Earl Warren died the next day, July 9. Warren, who had been a Republican governor of California (1943–53) and presidential running mate of Thomas Dewey in 1948, was, as chief justice of the United States, a robust force for social reform, particularly for racial equality and criminal rights. Warren embodied the liberalism that Nixon had opposed and Scalia abhorred. Especially irksome to the administration was the Warren Court's expansion of due process of law for criminal defendants. The Warren Court ensured that all persons had a right to see a lawyer before being questioned, that a poor defendant was entitled to a lawyer, and that evidence gathered through unlawful police methods generally was not admissible at trial.[25]

In a brief pause from all the recriminations of Watergate, Nixon, Silberman, and other top administration officials attended Warren's funeral at the Washington National Cathedral on July 12. Warren's successor, Chief Justice Warren Burger, and former colleagues at the Court, too, took a break from the exhausting negotiations over the Watergate tapes case. On July 10 Warren's casket had rested on the first floor of the Court; positioned behind it, the black-draped chair the chief justice had used during his sixteen years at the Court. Now at the National Cathedral, as the choir sang "Nearer, My God, to Thee" and benedictions were offered by an Episcopal bishop, a rabbi, and a Roman Catholic archbishop, Warren's legacy of legal protections for the "great and weak alike" was memorialized.[26]

Two weeks later, on July 24, the Supreme Court ruled 8–0 that Nixon had to turn over the Oval Office tapes.[27] The House Judiciary Committee quickly passed its first article of impeachment, charging Nixon with obstruction of justice in attempting to cover up the Watergate burglary. On August 5 the White House released transcripts of three incriminating conversations from June 23, 1972. These conversations had occurred six days after the break-in at the Democratic headquarters. The release forced Nixon to admit that he had ordered a stop to the investigation of the Watergate burglary and then had tried to keep evidence secret. The tapes also revealed that he tried to prevent the FBI from tracing the source of the money that went to the burglars.[28]

Nixon announced his resignation in a televised address on the evening of August 8. It was just two years after he had won reelection by trouncing the Democratic nominee George McGovern. The next day, Gerald Ford was sworn in as president. All of these events were disturbing to Scalia, but also a relief. "Anybody who was in the administration at the time was happy to get it over with," Scalia recalled. "Nixon had been twisting in the wind."[29]

After Ford took over the White House, he continued with Scalia's nomination to head the Office of Legal Counsel, and the U.S. Senate officially confirmed Scalia on August 22, 1974. For the impatient and striving Scalia who had left the private practice of law and then academia, it was a gratifying turn of events.

On the home front, the Scalias' seven children spanned from Matthew, a year old, to Ann, who was about to turn thirteen. The social and political upheaval of the mid-1970s challenged Scalia and his wife as parents, particularly as devout, conservative parents. The influences of Woodstock, women's liberation, drug experimentation, and—for Catholics—the Second Vatican Council were strongly disliked but ubiquitous. Vatican II, beginning in 1962, had transformed the liturgy, excised Latin, changed the role of priests, and encouraged the congregation to participate actively in the Mass. Vatican II also had sought a new openness and bonds with other Christian believers. For Scalia, who preferred the heavy incense and chanting of Latin, all these liberalizing developments were upsetting. As modern influences crept into his church in suburban McLean, Virginia, Scalia determined on Sunday mornings to drive his family into downtown Washington, D.C., for the Latin Mass and traditional organ music still offered at St. Matthew's Cathedral. Maureen strongly agreed with her husband on that choice, and they worked out arrangements together, despite the chiding of her own Catholic mother about the treks to different parts of town: "Why don't you people ever seem to live near churches?" she asked on one of her visits to their Virginia home.[30]

Regarding Vatican II, Scalia said later, "It was not on my hit parade—especially as somebody who had traveled in Europe. One of the nice things is that wherever you went, if you had your missal and you knew Latin, it was the same Mass. Maybe you couldn't understand the sermon, but who cares!"[31]

Scalia was not changing with the times. His children, who attended local public school, were generally not allowed to wear jeans.[32] Recalling the turbulent 1970s, Scalia said of his children, "They were being raised in a culture that wasn't supportive of our values, that was certainly true. But we were helped by the fact that we were such a large family. We had our own culture . . . The first thing you've got to teach your kids is what my parents used to tell me all the time, 'You're not everybody else . . . We have our own standards and they aren't the standards of the world in all respects, and the sooner you learn that the better.' "[33]

Scalia's old Trenton neighborhood declined in these years, bearing the scars of urban decay and the ravages of the riots that followed the 1968 murder of the Reverend Martin Luther King, Jr. Most of the downtown Trenton businesses Scalia had known as a child were burned or ransacked. Most of his relatives by this time were in the suburbs.

Amid this social upheaval and political anxiety Scalia cut his teeth at the center of government power. Watergate permeated everything, from the ideas of President Ford and his men about how to run the government, down to their daily routines. Those who formerly worked with Nixon were required to certify that all materials in their possession on August 9, the day he resigned, had been turned over to investigators.[34] When new tapes were discovered, they had to be handled as carefully as ticking time bombs. An August 13, 1974, memo labeled EYES ONLY to the new White House counsel Philip Buchen from Benton Becker, whom Ford had brought in to oversee the handling of Nixon materials, revealed the attention to details when a discovery was made: "Information developed today identified the location of what has been described as 900 reels of President Nixon's [audio] tapes . . . retained on the ground floor of the Old Executive Office Building in a converted closet across from the cafeteria—sealed and secure. The room is so small that it does not have a room number. The security of this room is under the jurisdiction of the Technical Security Division of the Secret Service. The tapes have been secured in this room since July 18, 1973, at which time combinations to locks were changed."[35]

A few weeks later Ford aides meticulously documented the opening of a safe removed from an office used by General Alexander Haig, Nixon's chief of staff: "The vault was opened in the presence of Hazel Fulton [an assistant in the Special Files Unit], two locksmiths, a TSD [Technical Security Division of the Secret Service] representative and Barry N. Roth."[36] At one point, Donald Rumsfeld, whom Ford chose to replace Haig as chief of staff, wrote to Buchen, "On Sunday, September 29, at approximately 7:30 p.m., my secretary, Brenda Williams, found, when looking for a White House telephone directory in one of the secretarial desks, the enclosed tape. The attached note characterizes it as 'Presidential Tape— March 8, 1971.' It is herewith delivered to your custody. Please acknowledge its receipt in writing."[37]

In the wake of the scandal and in this uneasy atmosphere Scalia's first assignment at the Office of Legal Counsel was to write an opinion determining whether Nixon owned the tapes and documents being sought by the special prosecutor Jaworski. Key administration players already had weighed in on the question. Becker, Ford's longtime confidant who had been hired to assist him in the transition and in the handling of Watergate materials, had concluded in a mid-August note to White House counsel Buchen that the records were indeed Nixon's property.[38] Similarly, Jerry Jones, special assistant to the president, had written an August 9 memo for the White House staff: "By custom and tradition, the files of the White House Office belong to the President in whose Administration they are accumulated. It has been the invariable practice, at the end of an Administration, for the outgoing President or his estate to authorize the depository or disposition to be made of such files."[39] Arthur Sampson, the head of the General Services Administration (GSA), too, had answered a skeptical query from a Ralph Nader–connected public interest litigation group by saying that presidents since George Washington had considered the papers accumulated in office their personal property.[40]

Scalia was thrust into the matter when Ford decided he needed a formal legal opinion on who owned the documents, tapes, and other materials Nixon was still trying to get out to his home in San Clemente.[41] James

Wilderotter, who with Jon Rose was a deputy to Silberman, said, "I thought, 'Welcome to the job, Nino!' Who owns the tapes and papers: it was clearly an issue that had to be resolved." Yet Wilderotter said that if anyone had a temperament to handle such a tumultuous issue, it was Scalia. He described Scalia as intellectually gifted, loving argument for argument's sake, and—when challenged—feisty to the point of flicking his fingers under his chin in the familiar Sicilian retort. "He would do that in the office all the time," Wilderotter recalled. "The mark of supreme disdain."[42]

Scalia projected high-energy confidence as he moved through trying situations; he walked with a kind of hop in his step that could seem comical but reinforced the image of an undaunted personality. Yet looking back, Scalia recalled the bunker mentality prevalent in the post-Nixon weeks. "We were under siege," he said.[43]

The fourteen-page opinion shepherded by Scalia said that Nixon's recordings and White House documents were his personal property. "To conclude that such materials are not the property of former President Nixon would be to reverse what has apparently been the almost unvaried understanding of all three branches of the Government since the beginning of the Republic, and to call into question the practices of our Presidents since the earliest times,"[44] Scalia's memo said. He asserted that the national custom had been that the president's papers were regarded as his personal property, and he made no distinction for papers that might—as in 1974—be part of a legal controversy. The opinion was released to the public on September 8 over the signature of Attorney General Saxbe. It was an opinion that reflected the institutional mind-set of the executive branch. It did not acknowledge the constitutional crisis of the moment, at the heart of which were the records and tapes that were evidence of a cover-up.

At the same time, an agreement between Nixon and the General Services administrator Sampson dictated that the tapes and documents would be sent to a secure storage facility under GSA control near San Clemente. That part of the deal said that the former president would be given one of two keys to the storage vault and that any subpoenas for the materials would be directed to him.

The most historic and controversial action that day, September 8, 1974, was President Ford's pardoning of Nixon. That had been the result of more delicate and secretive maneuvering among the president's and former president's men. It came down to Ford himself believing it was the right thing to do. On the morning of August 30, 1974, he had called to the Oval Office Buchen and two other close advisers, Robert Hartmann and Jack Marsh. General Haig was already there. According to Hartmann's account, the new president told the men that he favored granting Nixon immunity from criminal prosecution. There was such a deafening silence in the room, Hartmann later wrote, that when the pendulum of an antique clock on the Oval Office wall ticked loudly, it sounded like a burst of machine-gun fire. Ford wanted to put the ordeal of Watergate behind the nation and avoid the spectacle of dragging a former president into court.[45]

"What's the rush?" asked Hartmann, who had been a top aide to Ford since his congressional days. "Why not Christmas Eve, or a year from now, when things quiet down?" Ford said there was no reason to delay; he had decided this was what he wanted to do. In making public his pardon, Ford said of Nixon and his family, "Theirs is an American tragedy in which we all have played a part. It can go on and on, or someone must write 'The End' to it. I have concluded that only I can do that . . . My conscience tells me that only I, as president, have the constitutional power to firmly shut and seal this book."[46]

The pardon inflamed public passions and would affect Ford's personal prospects when he sought to keep the White House in the November 1976 election. At the time, there was little that Congress or the special prosecutor Jaworski could do about the pardon, but they vigorously opposed the agreement giving Nixon personal control over the tapes and presidential documents. Congress soon passed the 1974 Presidential Recordings and Materials Preservation Act, ensuring that Nixon's papers were not turned over to him. The act directed the GSA to assume immediate custody over the materials so they could be used in court and eventually be open to the public.[47]

Congress countered Scalia's opinion on Nixon's ownership of the tapes with barely a second thought. The episode would be one of several that caused Scalia to jealously guard executive power and, in an atmosphere of distrust and suspicion, to consider Congress an adversary.

·

Ford and his people tried to move past Watergate. The president wanted to demonstrate that his administration was open and accountable. Yet when the first test came with a measure specifically involving public access to government records, Ford, taking advice from Deputy Attorney General Silberman and his new assistant Scalia, turned in another direction. The test had to do with proposed amendments to the 1966 Freedom of Information Act intended to speed up the government's response to requests for information. One provision allowed citizens to recover attorney's fees if they had to resort to lawsuits to get requested information. Another provision, designed to prevent agency officials from routinely stamping documents "classified," permitted judges to review documents the executive branch wanted to keep from public view. Silberman and Scalia played a key role in Ford's opposition to the proposed amendments.

"Although President Nixon had been advised to veto [the amendments]," the White House counsel Buchen wrote to Ford after he took office, "it would be contrary to your policy of furthering openness and candor in government to oppose this legislation." Buchen believed that Ford should sign the bill, and he warned that Silberman wanted to delay Ford's signing so that Silberman could make the case for rejecting the amendments.[48]

Earlier in the 1970s, when Scalia was chairman of the Administrative Conference, trying to make the bureaucracy run more efficiently, he had made known his opposition to amendments designed to enhance people's ability to obtain government information. He had said the act's flaws "cannot be cured as long as we are dominated by the obsession that gave them birth—that the first line of defense against an arbitrary executive is do-it-yourself oversight by the public and its surrogate, the press." Scalia called the possibility of attorney's fees being paid a "bounty"—one that could spur class action litigation. He believed that some people sought information out of "idle curiosity" and that federal judges were not equipped to referee the classification disputes. He argued that judges should not be allowed to order information declassified unless an agency's reasons for withholding it were demonstrably unreasonable. In these matters, Scalia believed, a presumption should exist favoring an agency's holding back of information.[49]

Now, as an assistant attorney general, Scalia was in a position to help convince the president that the Freedom of Information Act amendments would thwart administration efforts related to law enforcement, the military, and foreign affairs. He was part of a small group of Ford officials opposed to the act's amendments—among them Dick Cheney, then deputy chief of staff to Ford.[50] Scalia sought out officials in agencies who objected to the amendments and urged them to voice their views. He told John S. Warner, the general counsel for the Central Intelligence Agency, to "move quickly to make" CIA opposition clear to Ford.[51]

At the time, Cheney reported directly to Rumsfeld, the former Illinois congressman whom Ford had chosen as his chief of staff.[52] Observations about their early relationship have proved to be enduringly fitting. Robert Hartmann, a Ford loyalist and former journalist, vividly recalled in his memoir the ability of the Rumsfeld-Cheney duo to undercut rivals (including Hartmann) and influence the president: "Cheney was a serious student of political power and derived both his employment and his enjoyment from it. Whenever his private ideology was exposed, he appeared somewhat to the right of Ford, Rumsfeld or, for that matter, Genghis Khan. Rumsfeld and Cheney were a rare match. Their differences reinforced the team. Rummy was darkly handsome, like Tyrone Power. Cheney was a presentable young man who could easily be lost in a gaggle of Jaycee executives. His most distinguishing features were snake-cold eyes, like a Cheyenne gambler's. Rummy was expansive and, when it suited him, all smiles. Cheney's demeanor was low-key and even dour."[53] The complementary relationship endured. Years later, as he traced the rise of Rumsfeld and Cheney on war policy, James Mann wrote, "[D]espite their contrasting styles, the two men tended to think alike. They were to work together, on and off, over a course of more than three decades without any strong differences of opinion emerging between them."[54]

While Cheney attacked the Freedom of Information Act amendments from his White House post, Silberman and Scalia took the lead at the Department of Justice to try to shoot them down. Silberman explained years later that he believed "it was going to cost enormous amounts [of money]."[55] Scalia prepared a "fact sheet" related to the amendments that highlighted their potential costs. He wrote that they would lead to "expenditure of literally incalculable amounts of tax funds, for purposes that will in many cases be entirely private, without any provision for compensating the public Treasury." Scalia then wrote that "there is no reliable estimate of the overall cost of this legislation, but those experienced in administering the present Act believe it will be substantial," and he put a possible half-billion-dollar price tag on the legislation.[56]

Such arguments gathered momentum among Ford's top advisers. In the end, Ford was convinced to veto the Freedom of Information Act amendments on October 17, 1974, five weeks after he had assumed the presidency from Nixon. Within weeks, Congress overrode the veto, by a vote of 371–31 in the House and 65–27 in the Senate. It is unlikely that Scalia had even tried to count the votes. He would prove time and again that he did not grasp—or care to grasp or bow to—the ways of Capitol Hill.[57]

It was a formative moment for Scalia and Cheney. It was part of the genesis of their respective concerns over a wearing down of executive power. Decades later, Cheney would trace to these months in 1974 a corrosion of executive authority that he would commit to recapturing. "Over the years there has been an erosion of presidential power and authority," Cheney, who would become vice president from 2001 to 2009, would say. "The president of the United States needs to have his constitutional powers unimpaired, if you will, in terms of the conduct of national security policy. That's my personal view."[58]

For his part, Scalia would for years continue to argue for the president's "exclusive" authority, as he had termed it, to withhold information. He believed the Freedom of Information Act had "turned out to be one of many modern factors sapping the vitality of" executive branch institutions, stripping them of the privacy necessary for their effective operation.[59]

Testifying to Congress years later, Scalia explained his continuing opposition to the Freedom of Information Act amendments by referring to a *Peanuts* cartoon that "one of the more philosophical" of his children had brought to his attention:

"A worldly wise and somewhat overbearing Lucy asks the good-hearted and somewhat naive Charlie Brown, 'Charlie, what would you rather do, be captain of the baseball team or marry the cute redheaded girl?' And Charlie replies innocently, 'Why can't I do both?' to which Lucy responds, 'It's the real world, Charlie Brown.' "[60]

Aligning himself with cynical Lucy rather than the optimist Charlie Brown, Scalia continued in his testimony by stating his own real-world view: "It is a world that imposes choices, even ultimately upon a good-hearted and well-intentioned government." Working with Cheney and others who had moved from the Nixon to Ford administrations, Scalia had learned to maneuver within the "real world" of the executive branch. His tenure there after Watergate also provided him with an unusual lens through which he would continue to see the ways of the nation's capital. He would grow more suspicious of the press, more condescending toward Congress. And along with others in the executive branch fraternity of the 1970s (most conspicuously Dick Cheney), he would come to adopt a very clear attitude: "You're either with us—or against us."

THREE

WITNESS FOR THE EXECUTIVE

In the fall of 1975 the Democratic senator Edmund Muskie of Maine was using his Senate Government Operations subcommittee to challenge Ford administration assertions of "executive privilege" as a way to keep information secret, specifically documents from the CIA and national security activities. The post-Watergate mind-set of Muskie—indeed, of all Congress—differed strikingly from that of President Ford and his administration aides. The new president and his men were convinced that requests for sensitive documents were encroachments on the authority of the executive branch. Members of Congress, on the other hand, saw a continuation of unwarranted secrecy and stonewalling from the Nixon years. Here was one battle in a larger war over the power of the respective branches of government. It was a battle Antonin Scalia, with his rhetorical ability and philosophical commitment, was ready to take up. The competition between the two political branches fed Scalia's ambition and taught him enduring lessons in the ways of Washington.

"I am hopeful that we never again will be faced with a constitutional confrontation like the one we faced a year ago," Senator Muskie declared as he opened the series of hearings in the wood-paneled Dirksen hearing room.[1] "But, as the events of this [year] have demonstrated already, the need to assure Congress access to information held by the executive branch is no less vital. Just in the past two months, the Congress has met with delay, and outright refusals of its requests for information from the President and other officials of the executive branch."

Muskie, a longtime Republican nemesis, was well known to the country. The former governor of Maine had run unsuccessfully for vice president in 1968 and for the Democratic presidential nomination in 1972. He was tall and angular, with a craggy face, and his accent was distinctly Yankee; and in a Senate hearing room, as on the campaign stump, he was known for forceful rhetoric and a passionate temperament. As the hearings continued over several weeks, Muskie's cantankerous side was matched by one pugnacious witness of equally passionate temperament, Assistant Attorney General Scalia, who had become the voice of executive branch prerogatives at congressional hearings. Sitting in a witness chair, taking questions from members of Congress on a raised dais, Scalia was a stubborn witness against entreaties for information. Nearly twenty years younger than Muskie and more compact (five feet nine to Muskie's six feet four), Scalia was as mercurial and brainy as his inquisitor in the chairman's seat. In high school at Xavier, then at Georgetown University, Scalia had excelled on the debate team. When he was fifteen years old, during the 1952 Eisenhower–Stevenson campaign, he had qualified for a spot in a student political forum that landed him on television. He had been a high school and college thespian as well, and now, at age thirty-nine before members of Congress, he was still a natural showman. Onstage, Scalia was sharp-tongued and never tentative.

"I realize that anyone saying a few kind words about executive privilege after the events of the last few years is in a position somewhat akin to the man preaching the virtues of water after the Johnstown flood, or the utility of fire after the burning of Chicago," Scalia said at Muskie's hearing in the fall of 1975. "But fire and water are, for all that, essential elements of human existence."[2]

Scalia was fending off Muskie-sponsored legislation that would have required the administration to keep congressional committees regularly informed about executive branch matters, including national security. "It is, in short, a scheme which, if it is to be effective, will require the creation and maintenance of an enormous shadow bureaucracy within each of the houses of the Congress," Scalia insisted.[3] He said that Congress had little right to executive branch documents or to be kept apprised of its daily activities. And he complained that the proposed legislation would penalize executive branch officials for not responding to letters from individual members of Congress; that idea, he said, was "extraordinary."

The struggle over information was, of course, part of the larger battle over the power of the three branches, and Scalia was firm about keeping executive branch information away from members of Congress and the press. With Vietnam and Communist threats in the background, he and other Ford officials linked assertions of executive privilege to national security as they sought leeway on domestic wiretaps and other surveillance.[4] Members of Congress, however, were acutely aware of government abuses from unchecked surveillance. In a separate ongoing committee investigation led by Senator Frank Church, an Idaho Democrat, evidence was mounting of how the Nixon administration had used domestic wiretaps to spy on civil rights leaders, antiwar protestors, and journalists—to serve political interests more than to address foreign espionage.[5]

Muskie said he was "astounded" by Scalia's arguments against executive branch disclosures. "The notion that the Congress has a . . . constitutional right to inquire into anything that happens in the executive branch is challenged by your logic . . . I will listen to the rest of your statement, but I have listened for 10 pages here to this logic that is the most incredible exposition . . . that I have been exposed to in all of the time I have been in the Senate.

"Before I know it, you are going to be challenging my right as an individual senator to bring up the question," Muskie continued. "How petty can you get?"

Muskie accused Scalia of engaging in verbal "fencing."

Scalia believed that the authority to assert executive privilege—that is, to resist congressional requests and searches—was indispensable to the separation of powers. When he appeared on the Hill, he was taking up the Ford administration line, but this was not difficult for Scalia. He had an authoritarian instinct and a natural inclination to jealously guard presidential papers and prerogatives. He was suspicious of members of Congress. "In those days," Scalia said decades later, in a 2007 interview, "if you gave it to Congress, you just as well might send it to *The Washington Post.*" Scalia struck that chord at a 2007 judicial conference in Ottawa, Canada, too. According to Charlie Savage in his book, *Takeover,* Scalia said that as he and other legal and intelligence officials met daily in the White House situation room, they "decided which of the nation's most highly guarded secrets that day would be turned over to Congress, with scant assurance in those days that they would not appear in the *Washington Post* the next morning."[6]

He was energized by his confrontations with members of Congress. In the fall of 1975, simultaneous with the Muskie tussles, he sparred with a special committee chaired by the U.S. representative Otis G. Pike, a Democrat from New York, that was looking into potential abuses by U.S. intelligence agencies. Pike's committee had recommended that Secretary of State Henry Kissinger be cited for contempt of Congress for failing to produce classified documents about U.S. covert operations abroad. It fell to Scalia to go to the Hill and explain why Ford was asserting executive privilege and refusing to disclose the State Department information. Committee members wanted to know what involvement Scalia, a top Justice Department lawyer, had had in keeping the documents secret and whether he was now simply part of administration delaying tactics.

"When did you become involved in this controversy and this struggle?" Representative Robert Giaimo, a Connecticut Democrat, asked Scalia during a November 20, 1975, hearing.[7]

"I have been outside of it—"

"I am not interested in how long you were on the outside," Giaimo responded. "I want to know when you got on the inside of it."

"It depends on what you mean by on the inside," Scalia responded, naturally reluctant.

Giaimo shot back, "That depends on what you mean by on the outside."

"I guess it does," Scalia said. "I guess we agree then."

"You have been making a lot of statements here to which I am trying to pay close attention," Giaimo continued. "After all, you are here speaking for the executive branch of the United States and I am a little saddened by this spectacle of two branches of Government seemingly appearing to be in bitter combat over what we both claim to want to do, and that is to enlighten the American people on what is going on in their Government. But I am curious as to how long you have been privy to these secret decisions in the area of intelligence, and also those decisions involving what the executive branch is going to do vis-à-vis the Congress and compliance. How long have you been involved?"

"Regularly, I think is the answer," Scalia answered. "I was not trying to be cute. I am regularly involved in assisting the Attorney General in such matters as his advice to the President on whether executive privilege should be asserted."

Later in the hearing, the U.S. representative Ronald Dellums, a California Democrat, questioned further why members could not obtain all the documents sought. Scalia said the administration didn't want to "let these documents float about the place."

"That is the precise point I am trying to address," Dellums said. "Your stipulation or your characterization of 'floating about.' . . . I do not believe you have the right to challenge the integrity of this committee. To assume the documents are 'floating around' someplace is absurd . . . We have not been about the business of leaking any materials, and no one can state that."

"I withdraw 'floating around,' " Scalia said. "I should not have put it that way. My point stands, however, that we want the minimum possible circulation of this material, even in very secure places."

Added Scalia, "[W]e don't mistrust you at all; it is just your safes. We would rather have them where we can look after them."

Chairman Pike interjected, "Now, this has just degenerated. You don't mistrust us. You mistrust our safes."

A frustrated Pike later told Scalia, "I will say this: Regardless of the outcome of today's meeting, I think you can go back to those who sent you and say you did indeed accomplish your purpose—you stopped the committee for one more day."

"That was not my purpose, Mr. Chairman," Scalia said. "It is a serious matter you are considering, and I think it is worth a couple of hours before you cite a Secretary of State for contempt for the first time in the history of the country."

Recalling the episode years later, Scalia said he spent long nights at the White House trying to resolve the dispute. His wife, Maureen, recalled this period of her husband's life as tense and exhausting. "The hours were terrible," she said. "He slept in the White House, and I don't mean the Lincoln bedroom." But, she said, the nerve-racking work did not take a toll on him: "He thrives on that."[8]

Scalia recollected the years sparring over executive privilege with gusto, claiming in a "bring 'em on" tone that he held the superior position and was readier with rhetorical points than members of Congress. In the end, the Pike committee and Ford lawyers reached a deal over access to the State Department papers about covert operations between 1962 and 1972. Most but not all information was turned over, and neither side wanted to push a showdown to the point of going to court, uncertain of who would prevail.[9]

In a separate contentious dispute, Scalia served as the face of the Ford administration in a fight over the so-called newsman's privilege—a reporter's freedom from being compelled to identify a source of information in court. The Supreme Court in its 1972 decision in *Branzburg v. Hayes* had rejected arguments that the First Amendment protects the rights of journalists to refuse to reveal the identity of sources. In response, news organizations urged members of Congress to pass legislation creating a national right to keep certain sources confidential. The legislation would have protected journalists from judicially compelled disclosure of sources in criminal cases, unless the information sought was clearly shown to be "indispensable to the establishment of the offense charged" and unavailable by any other means.[10]

At a House Judiciary subcommittee hearing on the "shield" bill, Scalia faced off against another liberal champion, the Massachusetts representative Father Robert Drinan, the Jesuit priest whom the pope would eventually force to leave elective office. The issue was protection for journalists investigating government activities and potential wrongdoing, still very much at the forefront in the year after the Watergate scandal had brought down Nixon.[11]

The subcommittee chairman Robert Kastenmeier, a Wisconsin Democrat, began the session by saying that the federal shield law proposal "involves the balancing of vital but sometimes conflicting principles. The first is the well-known rule that the Government has the right to secure the testimony of its citizens. The second is the equally urgent proposition that the public should have the greatest possible access to the news and other information, and that members of the press shall not be cut off from their sources."[12]

Scalia argued that if the "shield" legislation went through, police would not be able to obtain information that a newspaper had acquired about a kidnapping or a series of bombings. Scalia also insisted to committee members that the 1972 Supreme Court ruling that rejected a First Amendment privilege nonetheless offered reporters sufficient protection against any truly intrusive government action. "The Supreme Court has given some indication in the *Branzburg* opinions that the worst abuses, which constitute harassment of the press, will be prevented by the Court itself," Scalia said as he took an unusually broad reading of the Court decision.

The dramatic high point of the hearing came as Drinan began questioning Scalia. They were a feisty pair. Neither was inclined to hold back. Neither shied from sarcasm. As the Jesuit Drinan peered down from the dais at the Jesuit-trained Scalia, he said, "I'm afraid, sir, I must say that the Department of Justice seems to be regressing." Drinan noted that the department in earlier years "at least admitted that there was a problem" of reporters being vulnerable to subpoenas concerning their sources. Drinan took strong exception to Scalia's idea that no federal legislation was required, especially because Scalia testified that the number of requests for Justice Department approval of subpoenas for newsmen had risen markedly in recent years.[13]

Then the two got down to the nitty-gritty, and Drinan abandoned the pretentious language of the hearing room. "[Y]ou cannot cop out by saying that . . . there is no federal problem," Drinan insisted. Scalia protested that he was not "copping out."

When Drinan asked Scalia who ultimately was in charge of subpoenas issued against journalists, Scalia said the attorney general. Drinan scoffed and said, "We have had so many!" Spectators laughed, well aware of the Nixon-Ford succession of attorneys general: John Mitchell, Richard Kleindienst, Elliot Richardson, William Saxbe, and now Edward Levi.[14] Drinan had, in fact, been one of Nixon's staunchest critics. Long before the culmination of the Watergate scandal, Drinan had proposed that Nixon be impeached for the secret bombing of Cambodia.

At the hearing with Scalia, Drinan captured the essential differences between the dueling executive and legislative approaches. "Your first norm seems to be whatever is good for law enforcement is good for the country," Drinan declared. "[Y]ou should start from my point of view, from the First Amendment, and say let us maximize the rights [of individuals]."

Scalia responded, "Mr. Drinan, my problem is this: I do not see any great First Amendment problems, any great societal interests."

That, in a nutshell, was Scalia. He simply did not believe the press needed to shield its sources or the information it had dug up. He objected to the idea that the press truly represented the public's interest.

Three decades later, in a far different situation, but one that coincidentally involved the former Ford aide Dick Cheney, Scalia would again reveal disdain for the watchdog role of the press. When Scalia was challenged as a justice to step out of a case involving Cheney, who became vice president in 2001, on the grounds that they had gone on a hunting trip together as the dispute was pending, Scalia refused: "The people must have confidence in the integrity of the justices, and that cannot exist in a system that assumes them to be corruptible by the slightest friendship or favor, and in an atmosphere where the press will be eager to find foot-faults."[15]

During nearly forty years in the public eye, Scalia would deride the news media time and again for aggressive efforts to report on government officials. He often saw their efforts as a "gotcha" exercise rather than as a benefit to democracy.

Scalia and other Ford staffers not only embraced a proprietary interest in government information, they resisted putting things down on paper in the first place. "When President Ford took office last August," *The New York Times* observed in March 1975, "one of the first things he did was cut down on the record-keeping at the White House, where for years virtually everything relating to the President had been put on paper or tapes. It was the tape recordings and reams of memoranda that had brought the forced resignation of President Nixon. Mr. Ford was so sensitive to this fact that at first he resisted even the simple keeping of the log of his daily routine . . . [T]he old practice of memo-writing has been cut drastically, not only in the White House but in the departments."[16]

Scalia was not a natural chronicler. Years later he would be appalled at the notion that the Supreme Court justice Harry Blackmun kept all correspondence that crossed his desk and maintained a daily log. The trove was made public after Blackmun's death.[17]

Within an administration taking a hard line against Congress, Scalia was among those taking the hardest. That was seen in his drive to keep government records secret and also in his support for broad administration discretion on activities related to foreign intelligence. A hallmark of Nixon's tenure had been the centralization of power in the executive branch and the quest for secrecy. A lingering byproduct of that attitude and of the Cold War was unchecked domestic spying and other intelligence activities discovered by the Church Committee and detailed in its 1975 and 1976 reports. The committee findings generated widespread public and congressional alarm, including over whether the unchecked monitoring of telephone calls was infringing on Americans' privacy rights. The Ford administration faced both the consequences of prior administrations' intelligence abuses and pressure to end its own exclusive power over warrantless wiretaps. Scalia, who deemed the warrantless wiretaps "a practical necessity," opposed moves to remove executive branch control.[18]

"When counterintelligence agents have an opportunity to copy a codebook in the room of Colonel Abel, a Russian spy, they do not want to leave a warrant advising him that they have been there," Scalia wrote years later, referring to the notorious Soviet spy Rudolph Abel and drawing a worst-case scenario. "Indeed, there would probably be no legal basis to obtain a judicial warrant for such an entry . . . The Fourth Amendment, after all, does not require a warrant; it requires reasonable searches and seizures, and in the intelligence field reasonableness does not demand the service of a warrant."[19]

Scalia watched with apprehension as the pragmatic attorney general Edward Levi worked with Congress on a law to establish a panel of federal judges to review, in secret, domestic wiretap requests. (Levi, a respected former University of Chicago president and law dean who defied labels such as conservative or liberal, had been chosen by Ford to try to restore the reputation of the Justice Department.) The Foreign Intelligence Surveillance Act (FISA) passed Congress during the Carter administration in 1978. When asked years later about the transfer of domestic-wiretapping authority from the executive branch to the special Foreign Intelligence Surveillance Act court, Scalia said, "I had seen how [approval for secret wiretaps] worked under the executive, and it was not done irresponsibly. I don't like the secret court, which is what FISA is. I did not think that was an improvement. I think that given the times, it was inevitable. I don't know whether Ed [Levi] thought that as an original matter it was a good idea. But it wasn't an original matter. It was going to happen. So the thing was to try to make it as little harmful to the executive as possible."[20]

Scalia's idealism was being tempered by realism.

During his tenure in the Ford administration Scalia also observed close up the filling of a Supreme Court vacancy, caused by the retirement of William O. Douglas, and how valuable friends in the right places could be to a possible nominee. Although not directly involved in the 1975 selection of a successor to Douglas, Scalia followed Attorney General Levi's actions in the process that led to the appointment of John Paul

Stevens. The process Scalia witnessed flowed from a traditional approach to judicial selection. In time, Republican administrations would raise the stakes and move more boldly, to Scalia's advantage.

Douglas, named to the Court in 1939 and by 1975 setting a record for longevity, was the last of the Franklin D. Roosevelt appointees who had undertaken a major transformation of American law. This had occurred around the time of Scalia's birth. The judicial revolution—which brought new liberalism, then an eventual conservative backlash that helped to open the door to Scalia's own judicial ascendancy—began with Roosevelt's New Deal initiatives. In the midst of the Depression, he had proposed several programs to stimulate industrial production and provide some relief to workers. Businesses challenged the programs as unconstitutional expansions of federal power. On the day of Scalia's birth, in fact, March 11, 1936, the Supreme Court heard a case against one of the initiatives, the Guffey Bituminous Coal Conservation Act, which limited work hours and prescribed minimum wages for coal workers. Coal producers and operators claimed that the Guffey Coal Act interfered with their business practices and represented unconstitutional meddling with the states.

The pristine neoclassical Supreme Court building across the street from the Capitol had just been opened. Its courtroom was filled to capacity for the Coal Act oral arguments. More than a thousand spectators rotated in and out of a courtroom that held only 320 at a time. "The justices attended very closely to discussion of the coal case," *The New York Times* reported, "but only three questions were put from the bench during the entire argument."[21] (In the contemporary era, a hundred questions could easily be asked during an oral argument session.)

Two months later, in 1936, the Supreme Court ruled that Congress had exceeded its powers to regulate interstate commerce and struck down the Coal Act by a 6–3 vote.[22] The decision followed earlier rulings against Roosevelt's experiments intended to reverse the ill effects of the Depression, including the Railroad Retirement Act.[23] Roosevelt's initiatives tumbled down like a house of cards. After invalidating the Coal Act, the Court overturned the Municipal Bankruptcy Act and voided a New York state minimum wage law.[24]

Without question, the Court majority's view of the Constitution was dramatically at odds with that of Roosevelt, who declared on March 9, 1937, "We have . . . reached the point as a nation where we must take

action to save the Constitution from the Court and the Court from itself."
Roosevelt proposed the appointment of a new justice for every current
justice over age seventy. Six of the nine were over seventy at the time, most
of whom were antagonistic to his New Deal initiatives. The Court-packing
plan drew immediate, intense, and widespread opposition.[25] Roosevelt's
political miscalculation would endure with the Roosevelt legacy, but it was
not without effect on the sitting justices. Within weeks of Roosevelt's
announcement, the situation changed among a majority of the justices.
The Court reversed a stance it had taken against New York's minimum
wage law by upholding a Washington state requirement of minimum
wages for women and children.[26] Whether the switch was a response to
Roosevelt and public criticism or part of the justices' own legal evolution,
the new decision buried the notion that the "liberty" embodied in the due
process guarantee protected a business's "liberty to contract." The Court
also adopted a broader view of "interstate commerce" to enhance congressional authority, and thus ended the era of special protection for property
rights and favoring of business.

Douglas, a young beneficiary of Roosevelt's effort to remake the Court,
was appointed in 1939 and became a reliable vote for the expansion of
individual rights that marked the mid-century Court and would generate
the countermovement that would eventually advance Scalia. During
Douglas's record thirty-six years and seven months on the bench, he
became a champion of social causes, from free speech to personal privacy.
He penned the 1965 *Griswold v. Connecticut* decision finding a right to
privacy in the Constitution's Fourteenth Amendment and laying the
groundwork for the 1973 *Roe v. Wade* decision that made abortion legal
nationwide. Scalia vehemently disagreed with the *Roe* decision and believed that Douglas's ruling in *Griswold*—valuing personal liberty over
government interests—had gone beyond the bounds of constitutional
interpretation.

By late October 1975 it was becoming clear that Douglas was at the
end of his tenure. He had suffered a stroke several months earlier and was
increasingly frail. He had just turned seventy-seven and could barely participate in oral arguments and deliberations on cases.[27] Some of his colleagues were pressuring him to retire and even trying to take away his
vote, which heightened internal tensions among the brethren.

Justice Byron White, an appointee of John F. Kennedy's, complained to

Chief Justice Burger about the secret maneuverings to squeeze out Douglas: "I should like to register my protest against the decision of the Court not to assign the writing of any opinions to Mr. Justice Douglas." White's letter was an effort to fight the tide of the majority. In referring to Douglas as "Mr. Justice" rather than by his first name, as usually occurred in inner-office correspondence, White also was consciously attempting to restore some respect to his veteran colleague. White had personally hand-delivered copies of the letter to the other justices.[28]

In his letter, White reminded Burger that the Constitution says that justices can be removed from office only through impeachment by Congress. "If there is sufficient doubt about Justice Douglas' mental abilities that he should have no assignments of opinions and if his vote should not be counted in 5–4 cases when he is one of the five, I fail to see how his vote should be counted or considered in any case or why we should listen to him in conference at all," White wrote. He said that it was also unfair to the public and litigants to restrict Douglas's participation without making the action public.

As Douglas's colleagues struggled with the best way to handle the situation, Chief Justice Burger took the unusual step of going outside the Court's marble walls. In a letter to President Ford marked "confidential," Burger told Ford that the Supreme Court had "been functionally only a court of eight," rather than nine, for nearly a year because of Douglas's ill health. Burger suggested that Douglas might soon be stepping down and urged Ford to act quickly if he did and to consider someone who already had been a judge. Burger wanted Ford to look for someone under age sixty.

Two days later, on November 12, Douglas gave in and wrote to Ford that he would retire: "It was my hope, when I returned to Washington in September, that I would be able to continue to participate in the work of the Supreme Court. I have learned, however, after these last two months, that it would be inadvisable for me to attempt to carry on the duties required of a member of the Court. I have been bothered with incessant and demanding pain which depletes my energy to the extent that I have been unable to shoulder my full share of the burden."[29] Ford sent Douglas a note of appreciation. Yet there was some irony in Ford's being able to appoint Douglas's successor. When Ford was House minority leader in 1970, he had tried to spur impeachment of Douglas, partly for his judicial liberalism, partly for his sensational private life. Douglas, an adventurer who traveled the globe, was married four times, the last two times when he was in his sixties to women in their twenties. Ford's effort failed.[30]

Now Attorney General Levi was shepherding the selection process in his low-key style. Despite their differing personalities and ideological visions, Levi and Scalia developed a mutual respect and friendship. Once, when Scalia and Maureen invited Levi and his wife, along with Robert Bork and his wife, over for dinner, Scalia had to handle a delicate matter of etiquette rather than the law. After taking their orders for cocktails, Scalia discovered that the floor-level liquor cabinet was locked, and the key, usually in the lock, was missing. "The obvious culprit was our toddler, who had evidently taken the key and dropped it who knew where," Scalia later wrote. "I will never forget the image of the Attorney General, the Solicitor General, and I . . . crawling around on our hands and knees on the living room Oriental rug, feeling for the missing key."[31]

Levi gave Ford a list of ten possible successors, pared down from a broader field of about twice that number. Scalia's name was on the early, sweeping list of eighteen men Levi prepared.[32] But Scalia was still a relative youth (age thirty-nine), untested, and, as would be seen, much more suited toward a different model of judicial selection. Attorney General Levi, having prepared the new, more selective list, told Ford he "would place the greatest emphasis" on the U.S. Appeals Court judge John Paul Stevens, of Chicago, Solicitor General Bork, and Dallin Oaks, then president of Brigham Young University. Levi described Stevens, whom he knew from Chicago legal circles, as a "judge of the first rank, highly intelligent" and as "a moderate conservative in his approach to judicial problems."[33]

Stevens, whom Scalia knew by reputation but had not met, was fifty-five years old and just under an informal age limit set by administration lawyers to ensure that whomever they named had a significant tenure. His undergraduate degree was from the University of Chicago, his law degree from Northwestern University, and between college and law school Stevens had served in the navy. For helping to monitor secret Japanese transmissions during World War II, he had been awarded the Bronze Star. After Northwestern, where he coedited the law review, he had become a law clerk to the Supreme Court justice Wiley Rutledge. Returning to Chicago, Stevens specialized in antitrust cases. He first attained public prominence in 1969 with his leadership of a commission that investigated two Illinois Supreme Court justices accused of taking a bribe. His work, which forced the justices' resignations, led to an appointment by Nixon in 1970 to a federal appeals court and brought him more in the orbit of the University of Chicago president and former law dean Levi.

Scalia recalled Levi's reviewing all of Stevens's opinions. He was also very aware of their friendship. "They were both Lab schoolers," Scalia said years later, meaning that both men as children had attended the University of Chicago's laboratory prep school.[34] Both, too, had similarly unassuming personalities while favoring dapper suits and bow ties. Neither of them exuded the aggressiveness that would define the next Republican administration and its judicial agenda in the next decade.

As Ford waded through his options, he resisted pressure to go with a more conservative jurist or to name the first woman justice. First Lady Betty Ford especially was pushing for a woman nominee. Within a few days, Ford was down to the most promising contenders, including Stevens, Bork, and the U.S. Appeals Court judges Philip Tone of Illinois and Arlin Adams of Pennsylvania.

In a lesson to insiders like Scalia, who watched the machinations of the selection process, Ford appeared to be looking for someone with stellar credentials and little political or ideological baggage. That was a priority distinct to Ford and to the times. Of Bork, Levi had written in a memo to Ford, "Before his appointment [to solicitor general], Mr. Bork was generally known in the profession as one of the foremost conservative critics of the prevalent interpretation and enforcement of the antitrust laws. In constitutional law, Mr. Bork . . . [played a] prominent role, in the first term of President Nixon's administration, as one of the draftsmen and proponents of proposed legislation to eliminate busing as a judicial remedy for school segregation . . . If Mr. Bork was appointed to the Court, there would be little doubt of his intellectual capacity for the work. There would be equally little doubt that, on the Court, Mr. Bork would provide strong reinforcement to the Court's most conservative wing—particularly in the sense of a need to limit the extended role of the courts."[35]

Uninterested in an ideological lightning rod, Ford put a little "No. 4" next to Bork's name on a list he carried around. He gave Stevens No. 1. Ford also penned himself a separate note regarding Stevens: "Supreme Ct—good man."[36]

The day of the announcement, the Ford aide Max Friedersdorf first called the offices of several members of Congress. It was the Thanksgiving weekend, so Friedersdorf had trouble reaching some members. House Majority Leader Tip O'Neill, according to Friedersdorf's note recounting reactions to Stevens, said, "Who? . . . I never heard of him—who is [he]?" House Republican Whip Bob Michel was pleased that the nominee was from the upper Midwest Seventh Circuit. Strom Thurmond of the Senate Judiciary Committee asked, "Is he a strict constructionist?" Senate Majority Leader Mike Mansfield asked whether a reputed moderate would "cause trouble with the Reagan people" who were preparing to mount a presidential challenge to Ford.[37]

Stevens was regarded as a moderate jurist with nominally conservative credentials and little background or interest in politics.[38] He was also plainly Levi's man. In the end, he won Senate approval on a 98–0 vote. Afterward, Ford's personal list of names was turned over to chief of staff Cheney, who had not had a strong hand in the selection but did have an interest in keeping records secret. "This is extremely sensitive," Cheney wrote in a memo to an aide. "It should be locked up. Again, with the President's very personal papers."[39]

A few weeks later Scalia argued his first and only case before the Supreme Court, with Stevens newly seated. Scalia represented the Ford administration as it sided with Alfred Dunhill of London seeking money from Cuba for cigar exports. Justice Blackmun, who kept a log of arguments, regularly included notations on lawyers' appearances. He described Scalia as "plump." Years later Scalia remembered little about the arguments or the case, except that Ford's new justice did not sign the entirety of the majority opinion that favored the United States's position. Stevens concurred only in portions of the opinion and the bottom-line judgment for Dunhill.[40]

Patrick Buchanan, a former Nixon speechwriter who had a special interest in judicial nominations, was also watching the new justice. Buchanan had thrown his lot in with Ford after Watergate, but when he saw the Stevens nomination, he changed his mind. Buchanan later wrote, "In January of 1976, after a [televised] New Year's interview with President Ford, in which he said that Justice John Paul Stevens . . . represented the kind of appointments Ford would make, if elected in his own right, I publicly endorsed Ronald Reagan's challenge against President Ford in the primaries. Putting non-controversial moderates on the

United States Supreme Court was not why I had joined up with Richard Nixon."[41]

Such views simmering in other corners of conservatism would eventually benefit Scalia. The right wing would rise up, and Reagan and his men would ensure that they did not make another choice in the mold of Stevens. In fact, the model that produced an older, gentlemanly candidate would give way to one favoring the young and brash. For the time being, the Stevens episode yielded another lesson for Scalia. Still under forty years old, he had witnessed the workings of the executive and the importance of knowing the insiders and their motivations. Levi had been there for Stevens. Timing, Scalia could see, was everything.

Scalia could have remained in corporate law, which would have meant more money. He could have devoted himself to academia, which would have been the life of his father. But he opted for the federal government and in relatively short order had landed a powerful spot in the Justice Department that was exactly right for him. He developed important connections there, too. Of Cheney, Scalia would later say, "He knew who I was. He knew my qualifications. He knew I was on the right team."[42]

As it turned out, Scalia's political savvy, natural combativeness, and allegiance to the executive were ideally suited for the post-Watergate time. His authoritarian bent, rooted in a rule-oriented father and Catholic upbringing, fostered his concern for the erosion of the executive branch and encroachments on the presidency.

Yet Scalia's tenure with the Nixon and Ford administrations made him a realist and led him to acquire some patience, too. Despite his preference for the executive, Scalia wrote in an undated memo while assistant attorney general that "the doctrine of Executive privilege is (and probably should be) subject to the tugging and hauling of power between the branches of Government."[43] Scalia recognized that Congress had an arsenal of ways of getting people to talk, for example, by withholding action on nominations or other matters dear to the executive unless testimony was provided.

Scalia's time in the Situation Room and before congressional committees had taught him that power belongs to the vigilant. He was learning to play the long game.

FOUR

MEETING OF THE MINDS

———◆———

The former host of the quiz show *What's My Line?*, John Charles Daly, opened a December 1978 legal forum by paraphrasing Alexis de Tocqueville, observing that "there was hardly a political question in the United States that did not sooner or later turn into a judicial one."[1] The panel of lawyers had assembled at the American Enterprise Institute in Washington, D.C. The liberal-leaning Brookings Institution had pioneered the "think tank" scene in Washington decades earlier. Now the AEI was providing a counterweight and offering a home for conservative thinkers, particularly after Jimmy Carter won the White House from Gerald Ford in November 1976 and Ford's high-ranking partisans needed a place to land. After the election it was a natural next step for Antonin Scalia, looking for teaching jobs, to take an office at the institute, joining his friend from the Nixon and Ford administrations, Laurence Silberman. Even when Scalia and other former Ford aides moved on to more permanent jobs, they stayed within the AEI fraternity; in the fall of 1977 Scalia began teaching law at the University of Chicago but kept his affiliation as an adjunct scholar and editor of the AEI magazine, *Regulation*.[2]

The topic of the December 1978 evening—"An Imperial Judiciary: Fact or Myth?"—referred to an emerging notion that judges were exerting too much power in American life and usurping the legislative and executive branch roles. "The judiciary is now the target," Daly said, noting that in contemporary America, Tocqueville's assertion had a new twist. "The charge is now made that the courts function too broadly, and that their decisions culminate in a reordering of the economic, social, and political life of the nation. While we recently heard cries of an imperial presidency, we now hear of an imperial judiciary."

Scalia had long believed that judges were wrongly using their own personal values to decide legal issues. That viewpoint was gaining currency in the 1970s, as the Supreme Court guaranteed abortion rights and federal judges took control of segregated school systems and began managing poorly run prisons. Panelists at the forum moderated by Daly—a son-in-law of Earl Warren, whose tenure as chief justice embodied the notion of a commanding judiciary—were Scalia; Silberman; and, for balance, Abram Chayes, a Harvard law professor who had served in the Kennedy administration, and Ira Glasser, the executive director of the American Civil Liberties Union.

"Where do rights exist, and where do they not exist?" Scalia said as the discussion grew heated and he took aim at *Roe v. Wade*, which was decided in 1973 under Warren's successor, Chief Justice Warren Burger. "In the abortion situation, for example, what right exists—the right of the woman who wants an abortion to have one, or the right of the unborn child not to be aborted? In the past that was considered to be a societal decision that would be made through the democratic process. But now the courts have shown themselves willing to make that decision for us. That is the major objection most people have with the direction the courts are now taking, and it is the major reason why some people speak of an imperial judiciary."

Scalia, forty-two years old and free of the yoke of a government job, was becoming accustomed to having his say. He no longer had to "call it down the middle," as he said he did at the Justice Department Office of Legal Counsel.[3] His naturally confrontational style was surfacing. Teaching at the University of Chicago, recommended by his boss in the Ford administration, Edward Levi, Scalia liked to mix it up with students and get arguments going. He complained that he encountered too many students who had turned to law "to save the world." There are far better ways to save the world, he griped, than becoming a lawyer.[4]

Yet even as Scalia in middle age was developing a more rigid view of the law, he still had bursts of idealism. He would sometimes end the semester by reading to his students a passage from *A Man for All Seasons*, Robert Bolt's play about Sir Thomas More. Scalia liked to cite it as a tribute to fair legal processes. In it, More tells his son-in-law Roper, "Whoever hunts for me, Roper, God or Devil, will find me hiding in the thickets of the law! And I'll hide my daughter with me! Not hoist her up to the main-mast of your seagoing principles! They put about too nimbly!"[5]

Scalia found a hero in More, the Catholic lawyer who became lord chancellor of England and was beheaded in 1535 after refusing to approve of Henry VIII's marriage to Anne Boleyn and swear to Henry's ecclesiastical supremacy. Referring to Bolt's rendering of More's legal fidelity, Scalia said, "It's such a beautiful expression of the importance of law."[6] Beyond More's principles, Bolt was attracted to his protagonist because he "seized life in great variety and almost greedy quantities." Such words would resonate with Scalia, a connoisseur of food and drink, an opera lover, an enthusiast of many intellectual pursuits.

In Chicago's Hyde Park neighborhood, Scalia and Maureen bought an old fraternity house on Woodlawn Avenue. They now had eight children. Ann, the eldest, was seventeen in 1978, and their newest baby, Christopher, was two years old. In returning to teaching, Scalia was able to spend more time with his children. "Teaching," he said, "permits you time to live on a more human scale."[7] But he was not the kind of professor who settled into a life of writing and reflection. He yearned for an audience. The former high school and college debater was quick, bold, and singularly confident. At the AEI session, he asserted that judges were enforcing "rights, so-called, on which there is no societal agreement, from the abortion cases, at one extreme, to school dress codes and things of that sort."

The Harvard professor Chayes, who believed the judiciary was providing the appropriate check on legislative and executive power, held the opposite view. He argued that judges were not reaching out and grabbing power, but were legitimately trying to protect individual rights. Judges, Chayes countered, have "not only seen gray-area violations of rights; they have walked into mental institutions and prisons and seen people being tortured, having hoses forced down their throats, and things like that. Is a judge to sit idly by and disregard such things? As I look around at the audience here, I do not see any prisoners. I see a couple of women and very few blacks. Mainly, I see a bunch of middle-class lawyers like myself. The black, the poor, the women, the prisoners, and mental patients can get into the courts, even if they cannot get in here."

As the audience applauded, Scalia retorted, "Of course we are against forcing hoses down people's throats, and there the judiciary should step in forcefully. But I did not realize that was what we were talking about today. I thought we were talking about more frilly issues, such as the judiciary's prescription of so many air conditioners per room in mental institutions, or their prescriptions against school dress codes."

Glasser, newly at the helm of the ACLU, interjected, "If you are basing your entire argument about an imperial judiciary on dress codes, then you are trivializing the problem."[8]

"No, I'm not basing it on dress codes," Scalia responded. "I have mentioned the striking down of a referendum regarding open-housing laws, the overturning of local funding of schools, the imposition of mandatory busing—a number of instances."[9]

Glasser and Scalia went around and around on busing, a practice ordered by some judges for schools in the throes of desegregation. "The assertion that most people oppose busing is nonsense," Glasser said. "Nobody opposes busing in this country except people who oppose it for the purpose of integration . . . They do not object to being on the bus; they object to where the bus is going. You can disagree, but that is not the same thing as saying they oppose busing."

"We could say the same thing about a person who is kidnapped," Scalia countered with typical bite. "He does not mind being in the car. He just cares about where the car is going."

By the end of the AEI session, the panelists had trudged through all the legal battlegrounds of the 1970s—school busing, abortion, religion in the public schools. On all of these fronts, Scalia believed judges were meddling. He thought appointed judges were asserting their values (values Scalia often found suspect) into matters best left to elected lawmakers and majority votes. The man who had been part of the Nixon administration—branded an "imperial presidency"—firmly believed the federal bench was exceeding its constitutional limits and deserved the label of "imperial judiciary."

The school busing controversy arose from the reality that two decades after the Supreme Court's 1954 *Brown v. Board of Education*, many school districts still were failing to provide equal resources for black and white students. To try to end disparate opportunities and recurring segregation, federal judges ordered more tax money to be spent on certain districts or required the busing of black children into white neighborhoods and whites into black areas. It was the latter move that ignited protests and violence, most notably in Boston. In one notorious incident in April 1976, two years before the AEI forum and while Scalia was at the Justice Department, Theodore Landsmark, a black lawyer involved in a desegregation case, was attacked by a group of white teenagers as he was leaving City Hall. One of the youths, Joseph Rakes, wielded a flagpole as a spear against Landsmark, an indelible image that was caught on television and in the next day's newspapers.[10]

As the battle over abortion rights raged, hospitals and health clinics were the front lines. The Supreme Court's 1973 *Roe v. Wade* decision had found a right to abortion in the Fourteenth Amendment's due process guarantee of personal liberty.[11] The ruling, in the case of a Texas carnival worker who claimed she had been raped, generated the Right to Life movement and transformed American politics. When state and local governments tried to restrict when the abortion procedure could be performed, some physicians, hospitals, and women's rights groups sued to challenge the restriction as violations of the constitutional guarantee of *Roe v. Wade.*

The controversy over the role of religion in public life was as old as the nation. In the mid-1970s it emerged in challenges to government programs providing aid to religious schools. The Supreme Court allowed public money to be spent on textbooks and transportation for children in such schools but forbade them tuition reimbursement or tax credits. As a law professor, Scalia complained about the latter Supreme Court decisions denying aid. He shuttled back and forth between Chicago and Washington to testify before Congress in support of "vouchers"—public money for parents who chose to send their children to religious schools.[12]

Scalia acknowledged that Supreme Court rulings suggested such vouchers were unconstitutional. But he said Congress should proceed despite those rulings. "The reason is that the Court's decisions in this field set forth neither a settled, nor a consistent, nor even a rational line of authority that you could rely on even if you wanted to," he said during one hearing. "That is a strong statement, but it doesn't take much effort to demonstrate its truth." Scalia went on to explain mockingly that under the Court's rules, the state could pay for religion students' bus transportation to school, but not for field trips to a zoo or museum, and could pay for textbooks, but not supplementary materials such as maps.[13]

In Scalia's mind, society had many problems that simply were not the domain of judges. He believed the Constitution's commands were limited, and outside those limits, judges had no authority to go beyond applying the solution elected officials had commanded. He also was skeptical that judges could know what course was best for the country. "Put not your trust in princes," he would say, scornful of the idea that judges could solve the real problems of the people.[14]

Separating himself from many other commentators of the day, Scalia was not afraid to speak in confrontational, even brazen terms. And his sense of showmanship made him a captivating, memorable speaker. During an appearance at Washington University in St. Louis in 1978, Scalia offered a provocative critique of affirmative action on the job and in schools. "From racist principles flow racist results," he contended of programs that took account of a person's skin color to compensate for past discrimination.[15]

Congress had passed the Civil Rights Act in 1964 to try to bring equality in the workplace to blacks and whites and women and men. By the mid-1970s, many private and government measures to advance minorities and women had led to complaints of "reverse discrimination"—the claim was that qualified white men were being spurned to meet "quotas" for blacks or women. The Supreme Court began the long and tortuous process of addressing such complaints in the 1970s, when it held that Title VII's ban on discrimination allowed private employers to adopt race-conscious affirmative action programs to help blacks and Hispanics. In a separate ruling, the Court upheld college admissions policies that considered an applicant's race.[16] These decisions vexed Scalia, who believed that government should not compensate racial minorities, as a group, for wrongs of the past. He believed that such programs punished whites who had no hand in the original discrimination.

"My father came to this country when he was a teen-ager," Scalia said, launching into a lesson in ethnic resentment during his Washington University speech. "Not only had he never profited from the sweat of any black man's brow, I don't think he had ever seen a black man. There are, of course, many white ethnic groups that came to this country in great numbers relatively late in its history—Italians, Jews, Irish, Poles—who not only took no part in, and derived no profit from, the major historic suppression of the currently acknowledged minority groups, but were, in fact, themselves the object of discrimination by the dominant Anglo-Saxon majority . . . [T]o compare their racial debt . . . with that of those who plied the slave trade, and who maintained a formal caste system for many years hereafter, is to confuse a mountain with a molehill."[17]

Referring to the white judges who were responsible for such rulings, Scalia also said, "[C]uriously enough, we find that in the system of restorative justice established by the [John Minor] Wisdoms and the [Lewis F.] Powells and the [Byron R.] Whites, it is precisely *these* groups [the Italians, Jews, Irish, Poles] that do most of the restoring. It is they who, to a disproportionate degree, are the competitors with the urban blacks and Hispanics for jobs, housing, education—all those things that enable one to scramble to the top of the social heap where one can speak eloquently (and quite safely) of restorative justice."

In and out of scholarly circles, Scalia was a relatively lonely voice of defiant conservatism. But America was changing. On the political scene, the shift was evident in the figure of Ronald Reagan, who was running for president on an antigovernment domestic policy agenda. As he declared that the federal bureaucracy was the enemy of the people, he targeted so-called activist judges. The 1980 Republican platform, on which Reagan campaigned, described model judges as those who believed "in the decentralization of the federal government and efforts to return decision-making power to state and local elected officials . . . who respect traditional family values and the sanctity of innocent human life . . . [and] who share our commitment to judicial restraint."[18]

Scalia was not active in Reagan's presidential bid. In fact, as Scalia put it, he had not worked for any serious candidate since he went door-to-door for his uncle Vince Panaro, a Democrat, in local campaigns in the 1950s. But Scalia liked Reagan's conservative agenda. It mirrored his thinking.

Edwin Meese, a former prosecutor who had worked with Reagan since the 1960s, said Reagan believed that "the modern liberal mind-set" of the 1960s and 1970s had brought about a judicial "social engineering" related to abortion rights, school desegregation, and criminal defendants' protection. Writing later about how he and Reagan had wanted to transform the federal bench, Meese insisted that "abortion, banning prayer from schools, pornography, busing, and leniency toward crime all resulted from federal court decisions."[19]

With his complaints about judges, Reagan and his top aides were pulling a page from the Arizona Republican senator Barry Goldwater's unsuccessful presidential campaign in 1964 and from Richard Nixon's winning strategy in 1968 and 1972. But Reagan's message resonated with more force than that of his GOP predecessors. He spoke to the free-market desires of business conservatives—important to the corporate bent of the AEI crowd—and tapped into the moral outrage of social conservatives against abortion and for school prayer. Reagan also energized theorists such as Scalia who were propounding a search for the original meaning of the Constitution. Arguments for an "originalist" interpretation differed from the "institutional deference" view but aligned with it at this time and reinforced the contention that judges should broadly defer to elected officials on social policy concerns.

In November 1980 all of this moved beyond the theoretical as Reagan won the presidency, defeating Jimmy Carter by nearly 10 percent of the popular vote. Within weeks of the election, the former president Nixon offered Reagan advice related to judges. In an eleven-page memo that covered several topics, Nixon wrote, "I very deliberately appointed conservative justices to the [Supreme] Court who shared my philosophy that it was the responsibility of the Court to interpret the law rather than make it."

"Because he had a liberal attorney general," Nixon continued, referring to the moderate Edward Levi, "Ford appointed [John Paul] Stevens, who has lined up with the liberals on the Court in virtually every significant case . . . You will leave a great legacy both in your new approach to economic policy and in your foreign policy. But the most lasting legacy will be your impact on the Supreme Court."[20]

William French Smith, Reagan's longtime personal adviser from California and new attorney general, held on to Nixon's letter. "We believed that the groundswell of conservatism that swept Ronald Reagan into office in 1980," Smith recalled in his memoir, "made it an opportune time to urge upon the courts a return to fundamental legal principles, thereby diminishing judicial activism."[21]

From his perch as a University of Chicago professor, Scalia followed these developments closely. His former colleagues from the American Enterprise Institute were moving back into government. Scalia was feeling restless. He had been looking around for other teaching jobs and for deanships, including at Washington and Lee School of Law in Lexington, Virginia.[22] Earlier in 1980, with Maureen pregnant with their ninth child, he had uprooted his family for a temporary one-year position at Stanford University in California. Now Reagan's election opened new possibilities, and Scalia would have jumped at the chance to move back into the executive branch. He had ideas for the president. "One of the Reagan Administration's first tasks," he wrote in an editor's column of *Regulation* magazine, "should be to reduce the reach of the agencies and regulators: get them out of people's business [and] businesses' business."[23]

There would be a financial disadvantage to leaving his teaching post at the University of Chicago for government work. Scalia was making an estimated $50,000 as a professor, was paid about $15,000 by the American Enterprise Institute for editing *Regulation* magazine, and accepted a handful of consulting contracts on the side that brought him additional tens of thousands.[24] Most significantly, the University of Chicago had a policy of paying the college tuition of all faculty children. If a child did not attend the University of Chicago, the school provided reimbursement for tuition elsewhere. That benefit was worth hundreds of thousands of dollars to a man with a large family.

It was not enough, however, to keep Scalia from trying to win a high-ranking job in Reagan's social counterrevolution, or to keep him harnessed to a place he disliked. The University of Chicago's Hyde Park neighborhood was not a good match for the Scalias. They thought their children's school not academically rigorous enough. They found their neighborhood Catholic parish too liberal and drove into downtown Chicago in search of a more conservative place to worship. Born, reared, and educated on the East Coast, they were not happy in Chicago.

Scalia's first choice for a position in the Reagan administration was the solicitor general of the United States. In a top-ranking post at the Justice Department, the solicitor general represented the federal government at the Supreme Court. Attired in dark gray morning coat, gray striped pants, tie, and vest as he presented arguments from a tall lectern, the solicitor general was the picture of dignity. With his experience in the Justice Department's Office of Legal Counsel, Scalia considered himself ideally qualified for the "SG" post, as it was called. He saw the law as Reagan did and was a persuasive writer and forceful debater for the cause.

In early 1981 Scalia made the Reagan administration's short list for the job with two other men: Rex Lee, a former assistant attorney general for the Justice Department's civil division and a founding dean of Brigham

Young University Law School; and Dallin Oaks, the former president of Brigham Young University (1971–80) who had become a Utah Supreme Court justice. Scalia flew to Washington to meet with Attorney General Smith, who would make the SG decision.

The silver-haired, impeccably attired Smith was the scion of an old New England family. He had spent most of his professional life in California after joining the law firm of Gibson, Dunn and Crutcher in Los Angeles in 1946. Smith retained an aristocratic, passionless manner that contrasted with Scalia's volubility. Scalia thought the meeting in Smith's office at the Justice Department went well, and he remained optimistic. He was further encouraged when he heard that Oaks, settling in at Utah's top court and becoming more involved in the Mormon Church,[25] might be pulling out of the competition. Scalia believed the scholarly Oaks, a former clerk to Chief Justice Warren, was his real rival for the SG post, as opposed to Lee, who had, in Scalia's mind, a reputation as a trial court litigator rather than an appellate advocate. That, however, was not how Smith regarded Lee. Further, where Scalia had sharp edges, Lee had none. Lee was solicitous in his professional relations and less interested in challenging the existing state of the law.

Smith telephoned one morning when Scalia was teaching. Scalia returned the call after the class, but Smith was away from his desk. Scalia waited anxiously as several hours passed. When the attorney general finally called back, he said he had chosen Rex Lee.[26] Scalia was crushed. Maureen could not believe that administration officials would fly her husband to Washington only to reject him. She had her hands full with child rearing—her ninth child, Margaret, had just been born—and did not normally become so invested in her husband's work and aspirations. But in this case, she had. Uncharacteristically, she burst into tears when she heard the news.

"I was bitterly disappointed," Scalia said decades later. "I never forgot it."[27]

Scalia continued to put out feelers for an appointment in the Reagan administration. He was touted by the National Italian American Foundation, which since its inception in the Carter years had been trying to move Italian Americans into the upper ranks of the federal government. The group, founded by Frank Annunzio, a Democratic member of the House of Representatives from Chicago, and other political heavyweights, promoted both Democrats and Republicans. After Reagan's victory, the NIAF worked through Henry Salvatori—an early supporter of Reagan when he ran for governor, and ultimately a member of Reagan's "kitchen cabinet." Scalia was a natural for the group to support, and in 1981 the NIAF's president, Frank Stella, wrote to Reagan urging him to put Scalia on a prominent appeals court.[28]

A more legally dynamic organization was also expanding Scalia's network of politically useful connections. The Federalist Society, as it was called, was the 1981 brainchild of a woman and two men who had been undergraduates together at Yale College in the late 1970s: Lee Liberman, David McIntosh, and Steven Calabresi. They were tight personally (Liberman and Calabresi dated for a while) and discovered among themselves a brand of intellectualism that seemed peculiar on campus at the time. Liberman, a native of New York City, McIntosh, from Indiana, and Calabresi, reared in Providence, had thrived in the Yale Political Union, a long-standing debating society, and helped to invite speakers who were more conservative than the norm. The student-run newspaper often editorialized against their choices, which further spurred the three to search out speakers on the right.

When they each went on to law school in the fall of 1980, they wanted to try to create similar conservative debate forums at their new locales. Liberman and McIntosh were at the University of Chicago and students of Professor Scalia. Calabresi remained at Yale. "We had had tremendous fun in college with these debates," recalled Calabresi. "Our goal was to do the same at law school, to bring in some interesting thinkers on the right."[29] They had laid some plans in the summer before law school, hoping immediately to launch a new debating club, but they discovered that their first-year academic schedules were too busy for a major extracurricular undertaking.

Their objective did not fade and, in fact, grew stronger after the November 1980 election. "David and I noticed that there were all these student organizations and they all seemed to be, basically, on the left," Liberman recalled of what she and McIntosh witnessed at the University of Chicago. "We thought, that's kind of funny. After all, Reagan just won this presidential election. You'd have thought there would be some kind of conservative legal organization."[30]

Liberman and McIntosh were in constant telephone contact with Calabresi, who believed that his friends, who happened to be at a school known for its conservatism, were having an easier time finding soul mates.

The University of Chicago was also home to the "law and economics theory" that favored efficiency analysis over other, more equity-focused perspectives, suggesting judges' decisions should be informed by a cost-benefit analysis. "The climate at Chicago was not as hostile to conservatives as at Yale," said Calabresi, who was the nephew of the Yale law professor (and eventual dean, later judge) Guido Calabresi.[31]

As the three refined the agenda for their new student organization, they settled on a name, the Federalist Society, after the Federalist Papers, written by Alexander Hamilton, James Madison, and John Jay, which advocated ratification of the Constitution and evinced an ardent nationalism. A silhouette of Madison became their logo. The students did not think they were starting a national organization, but rather a couple of connected university chapters—if they were lucky, a half dozen.

At both campuses they needed faculty advisers. In New Haven, Calabresi turned to Professor Ralph Winter, Yale's most prominent conservative at the time. Professor Robert Bork had left New Haven a year earlier for private practice in Washington, D.C., and, soon after, was appointed by Reagan to a judgeship. In Chicago, Liberman reached out to Professor Scalia. They appreciated each other's up-front style, born of their respective upbringings in Queens and Manhattan. "He says what's actually on his mind," Liberman observed years later. "Sometimes here in Washington, that is looked upon as rude. In New York, it's not viewed as rude. It's normal." Liberman said she also found Scalia's approach commonsensical: "If something was so complicated that it was incapable of being explained to a regular person, he was skeptical of it. He had this character in his classes: What would Joe Sixpack say about this?"[32]

With his years in Washington and regular speaking gigs at other campuses, Scalia also was connected enough to help the Federalist Society network grow. Like the students he advised, Scalia realized the value of banding together to thrash out ideas. In those days, being a conservative made one feel "isolated, lonely . . . like a weirdo," Scalia recalled.[33] At the Chicago chapter's first meeting, he read from Federalist Number 49 a reference to the importance of strength in numbers: "If it be true that all governments rest on opinion, it is no less true that the strength of opinion in each individual, and its practical influence on his conduct, depend much on the number which he supposes to have entertained the same opinion. The reason of man, like man himself, is timid and cautious when left alone, and acquires firmness and confidence in proportion to the number with which it is associated." Years later, when asked about his choice of the Federalist passage, Scalia said he wanted something that addressed the benefits of organizing for "physical and intellectual courage."[34]

Liberman, McIntosh, and Calabresi connected with a Harvard student, Spencer Abraham, who had been editing the conservatively oriented *Journal of Law and Public Policy*. That journal would effectively become the flagship publication of the society, providing a forum for the group's arguments. The foursome began to plan a conference to be held at Yale in April 1982. They invited Richard Posner, a prominent adherent of the law-and-economics theory, and other high-profile conservative thinkers, as well as a handful of liberals, such as Judge Stephen Breyer, a Carter-appointed appeals judge who had been an aide to the Democratic senator Edward M. Kennedy of Massachusetts. The students believed that they needed to attract contrary thinkers to ensure lively debates and to build up the intellectual confidence of their own members. In fact, that goal of debate and the sharpening of conservative thinking remained at the core of their mission.

"We really didn't think about setting up student chapters everywhere," said McIntosh, who would eventually become a Republican member of the House of Representatives. "But then about a month out, after we had done advertising [for the Yale conference] in the *National Review* and elsewhere, we were getting RSVPs that said, 'How do we set up these at our schools?' "[35]

Two hundred students from about twenty law schools attended the inaugural Federalist Society symposium.[36] "We had to line up dorm-room floor space for sleeping bags," Calabresi said. "Suddenly there were all these conservatives milling around Yale Law School. It was a very strange experience."[37]

It was also a heady experience for the organizers, who had once felt relatively isolated in their ideas. Since at least the 1960s, liberalism had prevailed on college campuses, and, with it, attention to such topics as civil rights, school reform, and women's rights. Conservatives had been largely consigned to counterprotests or had simply remained silent. News media coverage of their agenda was nonexistent. Now it was as if the class geeks were suddenly popular. Discussion of economic rights and judicial restraint was in vogue. Major newspapers, including *The New York Times*, ran reports about their inaugural conference.[38]

The keynote speaker for the Yale event was Bork, newly appointed by Reagan to the U.S. Court of Appeals for the District of Columbia Circuit. In news media accounts at the time, Bork was regarded as the leading candidate for a future appointment to the Supreme Court. During his speech, he criticized the current Court for trying to "nationalize morality" and said that the justices were interpreting the law based on their own values rather than the Constitution's text.[39]

Bork's prominent participation lent the Federalist Society immediate credibility among students and professors. So did the attendance of Scalia, other well-known professors, and top Reagan Justice Department officials, including the White House counselor Meese and Assistant Attorney General Theodore Olson. Unlike other conservative groups with niche interests, the Federalist Society offered an environment for a range of conservatives and libertarians, drawing in those opposed to abortion and busing, along with free-market thinkers who were uninterested in a social policy agenda.

Calabresi had heard much about Scalia in his telephone conversations with Liberman and McIntosh. Years later he would vividly recollect Scalia in the flesh in a large lecture hall at the Sterling Law Building on Yale's campus. "He was very bright and very lively, just sort of bubbling over with ideas. He was a real intellectual and a tremendous lot of fun to talk to." On breaks in the presentations, Scalia yakked with students at the vending machines or as he had a smoke in the hallways.

Still, Scalia offered more than ideas and energy. He helped the students raise money. Liberman had obtained some early organizational funds from a University of Chicago student activities budget. Through Scalia's connections, she and the others were able to obtain a major $20,000 grant from the Institute for Educational Affairs, which had been cofounded by William Simon and Irving Kristol of the American Enterprise Institute. In time they also tapped into the New York–based John M. Olin Foundation, of which Simon became president and which was an early financial backer of the legal movement that promoted economically efficient rules, as well as the Milwaukee-based Lynde and Harry Bradley Foundation, supporting limited government, and the Pittsburgh-based Scaife Foundations, also backing conservative social causes.

By 1983 the Federalist Society had a national office in Washington, D.C., and had expanded beyond student members to include practicing lawyers. Fittingly, its first office was rented space at the American Enterprise Institute. By 1986 the Federalist Society budget had swelled to about $1 million.

There was hardly a big name in the conservative movement of the latter twentieth century who was not part of the original effort. "None of us would have thought anything like this would happen," Theodore Olson said of what became a 40,000-member student and professional organization.[40] The liberal *Washington Monthly* magazine called it "quite simply the best-organized, best-funded, and most effective legal network operating in this country."[41]

In his 2008 book, *The Rise of the Conservative Legal Movement*, the University of Maryland professor Steven Teles observed that the Federalist Society represented "the most vigorous, durable, and well-ordered organization to emerge from [the] rethinking of modern conservatism's political strategy."[42] Teles credited Scalia with much of the society's progress. "Perhaps the most important elite sponsor of the Society in its early years was then-professor Antonin Scalia, who first helped connect the Yale and Chicago contingents with the conservative law groups at Stanford, helped them with fund-raising, spoke at their first conference, hosted visiting Harvard Law Federalist Society members at his home when the Society had its conference at the University of Chicago Law School, and facilitated the Society's early move into an office at the American Enterprise Institute."[43]

For the student founders and Scalia, the Federalist Society meant the start of a mutually beneficial alliance that would exceed all expectations. "We thought we were just planting a flower among the weeds of academic liberalism," Scalia said. "It turned out to be an oak."[44]

The Federalist Society's timing was perfect. The three Yale undergraduates would not have gone as far with their dream of law-school-based groups if Reagan had not become president and issued his own call to conservatism. The students' effort also reflected a goal of some established conservatives, such as the lawyer Michael Horowitz, who would be general counsel of Reagan's Office of Management and Budget. In the late 1970s Horowitz wrote a paper financed by the Scaife Foundations pointing out the importance of broadening conservatism beyond the realm of big business and motivating law students.

Calabresi, Liberman, and McIntosh, too, were the right people with the right mission. They kept the emphasis on high-quality debate and first-rate networking. They built connections to prominent academics, federal judges, and Reagan administration officials and helped members get jobs in the Justice Department and judiciary.[45] All three eventually moved to the Justice Department and cycled in and out of one another's lives as they climbed the ladder of the law and politics, all the while helping to identify possible candidates for the federal bench. Stretching ahead of them was not merely a single Reagan term, but two, then George H. W. Bush's tenure, then the presidency of his son, George W. Bush. The student founders would be part of a broadscale transformation of the federal courts, and each of them would rise and remain on the stage of conservative policy and politics for decades.[46]

In the spring of 1982 Scalia was still smarting about having lost out as solicitor general, and at seeing Robert Bork get the first opening on the influential U.S. Court of Appeals for the District of Columbia Circuit. Reagan officials offered Scalia a life-tenured seat on the U.S. Court of Appeals for the Seventh Circuit. The court was based in Chicago and covered Illinois, Indiana, and Wisconsin. It would have meant staying in a place Scalia and his wife wanted to leave. If he were to end up with an appellate judgeship, Scalia thought, he preferred the federal appeals court for the District of Columbia Circuit, which specialized in regulatory matters and would mean a return to the Washington area. The choice before him was tough. There was a chance that he would eventually be offered a shot at the D.C. Circuit, but the Seventh Circuit was an opportunity actually in hand. Scalia considered his options, then decided, "Hell, I'll wait."[47]

The wait paid off. Later in the year, Reagan offered him a position on the appeals court in Washington, D.C. Scalia was getting the second opening (after Bork) on what was considered the nation's second-highest court. This reversal of the solicitor general rejection and his subsequent celebrity in the law would be in no small measure because of an alignment of conservatives and the times. The multiplying Federalist Society chapters gave him larger platforms. Where once Scalia was alone, a crowd was forming, and it was lifting his banner.

FIVE

RELENTLESS IN DISSENT

Judge Antonin Scalia was beginning his fourth year in the black robes of a federal judge when he entered the District of Columbia Circuit courtroom on October 3, 1985, for oral arguments in an important libel case. After three years on a federal appellate court, one step down from the Supreme Court, Scalia had acquired a reputation as a formidable conservative, critic of the press, and tenacious questioner. The dispute now before him and eight colleagues sitting en banc[1] would be an important test of his temperament and legal outlook. Seated at the bench, Scalia looked out at the crowd. Spectators had lined up two hours early to get seats for the First Amendment case, which was now in its sixth year and likely final chapter. The dispute pitted the Mobil Oil company president William Tavoulareas against *The Washington Post*. Attracting particular attention was the *Post*'s attorney, the trial lawyer Edward Bennett Williams, who had, over four decades practicing law, represented Joseph McCarthy, Frank Sinatra, and Jimmy Hoffa. Williams was as much an institution as the Washington Redskins football team, of which he was president, and the Baltimore Orioles, which he happened to own. Williams had been sick with cancer, in and out of the hospital, and was perhaps performing in the courtroom for the last time. For the argument he was about to make, he considered Judge Scalia his toughest customer.[2] In fact, it was in no small part because of Scalia that all were here. Scalia had helped write the ruling that *The Washington Post* was now appealing.

The case between Tavoulareas and *The Washington Post* traced back more than five years. Tavoulareas had sued the newspaper for a 1979 front-page report that said he "set up" his twenty-four-year-old son, Peter, as a partner in a shipping company, Atlas Maritime, which did millions of dollars in business with Mobil-owned vessels under exclusive, no-bid contracts. The implication in the article by Patrick Tyler was that the father had misused his position and corporate assets to provide his son a sweetheart deal. William Tavoulareas contended that he was defamed and that the *Post* had long been out to get him. After a trial in 1982, the jury had found against *The Washington Post* and Tyler under the standard derived from a First Amendment case, *New York Times v. Sullivan*. In that 1964 opinion by Justice William Brennan, the Court had said that even if a newspaper published a false statement about a public official, it could be held liable only if the statement was a "deliberate falsehood" or published in "reckless disregard of the truth."[3] Jurors had believed the Tavoulareas case met that definition and assessed $250,000 in actual damages and $1.8 million in punitive damages against *The Washington Post*.[4] The U.S. district court judge Oliver Gasch, however, had overturned the jury's verdict. He declared that there was not sufficient evidence for a finding that *The Washington Post* had deliberately or recklessly told a falsehood.

Another switch followed in April 1985. Cases at the District of Columbia Circuit, as in federal appeals courts nationwide, were routinely heard by three-judge panels, and in that spring of 1985 a D.C. Circuit panel reinstated the verdict by a 2–1 vote.[5] Judge Scalia and Judge George MacKinnon, a fellow conservative thirty years Scalia's senior, produced a 101-page opinion that declared the *Post* story "was published in reckless disregard of its falsity." MacKinnon and Scalia pointed to numerous "bricks" of evidence that they argued built a "wall" that warranted a ruling for Tavoulareas. One of the "bricks" they cited was the *Post*'s policy of pursuing "high impact investigative stories."[6] A factor like this—a newspaper's drive for attention-getting stories—was not typically part of the First Amendment libel analysis, but MacKinnon and Scalia maintained that such evidence should be allowed into a libel case for evidence of reckless falsehoods. Dissenting from the decision was Judge J. Skelly Wright. Wright said he feared the ruling could cause newspapers to "steer clear of unpleasant news stories" and to turn away from what the Supreme Court in the 1964 *New York Times v. Sullivan* milestone called the "profound national commitment to the principle that debate on public issues should be uninhibited, robust, and wide open."

Now, in October 1985, the full D.C. Circuit was considering *The Washington Post*'s appeal of the MacKinnon-Scalia judgment favoring Tavoulareas. Williams, the old battle horse, had pored over the trial transcripts for months to craft his arguments. He had roamed the halls of his law firm trying out lines for his arguments.[7] His surgery for liver cancer made him look older than his sixty-five years. He was hunched over and weary.[8]

Leaning on the lectern at first, then stepping back from it, Williams defended freedom of the press and emphasized how important it was for appellate judges to review closely the facts from a libel trial. He said the D.C. Circuit had to decide, after a fresh review rather than relying on the jury findings, whether the grounds existed to find a deliberate or reckless falsehood. With his voice rising, Williams told the court it was difficult for him "to discuss a liberty this precious without getting excited." Williams seemed to gain physical strength as his argument progressed.[9]

Scalia, at the right end of the bench, interjected that evidence from the trial showed that reporters were pushed to find groundbreaking stories that grabbed readers' attention. He asked Williams whether *Post* reporters were under pressure to produce "sensationalistic stories," a practice that Scalia suggested would be evidence of recklessness. Williams dismissed the question and called Scalia's characterization "a distortion and abortion of the record." Williams said evidence of hard-hitting stories was only mildly relevant. "It had a ticket of admission, but to the very cheapest seats of probative value," he declared, meaning that a jury could consider the *Post*'s practices but that they could not be used to determine whether the requisite proof of recklessness was met. Williams knew Scalia's question about the *Post*'s aggressiveness cut to the heart of the case because of Tavoulareas's claim that the *Post* wanted to bring him down and was inclined to publish reckless falsehoods.

Williams referred to Peter Tavoulareas's earlier job as a $14,000-a-year clerk at the shipping company before he became a 75 percent owner of the enterprise. "I say to you that anyone who would believe a $14,000-a-year-clerk went to a 75 percent owner . . . on the theory of meritocracy has to believe in the tooth fairy." The courtroom erupted in laughter, with the notable exception of Peter Tavoulareas, whom the *National Law Journal* reporter David Lauter described as "looking like someone who had just been punched in the gut."[10]

In contrast to Williams's theatrical performance, a restrained John J. Walsh represented Tavoulareas. Vigorous and, at age fifty-four, a half generation younger than Williams, Walsh warned the court that "the very integrity of the jury system is under fierce attack." Walsh, a partner in the New York firm of Cadwalader, Wickersham and Taft, had twice claimed victory in the long-running Tavoulareas case and wanted to hold on to the win he had with the three-member D.C. Circuit panel. The original jury verdict against the *Post* after a twenty-one-day trial had launched Walsh's reputation as a go-to counsel in libel cases. He was here at the D.C. Circuit only after having flown in from Hawaii the night before, during a break in a libel trial against the Gannett-run *Pacific Daily News* in Guam. "The plaintiff who wins a jury verdict is entitled to the most favorable view of the evidence," insisted Walsh, who had argued at trial that Tavoulareas was defamed by the story's implication that he misused Mobil's assets. "Appellate judges are simply looking at the cold record." Walsh hit points that particularly appealed to Scalia.[11]

When the hearing in the case was over, Scalia and the eight other D.C. Circuit judges voted in a private conference and began the task of drafting opinions. Their decision on whether the $2 million judgment against the *Post* should stand, and the larger question of rules for newspapers in libel trials, would not be issued for a year and a half.

That Scalia and MacKinnon had been the majority at the earlier stage of the case was a sign of how the D.C. Circuit had begun to evolve. Down Constitution Avenue from the Capitol, the D.C. Circuit was considered the second-ranking tribunal to the Supreme Court because of the significance of its caseload and the caliber of its judges. For decades it had been among the most liberal of all the federal courts of appeals. Its docket consisted mainly of disputes over federal regulation, and with liberal judges predominant, the D.C. Circuit had been a haven for labor unions, civil rights leaders, environmentalists, and consumer activists. The court regularly ordered agencies to act faster in complying with consumer-protection statutes or to revise procedures for more public accountability. In one ruling before Scalia joined the court, the D.C. Circuit had blocked decisions by the U.S. Nuclear Regulatory Commission to grant operating licenses for nuclear power plants in Vermont and Michigan. The court asserted in the 1976 opinion that the Nuclear Regulatory Commission had failed to consider adequately the environmental impact of nuclear fuel reprocessing and waste disposal. The D.C. Circuit wanted the commission to examine energy conservation as an alternative to nuclear power.[12] As a University of Chicago law professor at the time of the decision, Scalia had declared it improper "lawmaking." In an article that had helped gain him prominence among law professors, Scalia wrote, "It does not go too far to say that the D.C. Circuit was in the process of replacing the rudimentary procedural mandates" specified by Congress with its own rules. Scalia decried the ruling in *Natural Resources Defense Council v. NRC*, which because of one of the nuclear power plants involved became known as the "Vermont Yankee" decision, as "clearly contrary to the tenor of the Supreme Court decisions in the field."[13] (The Supreme Court later, in fact, reversed the D.C. Circuit.)

In June 1982, just before Scalia joined the D.C. Circuit, the court had reinstated a rule that all new cars must be equipped with air bags or automatic seat belts. That decision challenged the Reagan administration's agenda of less regulation by overturning the administration's rescission of the rule, which Reagan said would cost the auto industry $1 billion annually. (The Supreme Court essentially agreed with the D.C. Circuit, faulting regulators' rescission of the requirement for air bags or automatic seat belts.)[14]

The D.C. Circuit was "sort of the last bastion of liberalism," Joseph L. Rauh, Jr., a civil rights lawyer, observed in 1982 as he speculated that the era might be ending because of Reagan's appointments.[15] The Supreme Court itself was already well to the right of the D.C. Circuit. Many of its liberal decisions were reversed by the justices by lopsided margins.

No two judges were as emblematic of the D.C. Circuit's liberalism as David L. Bazelon, who had been the circuit's longtime chief judge and was known for his interest in protecting the rights of criminal defendants and the mentally ill, and Skelly Wright, who had dissented from the MacKinnon-Scalia April 1985 panel decision in the Tavoulareas case. Both had a decades-long history of finding innovative solutions for societal dilemmas.

Judge Bazelon was born in Superior, Wisconsin, in 1909, the youngest of ten children. His father died when he was two. He graduated from Northwestern Law School, worked as a federal prosecutor, and then joined the Justice Department lands division. President Truman appointed him to the D.C. Circuit in 1950. He had just turned forty. Early on, Bazelon took an interest in the sociology of criminal behavior. In the 1954 case of Monte Durham, a convicted burglar with a history of mental disturbances, Bazelon sought to revise a century-old rule that dictated that a defendant could be found insane only if he could not distinguish right from wrong. In his opinion, he tried to make it easier for a criminal defendant to establish an insanity defense, allowing the defense if the conduct was the product of mental disease or defect. Durham, Bazelon argued, should be confined in a hospital rather than prison. Bazelon's approach, the so-called Durham Rule, brought more attention to the problems of the criminally insane.

Skelly Wright, born in New Orleans in 1911, had been a federal prosecutor and then federal trial judge in his hometown. After the Supreme Court's 1954 *Brown v. Board of Education* decision, Wright, a Truman appointee, began ordering desegregation of the professional schools of Louisiana State University, pushing New Orleans to desegregate city parks and bus lines, and trying to ensure that blacks whose names had been taken off voting rolls were restored.[16] When the local school board failed to devise a desegregation plan, Wright, who had been a teacher before going to law school at Loyola University in New Orleans, ordered his own desegregation plan implemented in 1960. He became the target of southern segregationists who burned crosses in the yard of Wright's New Orleans home and threatened his family.

President Kennedy had considered promoting Wright to the U.S. Court of Appeals for the Fifth Circuit, which then covered Alabama, Florida, Georgia, Louisiana, Mississippi, and Texas. But Senator Russell Long, a Democrat from Louisiana, warned that he would block Wright's confirmation. So Kennedy nominated Wright to the D.C. Circuit in the nation's capital, and the Senate approved him in 1962.

Bazelon and Wright, with their different backgrounds and personalities—Bazelon cerebral, Wright loquacious—remained social innovators on the bench into the 1970s. In 1978, three years before Reagan would begin his many judicial appointments, Bazelon turned over the reins of the chief judgeship to Wright. *The New York Times* commented on the shift, saying of Bazelon's sixteen-year tenure as chief judge that he "used his prestige and powers to their fullest, speaking out boldly on and off the bench on matters of justice and civil liberties." Of Wright, the paper said, "Brand him an activist, deplore the length of his judicial opinions, but never call him dull. The Washington court will continue to have progressive—and interesting—leadership."[17]

Wright and Bazelon also were part of a liberal old boys club that schmoozed over lunch at Milton Kronheim's liquor warehouse on V Street in northeastern Washington, D.C. Kronheim, an old friend of Bazelon's, was one of the largest liquor distributors on the East Coast. He offered close friends a family-style lunch in a cleared-out corner of the warehouse. The large wooden table—no tablecloth—could seat up to a dozen. On the walls were hundreds of framed black-and-white photographs documenting Kronheim's decades of relations with Washington powers. One picture was from a birthday party for Chief Justice Earl Warren. Among the ten other men in the picture with the chief justice, crowded around the luncheon table, were Bazelon, Wright, and the Supreme Court justices William Brennan, Thurgood Marshall, and William O. Douglas. Bazelon's widow, Mickey Knox, said that Kronheim left the invitations to Bazelon, which meant those who attended were usually men of like-minded liberal views. "Milton was strictly a man's man," she said. "No women were invited to those lunches unless there was a special occasion." The fare was straightforward: homemade soup as a starter, then, typically, sliced beef, green beans, corn bread on the side. The conversation was free-ranging. "The first thing we do when we walk in the door is take off our jackets," Judge Wright said in 1979. "That sets the whole tone. Anywhere else we'd have to walk in frozen-faced."[18]

This tight liberal world was beginning to come apart. President Reagan would drastically alter the ideological character of the D.C. Circuit. Judges such as Bazelon and Wright, who embraced the notion of a "living Constitution," believing that it evolved to fit the needs of a society in every era, were about to face opposition from a new wave of conservative appointees, some of them proponents of originalism who believed the Constitution fixed by its eighteenth-century perspective. There were many variations, to be sure, among adherents of these dueling theories. Some liberals would not have gone as far as Justice Brennan, the leading proponent of the ideal of a "living Constitution," in expansively reading individual rights. And originalists varied in their degrees of rigidity and in exceptions for past non-originalist precedents.

Yet in the early 1980s on the D.C. Circuit a deep clash was developing between men who were some of the strongest believers of their respective approaches, men to whom other judges looked for guidance. For example, the doctrine of originalism, as embraced in the 1970s and early 1980s, owed much to the scholarly and prolific Yale Law professor Robert Bork, who would write, "A judge, no matter on what court he sits, may never create new constitutional rights or destroy old ones. Any time he does so, he violates not only the limits to his own authority but, and for that reason, also violates the rights of the legislature and the people."[19] To Scalia, who agreed with that approach, the Constitution had to be read with an eye to the social and moral perceptions at the time of its drafting.

Bork, the former U.S. solicitor general, became Reagan's first appointee to the D.C. Circuit, confirmed by the Senate in February 1982. Next was Scalia, confirmed in August 1982. Reagan would then add Kenneth Starr, in 1983; Laurence Silberman, 1985; James Buckley, 1985; Stephen Williams, 1986; Douglas Ginsburg, 1986; and David Sentelle, 1987. The scene at Kronheim's began to fade with the changed tone of the D.C. Circuit. Kronheim had a stroke in 1982 and died in 1986. Bazelon and Wright fell into ill health, too, and retired in the mid-1980s.[20]

Scalia was just forty-six when he joined the D.C. Circuit, and his vigorous manner contrasted with that of the balding Wright and the graying Bazelon. While the liberals had Kronheim's, and Scalia went a couple of times, he more often indulged his Italian-American roots with lunches at A.V. Ristorante, a downtown place where he favored pizza with anchovies.

Scalia liked Wright on a personal level, and he respected the man who had endured the burning of crosses on his lawn. Scalia found Bazelon more of a prickly soul. On the substance of the law, neither intimidated him. Scalia was the outsider who quickly learned to play the inside game. Bazelon's widow, Mickey, recalled seeing Scalia for the first time at the Watergate apartment of Judge Ruth Bader Ginsburg, a 1980 appointee of Jimmy Carter who was also on the D.C. Circuit. "Ruthie Ginsburg had me over to a little party when he joined the court, and everyone was calling him 'Nino,' " she said. "He made himself the centerpiece. He was very jovial, thinking himself very clever and full of himself. But nothing that was obnoxious. It was quite pleasant." Scalia was a rare animal who was not usually begrudged the attention he craved. "You feel it right away— the impact of his personality. I had no personal relationship with him, and neither did David. But I could feel it."[21]

Ruth Ginsburg was similarly struck by Scalia, but even more so. While she was a law professor at Columbia University, she had heard his speech railing against the D.C. Circuit's Vermont Yankee atomic energy ruling in the 1970s. She thoroughly disagreed with Scalia's position. She also was thoroughly charmed by him. "I was fascinated by him because he was so intelligent and so amusing," Ginsburg said. "You could still resist his position, but you just had to like him."[22] Ginsburg, a former women's rights advocate, was an unlikely chum to Scalia. Yet a deep friendship developed. Once he was appointed to the D.C. Circuit, two years after her 1980 appointment, Ginsburg and Scalia began celebrating New Year's Eve together with a formal dinner for themselves and their spouses.[23] Scalia attributed the friendship with Ginsburg to their shared backgrounds as law professors. They read each other's opinions with a scholarly eye and offered writing suggestions. Scalia treated Ginsburg like a faculty colleague and years later described her as "an intelligent woman and a nice woman and a considerate woman—all the qualities that you like in a person."[24]

At the courthouse, Scalia had an easygoing manner with his clerks. "We were a sounding board for him," recalled Michael Brody, a University of Chicago law graduate who worked for Scalia in his second year on the bench. When Scalia returned from meeting with his fellow judges over the resolution of a case, he would summon his clerks. Lighting up a pipe, he would run through the discussion that had transpired in the conference and the opinions he would be writing. (In these years, Scalia was trying to swap cigarettes for a pipe, but he kept losing the pipe and in time fell back on the cigarette habit.)

Scalia spent much time in the writing of opinions. He tinkered with phrases, sentences, paragraphs. This was classic Scalia. Colleagues back to his Nixon days recalled his interest in getting the words just right. Working with his trademark fountain pen, "he fussed and fussed over language," recounted Brian Lamb, who worked with Scalia in the White House's Office of Telecommunications Policy in 1971–72. "I used to say, 'Nino, stop, we have to get this out.' " Lamb, who would go on to found C-SPAN, was handling public relations for the office when Scalia was general counsel.[25] When Scalia was on the D.C. Circuit, he sat for a televised interview with Lamb and said of the process of judging, "I like the intellectual endeavor. I like playing with ideas and words and analyzing the meaning of statutes."[26]

In the 1980s, the ideological evolution at the D.C. Circuit was felt among the clerks. "You did have a sense that things were changing," Brody said. "We knew as law clerks that Scalia stood for something different."[27]

Scalia liked to spar intellectually and tried to hire one liberal each term among his stable of three clerks. In the spring of 1986 that was Joshua Rosenkranz. "He made no bones about it. I was his token liberal," recalled Rosenkranz, who said he viewed the Scalia clerkship as a way to test his own liberal principles. "I remember being struck by how much he liked to mix it up, but also how much fun he was, his gregariousness."[28]

One Christmas, a handful of clerks showed up at Scalia's door to sing carols, unannounced. They had been working their way across town, visiting the houses of D.C. Circuit judges. "We rang the doorbell, sang a song or two, and got back into our cars and went to the next house," Brody recounted. "Most of the judges smiled and were friendly, although a little nervous. Scalia was last—he was the farthest out of town. He invited us in without hesitation. Before long, he was at the piano, singing with the group . . . The kids were around, the dog was barking. But he was completely in his element."[29]

Yet the judge could turn it on and off. Some clerks for other judges dubbed him "the Ninopath," referring to what they regarded as an obsessive unwillingness to bend as opinions were drafted.[30] Correspondence from the era shows that Scalia could be impatient with some of his fellow judges. In the case of *United States v. Byers*, he wrote an opinion for the court finding a defendant who pleaded insanity could be forced to submit to psychiatric examination even without his lawyer being present. Judge Bazelon was writing a dissenting opinion and going at it slowly. Scalia tried to push him to finish up by writing a memo to all the court's members: "The majority opinion in the above case was circulated more than three months ago. I propose to issue it" soon.[31] Bazelon wrote back two days later apologizing for the delay and saying, "I understand your eagerness to issue an opinion. I am devoting my full attention to the case and expect to have a draft in two weeks or thereabouts . . . My crowded calendar and my failure to anticipate the grounds on which you would rest—coupled with some pesty health problems—have accounted for this delay." Bazelon, it later emerged, was in the initial stages of Alzheimer's disease. Judge Patricia Wald, a liberal appointed by President Carter, viewed Scalia's missives as in the spirit of judicial debate. "His legendary 'Ninograms' often set the stage for months of combat," she recalled.[32]

If words and small phrases mattered to Scalia, the substance of an opinion mattered even more. Lee Liberman, his student at the University of Chicago who helped found the Federalist Society, became a law clerk to him on the D.C. Circuit. She said Scalia was "tireless in chasing down and eliminating bad dicta from his colleagues' opinions," referring to phrases that could potentially broaden the reach of a ruling.[33]

Strands of Scalia's prior advocacy emerged in his opinions. He was skeptical of legislation that he believed encroached on prerogatives of the executive branch, a skepticism reinforced by his experience in the Nixon and Ford administrations.[34] He narrowly read individual rights. He continued to protest race-based and sex-based policies intended to compensate for past discrimination.[35] He remained no friend of the press and complained that the Supreme Court had "fulsomely," or excessively, protected the news media under the First Amendment in *New York Times v. Sullivan*.[36] Scalia would rail against that decision for decades, at one point telling the former *Time* magazine editor Norman Pearlstine that given the chance, he would probably vote to reverse it.[37]

Scalia vigorously laid groundwork in other areas of the law as well, and the effort drew the attention of Reagan lawyers monitoring their lower court judges and of Supreme Court justices who were apt to try to reverse decisions by the liberals who still dominated the D.C. Circuit. Scalia wanted judges to engage in less judicial review of federal regulators' actions, a staple of the D.C. Circuit docket. He sought higher hurdles for consumer and special interest groups trying to bring their grievances to court. And he wanted to reduce the tendency of judges to look beyond the text of a piece of legislation to determine its breadth. Scalia believed that the general practice at the time of relying on floor statements by members of Congress and committee reports led to unduly broad readings of federal statutes. All of these emphases in his early years in the black robe were part of an overarching view that society's problems should be left to the legislative and executive realms. He believed in adhering closely to a legal text, the opposite approach of the Bazelons and Wrights, who took a more flexible view of legal authority to address real-world consequences.

Scalia dissented in a pair of cases in which the majority said that consumer groups could sue the National Highway Traffic Safety Administration to contest a rule reducing fuel economy standards for light trucks. The groups claimed that the rule undermined energy conservation and conflicted with the Energy Policy and Conservation Act of 1975. Scalia's dissenting opinion was dripping with cynicism for such public efforts. "If the injuries hypothesized by the interest groups suing in the present cases are sufficient," he declared, "it is difficult to imagine a contemplated public benefit under any law which cannot—simply by believing in it ardently enough—be made the basis for judicial intrusion into the business of the political branches."[38]

Steven Calabresi, the former Yale student who met Scalia at the first Federalist Society conference, was a law clerk to Judge Bork when Scalia was on the D.C. Circuit. Calabresi found himself as committed to trying to limit courts' jurisdiction as Scalia was. "A few other law clerks and I became jurisdiction police," Calabresi said, recalling that they would scrutinize filings to ensure that the parties had a right to bring the claim and were in the proper court. "Bork was bemused by this. But Scalia was downright delighted by the notion that there was this group of twenty-six-year-olds as passionate about it as he was. I finished my clerkship with huge respect for Bork but also for Scalia."[39]

In the early 1980s, when liberals still had control of the bench, some of Scalia's strongest and most attention-getting statements naturally came in dissenting opinions regarding regulatory power. Reagan administration lawyers particularly noticed a dissent he wrote in the case of the convicted Texas murderer Larry Leon Chaney and seven other death row prisoners in Oklahoma and Texas who had challenged the drugs used for executions by lethal injection. The prisoners believed they had evidence that the barbiturates and paralytics used were not a "safe and effective means of executing people," and in fact posed a risk of torturous pain. They argued that the Food and Drug Administration was legally obliged to prevent the misuse of the approved medications. The FDA declined to take action, saying it lacked the authority to answer the prisoners' claim.

After the inmates appealed and the case was heard, the D.C. Circuit majority found that the FDA had the power, and indeed the duty, to address the complaint about the lethal mix. Judge Wright, who wrote the opinion for the court, said the FDA must examine evidence that the drugs used for lethal injections posed a substantial threat of torturous pain. He said the FDA acted "arbitrarily and capriciously" when it refused to consider the inmates' claim.

Scalia believed the majority's view usurped executive branch authority—a belief the Supreme Court then endorsed, reversing Wright's opinion. Scalia knocked Wright's comparison of prisoners to "consumers" of a drug regulated by the FDA. A "condemned prisoner executed by injection is no more the 'consumer' of the drug than is the prisoner executed by firing squad a consumer of the bullets," Scalia countered, arguing that "it must be acknowledged that the public health interest at issue is not widespread death or permanent disability, but—at most—a risk of temporary pain to a relatively small number of individuals."[40]

Reagan administration lawyers wrote a memo for their "Supreme Court candidates" file favorably noting Scalia's effort to stop judges from second-guessing federal regulators in the FDA lethal injection case.[41] Also noted in the file was Scalia's dissent in *Community for Creative Non-Violence v. Watt*, opposing the D.C. Circuit majority's view that demonstrators had a First Amendment "symbolic speech" right to sleep in Lafayette Park across from the White House to call attention to the plight of the poor and homeless. Scalia said the majority was stretching "the Constitution not only beyond its meaning but beyond reason, and beyond the capacity of any legal system to accommodate."[42] The Supreme Court later reversed the D.C. Circuit majority.

As an appeals court judge, Scalia planted the seeds that would lead to a change in how judges went about interpreting a statute at the heart of a dispute. It was common practice at the time for judges to use congressional committee reports, floor speeches, and other components of the legislative process to interpret a statute. Scalia believed that judges should look solely at the text of a law and related statutes, rather than at the artifacts of the legislative process. He dismissed the congressional reports that accompanied a bill to the floor as merely the work of staff and not representative of a sense of Congress. Scalia's reverence for the text, no doubt, flowed partly from the lessons of his scholarly Italian father, who taught him to value words. Scalia also doubted that statements made on the floor or otherwise not in the text of the bill truly represented the view of the majority.

For Scalia, the essential fact was that members of Congress voted on bills, not committee reports. Yet the bills themselves were every bit a product of staff work as the reports Scalia despised. And at the time of a floor vote, many senators and members of the House hustled into the chambers and, as they were going through the door, were told by aides whether to vote aye or nay. That was the nature of business on Capitol Hill. A committee report or floor statement might also genuinely explain what Congress as a whole understood by the words it enacted.

Scalia made his disdain for legislative history known in a concurring opinion in the 1985 case of *Hirschey v. Federal Energy Regulatory Commission.* "I think it time for courts to become concerned about the fact that routine deference to the detail of committee reports . . . [is] converting a system of judicial construction into a system of committee-staff prescription."[43] He insisted that the more judges resorted to reports as authoritative, the more staffers would try to affect the court's understanding of the thrust of the law with committee reports, and that understanding would not necessarily reflect the will of the House and Senate.

Scalia expanded on his position in a speech at various law schools in 1985 and early 1986. "The use of legislative history to give meaning to a statute is a relatively new development in our common-law system," he insisted. "Some creatures that seem pleasant and tractable in their infancy—tiger cubs, for example—are better abandoned when they reach their full natural development. Now that legislative history has reached its adulthood, perhaps it is time to reconsider whether we want to live with it." He noted that one of his predecessors on the D.C. Circuit, Harold Leventhal, once described the use of legislative history as the equivalent of looking over the faces of the crowd at a large cocktail party and picking out friends.[44]

A gifted stylist, Scalia could make otherwise dry topics such as legislative history come alive. One of his favorite opinions in that vein during these years flowed from a dispute in which the Community Nutrition Institute sued the agriculture secretary, John Block, over a regulation that permitted the use of machines to separate bones from meat in the making of hot dogs and other sausages. The institute had challenged the regulation because it allowed use of the machinery without disclosure on the food label that the meat product would contain bits of bones. Scalia opened the opinion saying, "This case, involving legal requirements for the content and labeling of meat products such as frankfurters, affords a rare opportunity to explore simultaneously both parts of Bismarck's aphorism that, 'No man should see how laws or sausages are made.' "[45] Years later, Scalia boasted, "Best opener I've ever had. I'll never have one as good."[46]

As Scalia was gaining attention for his opinions, he was making connections off the bench. He joined a monthly poker game that included Associate Justice William Rehnquist; the former Nixon lawyer Leonard Garment; the legendary Washington attorney Robert Bennett; his brother William Bennett, who became Reagan's secretary of education; and other power brokers. Scalia was a guy's guy who liked playing cards and smoking cigars.

He also began spending time with Arthur Gajarsa. Gajarsa had emigrated as a child from Norcia, Italy, studied engineering, and gone on to become a lawyer. A burly man, Gajarsa was on Outward Bound's board of trustees, and in 1984 he convinced Scalia to take part in an Outward Bound trip. "He was somewhat skeptical" at first, Gajarsa recalled. "He really wasn't quite sure whether Outward Bound was more of a survival course" or largely recreational. But Gajarsa prevailed, and Scalia, who had grown up in the urban environs of Trenton and Queens, found the excursions exhilarating. The adventure program was known for its physically challenging courses but was equally reputed for team building. Participants hiked, rafted, and rappelled together and shared the chore of carrying all the gear. Scalia enjoyed it all, including getting to know the others in a group—members of Congress and other Washingtonians handpicked by Gajarsa for the trips.[47]

Thomas Susman, a longtime Democrat who worked for the Massachusetts senator Edward M. Kennedy and joined in the Gajarsa trips, said that Scalia had "no trouble letting his hair down. He and I probably sang for two hours straight on a bus ride to one river. He knows all the old songs." Susman recalled that on another trip, as the group was gathered around the campfire, there was a rustle in the bushes. Scalia emerged in a dress and wig as "the wild woman of the marsh." Recalled Susman, "It was just for the gas of it, just for the laugh of it."[48]

As Gajarsa put it, "He is totally a different person when you get him out there . . . his robes off . . . in a bathing suit."[49]

Scalia earned the friendship of liberals, despite the enmity that would eventually come his way from organized critics on the left for his stances on the law. While he was still on the D.C. Circuit, he was rarely singled out for his rulings. Rather, he was lumped with Judge Bork and other Reagan appointees. The notable exception was the New York Times columnist William Safire, a former Nixon speechwriter, who disparaged Scalia, in particular for his positions on the First Amendment.

Soon after the MacKinnon-Scalia ruling in the dispute between Mobil's Tavoulareas and *The Washington Post* in early April 1985, Safire had penned a scorching critical piece, questioning not only Scalia's legal reasoning but also his motives. Safire had theorized that Scalia was making a conscious effort to appeal to President Reagan's far-right aides, and he portrayed Scalia as campaigning for promotion from the D.C. Circuit to the Supreme Court by marching "in the vanguard of the media-haters." Scalia, the columnist declared, was "the worst enemy of free speech in America today." Safire had asserted that Scalia probably won his seat on the D.C. Circuit because of such attitudes, and he concluded in the prescient April 29, 1985, piece, "At such a time, when recommendations for the High Court are made to the President by Ed Meese with a covering memo from Pat Buchanan, the posture of being the fiercest opponent of the First Amendment does not hurt a judge's chances."[50]

The full D.C. Circuit's long-awaited opinion in the Tavoulareas libel case was handed down in March 1987. Its final judgment: The full court reversed the MacKinnon-Scalia panel decision and threw out the libel award for Tavoulareas. The court said that the story about Tavoulareas's business dealings with his son was "substantially true" and not libelous. "Given [the] plentiful, undisputed evidence of Tavoulareas' personal involvement in the establishment and operation of Atlas [shipping company] to Peter's manifest benefit, we conclude that no reasonable jury could . . . find that the 'set up' allegation was false," wrote Judges Kenneth Starr and Skelly Wright jointly for the majority.

The full D.C. Circuit was troubled by the tack the MacKinnon-Scalia panel had taken on several points, including its criticism of the *Post*'s aggressive reporting. When it reversed the panel decision, the full court stressed that "as in other professions, an adversarial stance is fully consistent with professional, investigative reporting." Of particular significance to the newspaper industry, the D.C. Circuit majority said that the jury had wrongly considered evidence of *The Washington Post*'s newsroom practices and the reporter Tyler's personal views. (Tyler reportedly had boasted during his investigation that "it is not every day you knock off one of the Seven Sisters," a reference to the world's largest oil companies.) Commenting on its own profession of the law, the D.C. Circuit majority wrote, "These statements, not unknown to the vernacular of litigators, seem to us well within the everyday parlance of an investigative reporter." Further, Judges Starr and Wright wrote, if Tyler had indeed taken an adversarial stance toward Tavoulareas, that was "certainly not indicative of knowing or reckless falsity under the circumstances where, as here, the reporter conducted a detailed investigation and wrote a story that is substantially true." The D.C. Circuit vote was 7–1. Only Judge MacKinnon dissented. Scalia, the ninth judge who had heard the case, had no vote. He had already left the D.C. Circuit for the Supreme Court.[51]

A postscript is in order, however, because of Scalia's involvement in the D.C. Circuit libel case even as he was about to leave that court. He continued to work on it behind the scenes, revealing his commitment to narrowing First Amendment protection for the press. Yet as much as the Tavoulareas libel case against *The Washington Post* mattered to him until practically his last days at the D.C. Circuit, he sought to publicly minimize his role—also to the end.

During his Supreme Court confirmation hearings on August 5, 1986, Senator Paul Simon, a Democrat from Illinois, asked Scalia about his position as a member of the original three-judge panel in the case and his vote against *The Washington Post*. Scalia played it down as he answered Simon. "I can at least note that it was not my opinion," he told the Senate Judiciary Committee. "It was the opinion of Judge MacKinnon in which I joined . . . I think I had better not try to defend the holding at all, except to note that the opinion was not mine, it was an opinion in which I joined . . . The fact that I joined an opinion against the press doesn't prove anything."[52]

His statement implicitly contradicted how much the case had mattered to him at the time and continued to matter. Scalia had fully joined MacKinnon's opinion and had worked privately with him on the wording of the panel decision. Scalia had been adamant about using *The Washington Post*'s aggressive journalistic practices as grounds for the finding of libel, and MacKinnon had considered Scalia a full partner for their panel decision. The former clerk Liberman said that Scalia wrote a portion of the opinion "narrowly construing" Supreme Court precedent requiring appeals courts to independently review the facts of a libel dispute.

There would be even more Scalia involvement in the case than the public—and the Senate Judiciary Committee—would know. Three weeks after his comments to Simon at the Senate Judiciary Committee hearing, Scalia wrote a note to MacKinnon to recommend changes in what was— at that time, in the private D.C. Circuit negotiations—their joint dissent against the D.C. Circuit majority decision for *The Washington Post*.

"Attached, the three suggestions which I was unable to give you last Saturday," Scalia wrote in the memo to MacKinnon dated August 26, 1986.[53] Scalia suggested various additions, including one point of particular concern to the press—whether, in interpreting an article to determine whether it contained a falsehood, a jury could consider the reporter's internally expressed views about the article. As he privately reviewed MacKinnon's draft dissent—which originally had been written on behalf of the two of them—Scalia wanted MacKinnon to make clear that Tyler's newsroom memo expressing his personal views about Tavoulareas's nepotism should have been properly admitted into evidence to prove libel.[54] So, even as he had portrayed his role in this major press case to Senator Simon in the most insignificant terms, Scalia was still trying to shape MacKinnon's opinion.

Certainly it was appropriate for Scalia to be working on D.C. Circuit cases while his Supreme Court hearings and review were under way. But he had declined to tell the full story. In light of the new scrutiny he faced before the Senate Judiciary Committee, Scalia simply did not want to reveal how invested he was in the libel dispute. His continued involvement in the case—if it had been known to senators at the time—most likely would have provoked further questions.

MacKinnon adopted the substance of Scalia's suggestions. Two months later, in November 1986, as the D.C. Circuit was continuing its drafting process in the Tavoulareas matter, MacKinnon wrote to Justice Scalia to ask if he wanted MacKinnon to note that Scalia "orally concurred in [the dissenting opinion] prior to the shift to the Supreme Court."[55] Scalia said no, and when the D.C. Circuit was finally ready to issue opinions in the Tavoulareas libel dispute in March 1987, MacKinnon had changed all the "we" references to "I." Scalia had moved on.

SIX

"I HAVE NO AGENDA"

His nine children, ages five to twenty-four, were attired in suits and dresses and assembled behind him in two rows as Antonin Scalia sat down at a long, green-draped table. The Senate Judiciary Committee was about to begin a hearing on his Supreme Court nomination the morning of August 5, 1986. "Judge Scalia, we again welcome you to the committee, along with your wife, Maureen, and your family," the committee chairman, Strom Thurmond, intoned in his thick South Carolinian drawl as he opened the session in the grand, high-ceilinged hearing room of the Dirksen Senate Office Building. Scalia had appeared before the committee four years earlier for his nomination to the U.S. Court of Appeals for the District of Columbia Circuit. Since that time, Scalia had emerged from a competition with other conservative appeals court judges—most notably Robert Bork—to be President Reagan's choice for an opening on the Supreme Court. The selection of Scalia for this new lifetime appointment was the consequence of a screening process more systematic than any other in modern history.[1]

"I believe eight of your nine children are here, are they not?" Thurmond added hesitantly.

"Yes, Senator. I do not know what happened to the ninth," Scalia began. "He is supposed to be here, too." Scalia turned around and noticed that the late-arriving son was indeed in a seat. "He is here," Scalia said. "They are all here, Senator. I have a full house. I was worried about that."

Scalia was the beneficiary of a marvelous backdrop of wholesomeness and familial loyalty. Senators repeatedly referred to the good-looking family behind him. The fifty-year-old nominee had another advantage. He was appearing before the Senate Judiciary Committee just a week after the Supreme Court associate justice William Rehnquist had occupied the same seat. Nominated by Reagan to be chief justice of the United States, Rehnquist, sixty-one, had been hammered for a week by senators for his conservative record on the Court and his earlier work as a lawyer in Phoenix.

They had not questioned Rehnquist's competence. Everyone agreed to the brilliance of the man who had graduated first in his class from Stanford Law School, been a law clerk to the Supreme Court justice Robert Jackson, and served as an associate justice for fourteen years. Some Democrats opposed his conservative views, but they focused on his character and credibility. Democrats had strongly intimated that Rehnquist had misspoken—or outright lied—when he denied claims that he intimidated black and Hispanic voters in Phoenix in the early 1960s. Some senators thought he also had told untruths when he denied that he personally believed the Court should have voted differently in *Brown v. Board of Education* and upheld the separate-but-equal doctrine of school segregation. Rehnquist had written as much in a 1952 memo to Justice Jackson.[2] "I am concerned about his integrity," Senator Howard M. Metzenbaum of Ohio had said. "I don't know that he's willfully misstating the facts, but I have difficulty with it."[3] The Republican senator Alan Simpson of Wyoming had believed that Democratic senators were only "out to tack the 'pelt' of Bill Rehnquist on the wall of the den," simply interested in rejecting a Reagan conservative.[4]

Since his appointment as an associate justice in 1972, Rehnquist had been the Court's voice of the right: against abortion rights, for school prayer, against busing and other race-related policies to spur integration, and for the death penalty. He was a sharp opponent of some of the safeguards for criminal defendants announced by the Warren Court, such as a constitutional right to a lawyer before police questioning. Rehnquist's work prior to his becoming a justice was the sorer point for liberal senators. As a lawyer in Phoenix, Rehnquist had opposed a 1964 local antidiscrimination ordinance and testified against a 1967 school desegregation program. In work for the local Republican Party, he reportedly had harassed African American voters by demanding that they read the Constitution aloud before being allowed to vote.[5] One witness at the Senate

Judiciary Committee was James J. Brosnahan, a former assistant U.S. attorney who had investigated complaints at the Phoenix polls in 1962. He testified that black voters had pointed out Rehnquist as the man who tried to stop them when they came to vote. When the Utah Republican senator Orrin Hatch asked Brosnahan if this might have been a case of mistaken identity, Brosnahan responded, "Do you think I really would be here to testify about the qualifications of the chief justice after twenty-seven years of trying lawsuits if I wasn't absolutely sure? If it was even close, I would be at Jack's restaurant in San Francisco for my Friday afternoon lunch."[6] Senators had also expressed concern that immediately before Rehnquist had joined the high court, he had been, as an assistant attorney general in the Office of Legal Counsel, the Nixon administration's point man advocating enhanced wiretapping and citizen surveillance. Nevertheless, in the end, no matter how much Democrats pounded away at that background and at Rehnquist's record, he held on in the Republican-controlled Senate to majority support for confirmation to the chief justice post. Even if he had been rejected, Rehnquist would still have been on the bench as an associate justice.[7]

Scalia was a different story. He was at the gate for the first time, nominated to be a new associate justice, or as Senator Dennis DeConcini, an Arizona Democrat, put it, poised to be "a new voice for the Court." As Scalia sat before the committee, DeConcini, who was a fellow Italian American, reminded the committee during opening remarks from the dais, "Let no one say that the Judiciary Committee ignored its duty to examine the President's nominee for Associate Justice."

Yet senators did not wholeheartedly accept the task before them. Even the scene in the ornate hearing room as Scalia took his chair revealed how this nominee would not be scrutinized as Rehnquist was. There were fewer news reporters and photographers. The rows of spectators had thinned. Senators were exhausted.

The real drama had occurred months earlier. Scalia's nomination was the product of the administration's desire for a turnabout in American law. Attorney General Edwin Meese had demonstrated that in a series of speeches a year earlier. On July 9, 1985, Meese appeared before a special meeting of the American Bar Association in Washington, D.C., with a calculatedly provocative message. He declared that it was time for the Supreme Court to reform. Tall, hefty, with a clean-cut, ruddy face, Meese, fifty-three, was physically imposing and blunt spoken. "Far too many of the Court's opinions, on the whole, have been more policy choices than articulations of long-term constitutional principle," Meese declared in the ballroom of the Sheraton Washington Hotel to the ABA's five-hundred-member House of Delegates. The framers of the Constitution, Meese insisted, had intended that the document be interpreted as it was under-stood in the America of 1789.[8] He wanted a return to an earlier era, before the Court under Earl Warren had expanded individual rights, which Meese derided as "radical egalitarianism."[9] Meese also said that the Court was misinterpreting First Amendment provisions that addressed relations between church and state. He complained about decisions from the 1984–85 term that had struck down an Alabama law giving students a "moment of silence" for prayerlike reflection and had rejected New York and Michi-gan programs letting public school teachers offer remedial education in parochial classrooms.[10]

Meese argued for an approach contrary to constitutional interpreta-tions that had been in place for decades. Judges had taken leading roles in addressing society's problems—to desegregate schools, reapportion legis-latures, manage prisons, and monitor environmental risks.[11] Now Meese was declaring such social problems out of bounds and in fact trying to discredit those judicial efforts. Meese's position especially provoked Jus-tice William J. Brennan, Jr., who had been right-hand man to Chief Justice Warren. Brennan felt personally attacked. At age seventy-nine, in frail health, and no longer speaking frequently in public, he used the occasion of a lecture at Georgetown University on October 12, 1985, three months after Meese's pronouncement to the Bar Association, to answer the attor-ney general. "One does not forget how much may depend on the decision [rendered by the Court]," said Brennan, whose fervent speech made the front pages of national newspapers. "More than the litigants may be affected. The course of vital social, economic and political currents may be [altered]." Brennan said of Meese's "originalist" approach to the Con-stitution, "It is a view that feigns self-effacing deference to the specific judgments of those who forged our original social compact. But in truth it is little more than arrogance cloaked as humility."[12]

Undeterred, Meese continued to complain publicly about the Court.

At the same time, in 1985, lawyers at Reagan's Justice Department were working on another front toward similar goals. They were preparing a legal brief to the Supreme Court against the 1973 *Roe v. Wade* decision that made abortion legal nationwide. The brief would go further in challenging abortion rights than the former attorney general William French Smith and Solicitor General Rex Lee had advocated. Asking the justices to use a pending Pennsylvania abortion dispute to overturn the landmark *Roe*, Justice Department lawyers wrote, "The textual, doctrinal and historical basis for *Roe v. Wade*, is so far flawed and . . . is a source of such instability in the law that this Court should reconsider that decision."[13] In the same vein, the Justice Department was accelerating its efforts against affirmative action and busing.

A related effort, one that would affect the fate of Scalia, was occurring deeper behind the scenes. Lawyers at the Justice Department were making a list of potential Reagan nominees to the high court, even though there was no vacancy at the time. Meese had tapped William Bradford Reynolds, an assistant attorney general and Meese's close friend, to lead a team that quietly screened potential candidates. As head of the Justice Department's civil rights division, Reynolds had been the architect of the Reagan administration's opposition to affirmative action. Members of Congress had criticized him for lax enforcement of laws barring discrimination in voting and housing.[14] Reagan had wanted to promote Reynolds to associate attorney general, but the Senate Judiciary Committee had blocked the nomination.[15] In the special role Meese created for him, Reynolds had his teams divvy up names of potential nominees for the high court, read through their writings and speeches, and examine biographies for "red flags" that might put them at odds with Reagan's agenda or that might cause trouble with the Senate. Even as they undertook their work, they were aware that an appointment might not be made for many months and that the results of their efforts might not be seen for decades.[16]

"I think Reagan probably had a fairly broad but fairly definite idea of what he was looking for," recalled Lee Liberman, the former Scalia student and law clerk who became a Justice Department special assistant and worked with Reynolds to gather material on potential nominees. "Meese was in charge of figuring out what that meant in practice."[17] Steven Calabresi, who like Liberman had helped found the Federalist Society and then clerked on the D.C. Circuit, was also on the Justice Department screening team.

The Reynolds group focused on prominent U.S. appeals court judges, including Scalia, Robert Bork, Anthony Kennedy, and Ralph Winter. The gray-bearded Bork was a natural to head up any list of who might be next for the high court. As a former U.S. solicitor general and D.C. Circuit judge, he had the experience. And as a leading conservative thinker and prolific writer, he appeared to be the brightest star in the conservative legal constellation. A well-known advocate of judicial restraint, Bork had been among the first academics of the era to argue that courts should recognize only liberties and rights explicitly written in the Constitution. He denounced the Supreme Court's 1965 case of *Griswold v. Connecticut*, which said the Constitution covered the use of contraceptives by married couples.[18]

After Bork's tenure as solicitor general, he had returned to teaching at Yale Law School and then entered the private practice of law. When Reagan called in 1981 to offer him a spot on the D.C. Circuit, Bork had proved himself a good soldier by leaving a lucrative law firm job. Reagan aides had suggested that the move would put him first in line for the Supreme Court. The American Bar Association had deemed Bork "exceptionally well qualified," the group's highest credential, when he was nominated to the D.C. Circuit in 1981.

Yet by the mid-1980s, Scalia, nine years junior to Bork and seven months behind him on the D.C. Circuit, had established himself as a dominant personality. In 1985 *The American Lawyer* magazine ran a story about Scalia's emergence on the D.C. Circuit. The author, Stephen J. Adler, noted that lawyers had assumed Scalia would defer—at least initially—to the more senior Bork. Adler reported in the piece, "Scalia did nothing of the kind. Instead, he made it clear from the start that he didn't intend to ease into the job." The larger and present question in legal circles, Adler added, was, "Can he beat . . . Bork to the Supreme Court?"[19]

That question would become more than academic the following year, in 1986, when Chief Justice Warren Burger arrived at the White House in a black Court limousine for a private meeting with President Reagan. Burger had asked for the appointment on May 27 to tell Reagan he wanted to retire at the end of the Supreme Court's term, about a month away. At seventy-eight, weary of his work as chief justice, Burger said he wanted more time to devote to his leadership of the Commission on the Bicentennial of the U.S. Constitution. Reagan had hoped for retirements from Brennan, a 1956 Eisenhower appointee, and Justice Thurgood Marshall, Lyndon Johnson's 1967 groundbreaking black appointee, but he had not necessarily expected the resignation of Burger, Nixon's man of 1969. Still, Reagan did not try to dissuade Burger from leaving. Five years had passed since the president's first appointment, of Sandra Day O'Connor. Burger's timing was good, too. After the approaching November elections, a Democratic majority could be in control of the Senate. Winning approval of a Reagan nominee certainly would become harder.

The next day, Reagan's chief of staff, Donald Regan, told Meese, who had been waiting for this moment, and the White House counselor Peter Wallison about Burger's retirement. They decided that they alone would review candidates, using information from the Brad Reynolds group. It was better for them to privately undertake the screening before the press heard of the opening and began its scrutiny. Equally important, Regan wanted to prevent lower court judges from angling for a Supreme Court spot.

Foremost in the minds of Meese, Regan, and Wallison was this opportunity to shift the Court's direction. A lifetime appointment could help project components of the Reagan revolution far into the future. Reagan's appointment of O'Connor had fulfilled a campaign promise to place a woman on the Court. This new nomination could be more of a reflection of Reagan's quest for a remade judiciary.

As the calendar turned to early June, Reagan reached a decision to first move Associate Justice Rehnquist into the chief justice chair. When Reagan met with Rehnquist on June 12, 1986, to tell him that he was the "unanimous choice of all of us" for chief, the president mentioned that he was thinking about Bork and Scalia as possible candidates to succeed him. Rehnquist said he had high regard for both men and did not try to make a case for either.[20]

Scalia was not as highly credentialed as the former solicitor general Bork, but his stock in the Reagan administration was rising. It was not just that Scalia protégés such as Liberman and Calabresi were among those putting together information on candidates for the standing Supreme Court selection project. It was that the man who had stood between Scalia and an earlier ambition for the solicitor generalship, William French

Smith, was gone. Meese, even with his Princeton undergraduate and Yale law degrees, was more suited than Smith to the rough-and-tumble of Washington politics. He had served as Reagan's chief of staff in the tumult of the California governorship. He had always liked the scrappy Scalia and had even adapted some of his writings in the provocative speech to the American Bar Association. At least as much as Bork, the fifty-year-old Scalia embodied Reagan's legal counterrevolution. In addition, Scalia's personal story as the son of a Sicilian who had come to America through Ellis Island, in the shadow of Bartholdi's Statue of Liberty, was captivating. And, important in the context of nomination politics, Scalia's backers made their views known to the White House. Patrick Buchanan, the former Nixon speechwriter and TV commentator whom Don Regan had brought in to be communications director at the White House, had written a memo touting Scalia as a major contributor to the legal legacy Reagan hoped to leave.

When Buchanan was appointed to the White House staff in January 1985, he had very quickly set up what he called a "response desk" to take on the "liberal ideologues" and answer other Reagan critics. Buchanan's aggressive ways impressed Meese, and Don Regan regarded him as "the Thomas Paine of the Right." News commentators did not view Buchanan so generously. The *New York Times* columnist James Reston wrote, "We haven't had a really provocative political hatchet man around the White House since Spiro Agnew, but with the appointment of Patrick J. Buchanan . . . the old noisy tradition may not be lost."[21]

Trying to focus Reagan on the Court even before there was an opening, Buchanan had written in his Scalia memo, "The stakes here are immense—whether or not this President can leave behind a Supreme Court that will carry forward the ideas of the Reagan Revolution—into the 21st century." Buchanan's stance also reflected the political and strategic dimension of what Meese was seeking in the legal realm: "While Bork is [an] ex-Marine and a brilliant judge, I would lean to Scalia for the first seat [of Reagan's second term]. He is an Italian-American, a Roman Catholic, who would be the first Italian ever nominated—a tremendous achievement for what is America's largest ethnic minority, not yet fully assimilated into the melting pot—a minority which provides the GOP its crucial margins of victory in New Jersey, Connecticut and New York." Buchanan closed his memo by referring to "the cruciality of the Supreme

Court to the Right-to-Life Movement, to the School Prayer Movement, the anti-pornography people etc.—all of whom provide the Republicans with the decisive Presidential margins."[22]

Buchanan and Scalia were fervent antiabortion Catholics with street-fighter intensity. They had grown up in urban ethnic enclaves—Scalia in Queens, Buchanan in Washington, D.C.—and both had gone to Jesuit high schools and attended the Jesuit Georgetown University for their undergraduate degrees. Buchanan was known for his take-no-prisoners style. Scalia, on the other hand, had been called "a knife-fighter, but a friendly knife-fighter."[23]

Letters from Italian Americans had been flowing into the White House on behalf of Scalia for months. Unlike Buchanan or Meese, Italian American leaders were not looking at ideology. They sought ethnic representation.[24] Many Roman Catholics outside the Italian American community also were supportive of Scalia.[25]

What further boosted Scalia's chances in the selection roulette was the number of young Reagan insiders who were his followers. They devoured his opinions and were enamored of his verve. Years before this Supreme Court search got under way, soon after he had been appointed to the D.C. Circuit, Scalia was being mentioned in the same breath as Bork and other esteemed conservatives. In fact, John Roberts, then only two years out of Harvard Law and working in the White House Counsel's office, had invoked Scalia's name, along with those of more seasoned jurists, to argue against the proposed creation of an intermediate judicial panel to help the Supreme Court with its burgeoning caseload. Roberts argued that only the Supreme Court should be in a position to review opinions of appeals court judges of Scalia's stature.[26] Roberts's reference to Scalia—when Scalia had not been a judge for even a year—showed how quickly Scalia was earning standing. While Bork had long been embraced by establishment conservatives, Scalia was speaking to the new generation. He was a force to be contended with, as were the newly minted lawyers drawn to Reagan's mission and building the Federalist Society.

In the thick Justice Department notebooks prepared on each possible nominee, Bork and Scalia had been similarly portrayed as advocates of judicial restraint. But there was a bonus in the Scalia assessment prepared primarily by his former law clerk Liberman. Because of her time with Scalia, she was well positioned to convey his philosophy and to present him to best advantage. "In light of some of the Supreme Court's cases, our candidate will need a willingness to depart from previous cases, and a strategic grasp of how to go about doing so," according to the memo Liberman shepherded. "Scalia has a very strong record in this area, both on and off the bench." What followed in her memo was a persuasive detailed argument about how Scalia as a judge on the D.C. Circuit had been systematically arguing for narrower interpretations of liberal Supreme Court decisions on free speech and privacy rights.[27] She also noted that before becoming a judge, Scalia had testified before Congress that it need not be bound by the Supreme Court's rulings on separation of church and state—exactly what Meese had advocated in his July 1985 speech at the American Bar Association.

A final factor gave Scalia the definitive edge: his relative youth and good health. In 1986, administration officials did not know whether this would be Reagan's last appointment to the Supreme Court. They wanted to be as sure as possible that the nominee would have a long tenure. Bork was fifty-nine, a heavy smoker, and overweight. Scalia had a tobacco habit, too, but was favoring a pipe at the time. "There was enthusiasm for Bork from our standpoint," Meese recalled years later. "But the president had no idea whether he would get another appointment. He had to think about age and health."[28]

Scalia's dynamic conservatism, Italian American story, and comparatively good health made this his moment. Reagan told his aides to set up a meeting with Scalia.

Meese called Scalia on Friday, June 13, to arrange a visit to the White House for the following Monday. Scalia told only his wife about the call. The experience with the solicitor general position was fresh in his memory, and he was nervous. He had never really known what went wrong five years earlier when Attorney General William French Smith chose Rex Lee over him for the job. Could Smith have wanted someone less passionate and more restrained? Possibly, Scalia thought, saying decades later, "Maybe he wanted somebody smoother."[29] The time between Meese's Friday call and the Monday meeting with Reagan was an eternity. Said Scalia, "I was floating around all weekend, hoping it wouldn't end the way it did" when Smith called with the rejection for the solicitor general job.[30]

He arrived at the White House on the afternoon of Monday, June 16, in a battered compact car, which Don Regan found an amusing contrast to the visit three weeks earlier by Burger's shiny limousine.[31] As they sat in the Oval Office, Reagan immediately liked Scalia's direct style. Unlike Rehnquist, who was a shy soul outside the Court and often looked down at his Hush Puppies, Scalia was animated.[32] As he did with Rehnquist, Reagan came right to the point. "I would like you to consider whether you'd want to be on the Supreme Court." Scalia immediately said yes.[33]

In exactly twenty days, but after months of staff preparation and years of groundwork laid all around, Reagan had chosen a man for the Supreme Court whose view of the law tracked the agenda that Reagan and Meese had been pressing. Scalia, with his deep-seated conservatism and Christian orthodoxy, had come to his beliefs on his own. Going forward, ensconced on the high court, he had the potential, however, to become a more influential advocate for the conservative cause than the men now in the White House.

The next day, at the marble-columned courthouse, most of the Supreme Court justices found out about Burger's retirement when they were invited into the chief justice's wood-paneled conference room to watch Reagan on television announcing the Burger departure and his choices of Rehnquist and Scalia. Burger had given messengers copies of his retirement letter to deliver to his colleagues. The letter landed on their desks at 1:50 p.m., ten minutes before Reagan's news conference began on June 17.[34]

At the White House, shortly before Reagan's news conference was to start, when Meese and Wallison assembled their aides and told them about the nominations, Pat Buchanan's reaction stood out: "Yes!" he shouted, and pumped his fists in the air.[35]

Now, in the Dirksen hearing room with Scalia, Senate Judiciary Committee Democrats who might have been unrelenting critics responded positively to the nominee's youthful dynamism and Italian heritage. Some knew him from social occasions or shared athletic pursuits. In opening comments, Senator Metzenbaum revealed his attitude toward Scalia as he jokingly observed that Scalia had recently whipped him in a game of tennis. Scalia rejoined, "It was a case of my integrity overcoming my judgment, Senator."[36]

"Touché," said Metzenbaum as spectators broke up in laughter. The exchange reflected the cozy good-old-boy world of Washington, where Scalia had been welcomed.

In other introductory remarks, there were many references to Scalia's Italian roots. Senators Pete Domenici, a Republican from New Mexico, and Alfonse D'Amato, a Republican from New York, were not members of the Judiciary Committee, but they came to the hearing to praise him. The Italian emphasis prompted the Democratic senator Howell Heflin, a hefty former state judge from Alabama, to say, "I believe that almost every Senator that has an Italian American connection has come forward to welcome you to this or to participate in this hearing thus far. I would be remiss if I did not mention the fact that my great-great-grandfather married a widow who was married first to an Italian American."

Scalia, never missing a beat, rejoined to Heflin, "Senator, I have been to Alabama several times, too."

The nominee was at ease. His usual intensity was channeled into geniality. He had been coached by Justice Department lawyers and had sought counsel from Laurence Silberman and other politically savvy friends. Scalia, of course, also loved being onstage. As he sat before the microphones, he folded his hands in front of him. Sometimes he lifted his clasped hands up to his chin and leaned his face on his thumbs. Scalia's black hair was combed straight back from his broad forehead. He was the picture of dignity in a dark blue suit and starched white shirt with French cuffs. Since his nomination by Reagan, things had gone smoothly. Yet Scalia was aware that in a politically charged atmosphere anything could happen.

The initial comments by the committee chairman, Thurmond, immediately reassured him. Age eighty-three and a loyal Reagan team player, Thurmond began by speaking broadly about the importance of the endeavor the senators were about to undertake. Thurmond noted that the Supreme Court had the final word on what the law was and that its interpretation of the Constitution could be reversed only by a later Supreme Court ruling or by a constitutional amendment.

Thurmond then lightly delved into one of the areas for which Scalia had been getting the most criticism since his nomination by Reagan. Scalia's views on the First Amendment's protection of free speech were narrow. That was reflected in the panel decision in the high-profile *Wash-*

ington Post libel case that was undergoing full court review in the D.C. Circuit at the time of the hearing. More generally, Scalia took a skeptical view of the press and public requests for information from the government. In an essay about the Freedom of Information Act, Scalia called the law the "Taj Mahal of the Doctrine of Unanticipated Consequences, the Sistine Chapel of Cost Benefit Analysis Ignored." He further argued that "the defects of the Freedom of Information Act cannot be cured as long as we are dominated by the obsession that gave them birth—that the first line of defense against an arbitrary executive is do it yourself oversight by the public and its surrogate, the press."[37]

One of Scalia's most vocal critics, the *New York Times* columnist William Safire, had penned a new column after Reagan's selection, tracing Scalia's rapid rise in public office to "his espousal of greater government secrecy and tighter restrictions on freedom of speech." Referring to the former vice president Agnew, a vigorous media critic, Safire had concluded that Scalia was chosen by Reagan partly because he expressed "Agnewism with a scholarly face." Safire reminded readers that earlier he had declared Scalia "the worst enemy of free speech in America today."[38]

Without mentioning Safire's name, Thurmond said, "Would you please give the committee your view as to why your interpretation of the First Amendment, with regard to libel, led to this criticism?"

"Well, I have to say it must have been a misunderstanding," Scalia began. "I do not know of anything in my opinions, or my writings, that would display anything other than a high regard, and a desire to implement to the utmost the requirements of the First Amendment."

Scalia then accentuated his years as a law professor and the value of free speech to colleges and universities. "I have spent my life in the field that the First Amendment is most designed to protect," Scalia insisted. "In addition to having been a scholar, and a writer as a scholar, I think I am one of the few Supreme Court nominees that has been the editor of a magazine. So why anyone would think that I—if anything—if I were to have a skewed view of the First Amendment, Senator, it would be in just the opposite direction."

Yet Scalia had written an opinion on the D.C. Circuit complaining that the Supreme Court had too excessively protected the press.[39] He had consistently argued against an expansive Freedom of Information Act and a reporter's "shield" to keep sources confidential. Justice Department lawyers reviewing his past record had accurately concluded that "he favored overruling *New York Times v. Sullivan*," the 1964 landmark case that helped protect the media from libel judgments in situations involving public figures.[40] A senator who was interested in truly probing his record might have followed up with references to Scalia's specific writings. But Thurmond, who by this time in his tenure was largely a ceremonial chairman reading a script prepared by staff, went immediately to a question on a separate topic.

The exchange recalled what had happened four years earlier, when Thurmond was questioning Scalia during the confirmation hearing for the D.C. Circuit. Thurmond had brought up the same essay attacking the Freedom of Information Act as "the Taj Mahal of unanticipated consequences" because of its costs in terms of manpower and resources to federal agencies responding to information requests. When Thurmond asked in 1982 about Scalia's view that the act was more trouble than it was worth, Scalia responded, "Well, let me make clear at the outset, Mr. Chairman, that that article came from the days which, if I am confirmed, would be bygone days—days in which as a private citizen I could comment on the wisdom of laws which the Congress had enacted. Needless to say, my views on the wisdom would have nothing to do with my interpretation of it were I sitting as a judge."[41] In 1982, as in 1986, Thurmond went on to another subject.

Next up for the Supreme Court confirmation hearing was the Democratic senator Edward M. Kennedy of Massachusetts, who went directly to the question of abortion rights. More than a decade after the 1973 decision in *Roe v. Wade*, a national debate still raged on whether abortion should be legal nationwide and whether the Court had improperly found a constitutional right on the issue, allowing a woman to end her pregnancy. The Reagan administration, in the most recently completed term, had engaged in an unprecedented effort to get the Court to overturn the decision. Justice Department lawyers had told the Court in a legal brief that the *Roe v. Wade* opinion was flat wrong and that the Constitution historically could not contain a right for women to end a pregnancy. A majority of the justices had just rejected that position. The Court had struck down a Pennsylvania law requiring physicians to give women seeking abortion detailed information about the medical procedure; the law was intended to persuade young women to change their minds about having an abortion. The Court's opinion forcefully endorsed the abortion right.

Before he became a judge, Scalia had criticized the right to abortion and the modern Court's expansive view of individual privacy. In the materials prepared by the Justice Department screening team he was cast as "a strong believer in traditional values" and an opponent of *Roe v. Wade*.[42] Reagan had been asked by reporters about Scalia's position on abortion in the weeks leading up to the Senate Judiciary Committee hearings. In one meeting with *Los Angeles Times* reporters and editors in late June, Reagan had stressed that "abortion" was murder but said he had not used a "litmus test" on his Court nominees to ensure that they would want to reverse *Roe v. Wade*. The president suggested that such screening was not necessary, because he had "confidence in the fact that the one thing that I do seek [is] judges [who] will interpret the law and not write the law."[43]

With that in the backdrop, Senator Kennedy told Scalia, "If you were confirmed, do you expect to overrule *Roe v. Wade*? There have been at least some reports that that was one of the considerations in your nomination."[44]

"Excuse me?" Scalia said.

"Do you expect to overrule the *Roe v. Wade* Supreme Court decision if you are confirmed?" Kennedy repeated.

"Senator, I do not think it would be proper for me to answer that question." Scalia said he did not want to elaborate on his abortion position, because an abortion case might come before him as a justice. Scalia's natural instinct was to engage the question, to do battle. But he, his White House advisers, and his personal confidants had decided ahead of time that he should say as little as possible. Laurence Silberman, his friend from the Ford administration and a colleague on the D.C. Circuit, said years later, "We had agreed that it was terribly important that he not answer doctrinal questions."[45]

Kennedy pressed Scalia on how much weight Scalia would give *Roe v. Wade* as a precedent. Scalia declined, saying, "It can only be answered in the context of a particular case, and I do not think that I should answer anything in the context of a particular case." To try to set Kennedy's mind at rest, the nominee added, "I assure you, I have no agenda. I am not going onto the Court with a list of things that I want to do. My only agenda is to be a good judge."

Kennedy, first elected to the Senate in 1962 and now fifty-four years old, was among the chamber's most liberal members. At the time of the Scalia hearings, he was worn out from the Rehnquist hearings. What's more, his home state of Massachusetts had a sizable Italian American and Roman Catholic population. Kennedy decided not to back Scalia against a wall.

The Maryland Republican senator Charles McC. Mathias followed up in trying to probe Scalia's sentiment on abortion. "You have written on the subject of *Roe v. Wade* . . . I believe you have expressed doubts about that decision, both on moral as well as jurisprudential grounds," began Mathias, then sixty-four years old and a seventeen-year veteran of the Senate. Scalia interjected, "I am not sure the latter is true, Senator. I think I may have criticized the decision, but I do not recall passing moral judgment on the issue."

Mathias continued. "What does a judge do about a very deeply held personal position, a personal moral conviction, which may be pertinent to a matter before the Court?"

"Well, Senator," Scalia responded, "one of the moral obligations that a judge has is the obligation to live in a democratic society and to be bound by the determinations of that democratic society. If he feels that he cannot be, then he should not be sitting as a judge. There are doubtless laws on the books apart from abortion that I might not agree with, that I might think are misguided . . . In no way would I let that influence my determination of how they apply. And if indeed I felt that I could not separate my repugnance for the law from my impartial judgment of what the Constitution permits the society to do, I would recuse myself from that case."

It would turn out that Scalia had virtually no occasion to believe that his personal beliefs impaired his legal judgment. However, he accepted as true—but did not say so before his Senate audience—that a judge's moral perceptions were always in the background, and not for the worse. He recognized the existence of these perceptions, yet felt they could be kept at bay. "One would be foolish to deny the relevance of moral perceptions to law," Scalia had said in a 1985 speech. "There is no need to apologize for the phenomenon, even when the moral beliefs spring from a theological belief. In any case, it is useless to rail against the phenomenon because it is inevitable."[46]

Other senators returned to the subject of *Roe v. Wade*, but Scalia was resolute. He declined to say even whether he believed the Constitution contained a right of privacy for matters of procreation and contraceptive use, as the Court had first ruled in 1965.

Because of Reagan's objections to government racial policies, affirmative action was another recurring topic in the hearings on Scalia's nomination. Reagan officials had aggressively tried to eliminate the legal grounds for affirmative action by issuing executive orders against it and by joining lawsuits brought by white workers challenging programs that gave minorities a boost. Reagan administration officials believed that any preferential government treatment of blacks or other racial minorities could be justified only when an individual showed personal discrimination.

In the Court term completed before the hearings, the justices had resolved three affirmative action cases. In the most significant one, they had struck down a Michigan policy that allowed black teachers with less seniority to keep their jobs when white teachers were laid off.[47] But the Court nonetheless had said in *Wygant v. Jackson Board of Education* that a public employer could—in some situations—use numerical hiring goals that favored minorities to remedy past discrimination or for racial diversity among faculty. Reagan administration lawyers had urged the Court to take a harder stance against such programs. They were foiled by Justice O'Connor, the decisive fifth vote in *Wygant*, who declared in a concurring opinion, "[T]he Court has forged a degree of unanimity; it is agreed that a plan need not be limited to the remedying of specific instances of identified discrimination."[48]

At the Senate confirmation hearing, the Maryland Republican senator Mathias asked Scalia whether he believed that Justice O'Connor's statements in the *Wygant* case reflected a consensus in this divisive area. Scalia declined a direct answer: "[T]he one thing you can say for sure about the Supreme Court decisions is that they have not answered all the questions." Later, Senator Paul Simon, a Democrat from Illinois, returned to laws intended to help victims of race discrimination. Simon said that the consensus from his staff's review of Scalia's writings in this area was that Scalia would "interpret civil rights statutes narrowly" and that he would be an "ardent enemy of affirmative action."

Scalia said that was a misreading of his work. "There should be no doubt about my commitment to a society without discrimination," he said. Then Scalia referred to his Italian roots as giving him the status of a racial minority: "[H]aving any animosity toward racial minorities in my case would be a form of self-hate. I am a member of a racial minority myself, suffered, I expect, some minor discrimination in my years; nothing compared to what other racial groups have suffered. But it does not take a whole lot to make you know that it is bad stuff."[49]

Scalia noted that his Irish mother-in-law "remembers the days when there were signs in Boston that said 'No Irish need apply.' I find all of that terribly offensive . . . I have absolutely no racial prejudices, and I think I am probably at least as antagonistic as the average American, and probably much more so toward racial discrimination." Scalia also vowed to Simon that he would keep his views about the wisdom or effectiveness of government policies on affirmative action out of his calculus as a judge.

When Scalia had argued against affirmative action in a 1978 Washington University speech and subsequent law review essay, he conjured up a story about the Lone Ranger and his Indian companion, Tonto: "If you recall the famous radio serial, you know that Tonto never said much, but what he did say was (disguised beneath a Hollywood-Indian dialect) wisdom of an absolutely Solomonic caliber. On one occasion, it seems that the Lone Ranger was galloping along with Tonto, heading eastward, when they saw coming toward them a large band of Mohawk Indians in full war dress. The Lone Ranger reins in his horse, turns to Tonto, and asks, 'Tonto, what should we do?' Tonto says, 'Ugh, ride-um west.' So they wheel around and gallop off to the west until suddenly they encounter a large band of Sioux heading straight toward them. The Lone Ranger asks, 'Tonto, what should we do?' Tonto says, 'Ugh, ride-um north.' So they turn around and ride north, and sure enough, there's a whole tribe of Iroquois headed straight toward them. The Ranger asks, 'Tonto, what should we do?' And Tonto says, 'Ugh, ride-um south,' which they do until they see a war party of Apaches coming right for them. The Lone Ranger asks, 'Tonto, what should we do?' And Tonto says, 'Ugh, what you mean, "we," white man?' " Then Scalia wrote in the piece, "I have somewhat the same feeling when [U.S. district judge] John Minor Wisdom talks of the evils that 'we' whites have done to blacks and that 'we' must now make restoration for."[50]

Some senators were offended by Scalia's use of a comic Indian speech in the Washington University presentation. "I note that you used a rather interesting story to illustrate one of your objections of affirmative action, and that is the story of Tonto and the Lone Ranger," Metzenbaum said, continuing in a way that seemed designed not to put Scalia on the defensive. "I will not read the whole story . . . but the English dialect of the Indian, I am not quite so sure about . . . What do you think the Indians of this country might feel about your reciting that story with some of the quotes? . . . It's a rather cute story, but I wonder if your use of an Indian dialect would offend the Indians."

"I am fully aware of that sensitivity, Senator," Scalia responded, "which was why, when I began the story, I made it clear that Tonto's wisdom was always Solomonic, but it was disguised between what I referred to there as a 'Hollywood Indian dialect.' That is a disparaging term. I am fully aware that Indians do not talk that way. It is how Hollywood portrayed them. I thought I made it very clear in what I wrote, that Indians do not talk that way, but that is the way Hollywood wrongfully portrays them. Now if that is not enough of a disclaimer and the story has to be stricken from everyone's repertoire, I think that would be a great loss. And it does not work in non-Hollywood Indian. It really does not."

Scalia's wife had been following every word, even as their youngest, Meg, at one point put her head on her mother's lap. Maureen was startled by Metzenbaum's line of questions. She worried that it might reveal some real skepticism or hostility toward her husband. But in fact Metzenbaum really did not probe Scalia's beliefs at the core of the Washington University speech. The senator moved on.

No wonder Scalia exuded a breezy superiority at the hearing. He was not going to answer what he did not want to answer, and senators barely protested. They did not want to corner him.

Scalia had been a leading proponent of the notion that judges should adhere to the original understanding of the Constitution at the time of its adoption when deciding the breadth of individual rights. That had been a crucial factor in the Reagan team's selection of him. But when the Delaware Democratic senator Joseph R. Biden, Jr., asked about Scalia's philosophy, the nominee declined to be pinned down on the implications of his "originalist" approach. He did make clear that he would not use the phrase a "living Constitution," which was associated with Justice Brennan and envisioned a document that could be adapted to changing times and societal needs. "What I think is that the Constitution is obviously not meant to be evolvable so easily that in effect a court of nine judges can treat it as though it is a bring-along-with-me statute and fill it up with whatever content the current times seem to require."

Scalia later added that he preferred to think of his approach as "original meaning," rather than "original intent," and that he believed the Constitution should be interpreted in terms of the original understanding of its framers. "The starting point, in any case," Scalia continued, "is the text of the document and what it meant to the society that adopted it. I think it is part of my whole philosophy, which is essentially a democratic philosophy, that even the Constitution is, at bottom, a democratic document." He said that view protected "against the passions of the moment that may cause individual liberties to be disregarded."

At one point Biden tried to provoke Scalia. The senator commented that the hearing had been "pretty dull." He encouraged Scalia to engage more on substance. Scalia did not take the bait. His refrain was, "Nobody arguing a case before me should think that he is arguing to somebody who has made up his mind either way."

The Pennsylvania Republican senator Arlen Specter complained about Scalia's vague testimony. "How does a senator make a judgment on what a Supreme Court nominee is going to do?" Specter asked. Years later, Specter wrote that Scalia "was justifiably confident that he could get away with answering practically nothing. When captured in combat, U.S. military personnel should give only their name, rank, and serial number. Scalia gave his name and rank, but not his serial number. Feisty and combative by nature, he refused to answer even the most basic questions."[51]

Specter acknowledged that he was flummoxed by the nominee from the start. When Scalia came to see him on a customary courtesy call before his hearing, Specter asked a property law question designed to stump the nominee: "What's the difference between a shifting use and a springing use?"

Recounted Specter, "Maybe one lawyer out of a hundred thousand could answer that esoteric question, unless he practices in that field or was taking the bar exam the next day." But Scalia had an answer. "Well, I'll tell you, Senator," Scalia began. "It's like these two guys who were riding in taxicabs that had a collision in midtown Manhattan. And while the drivers were exchanging information, the passengers started to talk. And one said, 'What do you do?' And the other guy said, 'I'm a lawyer.' The first passenger said, 'Hey, that's interesting. So am I. Where do you work?' 'I work on

Wall Street.' 'Hey, you know, I do, too. Which firm?'" Scalia quoted one passenger as naming a firm, maybe White and Case. "The other passenger rejoined, 'Oh, I work at White and Case also. What branch are you in?' 'I'm in property law section.' 'I'm in property, too. What do you do?' 'Shifting uses.' 'Well, that's why I don't know you: I'm in springing uses.' " "By the time Scalia had finished his answer," Specter recalled, "I had almost forgotten my question."[52]

Asked about the Specter anecdote years later, Scalia could not remember whether he knew the answer to Specter's question. Scalia said he doubted it.[53]

One potentially embarrassing line of questioning during the Senate hearings revolved around Scalia's participation in a D.C. Circuit case involving AT&T, a company from which he had received a consulting fee of $25,800 three years earlier, on a matter separate from what the case involved. News reports at the time about the case quoted the former Hofstra Law School dean Monroe Freedman saying, "I think it does raise questions about his judicial judgment." Freedman called Scalia's participation in the AT&T case an "act of serious misjudgment." Other ethics commentators, however, disagreed and said that Scalia need not have disqualified himself. (Scalia had voted against AT&T in the end.)[54]

The Vermont Democratic senator Patrick Leahy asked why Scalia had heard the case after taking the fee, noting that Professor Freedman had said it was unethical. "It seemed to me," Scalia responded, "that two or three years disqualification from AT&T matters would be more than enough to eliminate any appearance of impropriety. In all of these cases, of course, it is not just a matter of interest on just one side and no interest on the other side. It is a cost to the court when I have to disqualify myself, of course, and it is unfair to the litigants . . . So I decided that I would recuse myself for a period of three years . . . After three years, I instructed the clerk to put me back in the pool for AT&T cases." Scalia reiterated comments from his 1982 hearings about when he would take himself out of a case because a conflict of interest might exist. He said he would sit out a case if "a reasonable person would believe that my judgment would be distorted."

At the end of his day in the witness chair Scalia thanked the committee and said, "I have genuinely enjoyed being here."

He often exuded an air of assurance even when he was not feeling very assured. In this situation, however, he had reason to be confident. The questioning was soft. In the few prickly areas raised, there were virtually no follow-up questions. No senators had asked him about his connection to the founding of the Federalist Society, which by 1986 had members throughout the administration and had become an influential partner in the screening of judicial candidates. His tenure with the Nixon and Ford administrations was barely touched upon.

Stirring up another hornet's nest of controversy after the Rehnquist hearings was not worth it to senators politically. As Herman Schwartz observed in *Packing the Courts*, "[I]t is the common wisdom that liberal and moderate senators hate the thought of more than one nomination fight at a time or within a brief period."[55] The media, too, had been far more vigilant in pursuing Rehnquist's record. When Reagan unveiled Scalia's nomination back on June 17, the White House press corps was caught off guard. Reporters asked repeatedly how to pronounce the nominee's name: Sca-LEE-ah.[56] News stories then emphasized his Italian American roots, his large family, and his engaging personality. Few reports delved into his record of strident comments against affirmative action, denunciations of abortion rights, and views of executive power dating to his work for Nixon and Ford.

When outside witnesses were called before the Senate Judiciary Committee, Joseph Rauh, the head of the Leadership Conference on Civil Rights, referred to Scalia's comments that any criticism of his opinions arose from a misunderstanding of what he had actually written. "All I can say is that is nonsense," said Rauh. "All I listen to are these people saying he is probably the most articulate writer in America, and now he is telling you he did not mean exactly what he said." Rauh said that Scalia's "original meaning" view and his "minimizing [of] the experience of black Americans" would lead to cramped views of the equality guarantee. "If you took his theory [on race], you would still have *Plessy v. Ferguson* [allowing separate public accommodations for blacks and whites]; you would not have *Loving v. Virginia* [striking down bans on interracial marriage]." Even if Senate Democrats believed there was some truth to that, they were not going to challenge seriously the first Italian American nominee, who turned out to be an expert at deflecting their queries. The Senate Judiciary Committee voted unanimously to recommend him to the full Senate.

There were six weeks between his August 5 hearing and the September 17 Senate confirmation vote. Scalia received numerous letters of congratulation during this time, including from Justice Harry Blackmun. Scalia's response to Blackmun revealed the deft charm that had helped carry Scalia through the confirmation process and would gain him audiences even when his views were aggravating. Scalia replied to Blackmun, "I'm sure you recall how awkward the period is between nomination and confirmation, when everyone congratulates you but there is not yet any solid reason. I have been told that when Felix Frankfurter was nominated, he received a telegram from Groucho Marx that read: 'Tentative congratulations. Send photograph if confirmed.'"[57]

In the end, on September 17, Constitution Day, the Senate voted for Scalia 98–0.[58] "I was greatly encouraged by Judge Scalia's statement that he does not have an agenda of cases he is seeking to overturn," Senator Biden declared during the floor debate. Referring to Rehnquist, Biden added, "There is a significant distinction between this nominee and the last one. One is that this nominee has demonstrated through his career that he has an intellectual flexibility. He is not a rigid man."[59]

Years later, Rehnquist, the man senators fought, would move toward the center of the Court's ideological spectrum. Scalia, the man they readily accepted, ended up to the right of Rehnquist. Some Democrats, including Biden, would say they wished they could have their votes back, and not in small measure because of the conservative force Scalia would become. In 1993, during the Senate Judiciary Committee hearings for Ruth Bader Ginsburg, the first Democratic nominee in a quarter century, Biden said, "The vote I most regret casting out of all the ones I ever cast was voting for [Scalia]—because he was so effective."[60]

Yet when senators were going through the constitutionally mandated confirmation process in 1986, there was faint will to truly probe the nominee. Senators found it difficult to concretely examine differences of judicial philosophy or constitutional theory. And for Scalia there were overriding aspects. His Italian American heritage created a strong motive to support him. The Democratic opponents of Rehnquist had just failed. As a result, although Scalia's record was, for all intents and purposes, in plain sight, he barely had to defend or explain it. Scalia took his seat with hardly a glance at the substance of his views.

SEVEN

"IS ANYBODY LISTENING?"

———————•◦•◦•———————

Several months before he was nominated to the Supreme Court, both of Antonin Scalia's parents died. His father, Salvatore Eugene, had a stroke just before Christmas 1985. Catherine, his wife of fifty-six years, found his body lying on the floor at their home in suburban Trenton. She suffered cardiac arrest and died immediately. Salvatore Eugene was rushed to a hospital, where for several days he slipped in and out of consciousness. "He lingered for a couple of weeks," Justice Scalia recalled, adding that before the incident, his father had been worrying about Catherine's fragile heart and whether he would be able to continue caring for her.[1]

When Salvatore Eugene Scalia died, on January 5, 1986, he had just passed the sixty-sixth anniversary of his arrival in America. The only son buried his parents in side-by-side graves in the Panaro plot in Trenton. To the everlasting regret of the justice, they did not survive to see him reach the pinnacle of the law. "It took some of the sweetness out of it," Scalia said. "Of all people, you want your parents there."[2]

So it was with particular satisfaction that soon after his appointment Scalia accepted an invitation to be an honored guest in the ancestral hometown of Sommatino on the island of Sicily. Giovanni Falcone, a celebrated Italian judge and anti-Mafia crusader, escorted Scalia on his visit. "A lovely guy," Scalia said years later of the Italian hero who was at his side. They rode in an armored car with a battery of police motorcyclists in front of and behind the vehicle.[3] Scalia described his experience in Sommatino as one that filled him with pride but also made him feel he had stepped onto a retrograde movie set. "There was a parade through the city," he recounted. "A dime band played. People gave speeches." These were his family's people, and they felt a part of his success. Scalia thought the villagers regarded him primarily as "a friend of Ronald Reagan." The culmination of the fanfare came when Scalia was presented to the people from a balcony. The crowd below cheered, *"Viva Scalia! Viva Scalia!"*

Recounting the scene, the justice joked, "I felt like Mussolini."[4]

In Washington during his first term on the Court, Scalia wondered how much his voice would be heard. The process for deciding each case struck him as bureaucratic and laden with the kind of compromises and concessions he detested. A vote occured in a justices-only meeting referred to as "the conference." These sessions were held behind closed doors in a small oak-paneled room off the chambers of the chief justice. Here, the nine voted on the cases heard in oral arguments and also reviewed pending petitions to decide which to grant hearings. Held on Wednesday and Friday during the weeks the Court heard arguments (less frequently at other times), the sessions were a decades-old ritual.[5] Serious business was conducted, but the conference also offered the justices an opportunity for collegiality. Before settling into their discussion at a rectangular table under an intricate glass chandelier, they shook hands all around, consumed pastries and coffee, and engaged in rare moments of pure social chatter: the weather, the doings of their children, the news of the day.

In Scalia's first term, William Rehnquist was not, for the first time in his fourteen years on the Court, one of the last justices to speak and cast a vote. An overriding tradition at the "Marble Palace" was seniority. Justices were seated on the bench according to seniority, and in the private conference they spoke according to rank and tenure. As the new chief justice, Rehnquist was now first and at the head of the table. He was acutely aware of all the years he had sat in the last seat or close to it.[6]

The loquaciousness of his more senior colleagues had annoyed Rehnquist. First he would have to hear Chief Justice Burger go on in a manner Rehnquist likened to "a southern senator conducting a filibuster."[7] By tradition, the chief justice laid out the case and framed the legal issue to be decided, but Burger often showed up without having fully prepared the case, and he rambled on. He also had the habit of saying that he wanted to wait to vote until the other justices had spoken. That would allow him to cast a deciding vote and strategically control the case. Bill Brennan would follow. Rehnquist thought Brennan sounded "like someone reading aloud a rather long and uninteresting recipe." Then would follow Harry Blackmun, who, Rehnquist thought, usually found "two or three sinister aspects of every case which 'disturb' him although they have nothing to do with the merits of the question."[8]

In his new position, Rehnquist resolved to speed up the conference deliberations. His manner was focused and fast. He would not allow any justice to speak twice until all had had a chance to make an initial argument. He also knew what he wanted in a decision, figured other justices did, too, and did not bother to try to persuade, let alone manipulate, his colleagues. In this way, the Wisconsin native who had been first in his class at Stanford Law School was better liked than the imperious Burger.

Rehnquist had turned sixty-two just as the new term with Scalia started. From 1969 to 1971 he had been an assistant attorney general for the Office of Legal Counsel, and earlier, as a lawyer in Phoenix, he had written speeches for the 1964 presidential campaign of his fellow Arizonan Barry Goldwater.[9] Rehnquist embodied the judicial conservatism that Ronald Reagan had heralded in both his campaigns, but that was a lonely stance to take during Rehnquist's early years on the bench. In 1980, when the extent of the Reagan judicial revolution could barely have been imagined, Rehnquist told a University of Missouri audience that he was weary of the judicial emphasis on the Bill of Rights. He conceded that it contained "important guarantees of individual rights against action by federal and state governments," but, he went on to say, "the Constitution as a whole is a charter which created a national government and empowered it to limit not only the authority of states but the liberties of individuals."[10] Now, with the addition of Scalia, Rehnquist would have his first ideological partner in fourteen years.

Rehnquist's elevation and the addition of Scalia had changed the lineup around the table and who spoke when. Now following Rehnquist was Brennan, appointed in 1956 by President Eisenhower and the chief strategist behind the Court's civil rights revolution. Brennan had a background with unusual parallels to Scalia's. He was the son of an immigrant (from County Roscommon, Ireland) who had settled in Newark. Brennan's father, William Sr., had worked at a local brewery shoveling coal and had become a shop steward and labor leader. His mother, Agnes McDermott

Brennan, was a homemaker who raised eight children, the second of whom was William. Like Scalia, Brennan was raised a Roman Catholic and regularly attended Mass. Brennan graduated from the University of Pennsylvania and then, like Scalia, obtained a law degree at Harvard. In private practice, Brennan specialized in labor law. He was appointed to New Jersey trial and appellate courts and then, in 1952, to the New Jersey Supreme Court. He served there four years before Eisenhower chose him to be a justice. Brennan's and Scalia's views of the law were worlds apart, and Brennan's approach—tied to the "essential dignity and worth of an individual"[11]—made him a regular target for the conservatives who held up Rehnquist and Scalia as heroes. As the political science professor Peter Irons observed in *Brennan vs. Rehnquist: The Battle for the Constitution*, "During the 1980s, members and supporters of the Reagan administration filled the pages of conservative journals with denunciations of Brennan, portraying him as a black-robed Svengali who hypnotized his colleagues and made them see 'fundamental rights' that were not there. These critics portrayed their diminutive adversary in almost superhuman terms."[12] Brennan's wife of fifty-four years, Marjorie, had died in 1982, before Scalia was seated on the Court. The following year, Brennan married his longtime secretary, Mary Fowler. "Just married, off to Bermuda," Brennan had written to the others after the D.C. Circuit judge David Bazelon did the honors at his Watergate apartment. As Scalia ascended the bench, Brennan, a slight man with a big grin, was in a new life, but at age eighty he was racked by health problems and tiring.

Coming next was Justice Byron White, sixty-nine, who was appointed by the Democratic president John F. Kennedy in 1962 but was increasingly in the camp of conservatives. White had been deputy attorney general to Robert Kennedy and had taken the lead for the administration in the spring of 1961 to protect the Freedom Riders protesting segregation in the South. White had graduated from Yale, earned a Rhodes scholarship, and then became a football star for the Detroit Lions (known by the nickname "Whizzer"). He had personally faced down the Alabama governor John Patterson, who was in league with the Ku Klux Klan and would not guarantee protection for the Freedom Riders. By 1986, however, White was growing impatient with lower court judges' attempts to force integration through busing and other policy choices he believed best left to elected legislators. Scalia, who considered equivocation a serious character flaw, admired White for his firm, definite views. He always knew where White stood on a case—even if White's reasoning was sometimes obscure and even if Scalia did not agree with him. Scalia's first impression was of White's painfully firm handshake. "You had to squeeze back hard or he would hurt you," Scalia recalled.[13]

Thurgood Marshall, seventy-eight, the nation's first black justice, was next in seniority. A tall, physically imposing man, Marshall had been appointed in 1967 by Lyndon B. Johnson. Marshall had been a U.S. solicitor general and a judge on the U.S. Court of Appeals for the Second Circuit. Earlier in his legal career, as a lawyer for the National Association for the Advancement of Colored People (NAACP), Marshall coordinated the attack on segregation in voting, housing, public accommodations, and education, and he made his most important mark as one of the attorneys who crafted the legal strategy for the *Brown v. Board of Education* series of cases. When President Johnson chose Marshall to be the first black justice, the president said it was "the right thing to do, the right time to do it, the right man and the right place." Nearly two decades later, Marshall was still sharing his pained stories of what life was like for black men in America, hoping to influence his colleagues. With the changed nine, he had become a bitter voice of dissent and, unlike the strategic liberal Brennan, did not want to compromise with more moderate positions to prevail.

Next was Blackmun, seventy-seven, appointed in 1970 by Richard Nixon from the U.S. Court of Appeals for the Eighth Circuit. Blackmun was a boyhood friend of Burger's and best man at his wedding. Blackmun spent his early years on the court trying to get out from under Burger's shadow. Journalists had dubbed them the "Minnesota Twins," and in the beginning, the two justices indeed voted in tandem. A turning point for Blackmun was his authorship of the 1973 *Roe v. Wade*. Blackmun, a former general counsel for the Mayo Clinic, highlighted the interests of physicians to be free from government interference in medical choices. As the decision became a banner for the women's movement, Blackmun emphasized women's privacy concerns in later abortion rulings. Just before Scalia joined the bench, for example, Blackmun wrote in an opinion, "Few decisions are more personal and intimate, more properly private, or more basic to individual dignity and autonomy, than a woman's decision—with the guidance of her physician and within the limits specified in *Roe*—whether to end her pregnancy."[14] That stance and an increasing regard for individual privacy transformed Blackmun into one of the more liberal justices. Blackmun and Scalia were opposites on the law, but they shared an obsession with their colleagues' occasional grammatical gaffes. Scalia easily persuaded Blackmun to join his one-man enterprise, "the Chancellor's English Society"—which, Scalia quipped, was intended "to identify and stamp out illiteracies and barbaric neologisms in legal writing—or at least to commiserate about them."[15]

Lewis F. Powell, Jr., appointed in 1972 on the same day as Rehnquist, was the gentleman justice who offered all a good word and a hand. He had tried to buck up Rehnquist and his family throughout his confirmation hearings for the chief justice spot. "Thanks a heap," Rehnquist's wife, Nan, had written to Powell's wife, Jo, when Rehnquist's hearings were over in early August 1986. "It is friends who make life bearable under these circumstances."[16] When Scalia was sworn in at the Supreme Court on September 26, Powell wrote a family letter to his grown children, telling them, "One of my pleasant memories is that the nine Scalia children, together with lovely and petite Mrs. Scalia, were seated on the front row. The entire family . . . is handsome. Justice Scalia also is as attractive as he is brilliant."[17] Within a few weeks, however, Powell, seventy-nine, was bristling at Scalia's belligerence and sharp elbows. "Scalia's cheerful lack of deference rubbed his senior colleague the wrong way," Powell's biographer John Jeffries wrote. "His volubility struck Powell as bad manners. In Scalia's first oral argument he asked so many questions that Powell finally leaned over to Marshall and whispered, 'Do you think he knows that the rest of us are here?' . . . Scalia's quick dismissal of conventional wisdom seemed to Powell more suited to an academic than to a judge."[18]

Next in line was John Paul Stevens, sixty-six, appointed in 1975 by Ford while Scalia was an assistant attorney general. Stevens had reached out to Scalia during his confirmation process, suggesting that he get an outside counsel and not rely only on advisers from the White House, who would not necessarily share Scalia's best interests. Stevens was predisposed to enjoy Scalia because they had mutual friends and colleagues in Chicago. By 1986 Stevens was an independent thinker who leaned to the left and whose singular approach to the law often found him penning lone dissents. He spent much of his time at a second home in Florida and engaged in many outside pursuits. He was an airplane pilot, a national bridge champion, and a competitive golfer and tennis player. Unlike others who joined in rhetorical combat with Scalia, Stevens, who had earned high honors as an undergraduate at the University of Chicago and graduated first in his class at Northwestern Law School, never felt that Scalia was questioning his intelligence when they quarreled. Among the justices, Stevens was probably the first to understand that the newest colleague simply wanted, as part of his mental makeup, to have the last word. It did not insult Stevens, a Bronze Star winner from World War II. It amused him.

Until Scalia's arrival, Sandra Day O'Connor, Reagan's 1981 appointee, was the most junior justice. Yet she was in her ascendance by 1986. The former Arizona legislator had learned to work the conference and count votes, mainly from the conservative side. Her positions were close to the center of the bench, which often gave her the edge to win a majority. Reagan officials preliminarily had considered O'Connor, then fifty-six years old, for the chief justice spot that opened up with Burger's retirement. But her emerging moderation made them nervous. In the 1985–86 term, O'Connor had voted against school voluntary prayer groups and was not willing to go as far as other conservatives on abortion rights and affirmative action. Early in Scalia's first term, when a sex discrimination case was on the table and Scalia ranted about the evils of hiring preferences based on sex and race, O'Connor rejoined, "Why, Nino, how do you think I got my job?" She and Scalia would prove to be opposites in their legal methods and manners. She was all civility, no matter how riled.[19]

Scalia's and O'Connor's distinct personalities were also revealed in how they each handled the first conference, held right before the official first-Monday-in-October opening of the term. O'Connor and Scalia were sworn into their respective seats in late September—O'Connor in 1981— just as their colleagues were ready to consider hundreds of petitions that had been filed over the summer. These were from people who had lost their cases in lower federal and state courts and were seeking a final appeal. O'Connor tried to get up to speed on the filings—a near impossible feat that produced considerable frustration as she sorted through mounds of paper to cast her vote with some knowledge of the legal issues in the cases. Scalia did not even try. "Since I have found more than enough to do in preparing for the first round of [oral] argument," he wrote to the other justices on September 24, 1986, "I have abandoned any attempt to read the cert petitions that have accumulated over the summer. I am therefore planning to absent myself from the opening conference next week."[20]

From the start, it was clear that the new junior justice would not be shy about speaking up. But he did feel other frustrations. Rehnquist wanted the justices to come to the sessions ready to vote. Scalia felt constrained by how quickly cases were resolved and upset by the lack of meaty discussions. "It was different because people on the D.C. Circuit actually did talk over cases," recalled Lee Liberman, Scalia's protégé from the University of Chicago and D.C. Circuit whom he chose as a law clerk his first term on the high court. "That was the biggest surprise—the Supreme Court justices didn't talk with one another about cases . . . Three people [on an appeals court panel] can talk about something; nine people can't talk about something."[21]

Laurence Silberman, who had known Scalia since the Nixon years and served with him on the D.C. Circuit, recalled, "In his first six months on the Court, I remember his calling me . . . He was frustrated by how quickly Rehnquist moved. He was also disappointed in the methodology that people were using to decide cases. He thought it was too policy-oriented."[22] That is, Scalia believed that a desire for particular outcomes, rather than fidelity to the law, drove the decisions.

Accepting the perfunctory nature of the Rehnquist-led conferences, Brennan and O'Connor knew that real negotiations took place outside the conference. As personally different as the old liberal guard and the first woman justice were, they understood that the decision-making process was collective and believed that several justices could win satisfaction at the end of the opinion-drafting process. Brennan would catch a colleague in his office or grab him by the arm when he was walking the halls to make a pitch about a case. He would also size up a situation early and try to work on colleagues before they went into a conference to cast a vote. O'Connor, who had been elected Senate majority leader in Arizona, was similarly inclined to try to build coalitions through personal visits, phone calls, and private notes.[23]

In the late 1980s, as Brennan and O'Connor dueled for the upper hand on ideological and politically charged cases, Scalia was in his own world in many respects. The newest justice had no feel for such delicate negotiations. He also was not interested in compromise or finding a middle way. Scalia was readier to challenge legal doctrines and the existing order of things. He laid down markers that showed him to be more conservative than Rehnquist and, more than any other justice, ready to rattle the sedate, polite rhythms of the high court. This was a pattern set early in life. From his years in Trenton, Scalia had a way of crashing onto the scene. He was not deferential, and he bluntly spoke his mind.

As part of the justices' conference process, each case was put to a vote within a few days of oral arguments. The most senior justice in the majority decided who would write the opinion for the Court. The most senior member of the losing side assigned the main opinion for the dissenting viewpoint. The other justices were free to write their own statements, but it was the majority opinion that spoke for the Court and established the rule for all similar disputes.

Scalia was not reluctant to ask for changes—big and tiny—in the draft opinions of his colleagues writing the majority. If the substance of the change was not adopted, he would refuse to sign the full opinion and would state his objection to a particular paragraph or even footnote. When Justice White declined to adopt a Scalia suggestion in a drug case he was writing, *United States v. Dunn,* Scalia asked him to tack onto the end of the opinion that he joined White's opinion "with the exception of [one] paragraph in Part II."[24]

His colleagues reacted to his intensity in varying fashion. Thurgood Marshall was among the least receptive. "Dear Nino: I have considered your letter . . . I am sorry not to be able to accept your suggestions," Marshall wrote in an exchange over a California savings and loan case.[25] In another instance in Scalia's first term, when he told Marshall he was particularly troubled by his interpretation of a congressional statute, Marshall wrote back that he believed he was being "completely faithful to current doctrine." Scalia returned the volley, saying, "It is in my view not 'faithful to current doctrine' to continue to refer to [a 1975 case] as though its analysis had not been effectively overruled by our later opinions . . . [W]ith all respect, I cannot join your opinion if you insist upon those [references]." When Marshall received Scalia's note, he scrawled a big "No" on it and declined to make changes.[26]

When he had been assigned the Court's opinion, Scalia sometimes lost the majority as he began writing. That happened early in his tenure with the case of *Bowen v. Massachusetts,* a dispute between the federal government and states over Medicaid expenditures. In their conference vote, Rehnquist and Brennan were among the five in the majority. Chief Justice Rehnquist assigned the opinion to Scalia. But once Scalia began drafting it, his approach turned off Brennan, who sent him a diplomatic note saying, "You have written a very persuasive opinion, but I would feel more comfortable waiting until all the writing is in [from other justices] before joining it. I hope you do not mind." Justice Stevens, who was writing for dissenting justices, soon developed an argument that Brennan found appealing. Sensing this, Scalia wrote to his colleagues, "I will be responding to John's dissent tomorrow. I hope those who have not yet voted will wait." Two days later, Brennan, who was casting the critical fifth vote, sent a note around: "I have agonized long about these cases. Although Nino has written a very persuasive opinion I have finally concluded that John has the better of the argument. I therefore will join John's opinion in the above. I apologize for any inconvenience." Rehnquist realized soon enough that if a contentious case had been won by a single vote, he should not assign the opinion to Scalia, lest the obstinate justice lose the majority.[27]

As Scalia shook up things behind the crimson velvet drapes of the Court, he quickly became a charming presence on the social circuit, attending embassy parties and galas at art galleries. He was an equal-opportunity man-about-town, socializing with Katharine Graham, the publisher of *The Washington Post,* and Phyllis Schlafly, the founder of the Eagle Forum. *Dossier* magazine reported that "unlike many of the other justices, who by virtue of age or health or personal inclination prefer only the most limited social lives conducted over sedate dinners in private homes, Scalia circulates happily and easily in Washington's more public social swirl. He jokes, he dances, he bellies up to the buffet lines with the best of them."[28] Scalia was charming and eminently interesting, as well as restless and fidgety.

Scalia continued to play poker with Rehnquist and other power brokers in the capital, but he declined to throw money into the betting pools that Rehnquist organized at the Court during political elections. At first he said he would join in the wagering, along with the regulars Powell, Stevens, and O'Connor. But Scalia begged off in the end once he saw how intently Rehnquist and O'Connor were studying national political races.

"I enclose the 'pop quiz' in political science which we discussed at the luncheon table," Rehnquist wrote in one typical solicitation to his betting colleagues in November 1988.[29] "Please fill out and return to my chambers by 1 p.m. Monday if you wish to participate in the election pool. Each entrant wagers $1 on the correctness of his bet [as to whether Michael Dukakis or George H. W. Bush will win] in each state, so the maximum exposure is $50." Scalia decided not to take Rehnquist up on his offer as four other justices did. After the election, Rehnquist detailed how much each participating justice lost, then said, "Sandra won $5.19 and I won $15.19. Those that owe should send their money to me and I will in turn send it to the winners."[30] In a later interview, Scalia mused of Rehnquist and O'Connor, "They always won" the pool.[31]

In many ways, Scalia also relinquished a chance to be a full player in negotiating the outcome of cases. Unlike Rehnquist, he would not yield on his conservatism. Around the time of his nomination, several legal analysts commented on how the charming Scalia might be like the magnetic Brennan in building coalitions. But Brennan had little pride of authorship and would acquiesce to individual colleagues on the wording and substantive reasoning to keep a vote and to get close enough to the outcome he sought. Brennan would famously settle for half a loaf rather than get none. Scalia had no interest in such compromises to reach the five needed for the majority. He believed it to be wrong, maybe even beneath him, to yield on the things that mattered—and most everything mattered.[32]

Disputes over sex-based or race-based government policies particularly elicited Scalia's rancor. He argued in vain among the justices that the Court should outright eliminate policies that gave women a preference or created special opportunities for blacks and Hispanics to compensate for past bias. In one early case he adamantly opposed a government plan to promote female public employees who had been kept in low-level jobs in Santa Clara County, California. The plan allowed Diane Joyce to be elevated to road dispatcher over Paul Johnson, who scored marginally higher on a qualifying interview. Johnson sued. Brennan won a majority to reject Johnson's challenge and to uphold the county's program as allowed by Title VII.[33] Scalia, in a dissenting opinion signed in full by only Rehnquist, scoffed,

The majority emphasizes, as though it is meaningful, that "No persons are automatically excluded from consideration; all are able to have their qualifications weighed against those of other applicants." One is reminded of the exchange from Shakespeare's Henry the Fourth, Part I:

GLENDOWER: I can call Spirits from the vasty Deep.

HOTSPUR: Why so can I, or so can any man. But will they come when you do call for them?

Scalia continued: "Johnson was indeed entitled to have his qualifications weighed against those of other applicants—but more to the point, he was virtually assured that, after the weighing, if there was any minimally qualified applicant from one of the favored groups, he would be rejected."[34]

The Shakespearean allusion became classic Scalia. The son of a Romance languages professor who had collected Italian lyrics also relied on song lyrics, poetry, and mythology to make his points. As he drafted his opinions, he was comfortable at a computer keyboard, unlike his older colleagues who wrote longhand on a legal pad, and he often played a record in the background. "You put on Bach—Bach really orders the mind. All of the things just line up," he said, and acknowledged that over the years, as he failed to break the smoking habit, he would have a cigarette in an ashtray at his side. He would work through several drafts, writing and revising. "Writing," he recalled in later years, "is a very painful process . . . But I love having written, to have a product that I have sweated over . . . honed to . . . perfection."[35]

His ear was so fine that he could predict which of his zingers would draw immediate attention from fellow justices and lawyers who devoured his opinions. His writing was sprightly and alive. It could also have a contemptuous tone. When Scalia wrote an opinion in his first term saying that states could execute condemned murderers who were as young as sixteen when they committed their crimes, he ridiculed what he termed "ethicoscientific" concerns about whether juveniles were "morally blameworthy" enough to be executed. O'Connor—who was the critical fifth vote for Scalia's proposition that no national consensus existed that juvenile executions amounted to unconstitutional "cruel and unusual punishment"—declined to sign that derisive portion of Scalia's opinion in *Stanford v. Kentucky*. Brennan, who wrote for the dissenters in the case, said that a national consensus could be inferred from the fact that, in addition to the twelve states that require offenders to be at least eighteen

years old at the time of a crime and three states that set the age at seventeen, thirteen states forbade executions entirely. Scalia rejoined in his
opinion, "The dissent's position is rather like discerning a national consensus that wagering on cockfights is inhumane by counting within that
consensus those states that bar all wagering."[36]

In his early years, Scalia reserved his sharpest cuts for Justice O'Connor. His rule-oriented approach clashed deeply with her incremental
pragmatism. She wrote for a plurality of four in the 1987 case of *O'Connor v. Ortega*, in which a former public employee brought a civil rights
action claiming that his boss violated the Fourth Amendment in searching
his desk and files. Justice O'Connor said that a reasonable expectation of
privacy under the Fourth Amendment might have controlled the situation, but that in this case the privacy expectation was weakened by the
terms of the employment relationship and office practices. Scalia concurred only in the bottom-line result against the employee. With his for-
malistic approach, Scalia argued that it was reasonable for public
employees to expect that their employers could routinely search their
offices, just as private employees expected that of their private sector
bosses, and he complained that O'Connor's case-by-case approach provided "a standard so devoid of content that it produces rather than elimi-
nates uncertainty in this field."[37]

The only child who became the father of nine, Scalia could also adopt
the tone of a scold. In 1989 he wrote the leading opinion in a 5–4 California case denying the paternity claim of a man who had fathered a child
with a married woman during an affair. The woman had returned to her
husband with the child, and the biological father was trying to obtain visitation rights. Under California law, a presumption existed that the husband was the father of the child, and visitation rights were denied. "The
facts of this case are, we hope, extraordinary," Scalia said as he opened his
opinion rejecting the biological father's claim.[38] He noted repeatedly that
the entire case of "Michael H.," as the petitioning father was known in
Court filings, began with an adulterous affair. He believed the Court's
cases in this area of the law protected the traditional family unit, not relationships that arose outside of it. Scalia stressed in the case of *Michael H.
v. Gerald D.* the importance of judges remaining faithful to "the society's
views" and "relevant tradition."[39]

In a dissenting opinion, Brennan responded that Scalia was in the land

of "make believe . . . beginning with the suggestion that the situation confronting us here does not repeat itself every day in every corner of the
country." He and the other dissenting justices believed Michael H. should
at least have a hearing at which he could demonstrate his paternity and
argue his rights to visitation with the child who, Brennan observed, had
called him "Daddy" in her early years.[40]

The following year, when the justices took up their first "right to die"
case, Scalia separated himself from Rehnquist and the traditional conservatives. The parents of Nancy Cruzan, who had been unconscious since a
1983 automobile accident, wanted to disconnect her life-support systems.
Cruzan was in what physicians called a "persistent vegetative state"
(meaning she exhibited motor reflexes but no signs of cognitive function)
and was being fed through a tube in her stomach that provided food and
water. Missouri officials objected to her parents' desire to end the feedings,
which would cause death, because Cruzan left no clear advance directive
of what she would have wanted in such a dire situation. Cruzan apparently had told a former housemate that she would not wish to continue
her life if sick or injured unless she could live at least halfway normally,
but the state said such statements were unreliable for the purpose of
determining her true intentions. In an opinion by Rehnquist, the Court by
a 5–4 vote sided with Missouri in declaring that a state may block parents'
intervention when a patient's wishes were not clearly known.[41]

"While I agree with the Court's analysis today, and therefore join in its
opinion," Scalia wrote in a concurring statement, "I would have preferred
that we announce, clearly and promptly, that the federal courts have no
business in this field; that American law has always accorded the State the
power to prevent, by force if necessary, suicide—including suicide by
refusing to take appropriate measures necessary to preserve one's life; that
the point at which life becomes 'worthless,' and the point at which the
means necessary to preserve it become 'extraordinary' or 'inappropriate,'
are neither set forth in the Constitution nor known to the nine Justices of
this Court any better than they are known to nine people picked at random from the Kansas City telephone directory."

On the broader issue of whether an individual has a constitutionally
protected right to decline lifesaving food and water, all justices but Scalia
said the due process guarantee protects an interest in refusing treatment.
He said it should be left to Missouri legislators whether any patient—even

one who had shown by clear and convincing evidence that she would want no extraordinary measures taken to save her life—has a "right to die."

Scalia believed the Constitution gave legislators considerable opportunity to regulate in the areas affecting end-of-life decisions and—as also was seen in his early years—abortion rights, but he did not believe it gave similar freedom to Congress in the separation-of-powers area. He had firm ideas about the respective powers of the branches of government, which he demonstrated in 1988 as the Court took up a challenge to a statute, enacted after Watergate, allowing judges to appoint special prosecutors. Scalia was ardent in his view that the statute in the case of *Morrison v. Olson* breached the bounds of executive power. He was the only justice who saw it that way. When he gave his colleagues the first draft of his dissenting opinion, some of them were surprised by its emotional tone. "Screams!" Justice Blackmun wrote on the copy he received in June 1988. "Without the screaming, it could have been said in about 10 pages," Blackmun added in a note to himself on the Scalia draft that went beyond thirty pages.[42]

That was the early and enduring Scalia: confident in his views, hot in his rhetoric. As he staked out positions, such as in the *Morrison v. Olson* case, he showed that not only would he have a difficult time pulling colleagues to his side, he might also alienate them along the way. That was often true with Blackmun, sometimes true with O'Connor.

Morrison v. Olson tested the law allowing judges to appoint, under special circumstances, an independent counsel to investigate potential executive branch wrongdoing. The 1978 Ethics in Government Act was intended to prevent conflicts of interest within the White House and executive branch agencies. To Scalia, the no-conflicts goal may have been worthwhile, but the method violated everything he believed about the constitutional separation of powers. He thought the law improperly sanctioned prosecutorial powers outside the executive branch.

Theodore Olson, who had been head of the Office of Legal Counsel a few years after Scalia and had become a friend, was being investigated by an independent prosecutor for allegedly lying to a congressional committee during a March 1983 hearing. The committee had concentrated on political manipulation of a toxic-waste cleanup program and the Reagan administration's refusal to turn over relevant Environmental Protection

Agency documents. Committee members alleged that Olson had given false and misleading testimony regarding the administration's efforts in the cleanup program. Upon receiving the complaint, Attorney General Ed Meese invoked the independent counsel law and referred the accusations to a three-judge federal panel, which in turn named the lawyer Alexia Morrison to investigate whether Olson had lied under oath to Congress. As Olson protested that his congressional testimony had been truthful, he also challenged the constitutionality of the independent counsel law. Olson won a favorable ruling from the D.C. Circuit, which agreed that the law improperly transferred executive prosecutorial authority to the judges. Morrison, the independent counsel, appealed to the Supreme Court.

Rehnquist was a strong supporter of executive power, but in this case he disagreed with the lower court ruling, which happened to be written by the D.C. Circuit judge Silberman, Scalia's friend from the Ford days and a fellow Reagan appointee. Rehnquist believed the 1978 Ethics in Government Act gave only limited responsibility to judges to choose prosecutors upon a request by the attorney general. He did not believe it usurped executive powers, because the independent counsel was subordinate to the attorney general and could indeed be fired by the attorney general, although only with good cause. Other justices agreed with Rehnquist.

Scalia—the last justice to speak around the table—tried to argue that the president's constitutionally assigned duties included *complete* control over investigation and prosecution of violations of the law. During the drafting process Scalia was not able to change any votes and in fact turned off such justices as Blackmun with his hard line and emotional tone. When the ruling in *Morrison v. Olson* was announced by Chief Justice Rehnquist on June 29, 1988, Scalia read portions of his dissent aloud from the bench.[43] Under the white-and-gold rosette ceiling panels, Scalia went on for nine minutes—three times longer than Rehnquist's explanation of the majority opinion. "What is at issue in this case is purely executive power, quintessentially executive power to prosecute," he declared. In his written dissent, thirty-eight pages long, Scalia said the law "enfeebles" the president and his people. And he penned one of his most enduring lines: "Frequently, an issue of this sort will come before the Court clad, so to speak, in sheep's clothing . . . But this wolf comes as a wolf."[44]

The following year, Scalia dissented in another dispute over the separation of powers. By an 8–1 vote, the Court said that Congress did not improperly delegate its legislative authority to the U.S. Sentencing Commission when it authorized the commission to set prison terms for federal defendants. Blackmun wrote for the majority that the Constitution does not prohibit Congress from assigning certain determinations about the ranges of possible sentences to a commission that includes judges and members chosen by the president. In his lone dissent, Scalia wrote, "Today's decision follows the regrettable tendency of our recent separation-of-powers jurisprudence to treat the Constitution as though it were no more than a generalized prescription that the functions of the Branches should not be commingled too much—how much is too much to be determined, case-by-case, by this Court . . . I think the Court errs . . . not so much because it mistakes the degree of commingling, but because it fails to recognize that this case is not about commingling, but about the creation of a new Branch altogether, a sort of junior-varsity Congress."[45]

The view and language were pure Scalia: certain, contemptuous, clever. A junior-varsity Congress? It was a pure put-down. As the Harvard law professor Charles Fried, a former Reagan U.S. solicitor general, later observed in an essay about Scalia's writing style, no justice had ever before used the "junior-varsity" term in any opinion unrelated to a sports team. "By writing simply, clearly, directly, and forcefully he makes a moral and political point about judging, about the law, and about the kind of institution the Supreme Court should be," Fried observed.[46] Some Scalia critics, however, believed that his rhetoric—no matter how engaging—promoted incivility among judges and offered a poor lesson for law students. "No justice in Supreme Court history has consistently written with the sarcasm of Justice Scalia," the University of Southern California Law School professor Erwin Chemerinsky observed, as he reviewed some of Scalia's early decisions. "No doubt, this makes his opinions among the most entertaining to read. He has a great flair for language and does not mince words when he disagrees with a position. But I think that this sends exactly the wrong message to law students and attorneys about what type of discourse is appropriate in a formal legal setting and how it is acceptable to speak to one another." To other critics, Scalia's rhetoric left the impression that he simply wanted to be noticed.[47]

Scalia's early reputation also was defined by a series of disputes over religion, again where he was mostly in dissent. The First Amendment barred government from making any "law respecting an establishment of religion" and from prohibiting its "free exercise." Scalia's approach to disputes over government involvement with religion immediately put him at odds with the Court majority, which in the mid-1980s was still favoring a high wall of separation between church and state. Scalia wanted that wall lowered to allow greater support for religion. He wanted greater leeway for state and local governments to erect crosses or display Nativity scenes on public property. He endorsed more public aid to religious schools through tuition tax credits and vouchers for "school choice" programs that would allow parents to send children to Christian schools with public money. When it came right down to it, he believed almost no government action would violate the Establishment Clause, short of outright coercing religious participation. On the "free exercise" side, Scalia appeared untroubled by the grievances of those from minority religions or those who had no religion. He believed that any protections for their nontraditional practices—such as observance of a Saturday Sabbath—should be left to legislators and the political process rather than to the courts.

In his first term, he dissented when the majority held that a Louisiana law requiring that public schools that teach the theory of evolution also teach "creation science" violated the Establishment Clause because the state legislature enacted it as a way to promote religion.[48] In blistering rhetoric, Scalia accused the majority of bias against fundamentalist teachings. "Even if one concedes, for the sake of argument, that a majority of the Louisiana Legislature voted for the Balanced Treatment Act partly in order to foster (rather than merely eliminate discrimination against) Christian fundamentalist beliefs, our cases establish that that alone would not suffice to invalidate the Act, so long as there was a genuine secular purpose as well," he wrote, joined only by Rehnquist. "The people of Louisiana, including those who are Christian fundamentalists, are quite entitled, as a secular matter, to have whatever scientific evidence there may be against evolution presented in their schools, just as Mr. Scopes was entitled to present whatever scientific evidence there was for it."[49] Scalia's derisive reference to the famous Monkey Trial of 1925, when the high school teacher John Scopes was charged with violating a Tennessee law against the teaching of evolution, seemed to put creationism on an equal footing with evolution.

Scalia also dissented not many years later when the Court struck down faculty-arranged prayer at public school graduations, which had been challenged by a middle school student in Providence, Rhode Island—Deborah Weisman—and her father, Daniel, who said the faculty control turned graduations into state-sponsored worship. The Court majority agreed, emphasizing how young students would feel pressured to follow their teachers. Scalia chastised the majority for its "psycho journey," which he said gave more weight to Freud than Blackstone. He accused the Court of trying to write prayer out of public life. He insisted that invocations were a part of American history, "a tradition as old as public school graduation ceremonies themselves."

In the opening of his opinion, mocking the Court's view that prayer exercises carried a risk of coercing young students into joining, he took a swipe at one of the most significant opinions of his retired D.C. Circuit colleague Judge David Bazelon: "As its instrument of destruction, the bulldozer of its social engineering, the Court invents a boundless, and boundlessly manipulable, test of psychological coercion, which promises to do for the Establishment Clause what the Durham rule [devised by Bazelon] did for the insanity defense. Today's opinion shows more forcefully than volumes of argumentation why our Nation's protection, that fortress which is our Constitution, cannot possibly rest upon the changeable philosophical predilections of the Justices of this Court, but must have deep foundations in the historic practices of our people."

Most revealingly, Scalia's opinion in the case of *Lee v. Weisman* demonstrated his regard for majority rules. "The reader has been told much in this case about the personal interest of Mr. Weisman and his daughter, and very little about the personal interests on the other side," Scalia wrote in dissent. "They are not inconsequential. Church and state would not be such a difficult subject if religion were, as the Court apparently thinks it to be, some purely personal avocation that can be indulged entirely in secret, like pornography, in the privacy of one's room. For most believers it is not that, and has never been. Religious men and women of almost all denominations have felt it necessary to acknowledge and beseech the blessing of God as a people, and not just as individuals."[50]

He was staking out ground for a shift toward more deference to the government. Toward this goal, Scalia repeatedly pushed his colleagues to abandon the prevailing test for when a government action violated the Constitution's Establishment Clause. The test derived from the 1971 case of *Lemon v. Kurtzman*. That ruling dictated that any constitutionally permissible mixing of church and state meet three criteria: The government action had to have a secular purpose. It could not advance or inhibit religion. And it could not foster excessive "entanglement" with religion.[51]

Beginning with the 1987 creation-science case of *Edwards v. Aguillard*, Scalia tried to convince his colleagues that the so-called *Lemon* test had not been uniformly applied and that it offered little guidance to schools and other government officials. Most important to Scalia, he felt the *Lemon* standard was being manipulated by the more liberal justices to keep religion out of public places, sometimes by framing the inquiry simply as whether a government action was "endorsing" religion. The liberals did not think this was manipulation; rather, this was what the Constitution required, and in fact, when Brennan wrote the Court's opinion against the Louisiana creation-science law, he said that it impermissibly endorsed religion by advancing the religious belief that a supernatural being was responsible for all creation.[52]

In a 1993 case, as part of his effort to win a majority for ditching the *Lemon* test, Scalia said he had counted "at least five sitting justices" who had criticized the test over time. Scalia went on to liken the inconsistently applied standards of the 1971 case to "some ghoul in a late-night horror movie that repeatedly sits up in its grave and shuffles abroad, after being repeatedly killed and buried . . . [stalking] our Establishment Clause jurisprudence once again, frightening the little children and school attorneys. Its most recent burial, only last term, was, to be sure, not fully six feet under."[53]

That attention-getting public opinion in the case of *Lamb's Chapel v. Center Moriches Union Free School District* had been preceded by a flurry of private—and heated—memos among the justices. The Court had voted unanimously that a Long Island public school district could not prevent a church group from using its classrooms to show a film series on child rearing simply because of the group's religious mission. But then the nine split badly over the legal rationale. Justice Byron White was writing the opinion based on the Court's 1971 *Lemon* standard. In a memo to White on May 6, 1993, with copies all around to the others, Scalia objected to the rationale and also faulted White for a portion of his decision declaring that the apparent endorsement of "religion in general" would violate the Establishment Clause. Before White could respond, Stevens jumped in:

"One controversial proposition that I thought our cases had firmly settled was the proposition that the endorsement of 'religion in general' does violate the Establishment Clause. If you make the changes . . . that Nino suggests, your opinion will therefore be incomplete." Scalia responded, again on the same day, "I could not disagree more with John's assertion that it is 'settled law' that the endorsement of 'religion in general' violates the Establishment Clause. Old dicta say that, but recent cases hold to the contrary."

Within hours, Stevens sent back a note to Scalia, again with copies all around: "You may not agree with the reasoning in *Wallace v. Jaffree* [a 1985 case striking down moment-of-silence laws intended to restore prayer in school], but I do not think it is fairly characterized as 'old dicta.' " Stevens, not incidentally, had authored that opinion, delivered a year before Scalia joined the Court.

Other justices interjected with memos taking sides.[54] For her part, O'Connor suggested that she might withdraw her vote for White's opinion if he made the changes Scalia wanted: "As you know," she wrote in her "Dear Byron" memo, "I have already joined your opinion. I did so because I thought you correctly reflected our jurisprudence. I would not like to see it changed." A few days later White responded to Scalia and Kennedy, who also expressed doubts about the brief reliance on *Lemon* in White's opinion. White reminded his colleagues that all he needed was five votes, a majority: "Dear Nino and Tony, Since there are five of us who prefer the present draft and another, the Chief, who does not insist on changing it, I do not intend to make the changes that you have suggested, at least as presently advised."

Scalia thanked White for his response and said, parroting back some of the language, "Since there are three of us who strongly disagree with the draft as presently formulated, and since at least five sitting justices have criticized the *Lemon* formulation, I am unable to join the Establishment Clause analysis in your opinion."[55] In the end, Justice White responded to Scalia's "ghoul in a late-night horror movie" line with a footnote in his majority opinion that said, "While we are somewhat diverted by Justice Scalia's evening at the cinema," the question of the *Lemon* standard need not be revisited in the case at hand.[56]

A year later, when Scalia was on the losing side as the majority struck down a New York law creating a special school district to serve the disabled children of a Hasidic sect, he suggested that the majority was turning its back on religious toleration, which he deemed "one of the glories of" America. Scalia declared to his colleagues around the conference table, "I look forward to dissent!"[57] Such was the fate of Scalia in cases testing the separation of church and state in most of his early terms.

Remarkably, he was able to capture a Court majority in an early dispute concerning individuals' free exercise of religion. That constitutional guarantee was at the heart of a 1963 case, *Sherbert v. Verner*, that had been the subject of questions at his Supreme Court confirmation hearing. The case had been brought by a Seventh-day Adventist who wanted to have Saturday off instead of Sunday and lost her job at a textile mill because she would not work on Saturday, the Sabbath. The Court had held that the denial of unemployment benefits to the worker violated the free exercise of religion because it essentially conditioned the benefits on a willingness to violate religious faith.

During his 1986 confirmation hearing Scalia had complained about the decision and said, "Doesn't [it] somehow amount to an establishment of religion to have the state make a special rule to accommodate the religious belief of this Sabbatarian?"[58] He did not think judges should carve out exemptions from general rules or laws for minority religions; he said any exemptions should be left to the political process. The high court in the *Sherbert v. Verner* case and later religion disputes had declared that only a "compelling" governmental interest, such as public health or safety, could justify a burden on an individual's religious practice. Scalia considered that standard wholly "invented" by Justice Brennan, the author of *Sherbert*, through an expansive reading of the Constitution.

The new case before the justices began with Alfred Smith and Galen Black, who worked as counselors at a private rehabilitation center in Oregon. Off the job, they attended a Native American church and engaged in the sacramental use of the drug peyote, a hallucinogen. After their boss at the rehabilitation center discovered that they used peyote, they were fired. Smith and Black were denied unemployment benefits because they had been prohibited by the terms of their employment at the center from using alcohol or illegal drugs. The men appealed the denial of their unemployment benefits and won in Oregon courts. The Oregon Supreme Court ruled that the denial of benefits violated their First Amendment right to the free exercise of religion. The court said that while the men normally would have broken a state antidrug law, which made possession of peyote a felony, there had to be an exception for a good-faith religious use of peyote. State unemployment officials appealed, and a case that seemed routine became a bombshell because of what Scalia did with it.

During discussions behind the scenes in the case, Scalia told his colleagues he did not believe *Sherbert v. Verner* was pertinent precedent when the state had an interest in prohibiting the conduct for which the employee was fired. Scalia, with the help of like-minded Rehnquist, successfully convinced a majority that illegal behavior did not merit free exercise protection. The final opinion Scalia wrote went further and declared that states need not show a "compelling" governmental interest if a generally worded law happens to infringe on religious practice. That meant that as long as the law's terms were neutral (that is, not targeted at a religious group), it could be enforced against religious adherents. Scalia was joined by Rehnquist, White, Stevens, and Kennedy.

The new standard Scalia articulated for general laws that affected religion was important. Many laws that impinged on practices were written to apply to everyone and were not designed to interfere with religious exercise, such as an ordinance prohibiting alcohol consumption that could incidentally bar a Jewish family from drinking wine at a seder dinner. Scalia acknowledged in his opinion that "it may fairly be said that leaving accommodation to the political process will place at a relative disadvantage those religious practices that are not widely engaged in; but that unavoidable consequence of democratic government must be preferred to a system in which each conscience is a law unto itself or in which judges weigh the social importance of all laws against the centrality of all religious beliefs."[59]

As he discarded the long-standing "compelling interest" test, Scalia said, "We cannot afford the luxury of deeming presumptively invalid . . . every regulation of conduct that does not protect an interest of the highest order." Neither side of the Oregon case had asked the Court to reconsider whether the "compelling interest" test should be abandoned in certain circumstances.

Justice O'Connor, who agreed with the position that the Oregon men should have lost their jobs, nonetheless vehemently dissented from Scalia's opinion. She said the notion that the compelling interest test was "a luxury" was an insult to "the very purpose of the Bill of Rights." As Scalia read portions of his opinion from the bench on April 17, 1990, she passed a note to Blackmun, who had also disagreed with the majority's stance: "Harry, the Court took the wrong turn today in the free exercise case in my view. It pains me."[60]

Many law professors who specialized in religion agreed with O'Connor's view and declared that Scalia's opinion constituted the most startling development in religious freedom jurisprudence in decades. Michael McConnell, a University of Chicago scholar and a vigorous proponent of an expansive view of the free exercise of religion, observed that Scalia's insistence that religious minorities turn to the legislative process for protection was "certainly impolitic, leaving the Court open to the charge of abandoning its traditional role as protector of minority rights against majoritarian oppression." McConnell noted that before *Employment Division v. Smith*, the Free Exercise Clause gave shelter to less popular religious faiths. A coalition of religious groups and civil libertarians began working with Congress to try to overturn parts of the *Smith* decision. The result was the Religious Freedom Restoration Act, passed in 1993, which dictated that laws imposing substantial burdens on religious practices could be justified only with a showing of a "compelling" governmental interest. Of that unanimously adopted law, Scalia later scoffed, "It doesn't prove anything that everyone thinks you're wrong."[61]

Scalia wore as a badge of honor his status as antihero. "Scalia really had his fangs out this year," the Northwestern University law professor Lawrence Marshall told David Savage of the *Los Angeles Times* in July 1990, after the term involving the peyote decision had come to a close. "His dissents seem to say that 'if you don't agree with me, you must be out of your mind.' "[62]

At the same time, Scalia continued his aversion for the news media. In August of 1990, four months after the free exercise dispute, he devoted a speech to what he viewed as problems with coverage of the Court. Speaking in Los Angeles at an event sponsored by Pepperdine University, he argued that legal affairs were too complicated for general-interest newspaper reporters to understand. He appealed "to the principle that law is a specialized field, fully comprehensible only to the expert."[63] He said that the process can matter more than the result and declared, "There, it is frequently the case that the operation is a success even though the patient dies. For in judging, process is a value unto itself and not, except in a very remote sense, merely a means to achieving a desirable end. The result is validated by the process, not the process by the result." Scalia, who was speaking in generalities rather than targeting particular news stories, went on to endorse what he deemed an ancient maxim that judges not engage in public debate over the rightness or wrongness of decisions. Scalia's message in 1990 centered on the substance of Court decisions. He would increasingly develop an uneasy relationship with the news media, to the point where he would eventually say that he believed that because of his conservatism, "much of the press is hostile to my message. I don't think it's a conspiracy. I do believe a large majority of the press consists of liberals, for whatever reason, that that profession attracts them."[64]

Scalia remained a hero to Federalist Society members and other conservatives. In early 1993, as the Democrat Bill Clinton prepared to take the White House, Jeffrey Rosen wrote in *The New Republic* that "conservatives now have only the courts to carry on their thirty-year battle against entitlement liberalism, and only Antonin Scalia to bear their standard. Scorning other justices, who have refused to take some of the positions for which they were appointed, conservatives hail Scalia as the only justice guided by principle rather than politics. Scalia is the purest archetype of the conservative legal movement that began in the 1960s in reaction to the Warren Court."[65]

Scalia was reaching out to an audience beyond the Court. He inspired conservatives who, after twelve years of Ronald Reagan and George H. W. Bush control, were about to be out of government. He spoke to law students and professors. The *Cardozo Law Review* devoted an entire volume to him before he had even reached his five-year anniversary as a justice. In one essay, the U.S. appeals court judge Alex Kozinski observed, "In major opinion after major opinion, Justice Scalia finds himself writing alone. One kind of expects that one of these days his dissents will start out, 'Hello!! Hello! Is anybody listening?' " Kozinski noted that Scalia had made little headway among his colleagues with his "originalism" theory.[66]

Yet, as Kozinski observed, Scalia also had brought with him from the D.C. Circuit a deep suspicion of the usual way of interpreting statutes by looking at legislative history for lawmakers' intent. In this area, he was changing the practices of his colleagues. "Our task, as I see it," he wrote in one early case, "is not to enter the minds of the Members of Congress—who need have nothing in mind in order for their votes to be both lawful and effective—but rather to give fair and reasonable meaning to the text of the United States Code, adopted by various Congresses at various times."[67] Kozinski, a fellow conservative, noted that while most judges continued to look at committee reports and floor speeches, "the fact is legislative history just ain't worth what it was a few years ago. It used to be that you would get briefs and opinions that started and ended their analyses with legislative history, never once mentioning the text of the statutes they were purporting to interpret. Such things are much rarer these days."[68]

And, in fact, Scalia was gaining attention from key members of Congress. In a 1991 House Judiciary Committee action on a sweeping crime bill, the Massachusetts Democratic representative Barney Frank warned his colleagues not to resolve a dispute by putting compromise language into a committee report. He said the report language might ultimately be judged irrelevant. To caution his colleagues, he used just two words: "Justice Scalia."[69]

So the iconoclastic justice with the forceful writing style was being heeded. Further, as Kozinski observed, "To fault Scalia for having failed to garner a consensus on a lot of issues is like blaming a farmer because he has not yet collected a harvest while he's still busy sowing the seed. The fact is a body of law cannot be changed overnight; doctrines established over decades of fuzzy thinking cannot be turned around through the stroke of a pen."

Not long after, the writer Joe Morgenstern sized up Scalia in a *Playboy* magazine profile as a justice simply at the beginning of a long crusade against individual rights. "As a jurist who won't turn 80 until the year 2016, he has plenty of time to expand his horizons," Morgenstern wrote. "For now, though, Scalia stands as the Supreme Court's clearest expression of where we were for the past 12 years [in the Reagan-Bush administrations], and the sharpest reminder of what those years cost us."[70]

In the early 1990s, the Court's direction—whether liberals or conservatives would prevail, and whether Scalia's brand of conservatism would ever catch on—could not be foreseen. O'Connor's moderate conservatism was dominating, but it was not far-fetched to suppose that in time new justices would have more regard for the jurist who most perfectly embodied Reagan's aspiration for the Court.

EIGHT

DILEMMAS OF RACE

———◆•◆•◆———

"The color of a defendant's skin [and] that of his victim" matter, the lawyer John Charles Boger declared as he began oral arguments challenging Georgia's death penalty on October 15, 1986.[1] Representing the NAACP Legal Defense and Educational Fund, Boger hoped to win for his client, Warren McCleskey, a new sentencing hearing. McCleskey, a black man, had killed a white police officer during a 1978 robbery of an Atlanta furniture store. As his three accomplices looked for cash in a back office, McCleskey kept customers quiet in the showroom of the Dixie Furniture Store. When a police officer answering a silent alarm came in the front door, McCleskey shot him in the head. A jury convicted McCleskey of murder and sentenced him to die.

Now Boger was presenting data from an academic study that found blacks in Georgia were more likely to have received a death sentence if they had killed a white person than if they had killed a black person. Boger's appeal was based on the Fourteenth Amendment's guarantee of equal protection of the law. He had lost in the lower courts. His appeal to the Supreme Court presented Antonin Scalia with his first race-related case as a justice.

"If the State of Georgia had criminal statutes that expressly imposed different penalties, harsher penalties, on black defendants simply because they were black, or on those who killed white victims, simply because those victims were white, the statutes would plainly violate the Constitution," Boger told the justices. "There was a time, of course, when the state of Georgia did have such statutes, before our nation's Civil War, when free blacks and slaves alike could be given a death sentence merely for the crime of assault on a Georgia white citizen. With the ratification of the Fourteenth Amendment, such criminal statutes came explicitly no longer to be written. Yet the old habits of mind, the racial attitudes of that time have survived, as this Court well knows, into the current century." (The Fourteenth Amendment, ratified in 1868, said "no state shall . . . deny to any person within its jurisdiction the equal protection of the laws.")

Racial bias endured as an open wound in America in the mid-1980s. It revealed itself in de facto segregated schools and divided neighborhoods, in the pay gap between white and black workers, and in how black and white criminal suspects were treated. "Race is the pre-eminent factor in deciding who lives and who dies in capital punishment cases, particularly here in the death-belt states," Stephen Bright, of the Georgia-based Southern Prisoners' Defense Committee, told a reporter writing about the McCleskey case. "When you kill the organist at the Methodist church who is white, you're going to get the death penalty, but if you kill the black Baptist organist, the likelihood is that it'll be plea bargained down to a life sentence."[2]

At the Supreme Court, racially charged disputes ran the gamut from death penalty cases such as McCleskey's, to dilemmas in the screening of jurors, to more direct questions of compensation for past bias, such as with affirmative action. Scalia held fervent views in these areas, largely deriving from his conviction that racial minorities in court cases should be regarded as individuals and not part of an aggrieved group, despite the nation's history of discrimination. Classifying people by their skin color only exacerbated the original discrimination, he argued. And when it came to affirmative action, he scoffed at the notion of a "creditor or debtor race" and insisted that government remedies for discrimination should go only to individuals who make an individual case. Scalia found the concept of race-based restorative justice "thoroughly offensive," and wrote in a 1979 essay, "I owe no man anything, nor he me, because of the blood that flows through our veins."[3]

Such long-held feelings would be incited in a range of race-related cases in Scalia's early years on the bench, testing the reach of the Constitution's equality guarantees and the interpretation of various civil rights statutes. The question in the Georgia furniture store murder case was whether a state's capital punishment system could be deemed unconstitutional if data showed that murderers of white people were more likely to be sentenced to die than murderers of black people.

The justices let Boger talk for several minutes in his steady voice before they began their questioning. "Our evidence demonstrates that Georgia sentences the killers of its white citizens at a rate nearly eleven times that to which it sentences to death the killers of its black citizens," Boger said, explaining the study known by its lead researcher, the University of Iowa law professor David Baldus. Professor Baldus had focused on Georgia's capital sentencing system from 1973 to 1979. "Even after most of the legitimate sentencing considerations had been taken into account, a defendant remains over four times [more] likely to receive a capital sentence if his victim chanced to be white," Boger explained.

He tried to emphasize the integrity of the data and how the researchers had not been wedded to any particular conclusion. Yet Justice Byron White remained suspicious about the data underlying the NAACP Legal Defense Fund's position. Who collected the information from trial transcripts? White asked. Law students, Boger answered. White suggested that some of the information about the defendants and their victims might have been miscoded; he wondered whether the data truly showed discrimination. Boger stressed that Baldus had rechecked it all.

Questions from other justices focused on what could be done to remedy the problem Boger insisted existed. "What's the remedy?" Justice Sandra Day O'Connor asked. "Is it to execute more people?"

Justice Lewis Powell concentrated on McCleskey's violent actions at the scene of the crime and the cold-blooded killing of a police officer. That is when Justice Scalia entered the give-and-take, following up on Powell's questioning: "Wasn't the shot which the police officer suffered in the head . . . at very close range, indicating that there was a conscious attempt to kill the man?" he asked. He noted that such an "aggravating factor" made McCleskey's crime all the worse and suggested that his death penalty might have indeed fitted the crime.

Boger protested that such a shooting was not typically one that warranted a death sentence. He said he believed the shot was fired from ten or twelve feet. "It was not an execution-style slaying, in that sense," he said. "There's no doubt that the crime is a serious one. What the evidence shows, though [is that] it's not the kind of crime that gets death in Fulton County, or indeed, statewide, on any regular basis . . . It's the torture murderers and the multiple killers in Fulton County who receive death." Boger strongly suggested that McCleskey would be looking at life in prison, not death, if he were white or his victim were black.

Scalia questioned whether there would be a problem if statistics showed that there were patterns of discrimination based on physical characteristics beyond race. "You wouldn't say we can convict people more readily because they're ugly, or because they're shifty-eyed," he posited. "Now, what if you do a statistical study that shows beyond question that people who are naturally shifty-eyed are to a disproportionate extent convicted in criminal cases? Does that make the criminal process unlawful?"

"I don't think the Court has afforded the same kind of protection, constitutionally, to shifty-eyed or those other characteristics," Boger said, understating the obvious—that the Constitution treated race differently based on the nation's legacy of slavery and segregation. Scalia's suggestion that one's race could be equated with other physical characteristics—characteristics not linked to one's cultural identity—would surface as Scalia negotiated behind the scenes with his colleagues, too.

Next at the lectern was Mary Beth Westmoreland, a Georgia assistant attorney general. She reminded the justices that a police officer was killed "in broad daylight, in a store in which approximately seven people were held hostage, all of whom were forced to lie on the floor, many of whom were tied up during the commission of this crime." She said the fatal shot hit the officer in the eye. A second shot happened to bounce off a cigarette lighter in his pocket, directly over his heart. The facts of the crime plainly supported the death penalty, Westmoreland insisted.

Justice Thurgood Marshall challenged Westmoreland on the state's attempt to undermine the statistical evidence without any statistical evidence of its own. "So what basis do you have for saying that this material missed the mark?" Marshall asked. Westmoreland said statisticians who testified for the state found that no data could be reliable. "The bottom line," she said, "is you cannot come up with two similar cases to compare, because each case is unique on its own individual facts."

Westmoreland explained that Georgia had found that crimes against white victims usually involved more aggravating factors. She said murders of black people often grew out of family disputes. "Those types of disputes occur so frequently in black victim cases that they do tend to fall out of the system much earlier . . . And for whatever reason, frequently more times we'll see torture cases involving white victim cases than you do in black victim cases."

Two days after the hearing in *McCleskey v. Kemp*, Chief Justice William Rehnquist began the vote in the justices' private conference. Rehnquist said he wanted to affirm the lower court ruling against McCleskey. The chief justice believed that anyone asserting a violation of the Constitution's equality guarantee had to show, in this kind of situation, intentional discrimination based on race. William Brennan, speaking next, disagreed. He thought McCleskey had made a sufficient case for a violation under the Fourteenth Amendment. In addition, Brennan found good justification for a violation under the Eighth Amendment prohibition on cruel and unusual punishment, even aside from his view that the death penalty always violated that prohibition. Brennan voted to throw out the death sentence. Up next was White, who was with Rehnquist in believing there was not enough evidence to show McCleskey was a victim of bias. Then Marshall cast a second vote to reverse. He said data showing that defendants were more likely to get death for killing a white than a black reflected the reality that defendants—white or black—were rarely sentenced to die for killing black people. Blackmun wanted to reverse, too. Powell said he would affirm. Stevens brought up the history of the death penalty in the South and its disproportionate use against blacks. He said he wanted to reverse McCleskey's sentence. O'Connor joined Rehnquist, White, and Powell in saying she wanted to affirm the sentence. The vote was tied up at 4–4. Scalia cast a vote to affirm McCleskey's death sentence, giving the conservative justices the win.[4]

Because he came last around the table, Scalia had cast the deciding vote. Yet based on his past record, Scalia's position was predictable. Powell was the one who had wavered and was therefore the critical vote. He was uneasy with the statistical evidence. Still, he was convinced that Georgia had not discriminated against McCleskey and that the state had instituted safeguards in the trial process to minimize racial bias. Rehnquist assigned Powell the opinion, a step that would tend to ensure that Powell stuck with the majority. "We hold that the Baldus study does not demonstrate a constitutionally significant risk of racial bias affecting the Georgia capital-sentencing process," Powell wrote as he began drafting his opinion for the majority.[5]

Scalia planned to join Powell's opinion but had some reservations. "I do not share the view, implicit in the [draft] opinion," he told Powell, "that an effect of racial factors upon sentencing, if it could only be shown by sufficiently strong statistical evidence, would require reversal. Since it is my view that the unconscious operation of irrational sympathies and antipathies, including racial, upon jury decisions and (hence) prosecutorial decisions is real, acknowledged in the decisions of this Court, and ineradicable, I cannot honestly say that all I need is more proof."[6] Scalia believed that biases were woven into American life and that the reality of individual prejudices was not enough to override the state's interest in carrying out the death penalty for a horrible murder. With this one brief memo, Scalia was demonstrating at the very beginning of his tenure that on issues of race he was willing to go where even his most conservative colleagues would not venture.

In the end, Scalia's extreme view on the McCleskey case did not see the light of day. For reasons that he later said he could not remember, he did not write a separate opinion expressing his views about "ineradicable" racial biases.[7] The Supreme Court issued its opinion in *McCleskey v. Kemp* in April 1987, and three years later McCleskey exhausted all other grounds for appeal.[8] He was executed in Georgia's electric chair on September 25, 1991.

After he retired, Justice Powell had second thoughts about his position on the death penalty. He told his biographer, the University of Virginia law professor John C. Jeffries, Jr., that if he had it to do over, he would change his vote to side with McCleskey. Powell had long been ambivalent about how the nation should respond to its history of racial discrimination. He had cast the deciding vote in the 1978 case of *Regents of the University of California v. Bakke*, which had allowed race to be considered in college admissions for diversity but had banned the use of rigid quotas for minority applicants. Before he joined the bench Scalia had publicly derided the *Bakke* opinion as "thoroughly unconvincing as an honest, hard-minded, reasoned analysis."[9] Dilemmas of race aside, Powell's regret in McCleskey's case flowed in great measure from his changing views on the death penalty. "I have come to think that capital punishment should be abolished," Powell told Jeffries. He referred to the protracted appeals in the system that undercut any deterrence effect and said the death penalty "serves no useful purpose."[10]

Scalia was an unflinching, unyielding justice. His position on the death penalty and, separately, on race-conscious policies endured term after term. In another racially charged criminal case in his early years on the Court, Scalia dissented when a majority expanded the rule of *Batson v. Kentucky*. Rendered in 1986, months before Scalia joined the Court, the *Batson* ruling had barred prosecutors from using their allotted "peremptory," or discretionary, challenges during jury selection to dismiss a juror because of race. Such peremptory strikes were allowed above and beyond challenges that lawyers made to a potential juror "for cause"—that is, if they believed a juror could not be objective or fair. Each side received a set number of peremptory strikes to eliminate individuals without giving a reason and to shape a jury open to their respective arguments.

In its *Batson* decision, the Court had determined that using peremptory strikes to eliminate someone because of race violated the constitutional guarantee of equal protection of the law. In a practical sense, the justices said, it undermined the integrity of the justice system.[11] The *Batson* case had been brought by a black defendant who complained about the prosecution's screening out black jurors. In the new case Scalia would hear, and that a majority would use to expand the *Batson* rule, a white defendant convicted of murdering two white men in Columbus, Ohio, objected to the exclusion of potential jurors who were black. By a 7–2 vote in the 1991 *Powers v. Ohio*, the Court ruled that strikes based on skin color are unconstitutional, irrespective of the race of the defendant or of the jurors. "Racial discrimination in the selection of jurors casts doubt on the integrity of the judicial process and places the fairness of a criminal proceeding in doubt," the Court majority said. Scalia and Rehnquist dissented.

Scalia objected to the assumptions in the majority opinion. Joined by Rehnquist, he wrote, "Unlike the categorical exclusion of a group from jury service, which implies that all its members are incompetent or untrustworthy, a peremptory strike on the basis of group membership implies nothing more than the undeniable reality (upon which the peremptory strike system is largely based) that all groups tend to have particular sympathies and hostilities—most notably, sympathies towards their own group members." Scalia worried that attention to blacks as a group prevented individual litigants from using their legitimate intuitions in jury selection.

He closed his dissenting opinion in *Powers v. Ohio* with a jab at the

Court's jury-selection approach: "Today's supposed blow against racism, while enormously self-satisfying, is unmeasured and misdirected. If for any reason the State is unable to reconvict [Larry Joe] Powers for the double murder at issue here, later victims may pay the price for our extravagance." Scalia's opinion reflected his distaste for what he regarded as a certain elitist, or "politically correct," way of thinking about race. The reference to a "self-satisfying . . . supposed blow against racism" was classic Scalia. Later, in a lower court proceeding, it turned out there was not enough evidence to show that jurors had been removed because of their race, and Powers's life sentence was upheld.[12]

Scalia's determinations on race and jury selection were evident in another jury-selection case around the same time. Scalia wrote for a five-justice majority that found that the Sixth Amendment guarantee that a jury be drawn from a fair cross section of the people did not require a "representative jury" but "an impartial jury." Daniel Holland, a white Chicago man charged with kidnapping, rape, and robbery, argued that his jury was not fair because a prosecutor had eliminated the only two potential jurors who were black (of the total thirty potential jurors in the pool assembled). Scalia wrote that a requirement that a jury be representative "would cripple the device of peremptory challenge."[13]

In dissent, Justice Marshall declared that Scalia's opinion for the majority "insulates an especially invidious form of racial discrimination" in jury selection from scrutiny. He said the majority's view exaggerated the threat to the peremptory-challenge system and trivialized the goal of eliminating racial discrimination in the criminal justice system.

Scalia fired back in his written opinion: "Justice Marshall's dissent rolls out the ultimate weapon, the accusation of insensitivity to racial discrimination—which will lose its intimidating effect if it continues to be fired so randomly." Scalia was not deterred from using sharp words regarding race against a man who had been kept from restaurants, restrooms, and other public places simply because of the color of his skin. For the case at hand, Scalia insisted that the Court in *Holland v. Illinois* was not backtracking on *Batson*'s ban on the systematic exclusion of blacks from juries, rather it was saying that a defendant does not have a Sixth Amendment claim to a representative jury.

Scalia's position never wavered. He believed judges should not try to impose their notions of correct societal behavior onto jury selection. He wanted parties to be able to eliminate potentially hostile people from juries for any reason, even based on a racial stereotype. He thought peremptory strikes rightly allowed each side to exercise its biases and sympathies.

He would say this over and over, resolute in his dissenting point of view. That was evident in 2008, when a seven-justice majority threw out the conviction and death sentence of a black man whose prosecutor eliminated all blacks from the jury pool and then invoked the racially charged O. J. Simpson case to urge the death penalty rather than life in prison for the defendant.[14] The defendant, Alan Snyder, was tried in 1996 for the killing of his estranged wife's friend. It was less than a year after the football star O. J. Simpson had been acquitted of murdering his wife and her friend. During the sentencing phase of the Snyder case, the prosecutor, Jim Williams, had slyly referred to the famous California trial and said that the "perpetrator" in that case "got away with it." Snyder's lawyers used the prosecutor's Simpson-related remarks as evidence that he had improperly removed prospective jurors based on their race. The seven-justice majority that sided with Snyder said the trial judge had wrongly accepted the prosecutor's rationales, which the Court termed "suspicious," for striking blacks from the jury pool.[15]

About a month after the ruling in *Snyder v. Louisiana*, Scalia elaborated in an interview, "I think blacks ought to be able to strike whites from the jury if they think they will get a fairer shake from a black jury, and vice versa. I think you ought to be able to strike Methodists because Methodists will have something against you because you're a Catholic. It is crazy to try to turn discretionary strikes into rational strikes. They were never intended to be rational. They were intended to satisfy you that this is a panel you'd feel comfortable with, for whatever crazy reasons."[16]

Overall, Scalia, the originalist, found the Constitution's equality guarantee to be one of its thinnest protections. This was not a subject on which Scalia was tepid. He wrote in scalding terms, suggesting that he viewed the stakes as not just societal but personal. He believed that efforts to counteract discrimination against blacks or other minorities, as a group, necessarily led to policies that were racist against individuals.

Nowhere was Scalia's opposition to racial considerations so forcefully expressed as in cases involving education and workplace affirmative action. Inaugurated by President Johnson in the mid-1960s, affirmative action programs were aimed at more than an end to illegal discrimination. They were based on the notion that amends were required for the people who had long been excluded and subjected to prejudice in overwhelmingly white America. The words "affirmative action" encompassed many types of programs, some rigid, some goal-oriented. In the context of the legal challenges that came before the justices, "affirmative action" referred to policies for hiring and firing that explicitly favored blacks or other minorities over whites.

Scalia's position on affirmative action was made clear in his third year on the bench. The justices were considering a Richmond, Virginia, ordinance that required businesses contracting with the city to set aside 30 percent of their subcontracting work for companies owned by "black, Spanish-speaking, Oriental, Indian, Eskimo, or Aleut" people. The requirement adopted by the city in 1983 particularly benefited blacks and Spanish-speaking subcontractors because there were virtually no other racial minorities in the region. The J. A. Croson Company, which lost a contract for installing plumbing fixtures at the city jail because it lacked the requisite minority subcontractors, sued the city over the policy.

Croson prevailed before the U.S. Court of Appeals for the Fourth Circuit, and Richmond's appeal came to the Supreme Court in October 1988. Representing the city, John Payton told the justices at the start of oral arguments that "Richmond was attempting to address one of the most difficult problems confronting our nation and its cities and states. Identified racial discrimination is a scourge of our society." Speaking for the Croson company, Walter H. Ryland countered that if the city wanted to address bias, it could have done it by putting "the effort into enforcing" an antidiscrimination law already on the books for the awarding of public contracts.[17]

In the justices' private session, Scalia and the other conservatives had enough votes for a decision finding that the Richmond set-aside plan was too rigidly designed around the 30 percent figure and not justified by any findings of past discrimination. The majority decided that any state or local government set-aside plan could survive only if the government had a "compelling interest" in creating the program and it was narrowly tailored to that interest. The decision marked the first time the Court said

that public contracting policies involving racial or ethnic group preferences for minorities must hold up under the most rigorous judicial
scrutiny. It put affirmative action that benefited minorities to the same
test as the Jim Crow rules of the Old South that kept blacks down. The
Reagan administration had long advocated such an approach as a way to
eliminate government programs that gave blacks an advantage simply
because they were black. When the decision was released, just months
after Reagan finished his two terms in the White House, the former solicitor general Charles Fried declared that *Richmond v. Croson* was "great
news." Fried told *The New York Times* that the decision would have made
his four years in the job "worth it," even if he had accomplished nothing
else.[18]

Yet the decision was not entirely what opponents of affirmative action
had long sought. Chief Justice Rehnquist had assigned the opinion to Justice O'Connor to ensure that he kept her vote. And she had closed her
opinion with a caveat: "Nothing we say today precludes a state or local
entity from taking action to rectify the effects of identified discrimination
within its jurisdiction. If the city of Richmond had evidence before it that
nonminority contractors were systematically excluding minority businesses from subcontracting opportunities, it could take action to end the
discriminatory exclusion."

That concession infuriated Scalia. He wrote a separate opinion, signed
by no other justice, declaring that such race-based remedies were immoral
and destructive of society. Scalia believed such policies were not a solution
to past bias, but rather a continuation of the problem. "The benign purpose of compensating for social disadvantages, whether they have been
acquired by reason of prior discrimination or otherwise, can no more be
pursued by the illegitimate means of racial discrimination than can other
assertedly benign purposes we have repeatedly rejected," he wrote.[19]

Scalia argued that the Richmond ordinance furthered the notion that
blacks were a separate class, to be treated as a group rather than as individuals. "The difficulty of overcoming the effects of past discrimination,"
Scalia continued, "is nothing as compared with the difficulty of eradicat-
ing from our society the source of those effects, which is the tendency—
fatal to a Nation such as ours—to classify and judge men and women on
the basis of their country of origin or the color of their skin."

Scalia pointed out in his opinion, as O'Connor had in hers for the
Court, that the Richmond city council was majority black and arguably

giving its own people the contracting benefit. "The same thing has no doubt happened before in other cities," Scalia wrote, ". . . and blacks have often been on the receiving end of the injustice. Where injustice is the game, however, turnabout is not fair play." Scalia acknowledged that "blacks have suffered discrimination immeasurably greater than any directed at other racial groups," yet, he insisted, "those who believe that racial preferences can help to 'even the score' display, and reinforce, a manner of thinking by race that was the source of the injustice and that will, if it endures within our society, be the source of more injustice still. The relevant proposition is not that it was blacks, or Jews, or Irish who were discriminated against, but that it was individual men and women, 'created equal,' who were discriminated against."

Justice Marshall, joined by Brennan and Blackmun, considered the decision "a giant step backward." They recalled the history of bias in Richmond and the Deep South: "It is a welcome symbol of racial progress when the former capital of the Confederacy acts forthrightly to confront the effects of racial discrimination in its midst . . . As much as any municipality in the United States, Richmond knows what racial discrimination is; a century of decisions by this and other federal courts has richly documented the city's disgraceful history of public and private racial discrimination."[20]

Marshall complained of Scalia's "artful distinction" between the Richmond program and the permissible remedies of the school desegregation cases.[21] Addressing Scalia's lumping of all race conscious programs into the same prohibited category, Marshall said, "A profound difference separates governmental actions that themselves are racist, and governmental actions that seek to remedy the effects of prior racism or to prevent neutral governmental activity from perpetuating the effects of such racism."

This was anathema to Scalia, who a decade earlier had said the law of affirmative action was marked by "pretense and self-delusion" and was "an embarrassment to teach."[22]

In a later interview explaining his views on race, Scalia said, "The law can't treat races unequally. That's my whole objection to affirmative action: that it violates the principle of equality, that it is the state preferring one race over another—perhaps for very benign reasons. But nonetheless the Constitution forbids it. Jim Crow laws are bad. I just don't think it is any better when it is directed at the majority."[23]

Those notions developed long before Scalia donned a black robe. "I

was a law professor," Scalia recalled of the time when he first began publicly laying out his opposition to race-conscious policies. "I had no idea
that I would be cast in the role of having to decide things of this sort," he
said in an interview and then, referring to an influential justice whose
legal theories endorsed race-conscious remedies, said, "But I certainly felt
that the Lewis Powells of the world were not going to bear the burden that
they were creating. It wasn't their kids. It was the Polish factory worker's
kid who was going to be out of a job."[24]

That view resonated more with disaffected Middle America than with
the Ivy Leaguers Scalia had joined. Michael Klarman, a University of Virginia law professor who traced the modern development of civil rights
law, correctly observed that Justice Scalia was an exception to the general
rule that the justices—typically products of affluent homes and superb
educations—reflected elite opinion on issues such as race. Klarman wrote
that Scalia was a member of the cultural elite but did "not share its liberal
political propensities."[25] In fact, on many cultural issues, notably involving
race and gay rights, Scalia expressly challenged the "legal elite," and what
he argued was its flawed injection of social attitudes into the law.

In 1989 the Supreme Court did not stop with *Richmond v. Croson* and the
setback for government policies intended to help minorities who had
been excluded from public contracting. A succession of decisions in the
final months of the 1988–89 term would jar the nation's civil rights community, which in turn would issue a call to arms. "The Supreme Court
term now ending [in summer 1989] should be viewed with alarm by anyone committed to the eradication of racial oppression in America," wrote
Randall L. Kennedy, a Harvard Law School professor, in an opinion piece
in the *Los Angeles Times.* "The Court did not uniformly rule against
minority claimants. But by and large they have found the court a hostile
forum—a 'white man's court' rather than one sensitive to the just claims
of all who come before it."[26] In a stunning series of cases, a five-justice
Court majority, including Scalia, reduced back pay and other remedies for
discrimination across a swath of law. The Court announced more onerous
proof and procedural requirements for workers bringing discrimination
claims.[27] In a case known as *Wards Cove Packing Co. v. Atonio*, Scalia, in
fact, had taken the lead behind the scenes to put more of a legal burden on

workers who tried to get to court to claim that a company's practices, while not intentionally discriminatory, had a "disparate impact" on blacks or other minorities. Such practices typically included physical tests and academic requirements that were ostensibly neutral but had an adverse impact on a particular group of people. The *Wards Cove* decision made it harder for workers to challenge such practices.[28]

To civil rights advocates such as Professor Kennedy, "The court's handling of these cases reveals . . . a disaffection with such laws [forbidding bias], an aversion manifested by a militant insistence on interpreting civil rights statutes as narrowly as possible." He was writing about the full majority, but in that fivesome the most militant was Scalia. (Pressure from the civil rights community induced Congress to set about reversing the effects of several of the rulings through new legislation. The result, after two years of negotiations, was the Civil Rights Act of 1991, offering workers more protection against bias than the Court had read into the law and, for those individuals who prevailed in court, greater money damages and reimbursement of costs.[29])

Driving the decisions of the watershed 1988–89 term was a new conservative bloc that had coalesced with Reagan's final appointment in February 1988. Confirmed for the seat that opened when Lewis Powell retired in the summer of 1987, Anthony Kennedy had been a twelve-year veteran of the U.S. Court of Appeals for the Ninth Circuit, based in California. His Senate confirmation followed the tumultuous rejection of Robert Bork, Scalia's colleague from the D.C. Circuit and fellow constitutional originalist.

Bork had spent years on presidents' short lists for the Supreme Court. In the summer of 1987, when Powell revealed that he was stepping down, Reagan decided Bork's time had come. The president and his aides rightly suspected it would be the last nomination of Reagan's two-term administration and the last chance to seal Reagan's legacy of conservatism at the nation's highest court. But it was just what they liked in Bork—his extensive, intellectually developed record—that proved too great a weight as he moved through the confirmation process. Unlike the situation when Scalia cleared the Senate a year earlier, Democrats now had a majority in the chamber and controlled the committee hearings. This would not be the Republican chairman Strom Thurmond going through the motions— even, in Scalia's estimation, pitching softballs. This was the Democrat

Joseph Biden in the chairman's chair insisting on a real constitutional debate. As a result, Bork's hearings became a forum for argument over the direction of the Court at a pivotal moment—and in no small measure because of the threat Bork's critics said he posed to civil liberties. A tone was set when, after Reagan announced the nomination of Bork to succeed Powell, the Massachusetts Democratic senator Edward Kennedy took the Senate floor and declared, with hyperbole, "Robert Bork's America is a land in which women would be forced into back-alley abortions, blacks would sit at segregated lunch counters, rogue police could break down citizens' doors in midnight raids, children could not be taught about evolution, writers and artists could be censored at the whim of government."[30]

During Bork's contentious hearing, which got down to the substance of his views, he continued to insist that the Constitution should be read narrowly to contain only the rights explicitly granted in its text. His views seemed outdated, insensitive to the dilemmas of racial minorities, even— as they were portrayed by his critics—dangerous to all Americans. As Ethan Bronner, who chronicled the Bork hearings as a journalist, later wrote in his book on the nomination fight, "Bork would hardly have been the first justice lacking passion for the plight of black Americans. But the harsh nature of his writings, the well-established aims of his [Reagan administration] sponsors, and the political circumstances of the moment conspired to elevate his nomination into a Rorschach test of American values."[31]

Bork was defeated on a vote of 58–42. Three months later he decided to leave his judgeship on the D.C. Circuit so that he could more fully speak his mind. He chalked his defeat up to "an essentially unanswered campaign of misinformation and political slogans." He defended his view that judges should look to the original intentions of the Constitution's framers, saying, "That philosophy is essential if courts are to govern according to the rule of law." In the end, the Bork battle was far larger than the fate of one intellectual giant of the right. It offered a defining battle between conservatives, on the brink of real control of the judiciary, and liberals, trying to hold tight to the control they had. When Bork resigned, the Harvard Law professor Laurence Tribe, who had opposed his nomination, said, "The right wing lost the constitutional referendum of 1987. That is what galls them most about the loss of Robert Bork. Not pity for a man who had so long wanted to serve on the Court and whose credentials were so superb. It is pity for an agenda that was dramatically, decisively repudiated."[32]

Political and legal conservatives vowed to never forget. The term "to bork" became part of the political lexicon, invoked by conservatives to mean to caricature a nominee for partisan gain.[33] Before Reagan settled on Anthony Kennedy to succeed Powell, he made the short-lived choice of the U.S. appeals court judge Douglas Ginsburg, also of the D.C. Circuit. But Ginsburg's name had to be withdrawn within days of Reagan's announcement because of reports that Ginsburg had smoked marijuana while a professor at Harvard Law School.[34]

So it was Judge Anthony Kennedy, a conservative jurist but with a milder, less distinct profile than Bork. Age fifty-two when the president tapped him, Kennedy had grown up in a politically connected Sacramento family and had spent most of his life in the California capital, where his father was a lawyer and lobbyist. After Stanford University, the London School of Economics, and Harvard Law School, Kennedy worked for a San Francisco firm. Within a year, however, his father's sudden death forced him to move back to Sacramento and take over the family law and lobbying practice. With friends in Governor Reagan's administration, where Kennedy had done some consulting work, and a growing legal reputation, his name was passed on to the White House for judicial nominations. In 1975 President Ford appointed Kennedy, then just age thirty-eight, to the U.S. Court of Appeals for the Ninth Circuit.

Kennedy and Scalia were the same age, yet where Scalia was all looseness in his manner, Kennedy, with his coordinated tie and pocket handkerchief, could be formal to the point of being stiff. On the festering racial issues of the day, the men were largely of the same mind.

A month after he joined the Court, in February 1988, Kennedy provided the key fifth vote that ordered new arguments on the scope of a major post–Civil War law. The 1866 law, a hallmark of the Reconstruction era, gave blacks the same right to contract as whites. The question of the reach of the law arose in the context of a case started by Brenda Patterson, who had worked as a teller and file clerk at a North Carolina–based credit union for ten years. When she was laid off in 1982, she sued for racial harassment, claiming she had been subjected to racial slurs and asked to do such menial tasks as dusting and sweeping, tasks that white workers were not asked to do.[35]

The case of *Patterson v. McLean Credit Union* specifically tested whether the 1866 law ("Section 1981") covered racial harassment and other discriminatory treatment on the job, or only discrimination in the initial hiring process. A 1976 case, *Runyon v. McCrary*, had held that the 1866 law applied not only to discriminatory government actions but also to private contracts, such as between companies and their workers. The *Runyon* case had allowed two sets of black parents to sue private schools in Virginia that had denied their children admission because of their skin color.[36]

As the Court was considering Brenda Patterson's claim, the conservative bloc (Rehnquist, White, O'Connor, Scalia, and Kennedy) decided it wanted to further examine the reach of the 1866 law, so it issued an order requesting new arguments in the Patterson case focused on whether *Runyon* should be reversed. Rehnquist and White had been the lone dissents from the 1976 *Runyon* decision. They said the law should be reserved for government, not private, discrimination. Scalia also thought the 1976 *Runyon v. McCrary* case had been wide of the mark. "*Runyon* was plainly wrong," he said at one of the justices' conferences.[37]

The more liberal justices were indignant when Rehnquist was able to muster the five votes, which included Scalia's, to set new arguments on the larger question of the breadth of the 1866 law. "I am at a loss to understand the motivation of five Members of this Court to reconsider an interpretation of a civil rights statute that so clearly reflects our society's earnest commitment to ending racial discrimination, and in which Congress so evidently has acquiesced," Blackmun wrote in his dissenting statement, referring to the fact that after the Court had ruled in 1976 that the 1866 law covered private discrimination, Congress did not rewrite the law. Blackmun was joined by Brennan, Marshall, and Stevens.[38] Stevens wrote a separate dissent from the Patterson case reargument order, saying, "The Court's order today will, by itself, have a deleterious effect on the faith reposed by racial minorities in the continuing stability of a rule of law that guarantees them the 'same right' as 'white citizens.' To recognize an equality right—a right that 12 years ago we thought 'well established'— and then to declare unceremoniously that perhaps we were wrong and had better reconsider our prior judgment, is to replace what is ideally a sense of guaranteed right with the uneasiness of unsecured privilege. Time alone will tell whether the erosion in faith is unnecessarily precipitous, but in the meantime, some of the harm that will flow from today's order may never be completely undone."[39] Stevens's point was that the mere suggestion that the Court could move backward from *Runyon* undermined its integrity and status in society as a guardian of individual rights.

The new justice, Kennedy, was offended by such sentiment. He wrote to Rehnquist, Scalia, and the other conservatives that he was in "full agreement" with Rehnquist's opinion announcing the new arguments. "I might add the dissents still do not sit well with me, and are more [than] disappointing," Kennedy said.[40]

The Reagan administration had not asked for reconsideration of the *Runyon* ruling. Yet the order for new arguments was viewed in some quarters as a reflection of Reagan's thinking. The *Miami Herald* cartoonist Jim Morin drew a caricature of Ronald Reagan sticking his tongue out at Abraham Lincoln in his chair at the memorial. Lincoln holds his head in his hand. The headline: SUPREME COURT VOTES TO RECONSIDER MAJOR CIVIL RIGHTS LAW. The nation's most prominent newspapers similarly condemned the move.[41]

During the new oral arguments in October 1988, Julius LeVonne Chambers, director-counsel of the NAACP Legal Defense Fund, maintained that the Reconstruction-era law should provide a remedy for private as well as government racial discrimination. Chambers was born in Mount Gilead, North Carolina, in 1936, the same year that Scalia was born in Trenton. Witnessing firsthand an era of Jim Crow laws and racial intolerance, Chambers had been motivated to become a lawyer. He graduated first in his law school class at the University of North Carolina and was the first black editor in chief of the law review. He set up his own firm in Charlotte and began working on cases for the NAACP's legal fund, mentored by Thurgood Marshall.

"*Runyon* and Section 1981 have become a significant part of the web of joint congressional and judicial efforts to rid the country of public and private discrimination," Chambers told the justices. He emphasized that in 1866 Congress was concerned not just about state practices but also about "pervasive practices by private individuals who were placing blacks back in slavery as before.[42]

"We all concede that the Thirteenth Amendment reaches private and public acts," Chambers continued. "We all concede that in 1866, the government approved of reaching private practices. And so Congress in enacting the 1866 Act, was trying to cover public and private practices to rid the country of the slavery that we had just enacted the Thirteenth Amendment to cover."

Next up at the lectern was Roger Kaplan, a New York–based management lawyer, representing the McLean Credit Union and seeking reversal of *Runyon*, under which his client had been sued. Kaplan initially had not sought reversal of *Runyon*—no party before the Court had—but the justices had forced him into that argument with their order that the Patterson case be reargued along with the question of the soundness of *Runyon*.

Kaplan urged the justices to look back to 1883, not just 1866, to the Court's ruling on several civil rights cases concerning acts of public, not private, discrimination. He said it followed that "what the Congress was concerned with in the post–Civil War era were these statutes and rules and procedures that were growing up in the states which threatened to deprive the freedmen of their ability to make contracts and to enforce them." Kaplan rejected the notion that Congress had been targeting private discrimination in the South.

Scalia believed Kaplan's arguments fell short. He said Kaplan needed something stronger to induce the Court to reverse its precedent allowing Section 1981 to cover private discrimination.

"Why should we go back and change a decision that we've made?" Scalia asked him. "What is special about this statute?"

"It intrudes on the operation of Congress," Kaplan said. "That's basically where the fundamental problem lies."

"If that's all you have, Mr. Kaplan, I'm afraid it's nothing because that's always the case when we interpret a statute incorrectly," Scalia said, noting that an incorrect statutory ruling inherently displaces Congress's choice. Also, Congress always can amend a statute to reverse the high court's interpretation. It had not done that after the *Runyon* ruling.

Scalia nailed it. Despite his interest in overturning *Runyon*, and that of Rehnquist and White lingering from 1976, the case for its reversal had not been made. The interpretation of Section 1981 to cover private action was woven into American efforts to end race discrimination. O'Connor and Kennedy were especially sensitive to the public outcry that had greeted the order to even reconsider that reach.

Yet Brenda Patterson still lost her case. The five conservative justices said the 1866 law could not be used to cover harassment or any other conduct that occurred after the initial employment contract was signed. "What the Court declines to snatch away with one hand, it takes with the other," Justice Brennan wrote for the four dissenters. "Though the Court today reaffirms [the 1866 law's] applicability to private conduct, it simultaneously gives this landmark civil rights statute a needlessly cramped interpretation."[43]

In his opinion for the majority, Kennedy said that the law is limited to its literal wording about the making of contracts and does not extend to on-the-job bias. Yet Kennedy also spoke approvingly of "state and federal legislation . . . enacted to prohibit private racial discrimination in many aspects of our society [and] . . . our society's deep commitment to the eradication of discrimination based on a person's race or the color of his or her skin."

Intriguingly for his colleagues trying to figure him out, Kennedy had at one point voted in the justices' private conference to allow the 1866 law to cover racial harassment. That had initially given liberal Justice Brennan the majority opinion for the Court to side with Patterson. But Kennedy ended up switching his vote and then taking authorship of the opinion.[44]

His stance in the case was a blow to liberals on the Court and off, particularly because he had been presumed as more in the Powell mode than that of Bork. Kennedy's early moves particularly burned Brennan. For a generation, he had been able, through cajoling memos and gentle arm-twisting, to preserve most of the Warren Court legacy on civil rights. In the final negotiations on the Patterson case, after Rehnquist had reassigned it to Kennedy for the majority opinion, Brennan uncharacteristically displayed his frustration and anger. In a draft of his dissenting opinion he wrote, "The Court's fine phrases about our commitment to the eradication of racial discrimination . . . seem to count for little in practice." Justice Kennedy countered by adding a footnote to his draft opinion that accused Brennan of thinking "it judicious to bolster his position by questioning the court's understanding of the necessity to eradicate racial discrimination. The commitment to equality, fairness, and compassion is not a treasured monopoly of our colleagues in dissent." Before the opinions were released to the public, both Brennan and Kennedy deleted those comments.[45]

While conservatives were gaining the upper hand in their push to narrow civil rights law and Scalia's ideas seemed in ascendance, liberal justices in the early 1990s carved out some exceptions to that pattern. These cases were part of the constant tugging and pulling between the two ideological blocs and raised the public anticipation and anxiety about how long the old liberal warhorses—the eldest members of the Court—would last. Justice Brennan won one last civil rights victory before his retirement. Over Scalia's dissent, he wrote that Congress may order preferential treatment of blacks and other minorities to increase their ownership of broadcast licenses. After Metro Broadcasting, Inc., lost a proposal to construct and operate a new UHF station in the Orlando, Florida, area, it had challenged a Federal Communications Commission policy giving preference to minority owners. In upholding the FCC policy, Brennan distinguished the decision from the *Richmond v. Croson* decision of a year earlier: he said the federal government had more latitude than states and municipalities to favor minorities—here as necessary for broadcast diversity.[46] Justice White provided the fifth vote in the case that highlighted federal authority.

The next year, the liberal bloc prevailed again in a case that tested whether the landmark 1965 Voting Rights Act applied to elections for judges, just as its antibias provisions did for legislators. In this case, black voters in New Orleans had complained that a sprawling state-drawn judicial district covering the greater New Orleans area diluted their voting strength. The Voting Rights Act actually had long been thought to cover judicial elections along with contests for legislative and executive offices. Yet some confusion arose under a 1982 amendment to the act.[47] In the amendment, federal lawmakers had referred to the ability of voting blocs "to elect representatives of their choice." A lower federal appeals court hearing the New Orleans case had determined, based on the 1982 amendments, that the Voting Rights Act did not apply to judges, because they were not "representatives."

A Supreme Court majority voted to reverse the lower court and to hold that in the 1982 amendments Congress did intend the law to apply to judicial elections, too. Scalia, Rehnquist, and Kennedy dissented. Scalia began drafting a dissenting opinion that not only would have restricted the Voting Rights Act coverage to legislators but would have dramatically curtailed its protections against any kind of redistricting that diluted African American voting strength.[48]

Seeing Scalia's position, Justice Blackmun wrote to his colleagues, "I cannot reconcile Nino's approach with the prohibition of intentional acts of discrimination clearly embodied in Section 2 [of the Voting Rights Act]. Under Nino's reading of the Act, if the Louisiana Legislature were to gerrymander the judicial districts of the state with the sole purpose of diluting African American voting strength, Section 2 would provide no remedy. This is a strange result and one which the language, structure, and history of Section 2 do not support."[49]

Scalia objected to the Court majority's interpretation of the word "representatives" and what he believed was a generally expansive approach to the civil rights law. As a preliminary matter, he complained about the majority's method for reading the statute. "The Court transforms the meaning of [the provision referring to 'representatives'] not because the ordinary meaning is irrational, or inconsistent with other parts of the statute . . . but because it does not fit the Court's conception of what Congress must have had in mind. When we adopt a method that psychoanalyzes Congress rather than reads its laws, when we employ a tinkerer's toolbox, we do great harm. Not only do we reach the wrong result with respect to the statute at hand, but we poison the well of future legislation, depriving legislators of the assurance that ordinary terms, used in an ordinary context, will be given a predictable meaning."

Scalia also insisted that the majority was turning the Voting Rights Act into "some all-purpose weapon for well-intentioned judges to wield as they please in the battle against discrimination." He was offended by the notion of an all-knowing, all-protecting judiciary and did not believe the judiciary up to the task of making the world a better place. Scalia's position on race would recall an assessment of the University of Virginia law professor John C. Jeffries, Jr. (who was also Powell's biographer), on Scalia's idea of judges: "It is not merely that he doubts the *authority* of judges to make bets on the future; he doubts their *capacity* to do so with anything like consistent success . . . He knows that untold suffering has flowed from utopian visions and that even the soft utopias of the 1960s have had their costs."[50]

The two judicial lions whose views most contrasted with Scalia's retired in the early 1990s. First, Brennan, age eighty-four, announced after suffering a stroke in the summer of 1990 that he would have to step down. Brennan, on the bench since 1956, was able to prevail in his liberal vision nearly to the end, keeping majorities together on the separation of church and state, pulling out a few more victories on programs favoring minorities, and continuing to craft decisions that robustly protected free expression. He wrote the opinions for the Court in 1989 and 1990, right before he had to retire, that upheld a constitutional right to burn the American flag as political protest.[51] Marshall, the champion of racial justice, retired the following year at age eighty-three. He had devised the legal strategy to take on the "separate but equal" doctrine in the nation's schools and fought segregation on a host of legal fronts, traveling in the Deep South, where he was forbidden from using "whites only" drinking fountains and restrooms, and becoming the most important civil rights lawyer of his time. Both Brennan and Marshall absolutely opposed capital punishment.

President George H. W. Bush's appointments of successors in 1990 and 1991 diminished that old-style liberalism and enhanced Scalia's ability to prevail with his conservatism—but to strikingly different degrees. As the replacement to Brennan, Bush named David Souter, a New Hampshire Supreme Court justice whom Bush, three months earlier, in 1990, had appointed to the U.S. Court of Appeals for the First Circuit. Souter was born in Melrose, Massachusetts, in 1939 but spent most of his childhood in New Hampshire. A Rhodes scholar who attended both Harvard College and Harvard Law School, he had worked his way up in New Hampshire government, eventually serving as attorney general and then as a trial judge before being appointed to the state high court in 1983 by Governor John Sununu. It was Sununu, who had become President Bush's chief of staff, who brought Souter to Bush's attention, as did Souter's close friend Senator Warren Rudman, a New Hampshire Republican. "A home run for conservatives," declared Sununu, who was famously wrong, as would become evident in just a few years.

At the start of the Senate Judiciary Committee confirmation hearings in September 1990, Chairman Joseph R. Biden, Jr., declared that less was known about Souter than any other high court nominee in a quarter century. A few weeks earlier, a reporter had asked Souter how it felt to be snatched from obscurity. The sardonic nominee responded, "I must say, I never thought of myself as that obscure."

Souter's dry wit was a constant. But his record on the substance of the law changed after he was seated on the Court. In his first year, the new justice aligned himself with the conservatives on some of the ideological litmus test cases.[52] Within a few years, however, the man who became a close friend of his predecessor, Brennan, found his way squarely into the liberal camp.[53] A bachelor who was content to eat a lunch of yogurt and apple alone at his desk, Souter adopted an empathetic view that—while not as far to the left as Brennan's—found him siding with the poor, the weak, and many others whose paths Souter rarely crossed.

The following year, President Bush appointed a second justice, Clarence Thomas, who was very much unlike his predecessor, Thurgood Marshall. Thomas, who would become the nation's second African American justice, would, in fact, significantly reinforce Scalia's positions. Like Scalia, Thomas felt strongly about how government responded to problems of race. Yet Thomas's views arose from a completely different life story.

He was born in poverty in 1948 in a hamlet called Pin Point, near Savannah, Georgia. When Thomas was two years old, his father abandoned the family and his mother soon sent him and his brother to live with their grandfather, Myers Anderson, in Savannah. Anderson was a demanding taskmaster whom Thomas credited for helping him work hard in school and make something of himself. "Whenever one pang of self-pity even remotely touches me, I look at him," said Thomas of his grandfather, who never made it past third grade and endured the harsh segregation of the Deep South. Thomas graduated from Holy Cross College in 1971, then Yale Law School in 1974. He worked as a staff lawyer for the Missouri attorney general, John Danforth, who would be elected to the U.S. Senate in 1976 and eventually would be instrumental in Thomas's high court confirmation. Thomas first came to Washington to work as a legislative assistant to Danforth from 1979 to 1981. Drawn to Reagan's counterrevolution, Thomas then became an assistant secretary of education for civil rights (1981–82) and, after that, chairman of the Equal Employment Opportunity Commission (1982–90).

About a year before President Bush selected him for the high court, Bush had appointed Thomas to the U.S. Court of Appeals for the D.C. Circuit, the powerful bench where Scalia had served. Thomas's tenure there was only about eighteen months, longer than Souter's on a federal appeals court but still not significant experience. Nonetheless, when Bush nominated Thomas, he proclaimed him "the best person for this position."[54] A reporter asked Bush whether race was "a factor whatsoever in the selection," and the President said, "I don't see it at all . . . I kept my word to the American people and to the Senate by picking the best man for the job on the merits. And the fact he's [a] minority, so much the better. But that is not the factor, and I would strongly resent any charge that might be forthcoming on quotas when it relates to appointing the best man to the Court."[55]

As Thomas was being named to succeed the Court's first black justice, Marshall, these comments spurred public derision that hit Thomas hard. He had always felt stigmatized by affirmative action, first at Yale and then in his political appointments. He later wrote that he asked Bush's White House counsel Boyden Gray if he had been chosen for the Supreme Court because he was black. "Boyden replied that in fact my race had actually worked against me," Thomas recalled seventeen years after his appointment. "The initial plan," he said, "had been to have me replace Justice [William] Brennan in order to avoid appointing me to what was widely perceived as the court's 'black' seat, thus making the confirmation even more contentious. But Justice Brennan retired earlier than expected [in 1990], and everyone in the White House agreed that I needed more time on the D.C. Circuit in order to pass muster as a Supreme Court nominee."[56]

The NAACP opposed Thomas's nomination, as did the AFL-CIO, the National Abortion Rights Action League, and several major civil rights groups. The groups and numerous senators were deeply troubled by substantive positions he had taken. Even as the chairman of the Equal Employment Opportunity Commission, Thomas had criticized affirmative action. He had also complained that Congress was regularly interfering with the business of the executive branch. He had suggested that he opposed abortion rights. Such views put Thomas out of the mainstream, some Democratic senators complained. But all challenges to Thomas's stance on the issues were overwhelmed by the eleventh-hour revelation that one of his former employees, Anita Hill, was prepared to testify that Thomas had sexually harassed her.[57]

Hill, then a University of Oklahoma law professor, had been an attorney-adviser to Thomas from 1981 to 1982, when he was assistant secretary for the Department of Education's civil rights division, and she was a special assistant, in 1982–83, to Thomas as EEOC chairman. The youngest of thirteen children, she had been raised in a devout Baptist family in Oklahoma. Like Thomas, she was a striver and had earned a Yale law degree.

On October 11, 1991, before an uncomfortable Senate Judiciary Committee and a rapt national television audience, Hill presented her accusations in graphic detail. She said that Thomas repeatedly asked her out despite her discouragement. She said he then harassed her with comments about women's breasts, the size of his penis, and accounts of movies of group sex and bestiality. "Because I was extremely uncomfortable talking about sex with him at all, and particularly in such a graphic way, I told him that I did not want to talk about this subject," she told the committee as she spoke slowly, thoroughly composed. "My efforts to change the subject were rarely successful." She then added in her calm voice, "Telling the world is the most difficult experience of my life, but it is very close to having to live through the experience that occasioned this meeting."

Hill went on for seven hours, recounting how Thomas humiliated her. Some Republican senators challenged her to explain why she had not come forward with a complaint at the time. "I confess that I am very sorry that I did not do something, or say something. But at the time that was my best judgment. Maybe it was a poor judgment, but it wasn't a dishonest [one], and it wasn't a completely unreasonable choice that I made, given the circumstances."[58]

Television audiences were riveted. Hill's testimony that Friday, October 11, drew a larger prime-time audience than a major-league baseball play-off game, a combined 26.5 rating on NBC and ABC, according to the Associated Press. (Each rating point equaled 921,000 homes.) Hill's accusations similarly became Topic A in offices and classrooms, around dinner tables, in restaurants, and anywhere people gathered.[59]

After nightfall on that first day of what would become three days of intense hearings, Thomas returned to the witness chair and categorically denied her accusations. "This is a circus," he said. "It's a national disgrace, and from my standpoint as a black American, it's a high-tech lynching for an uppity black who in any way deigns to think for himself."

Thomas would later compare himself to the black defendant wrongly charged with rape in the Harper Lee classic *To Kill a Mockingbird*. He likened the experience of being accused of sexual harassment by Hill to finding himself alone in a hostile white neighborhood. "One of the things we were fearful of in southeast Georgia is that if you got off the beaten

path as blacks and you were in some place where you didn't know the
rules and there was no order, there was always this sense of vulnerability,
that somebody was going to pick you up, beat your brains out or arrest
you and put you in jail and you couldn't get out."[60]

In such a charged atmosphere, senators found themselves at a he-said-
she-said impasse. But just two days after this second round of hearings,
in part because of votes Senator Danforth, a well-respected moderate
Republican and Thomas booster, had earlier secured for his former
employee, the Senate confirmed Thomas by a vote of 52–48. Eleven
Democrats, mostly southerners, voted for him,[61] and only two Republicans voted against him, Jim Jeffords of Vermont and Robert Packwood of
Oregon. Thomas took his seat in October 1991. Soon after, Scalia and his
wife, Maureen, held a black-tie dinner in honor of the new justice and
his wife, Virginia, at the Court.[62]

The nation's second African American justice became a reliable second
vote for Scalia's position on race-oriented cases. Thomas's position
emerged from different concerns. "My thinking about race started under
segregation," Thomas said in an interview. "The nuns [who taught grade
school] and my grandparents told us we were equal and we should be
treated the same" as whites. He said he wanted to be consistent when a
decade later affirmative action was available to help blacks. "I said, wait a
minute, this violates the equal treatment rule. Are you only for the principle when it works to your advantage?" He also worried about the stigma of
being thought inferior that blacks carried. At one point when he defended
his opposition to affirmative action, he said, "I do not believe that kneeling
is a position of strength. Nor do I believe that begging is an effective tac-
tic."[63] Thomas believed affirmative action sent the message that blacks
needed a handout because they could not make it on their own.

Scalia's opposition, on the other hand, grew partly from his identification with the group that did not get the special benefit of affirmative
action. As the grandson of an Italian factory worker, Scalia repeatedly
adopted the point of view of the white person who was subjected to
reverse discrimination—as he would say through the years, "the Polish
factory worker's kid."

Scalia and Thomas were together in the majority in 1993 when the
Court for the first time allowed white voters to challenge in court black-
majority congressional districts that sought to consolidate minorities to

boost their voting power. These districts tended to be oddly shaped as they tracked barely contiguous black or Hispanic neighborhoods and cities. Such "majority-minority" districts, a record number after the 1990 census, were part of a U.S. Justice Department policy to spur local legislators to try to compensate for past bias that had kept blacks from casting ballots or that diluted the power of their votes through districts drawn to favor whites.

The 1993 Court case centered on North Carolina's Twelfth Congressional District, a serpentine 160-mile-long district that meandered through black neighborhoods as it followed Interstate 85. A group of white voters in North Carolina contended that the state's redistricting plan created "a racially discriminatory voting process" and deprived them of the right to vote in a "color-blind" election. A lower federal court had rejected their challenge. The Supreme Court reinstated the complaint in an opinion by Justice O'Connor. She said some districts could be so "bizarrely" drawn that they could be understood only as an effort to segregate voters by race and, therefore, violated the Fourteenth Amendment equality guarantee. "A racial gerrymander may exacerbate the very patterns of racial bloc voting that majority-minority districting is sometimes said to counteract," she wrote, joined by Scalia, Thomas, Rehnquist, and Kennedy.

Justice Souter originally had been on O'Connor's side in the case, but he switched to a dissent. He said that her opinion reneged on two decades of voting rights remediation and history. Souter also criticized her standard based on the "appearances" of any district. Justice White—who, as a deputy U.S. attorney general in the Kennedy administration, had personally confronted the Ku Klux Klan sympathizer Alabama governor John Patterson and faced down southern segregationists—wrote the lead dissent in the case of *Shaw v. Reno*. White said that "majority-minority" districts did not deprive white voters of any rights. Until the June 1993 decision, the usual voting rights challenge had not been to the shape of a district, but rather to a practice, such as a literacy test or poll tax, designed to keep someone from casting a ballot. Justice White said it was "both a fiction and a departure from settled equal protection principles" to regard the white voters as having a claim. Signing on with Justice White were Souter, Blackmun, and Stevens.

A year later, Scalia and Thomas demonstrated that they would take an

even stronger position against redistricting efforts designed to help formerly disenfranchised minorities. The 1994 case of *Holder v. Hall* tested
whether a Georgia county's single-commissioner form of government
violated black residents' rights. A group of blacks had sought to enlarge
the commission to five members because the single-commissioner system,
combined with Bleckley County's history of racial bloc voting, made
it impossible to elect a black commissioner. The precise question was
whether the size of a county government institution was covered by the
Voting Rights Act as a "standard, practice or procedure" that potentially
deprived minority voters of the franchise. The single-member commission that black voters were protesting allowed one elected official to exercise all executive and legislative power in the county. A lower federal
appeals court had said the voters' challenge could go forward and told a
trial judge to consider a five-member commission so that blacks, who
made up 20 percent of the county population, might be able to elect one
of their own. The Supreme Court was ready to reverse the appeals court in
Holder v. Hall and say the Voting Rights Act did not allow a challenge to
the size of a county commission or other government structure.

Chief Justice Rehnquist originally assigned the opinion for the Court
to Scalia. Over several months of drafting, however, Scalia went beyond
the majority's view that the challengers had not made a sufficient case
against the single-commissioner system, and he lodged a full-scale attack
on the breadth of the 1965 Voting Rights Act. "It is, in a word, unthinkable
that the sizes of all state and local institutions, from City Councils to
Houses of Representatives to state Supreme Courts, were meant to be
determined under the Voting Rights Act," Scalia wrote, warning later in
his draft opinion that the Court should consider the "practical considerations" of broadly reading the law. Scalia implicitly dismissed the historic
purpose of the Voting Rights Act to remedy long-standing black disen-
franchisement. His approach turned off his fellow justices and began to
cost him the majority opinion. Moderately conservative Justice O'Connor
was dismayed, as were the liberal dissenters. One of the latter, Blackmun,
discussed Scalia's direction with one of his clerks, who wrote a note back
to Blackmun that said, "I would like to see you pull the rug out from Justice Scalia's duplicitous, pernicious opinion."[64]

With time ticking away toward the traditional July 1 end-of-term
deadline, the five most conservative justices (Rehnquist, O'Connor,

Kennedy, Scalia, and Thomas) continued to believe that the black voters had not demonstrated that the size of the commission was covered by the act, but most of the majority had bailed from Scalia's opinion. Rehnquist reassigned the Court's opinion to Kennedy.

Scalia then worked with Thomas, who was elaborating on his own problems with the Voting Rights Act. The Court's only African American justice termed Court precedent on the 1965 law "a disastrous misadventure in judicial policymaking." Signed by Scalia, that Thomas opinion drew more attention than the main opinion for the Court, written by Kennedy, rejecting the challenge to the Georgia district.[65] Thomas and Scalia insisted that the law should cover only state laws that limit people's access to the ballot and should not be construed to cover other government practices, such as the size of a governing body, that dilute minority voting strength. Thomas's opinion was an indictment of the law that had been used for decades to counteract the dilution of black voter strength through the drawing of districts, particularly in the South. Justice Stevens, joined by the three other dissenters, wrote an opinion that said the Thomas-Scalia approach flew in the face of civil rights law history. Stevens termed their approach "radical" and said that if it were adopted, it would require the reversal of dozens of prior rulings.

"When a statute has been authoritatively, repeatedly, and consistently construed for more than a quarter century, and when Congress has re-enacted and extended the statute several times with full awareness of that construction, judges have an especially clear obligation to obey settled law," Stevens wrote. "Whether Justice Thomas is correct that the Court's settled construction of the Voting Rights Act has been 'a disastrous misadventure,' should not affect the decision in this case."[66]

Scalia and Thomas broke from Rehnquist and other fellow conservatives again the next year, in a 1995 case that began when a guardrail construction company, Adarand Constructors, challenged a U.S. Department of Transportation program favoring firms that awarded subcontracts to minority-owned businesses. Adarand Constructors was a white-owned Colorado Springs firm that lost a guardrail project in the San Juan National Forest even though it had submitted the low bid. A Hispanic company with a higher bid won out under a "disadvantaged business enterprises" program that presumed minorities were socially and economically disadvantaged.

Justice O'Connor wrote the Court's opinion allowing the challenge to go forward and requiring the most searching judicial scrutiny for all government policies based on race, even a congressionally mandated one. By doing this, the conservative majority reinforced O'Connor's decision in *Richmond v. Croson* and reversed Brennan's liberal decision in *Metro Broadcasting v. Federal Communications Commission*, which had upheld a federal preference program for minority broadcasters.[67] Writing for the four dissenting justices, Stevens said the Court's drive for "consistency" in racial policies erased any distinction between hurtful and beneficial treatment toward blacks and "would treat a Dixiecrat Senator's decision to vote against Thurgood Marshall's confirmation in order to keep African Americans off the Supreme Court on par with President Johnson's evaluation of his nominee's race as a positive factor."

Yet once again O'Connor left the door slightly ajar by saying that the Court's new standard for federal affirmative action need not always be "fatal" to such programs. She wrote that government may address "the unhappy persistence of both the practice and the lingering effects of racial discrimination." She did not explain how they could be justified, beyond possible evidence of "pervasive, systematic, and obstinate discriminatory conduct" by government against blacks or other minorities.

Taking up his pen, Scalia insisted that nothing could justify affirmative action. In a separate statement in the *Adarand Constructors v. Peña* case, Scalia said, "In my view, government can never have a 'compelling interest' in discriminating on the basis of race in order to 'make up' for past racial discrimination in the opposite direction." His concurrence was signed only by Thomas.

Scalia reached back to his views of no "creditor or debtor race" first articulated when he was a law professor: "Individuals who have been wronged by unlawful racial discrimination should be made whole; but under our Constitution there can be no such thing as either a creditor or a debtor race. That concept is alien to the Constitution's focus upon the individual. To pursue the concept of racial entitlement—even for the most admirable and benign of purposes—is to reinforce and preserve for future mischief the way of thinking that produced race slavery, race privilege and race hatred. In the eyes of government, we are just one race here. It is American."[68] Given Scalia's mind-set, it was easy for him to compare the "way of thinking" that caused slavery with affirmative action and other measures to counteract racial discrimination.

Justice Thomas wrote a separate concurring statement voicing his concerns about a stamp of inferiority: "So-called 'benign' discrimination teaches many that because of chronic and apparently immutable handicaps, minorities cannot compete with them without their patronizing indulgence . . . Inevitably, such programs engender attitudes of superiority or, alternatively, provoke resentment among those who believe that they have been wronged by the government's use of race. These programs stamp minorities with a badge of inferiority and may cause them to develop dependencies or to adopt an attitude that they are 'entitled' to preferences."[69]

Throughout the 1990s Scalia and Thomas voted together more than any other pair on the nine-member bench. Further, because Scalia already had established himself and Thomas rarely said a word during oral arguments, some commentators asserted that Thomas was merely following Scalia's lead. "I think Thomas is basically in Scalia's pocket," Bruce Fein, an associate deputy attorney general in the Reagan administration, said in 1994.[70]

Thomas appeared to brush it off. "People say that because I'm black, Justice Scalia does my work for me," Thomas told students at the University of Louisville in 2000. "But I rarely see him, so he must have a chip in my brain."[71] Thomas said in a later interview that criticism about his abilities was easy to dismiss. "I grew up brushing off racial slurs," he said. "It's a long road from Savannah, and a lot has happened along the way. That is not the worst that has happened to me in my life or been said about me." He said he had an "easy friendship" with Scalia and told him when critics said he was merely a Scalia clone, "Don't worry about that, buddy. I've been called worse." Scalia agreed that such criticism never caused awkwardness between the two men. "He knew that it was all a lie," Scalia said. "He didn't take it too much to heart." Noting that reporters had tagged the former chief justice Warren Burger and Justice Harry Blackmun as "the Minnesota Twins" (irritating Blackmun especially), Scalia continued, "As I recall, as luck would have it, the first time the press tried to do the Minnesota Twins number on us, paint us as two peas in a pod, was a case in which I had originally been on the other side. It was Clarence who drew me to his side. I don't remember at all what kind of case it was. I just recall vividly thinking that Clarence really won't take this to heart because he knows that the only reason I'm there is because he persuaded me to be there."[72]

With their views on race departing from even their fellow conservatives, Scalia said, there was an advantage to their alliance: "There are times
when I think I've been a comfort to him and he's been a comfort to me.
Nobody else seemed to see things our way. It's nice to have at least one
other person who you can sympathize with."

Justice O'Connor, whose vote continued to be the decisive one on the
Court's race cases, moved further away from them as the page turned to a
new century. In 2001 she voted for the first time to uphold the drawing of
a heavily black congressional district designed to try to give blacks a
chance to elect one of their own. Joining the Court's four more liberal justices at the time, O'Connor took the position that race consciousness in
redistricting is not automatically unconstitutional. Her altered position
occurred in a dispute over the redrawn Twelfth District in North Carolina.

"Race in this case closely correlates with political behavior," the majority said as it adopted arguments from North Carolina officials that politicians who drew the map were trying to protect a black Democratic
incumbent and shore up party strength rather than merely segregate voters by race. The Court in the new 2001 case said that when race can be
linked to political affiliation, the white voters who are challenging a district must show at least that the legislature could have achieved its political objectives in ways that would have ended with greater racial balance.[73]

Scalia voted with dissenting justices in an opinion by Thomas that
faulted the North Carolina legislature for drawing a district that Thomas
said was "based on the stereotype that blacks are reliable Democratic
voters."

Two years later O'Connor again made the difference—to Scalia's further consternation—in an affirmative action case from the University of
Michigan. In their admissions process, administrators at the campus in
Ann Arbor had favored blacks, Hispanics, and Native Americans on the
theory that racial diversity was central to its academic mission. The
undergraduate admissions policy automatically assigned extra points to
minority applicants. The law school had a more individualized screening
system that required applicants to be reviewed on a case-by-case basis and
allowed a "plus" factor for racial minorities. Jennifer Gratz and Patrick
Hamacher, who had been denied admission as undergraduates, and Barbara Grutter, who had been rejected for the law school, sued. All three
white students claimed that the credentials of black students who had
been admitted were weaker than theirs.

The Supreme Court, with critical votes by O'Connor, upheld the Michigan Law School program but rejected the undergraduate admissions system. Schools must individually assess applicants, she wrote, even as they consider race. O'Connor stressed the importance of campuses' being open to all races: "Effective participation by members of all racial and ethnic groups in the civic life of our Nation is essential if the dream of one Nation, indivisible, is to be realized," she wrote.[74] The decision enshrined the rationale of the 1978 *Bakke* case that first endorsed affirmative action in higher education and ushered in an era of policies designed to bring minorities to prestigious campuses. That opinion had infuriated Scalia and prompted him to denigrate the "Lewis Powells" of the world who were making it tough for the sons of the working class.

In Scalia's dissent in the 2003 University of Michigan Law School case, he mocked notions of diversity and "cross-racial understanding" highlighted by the majority: "This is not, of course, an 'educational benefit' on which students will be graded on their Law School transcript (Works and Plays Well with Others: B+) or tested by the bar examiners (Q: Describe in 500 words or less your cross-racial understanding)."[75]

Scalia also derided the university's goal of a "critical mass" of minorities that would encourage black and Hispanic students to participate in classes and not feel isolated. "If it is appropriate for the University of Michigan Law School to use racial discrimination for the purpose of putting together a 'critical mass' that will convey generic lessons in socialization and good citizenship," Scalia wrote, "surely it is no less appropriate—indeed, particularly appropriate—for the civil service system of the State of Michigan to do so. There, also, those exposed to 'critical masses' of certain races will presumably become better Americans, better Michiganders, better civil servants. And surely private employers cannot be criticized—indeed, should be praised—if they also 'teach' good citizenship to their adult employees through a patriotic, all-American system of racial discrimination in hiring . . . The Constitution proscribes government discrimination on the basis of race, and state-provided education is no exception."

Scalia had a bottom line: the Constitution bans all government classifications on the basis of race. Yet beyond legalities and what he believed the Constitution dictated, there was also the long-standing resentment he believed such programs engendered. Thomas signed his dissent but again demonstrated in his own separate statement how his concern was what affirmative action did to racial minorities. "The majority of blacks are admitted to the Law School because of discrimination, and because of this policy all are tarred as undeserving," Thomas wrote in the Michigan case.

Over more than two decades on the bench Scalia made clear that he saw affirmative action through the eyes of those denied jobs or school admissions. During oral arguments in the University of Michigan case, Scalia had told a lawyer defending the programs, "The people you want to talk to are the high school seniors who have seen people visibly less qualified than they are get into prestigious institutions where they are rejected. If you think that is not creating resentment, you are just wrong." This was Scalia's emphasis—his alone on the Court. Maybe it arose from his personal experience. Maybe it was his more general social perception. It expressly informed his no-discrimination rule.

A pair of blockbuster cases four years later demonstrated how dug in Scalia was. This time, however, because of the newly changed membership of the Court, his views helped carry the day rather than be heard only in dissent. It was no longer Scalia and Thomas off on their own. This time a new chief justice, John Roberts, would strongly echo Scalia's sentiment: "The way to stop discrimination on the basis of race," Chief Justice Roberts wrote, "is to stop discriminating on the basis of race."[76]

Roberts penned those words as the justices were reviewing, in 2007, Seattle and Louisville area school district policies that considered students' race in deciding which schools they should be assigned to in order to maintain racial balance in the district. During the hearings on those cases, Scalia was, as usual, active and argumentative. To the lawyer for the Seattle School District, Scalia asked, "Could the government achieve that objective [of racial integration] by barring people from moving into Little Italy or giving a preference to some people to buy real estate in Little Italy if they are of Italian ancestry? Could it do that? Absolutely not, right?"

"I would agree with you," the school district lawyer Michael Madden answered.

"So it would appear that even if the objective is okay, you cannot achieve it by any means whatever. And the mere fact that the objective of achieving a diverse balanced society is perfectly all right, although certainly not the only objective in the world. The mere fact that it's okay doesn't mean you can achieve it by any means whatever?"

Madden responded, "I would submit that there's a fundamental difference between the circumstances you've described and a school system which takes all comers and is asked to educate them by preparing them to live in a pluralistic society."

Fielding questions from other justices and continuing to try to distinguish between the two types of policies that would take account of a student's race, Madden said, "Segregation is harmful. Integration . . . has benefits."

"Well," rejoined Scalia, "but it seems to me you're saying you can't make an omelet without breaking eggs. Can you think of any other area of the law in which we say whatever it takes, so long as there's a real need, whatever it takes . . . I mean, if we have a lot of crime out there and the only way to get rid of it is to use warrantless searches, you know, fudge on some of the protections of the Bill of Rights, whatever it takes, we've got to do it? Is there any area of the law that doesn't have some absolute restrictions? . . . I had thought that that was one of the absolute restrictions, that you cannot judge and classify people on the basis of their race. You can pursue the objectives that your school board is pursuing, but at some point you come up against an absolute, and aren't you just denying that?"

Madden insisted that in the 2003 University of Michigan cases the Court had rejected such absolutes and left room for educators to look at race to achieve their goals. He ended up losing the Seattle case, as the justices by a 5–4 vote—with Scalia in the majority—struck down programs in Seattle and Louisville that used students' race as a factor in school placement to build diversity across a district. Chief Justice Roberts, who wrote an opinion that so appealed to Scalia that he wrote no separate statement this time, said, "Classifying and assigning schoolchildren according to . . . race is an extreme approach."[77]

Scalia's views no doubt tapped into deep feelings among some Americans. By 2008, through university policies and public referenda, affirmative action in higher education was on the wane.[78] Affirmative action had greatly added to the number of blacks who went to college and earned degrees. But state-sanctioned requirements appeared to have run their course. On the thirtieth anniversary of the 1978 _Bakke_ decision, the Yale law professor Stephen L. Carter wrote that the continuing fight over affirmative action was obscuring the real problems of racial injustice. "Those who suffer most from the legacy of racial oppression are not competing for spaces in the entering classes of the nation's most selective colleges. Millions of them are not finishing high school. We countenance vast disparities in education in America, in where children start and where they come out. And we do not even want to talk about it."[79]

Scalia considered that sentiment undeniable. At the same time, he was certain that if anyone were to take a lead in that discussion, it should not be the nation's judges. Their role in the dilemmas of race was limited, he insisted, no matter how dire the problems, no matter how much legislatures might fail to respond to the historic needs of minorities. He challenged the long-standing argument that special protection should be given the disenfranchised and disadvantaged. In that view, some critics argued, he was abandoning the core responsibility of courts in America because the neutral rules he advocated could not bring about racial equality. "He has asserted that these programs [favoring disadvantaged classes] are pathological. They divide Americans, award special privileges, and undercut majority rule," wrote Richard Brisbin in his book *Justice Antonin Scalia and the Conservative Revival.* "However, he has provided no evidence that neutral rules . . . can really cure the pathologies inherent in existing racial [divisions]." Brisbin suggested that Scalia was simply hostile to governmental action to bring about racial equality.[80]

Not surprisingly, Scalia was unmoved by his critics. Judges should become involved only when an individual had been denied "something that the individual was properly entitled to," he said, elaborating on his views in an interview. "If he has been discriminated against on the basis of his race, that's a reason [for court action]. But to set one race against another by giving racial preferences does not solve the problem. It just further ingrains the problem."[81]

Scalia's mind was settled, no matter how much remained unsettled in racially divided America.

PASSIONS OF HIS MIND

———•◦•———

In the heart of downtown Washington, D.C., looms the Cathedral of St. Matthew the Apostle, a redbrick and terra-cotta structure marked by a distinctive copper dome. Built in the 1890s and a hybrid of Byzantine and Romanesque architecture, it was here, among its mosaics and multihued murals, that President Kennedy's funeral service was held in 1963, and it was the setting for a Mass by Pope John Paul II in 1979. It also became the place for a traditional "Red Mass" on the Sunday before the first Monday in October and the start of the Supreme Court's annual term. The ancient Red Mass, dating to thirteenth-century Europe and named for the scarlet vestments bishops wore for the occasion, had come to mark the start of a judicial year and celebrated the community's lawyers. For many of the Supreme Court justices, St. Matthew's was a ceremonial home.[1] For Antonin Scalia, it was a regular sanctuary.

In the 1970s, when he worked for Presidents Nixon and Ford, Scalia often drove his family over from their northern Virginia home to attend services at St. Matthew's. In those years American Catholicism was veering away from solemn organ music toward folksier guitar masses. But St. Matthew's still offered the Latin Mass, and Scalia sought it out. The extra hour of driving to a just-right church became part of the routine of the Scalia children's upbringing. When the family lived in Chicago and Charlottesville, too, Scalia looked for a church with a High Mass and the reverence he desired. "My father views the Catholic faith today as the inheritor of a cultural heritage, the great art, the music, the Latin tradition," said Scalia's eldest son, Eugene. "To him, it's Bach and Beethoven versus a guitar Mass. I don't think for him it's a conservative thing, or right-wing thing. He wants the tradition."[2] It was family lore that on one Palm Sunday, a priest at a parish church in suburban Virginia drove a Volkswagen Beetle down the aisle to replicate Christ's journey to crucifixion. Whether true or not, the story reinforced the lesson among the children that the Scalia parents would not partake of the experimental or modern.[3]

"We have always traveled long distances to go to a church that we thought had a really reverent Mass, the kind of church that when you go in, it is quiet—not that kind of church where it is like a community hall and everybody is talking," Justice Scalia explained in an interview. "We used to travel in Chicago . . . [At first] we went to the church that was closest . . . in Hyde Park. I remember the last straw there. And it was around Christmas time and they had some smart-ass young Jesuit who said the Mass and gave the sermon, and he said, 'Of course, we know that all of this about the manger and all . . . is fanciful.' "

Scalia, who was then a professor at the University of Chicago, was furious that a priest would denigrate the biblical story of Jesus Christ's birth in a stable. The remark cast doubt on the depiction of Mary laying Jesus in a manger, a story from St. Luke's Gospel that Scalia and his wife, Maureen, taught their children. Justice Scalia recalled his encounter with the priest: "I went up to him afterward and I said, 'We never lied to them about Santa Claus. And here it was as if I've been lying to them about the manger. We're out of here.'[4]

"So we used to go downtown [in Chicago] to a little church near the Merchandise Mart," Scalia continued, "a little church run by an Italian order, the Servites, and they had a very devout Mass. I did the same in Charlottesville. We had to go to that university church. They had some crazy Dominicans. After one sermon when it was relativist morality, I went up to the priest afterwards and I said, 'What is this stuff?' And he said, 'Well, you know, the teaching of the church changes.' . . . So I was out of there . . . Really, we've always traveled some distance."

Like his Italian roots and devotion to family, traditional Catholicism was integral to Scalia's identity. "It's pretty clear to me that he believes the Catholic Church is the one true church," said Leonard Leo, a Washington lawyer and friend of Scalia's from the Federalist Society. "He makes no bones about it. He has said as much. He is very much committed to the magisterial traditions of the Church. He believes those traditions have a purpose and meaning. You'll hear the justice complain about church architecture or liturgies that are too modernistic. At first blush, you might just think he's a rigid Catholic. In reality that's not true. You come to realize that those traditions, that architecture, that music, the incense, all of those things are there to deliver up a sense of piety, reverence for the person attending Mass. What those outward manifestations allow him to do is to focus on faith and to achieve a level of spirituality."[5]

Scalia's longtime friend Arthur Gajarsa, who became a federal appeals judge in 1997, characterized Scalia as defined by his Catholicism. "I think his faithful belief in the Catholic doctrine is what makes him run. I think he is a true believer."[6] Yet Gajarsa also said that Scalia, as a justice, was more generally directed by a personal moral compass. "His ethics are much more broadly ingrained . . . Catholicism is part of it."[7]

When Scalia joined the Supreme Court as the 103rd justice in 1986, six Roman Catholics already had been appointed to the Court over the years, beginning with Chief Justice Roger Taney in 1836.[8] The Catholic William Brennan, a 1956 appointee, was still on the Court when Scalia was named. Other Catholic jurists would serve in the subsequent years of his tenure.[9] But more than any of them, Scalia was identified as a Catholic justice. He publicly presented himself in this way, and news media coverage reinforced the importance of Catholicism to his life and his sense of himself.

During an interview on CBS's *60 Minutes*, Lesley Stahl asked Scalia about the fact that he and Maureen had nine children. "We didn't set out to have nine children," Scalia said. "We're just old-fashioned Catholics, playing what used to be known as 'Vatican roulette.'"[10] Around the same time, he gave a similar answer to a lighthearted inquiry from NBC's Tim Russert, also a Catholic: "I didn't set out to have nine. It just happened that way."[11] One of Scalia's sons, Paul, had become a priest, and in the *60 Minutes* interview Scalia joked, "If in an old-fashioned Catholic family with five sons you don't get one priest out of it, we're in big trouble, right? I will say that the other four were very happy when Paul announced that he was going to take one for the team."[12]

Paul became a diocesan priest and shared his father's disdain of the modern liturgy—and his father's tendency to speak out. "As priests, we shouldn't be afraid to preach about abortion," Father Paul said in an interview reprinted in the *Priests for Life* newsletter. "Yes, we may take a few lumps; and yes, some parishioners might get mad at us and write hasty letters. But you never know who is going to be affected by what you say. If we don't preach about this, how is that woman sitting in the pews who is considering having an abortion going to hear the message."[13]

Justice Scalia actively encouraged fidelity to the Church's traditional values. In a speech to a Knights of Columbus council in Baton Rouge, he praised, according to the local paper *The Advocate*, "traditional Catholics" who say the Rosary, go on pilgrimages, kneel during the Eucharist, and "follow religiously the teaching of the Pope."[14] A few of his law clerks who were Catholic said the justice took a strong interest in commitment. He wanted to make sure they observed Ash Wednesday and all holy days and followed Catholic teaching. One of his greatest sources of pride, he said, was that all nine of his children attended regular Sunday Mass.

No one on the contemporary Court spoke out on religion before audiences as Scalia did. Some earlier Catholics on the Court had even taken pains to downplay their religion—perhaps in response to earlier anti-Catholic bigotry.[15] Justice Brennan, for example, believed that the Constitution required strict separation of church and state and told an interviewer that his hardest case was a 1963 dispute that led the justices to strike down organized prayer in public school. "In the face of my whole lifelong experience as a Roman Catholic," Brennan explained in a 1986 interview, "to say that prayer was not an appropriate thing in public schools, that gave me quite a hard time. I struggled." He added, "I had settled in my mind that I had an obligation under the Constitution which could not be influenced by any of my religious principles."[16]

In 1996 Scalia appeared at an event sponsored by the Christian Legal Society at the Mississippi College School of Law and struck a decidedly different tone. He told the audience to stand up for their religious beliefs. "We must pray for the courage to endure the scorn of the sophisticated world," he declared, and, adopting the language of Saint Paul, urged the audience to be "fools for Christ's sake." Scalia then offered a contemptuous portrayal of a society that viewed miracles skeptically and disparaged religious believers. The "worldly wise," he said, do not believe in the resurrection of the dead and "just will not have anything to do with miracles." He was drawing a line between the reverent, the "true believers," and all others, and in fact he later acknowledged an us-versus-them dimension to his message: "You have to be prepared to be regarded as idiots by sophisticated modern society," he said of his meaning. "You know, don't get upset by it."[17]

As might have been expected at the 1996 appearance before the Christian Legal Society at the Southern Baptist school, he received a standing ovation.[18] But news reports of the event were grist for critics who thought that, in a society founded on the notion of separation of church and state, Scalia had gone too far in his personal identification with religious believers. His remark about the "worldly wise" provoked the *Washington Post* cartoonist Herb Block to sketch a cartoon of Scalia on the bench: the justice sits alongside his colleagues reading the Bible and fuming about the "worldly wise guys." The *American Lawyer* magazine columnist Stuart Taylor accused Scalia of having a "persecution complex." He referred to Scalia's "flirtation with Christian victimology" and wrote that the justice was parroting unthinkingly "the kind of nonsense that is often heard from the likes of [the television evangelist] Pat Robertson and [the conservative commentator] Patrick Buchanan."[19] The following year, the law professors Michael Stokes Paulsen and Steffen N. Johnson defended Scalia in the *Notre Dame Law Review*, casting him as "a priest, seeking to help his fellow believers." Expressing sympathy, they wrote, "For Christian law students (and Christian lawyers), the tension between being a Christian and the study and practice of law can be very real."[20]

There would be other incidents, some generating more storms than others. The result was a constant spotlight on Justice Scalia's religious identity and questions about how it affected his rulings. One episode occurred after he had attended a Red Mass at the Cathedral of the Holy Cross in Boston in 2006. As reporters and photographers gathered around for an impromptu Q and A in the vestibule of the church, the *Boston Herald* reporter Laurel Sweet asked Scalia whether he had to fend off "a lot of flak for publicly celebrating" Roman Catholic beliefs.[21] The angry Scalia replied, "You know what I say to those people?" then flicked his fingers under his chin in the familiar Sicilian brush-off. Scalia had turned right toward the photographer Peter Smith, who immediately immortalized the finger flick. Smith gave the picture to the *Herald*. (At the time, Smith was freelancing for *The Pilot*, the paper of the Archdiocese of Boston, which terminated his contract after the incident.) The *Boston Herald* reported that Scalia had engaged in an obscene gesture, such as the raising of the middle finger. That assertion induced Scalia to write the *Herald* a letter that said the chin flick actually meant, "I couldn't care less. It's no business of mine. Count me out." Scalia continued with his vintage sarcasm in his letter to the newspaper: "From watching too many episodes of the Sopranos, your staff seems to have acquired the belief that any Sicilian gesture is obscene—especially when made by an 'Italian jurist.' (I am, by the way, an American jurist.)"[22] The *Boston Herald* backed down, saying in an editorial addressing Scalia's letter that the gesture may not have been obscene, but "it's still not something you'd do to your mother."[23]

The confrontation offered yet another reminder of how singularly outspoken Scalia was when it came to religion. In an interview three years after he brushed off the reporter with a chin flick, Justice Scalia said that he mainly had objected to being confronted as he was leaving a service. Generally, he said, he thought questions about his views on religion were fair game. "People know I'm serious about my religion," he said in the interview. "It doesn't seem to me an unreasonable question. It doesn't annoy me."[24]

Questions and criticism about Scalia's views on religion naturally collected around disputes involving the religion clauses of the First Amendment, which said government "shall make no law respecting the establishment of religion" and which guaranteed "the free exercise" of religion. Yet controversy tied to Scalia and his religion went beyond such areas of the law: it extended most notably to abortion rights. In time, particularly as more Catholics joined Scalia on the bench, attention began to focus on whether a justice's religion mattered in votes on abortion. "The discussion was probably inevitable," wrote Robin Toner in *The New York Times*. "Catholics, for the first time, hold a majority of seats on the Supreme Court, after decades when there were, typically, only one or maybe two 'Catholic seats' on the bench."[25]

For his part, Justice Scalia believed he should not be criticized or praised for any shadow of his Catholicism in his opinions. "I am sometimes embarrassed when I come out of Mass and people come up and say, 'I want to thank you for all you've done for the pro-life cause.' It embarrasses me because I have to tell them that, no, indeed, if I thought the Constitution said [otherwise], I would have come out that way. It has nothing whatever to do with my being a Catholic. It has to do with my being a good lawyer. I've said that in speeches, and I have said it to people after Mass. I'm embarrassed for the praise, because they're praising me for the wrong thing."[26]

What could be said, however, was this: Scalia expressed with unique fervor two passions—for his religion and for a repudiation of the view that the Constitution contains a right to abortion. From everything Scalia said, these were separate, parallel passions: "I am always reading a text and trying to give it the fairest interpretation possible. That's all I do. How can my religious views have anything to do with that? . . . I will strike down *Roe v. Wade*, but I will also strike down a law that is the opposite of *Roe v. Wade* . . . I have religious views on the subject. But they have nothing whatsoever to do with my job."[27]

Yet there was no ignoring that his repudiation of abortion rights and support for prayer in schools were in sync with his strongly stated religious views. As a result, the connection between these two emphases of Scalia's became part of the political landscape and a topic of conversation among Court observers. Sometimes thoughts about how Scalia's Catholicism influenced his brand of judging were expressed only in private, reflecting the discomfort among lawyers with the suggestion that either Scalia was disingenuous about how his beliefs influenced him or that serious Catholics could not think nonreligiously about legal matters. Sometimes observations played out loudly, however, as such critics as Geoffrey Stone at the University of Chicago publicly expressed views that Scalia's Catholicism affected his anti-abortion-rights vote. Still others saw a more methodological connection between Scalia's Catholicism and his rulings. In an early review of Scalia's Supreme Court decisions, the SUNY-Buffalo law professor George Kannar linked Scalia's text-driven legal approach with his "catechism" roots as the son of observant Catholics and a graduate of the Jesuit-run Xavier High School and Georgetown University. Kannar highlighted the likely influence of Scalia's father, who worked as a translator and had high regard for the authority of texts. "The experience of growing up Catholic in pre-Vatican II America was that of inhabiting a world of quaint legalisms, similar to that created by a quaint originalist Constitution," Kannar wrote in his 1990 "The Constitutional Catechism of Antonin Scalia," published in *The Yale Law Journal*.[28]

Scalia repeatedly rejected the notion that his Catholicism directed his rulings. He did, however, readily acknowledge that, like his religion, his insistence on the wrongness of *Roe* stirred his deepest emotions. "*Roe v. Wade* was a lie, [and] even those who favor the outcome acknowledge that the reasoning in the opinion was terrible," he said, explaining why he wanted to overturn the 1973 case. "It was not generally accepted. It still hasn't been. It still tears the society apart and becomes a national political

issue. And . . . this is the most important, for me as somebody who is trying to be a jurist: it does not allow me to operate as a lawyer, because the
new version of *Roe*, which is *Casey*, [asks]: Is this state law an 'undue burden' [on the abortion right]? What the hell does that mean?"[29] It was an
unanswerable legal dilemma, he insisted. "I run to the law books. And
what do you know?" he asked derisively. "No law was an 'undue burden'
for two centuries . . . This is a judgment call, but it is a judgment call for
legislators, not for lawyers, not for judges. I'll be damned if I'm going to
do that."[30]

The first abortion case Scalia took up as a justice came when he was in his
third year on the bench. The dispute from Missouri arose just as Ronald
Reagan was leaving the White House, to be succeeded by George H. W.
Bush, who had been Reagan's vice president and had defeated the Democratic governor Michael Dukakis, Scalia's Harvard classmate, in the
November 1988 election. On January 23, 1989, the sixteenth anniversary
of *Roe v. Wade*, the newly installed president Bush told a cheering crowd
of antiabortion demonstrators on the Ellipse that he would work for
reversal of the 1973 landmark that established abortion rights. As he
spoke to the crowd over an amplified telephone hookup, Bush said *Roe v.
Wade* was wrong and echoed the sentiment of Reagan during his two
terms.[31]

The Reagan, and then Bush, administrations endorsed Missouri's disputed abortion regulation, which opened with the assertion that life
begins at conception and that the unborn have "protectable interests in
life, health and well-being." The law at the core of the new case, *Webster v.
Reproductive Health Services*, prevented public hospitals and public
employees from performing abortions not required to save a mother's life.
If a woman seeking an abortion appeared to be at least twenty weeks pregnant, physicians were required to perform tests to see if the fetus could
live outside the womb. The Missouri law had been partially invalidated in
lower courts. State officials, now backed by Bush administration lawyers,
appealed.

The abortion dilemma was crucially important for the Catholic
Church, too. "Abortion has . . . taken on symbolic weight," the reporter
Ethan Bronner wrote in *The Boston Globe* in the spring of 1989 as the case

was about to be heard. "It is the flagship of a fleet of issues, equivalent in the Catholic community to Israel in the Jewish community. It stands for changing mores, for the conflict over women and family values."[32]

Before becoming a judge, Scalia had criticized the Court's regard for reproductive rights. He believed that if abortion was to be legal, it should not be through decisions like *Roe v. Wade*, which put judges in the "abortion-umpiring business," as he called it. When the Missouri case was argued in April 1989, Scalia left no doubt that the views he voiced before he donned the black robe still guided his thinking. He asked the lawyer Frank Susman, who represented the challengers to the Missouri law: How can the right to abortion be defended as fundamental "unless you make the determination that the organism that is destroyed is not a human life?" The question of when life begins, Susman responded, "is a question verifiable only by reliance upon faith." Susman noted that the two sides disagreed on "what you call that collection of physiological facts."[33]

"But what conclusion does that lead you to?" Scalia asked. "That, therefore, there must be a fundamental right on the part of the woman to destroy this thing that we don't know what it is or, rather, that whether there is or isn't is a matter that you vote upon; since we don't know the answer, people have to make up their minds the best they can."

Justice Scalia, of course, was of the latter mind. He strongly believed that the question of an abortion right should be left to the democratic process, not to unelected judges. Two days after the justices' oral argument, in their private conference, Scalia voted to uphold the Missouri regulations, and he pushed his colleagues also to overturn *Roe v. Wade*. "I just disagree with it," he said, insisting that the decision had gotten "no better as time" went on.[34] Four other justices were ready to reinstate the Missouri law: Rehnquist, White, O'Connor, and Kennedy.

Yet there were divisions among that five-justice majority over how to handle *Roe v. Wade*. Whether it should be reexamined was not squarely before the justices and had not been subjected to full briefing from both sides of the dispute as had the specific provisions of Missouri's law. Even Rehnquist and White, the lone dissenters in the 1973 *Roe v. Wade* case, were reluctant to use *Webster v. Reproductive Health Services* to directly attack *Roe*. The chief justice began writing an opinion for the majority that would allow abortion restrictions to stand if they "reasonably further the state's interest in protecting potential human life." That standard was a far more lenient test of abortion regulations and a major departure from *Roe*. Justice Stevens, a dissenter, wrote to Rehnquist, "Because the test really rejects *Roe v. Wade* in its entirety, I would think that it would be much better for the Court, as an institution, to do so forthrightly rather than indirectly." Stevens continued, "As you know, I am not in favor of overruling *Roe v. Wade*, but if the deed is to be done, I would rather see the Court give the case a decent burial instead of tossing it out the window of a fast-moving caboose."

Only Scalia was ready to give *Roe* that public burial. Blackmun, the author of *Roe v. Wade*, was disturbed by Rehnquist's aim of silently overruling it and alarmed by Scalia's wanting it explicitly rejected. Blackmun did not want to return this intense issue to state control for what he termed "the quintessentially intimate, personal, and life-directing decision whether to carry a fetus to term."[35]

Further, to address specifically Scalia's attempt to leave the matter to the democratic process, Blackmun included in the opinion he was drafting a quote from the Court's 1943 *West Virginia State Board of Education v. Barnette* decision: "The very purpose of a Bill of Rights was to withdraw certain subjects from the vicissitudes of political controversy, to place them beyond the reach of majorities and officials and to establish them as legal principles to be applied by the Courts."[36] Blackmun continued, "In a Nation that cherishes liberty, the ability of a woman to control the biological operation of her body and to determine with her responsible physician whether or not to carry a fetus to term, must lie within that limited sphere of individual autonomy that lies beyond the will or the power of any transient majority. This Court stands as the ultimate guarantor of that zone of privacy, regardless of the bitter disputes to which our decisions may give rise."

The outcome of the case was determined by Justice O'Connor, who in the spring of 1989 was emerging as a crucial, influential justice on numerous dilemmas before the Court. The addition of the conservative Kennedy a year earlier had put her squarely in the middle of a divided bench. A naturally tentative jurist who kept an eye on trends in state legislatures, O'Connor's personal inclination was not to move the law much in either direction. She agreed to uphold the Missouri regulations but declined to join any of Rehnquist's undermining of *Roe*. Justice O'Connor, who only six years earlier had disparaged the reasoning of *Roe* as she voted to uphold strict Ohio abortion regulations, had no interest in being the fifth vote to overrule *Roe* at present. In sketching out her objections to Rehnquist's opinion, which was still joined by Scalia, White, and Kennedy, she wrote, "When the constitutional invalidity of a State's abortion statute actually turns on the constitutional validity of *Roe v. Wade*, there will be time enough to reexamine *Roe*. And to do so carefully." It would emerge that O'Connor was slowly reconsidering whether *Roe* should ever be overturned.

Since she would have been the key fifth vote to gut *Roe*, Scalia was livid about O'Connor's equivocation: "We can now look forward to at least another term with carts full of mail from the public, and streets full of demonstrators, urging us—their unelected and life-tenured judges who have been awarded those extraordinary, undemocratic characteristics precisely in order that we might follow the law despite the popular will—to follow the popular will. Indeed, I expect we can look forward to even more of that than before, given our indecisive decision today." Taking specific aim at O'Connor's opinion, Scalia wrote that her rationale "cannot be taken seriously" and that "of the four courses we might have chosen today—to reaffirm *Roe*, to overrule it explicitly, to overrule it sub silentio, or to avoid the question—the last is the least responsible."

That Scalia statement in *Webster v. Reproductive Health Services* probably was on the mind of the retired Justice Powell when he wrote to O'Connor a few days later: "I cannot recall a previous term in which there were as many concurring and dissenting opinions. Some of the intemperate language in dissents reached the level of personal criticism. This, if this trend continues, could lessen public respect for the Court as an institution."[37]

Scalia's strong language reflected the passion he felt about this issue. He viewed *Roe* as perhaps uniquely offensive as a judicial usurpation of a choice that, given the moral claims on both sides and the absence of a specific answer in the Constitution's text, had to remain one for the political process. And he thought that the contrary lesson about the proper judicial role taught by *Roe* was so pernicious that the usual imperative to decide cases narrowly should be overridden. In pressing his colleagues to reach out and overturn *Roe v. Wade*, he wrote, "The real question . . . is whether there are valid reasons to go beyond the most stingy possible holding today. It seems to me there are not only valid but compelling ones. Ordinarily, speaking no more broadly than is absolutely required avoids throwing settled law into confusion; doing so today preserves a chaos that is evident to anyone who can read and count. Alone sufficient to justify a broad holding is the fact that our retaining control, through *Roe*, of what I believe to be, and many of our citizens recognize to be, a political issue, continuously distorts the public perception of the role of this Court."

Scalia certainly held views—fervent views consistent with his religious beliefs—about the moral issue of whether women should have abortions and the policy issue of whether laws should permit or forbid that choice. But he repeatedly insisted that his fervidly argued position in the Supreme Court cases was a legal one—simply about whether the Constitution spoke on the matter. "My difficulty with *Roe v. Wade* is a legal rather than a moral one," Scalia said in a 2002 appearance. "I do not believe—and no one believed for 200 years—that the Constitution contains a right to abortion. And if a state were to permit abortion on demand, I would and could in good conscience vote against an attempt to invalidate that law, for the same reason that I vote against invalidation of laws that contradict *Roe v. Wade*; namely, simply because the Constitution gives the federal government and, hence, me no power over the matter."[38]

After the Missouri case ruling, there was virtually no commentary on the religious affiliations of the justices. After all, while the Catholics Scalia and Kennedy were in the majority to uphold the abortion restriction, the Catholic Brennan voted to strike it down. Yet perhaps foreshadowing the kind of commentary that would come in later years, some legal analysts noted in a more general vein that the addition of Kennedy (in February 1988) meant that for the first time in the Court's two-hundred-year history, three Roman Catholics were serving at the same time. As a result, the Sweet Briar College professor Barbara Perry noted in a 1990 article in the *Journal of Law and Politics*, "the questions concerning the relationship between religion and nominations to the Supreme Court have now assumed a more urgent character."[39]

When abortion returned to the Court three years later, Scalia believed he now could have a majority to win reversal of *Roe v. Wade*. By 1992 Clarence Thomas, an opponent of abortion rights, had succeeded Thurgood Marshall, an abortion rights advocate. So if the same foursome from the 1989 Missouri case stuck together (Rehnquist, White, Scalia, and Kennedy), there would be a five-justice majority to overturn *Roe v. Wade*. David Souter, who succeeded Brennan in 1990, had made clear to his colleagues that he did not want to reconsider the constitutional right to abortion. Scalia was not counting on him. Scalia was, however, counting on Kennedy. And the prospect of finally reversing *Roe* heartened Scalia.

The Pennsylvania law in dispute required a woman to tell her husband of her intention to obtain an abortion. The statute also imposed a twenty-four-hour waiting period and required that physicians, to obtain an "informed consent," provide exhaustive information about the fetus and the abortion ahead of time. A federal appeals court had upheld the provision, and Planned Parenthood of Southeastern Pennsylvania had appealed to the justices.

Three years earlier, O'Connor had hedged. Now Kennedy was shifting his position. After oral arguments in the case, Kennedy joined a secret alliance with O'Connor and Souter to endorse the principles of *Roe v. Wade*. Kennedy had concluded that an abortion decision was a personal choice protected by the concept of privacy within the Constitution's prohibition on deprivations of liberty without due process. With O'Connor's past writings as a starting point for their rationale, the threesome worked quickly together, dividing up the writing of the opinion, and kept their efforts quiet from the other justices to avoid being pressured by either side. Shortly before they would make their determinative draft opinion available to their colleagues, Kennedy wrote a personal note to Blackmun, the author of the 1973 *Roe v. Wade*. "I need to see you as soon as you have a few free moments. I want to tell you about some developments in *Planned Parenthood v. Casey*, and I think part of what I say should come as welcome news."

When Scalia got wind of what was going on, he was furious. "It was no more than a couple of days [before] the opinion of the three of them circulated" to colleagues for comment, Scalia recalled when asked about how he discovered Kennedy's changed position. Scalia was reluctant in a later interview to reveal how much he had tried to convince Kennedy to stick with his prior position that *Roe* should be overruled. "I talked to Tony about it," Scalia said. "I don't recall that I talked to him after [the joint opinion] had circulated. But I talked to him when he had not yet joined the majority."[40] The opinion by Justices O'Connor, Kennedy, and Souter was largely endorsed by the liberal Justices Blackmun and Stevens to form a majority affirming *Roe v. Wade*.

In their first paragraph, O'Connor, Kennedy, and Souter noted with some exasperation that five times in the last decade the Reagan and Bush administrations had asked that they invalidate *Roe.* "Liberty finds no refuge in a jurisprudence of doubt," they declared. The justices went on to describe how the right to end a pregnancy had become part of women's economic liberation and part of contemporary America's way of life.[41] They emphasized that however they may feel personally about abortion, the right had become part of liberty in America. "Some of us as individuals find abortion offensive . . . but that cannot control our decision," they wrote, referring to the reality that for two decades people had lived their lives with the freedom to have abortions and that any change would have great social repercussions.

In his dissent, Scalia first mocked the opening line of the plurality's opinion—"Liberty finds no refuge in a jurisprudence of doubt"—and asserted that the opinion made little clear. "There is a poignant aspect to today's opinion," he wrote. "Its length, and what might be called its epic tone, suggest that its authors believe they are bringing to an end a troublesome era in the history of our nation, and of our Court. 'It is the dimension' of authority, they say, to call the contending sides of national controversy to end their national division by accepting a common mandate rooted in the Constitution." Scalia warned that it would never happen, and he concluded, "We should get out of this area, where we have no right to be, and where we do neither ourselves nor the country any good by remaining."

After the Court's stunning decision was made public on June 29, 1992, the columnists Rowland Evans and Robert Novak suggested that Kennedy's switch was due to the influence of the liberal Harvard law professor Laurence H. Tribe. The columnists also said that Scalia had driven to Kennedy's home "to argue with him about his reversal."[42] Years later, Scalia declined to talk about what happened between him and Kennedy.

Kennedy's changed position diffused any discussion at that point, however, over whether justices generally were voting their Catholicism in abortion cases. Of the Court's two practicing Catholics, one voted to overturn *Roe,* one to affirm it. (The Catholic Brennan retired two years before the *Planned Parenthood v. Casey* decision.)

Four years later the Court gained a third practicing Catholic as Justice Thomas revealed that—after years of attending a Pentecostal church—he had returned to the Catholicism of his youth. Thomas, in fact, had once considered becoming a priest and attended seminary school. Thomas's new Catholicism, and the addition of two Jewish members at that point (Justices Ruth Bader Ginsburg and Stephen Breyer), meant that for the first time in the nation's history, there was no longer a Protestant majority on the Court. It was a shift that passed almost unnoticed by the news media, largely because it was a symbolic rather than substantive transformation. It was, however, remarkable in a nation that had been shaped by a strong Protestant ethos. The University of Texas law professor Douglas Laycock observed in an interview at the time, "In terms of the long run of history, the Protestant dominance has been overwhelming. Here is a very elite institution where for the first time Protestants are in a minority. This serves as a marking point as we look to a future with a more pluralistic society." Laycock also noted in 1996 that where once the country had been marked by divisions between Protestants and Catholics, new divisions had emerged between fundamentalists of any faith and those who were more willing to adapt their beliefs to contemporary society.[43] Perhaps that was why someone devoted to traditional Catholicism might find himself more aligned with evangelical Protestants than with Catholics who inconsistently adhered to the teachings of Rome.

The abortion debate turned more emotional eight years later, in 2000, when the justices took up a challenge to a procedure its critics called "partial birth." The method, used midterm before a fetus would be capable of living outside the mother, was known medically as dilation and extraction (or D&X). It involved dilating a woman's cervix to allow most of the fetus to emerge into the vagina intact rather than dismembering the fetus in the uterus by using forceps and other instruments. Critics likened the method, which medical advocates said could be the safest procedure for some women, to infanticide.

Nebraska, along with thirty other states, banned the procedure. The Omaha physician Leroy Carhart challenged the law as a burden on a woman's right to end a pregnancy. He said the method was sometimes the best for the woman in the second trimester because it could mean less trauma and injury to the uterus. He also contended that the Nebraska law was so vaguely worded that it could cover and criminalize other abortion procedures. The statute defined the banned method as "an abortion procedure in which the person performing the abortion partially delivers vaginally a living unborn child, or a substantial portion thereof" before causing the fetus's death and ending the pregnancy.

The so-called partial-birth procedure was used in only a small fraction of abortions performed each year, yet the controversial method took on great significance legally and politically, especially since the dispute over it came during a presidential election season where the candidates were the Texas Republican governor, George Bush, and the Democratic vice president, Al Gore. Unlike the basic question of whether women should have the right to end a pregnancy, the dispute over this particular abortion method conjured up more complicated social, and ultimately legal, questions.

Carhart won in lower courts, and after the justices heard the state's appeal in *Stenberg v. Carhart*, their vote was another narrow, bitter 5–4 to strike down the Nebraska ban. In the majority were Justices Stevens, O'Connor, Souter, Ruth Bader Ginsburg (who had succeeded the abortion rights opponent White), and Stephen Breyer (who had succeeded the abortion rights supporter Blackmun). The majority faulted Nebraska for a vaguely written statute that could have covered not only the contentious, purportedly infanticidal D&X method but also a more commonly used method known as dilation and evacuation (D&E). "All those who perform abortion procedures using that (D&E) method must fear prosecution, conviction, and imprisonment," Justice Breyer wrote for the majority. "The result is an undue burden upon a woman's right to make an abortion decision." He also said on behalf of the majority that the law should have provided an exception for when a physician may find the method the best for the mother.

Addressing the broader national feelings invoked in the case, Breyer wrote, "Millions of Americans believe that life begins at conception and consequently that an abortion is akin to causing the death of an innocent child; they recoil at the thought of a law that would permit it. Other millions fear that a law that forbids abortion would condemn many American women to lives that lack dignity, depriving them of equal liberty and leading those with least resources to undergo illegal abortions with the attendant risks of death and suffering."[44]

Justice O'Connor cast the critical fifth vote. She agreed that the banned procedure could, in some situations for some women, be the safest method of ending a pregnancy. She wrote a separate statement detailing how such a "partial-birth" ban could be constitutional if it had an exception to protect women's health. This time around, Justice Kennedy dissented, declaring that he felt betrayed by his fellow justices from the 1992 *Planned Parenthood v. Casey* case.

Kennedy called the disputed procedure "abhorrent" and said that elected lawmakers, not judges, should decide which abortion methods should be permitted and whether one is so extreme it never need be used. "Ignoring substantial medical and ethical opinion," Kennedy wrote, "the Court substitutes its own judgment for the judgment of Nebraska and some 30 other states and sweeps the law away." He also accused the majority of corrupting the standard articulated in the 1992 *Casey* decision. Kennedy insisted that the joint opinion from *Casey* had left states an "important constitutional role in defining their interests in the abortion debate," and he said that Nebraska was exercising "concern for the life of the unborn and for the partially born." Kennedy's fellow dissenters, Chief Justice Rehnquist and Justices Scalia and Thomas, also wrote separate statements opposing the majority's position.

As usual, Scalia's opinion stood out. Although Kennedy was on Scalia's side, Scalia fired shots specifically at him. "There is no cause for anyone who believes in *Casey* to feel betrayed by this outcome," Scalia wrote. "It has been arrived at by precisely the process *Casey* promised—a democratic vote by nine lawyers, not on the question whether the text of the Constitution has anything to say about this subject (it obviously does not); nor even on the question (also appropriate for lawyers) whether the legal traditions of the American people would have sustained such a limitation upon abortion (they obviously would); but upon the pure policy question whether this limitation upon abortion is 'undue,'—i.e., goes too far . . . While I am in an I-told-you-so mood, I must recall my bemusement, in *Casey*, at the joint opinion's expressed belief that *Roe v. Wade* had 'call[ed] the contending sides of a national controversy to end their national divisions.' "

Scalia had opened his dissent from the June 28, 2000, majority opinion by saying, "I am optimistic enough to believe that, one day, *Stenberg v. Carhart* will be assigned its rightful place in the history of this Court's jurisprudence beside *Korematsu* [upholding the Japanese internment during World War II] and *Dred Scott* [allowing slavery and helping to start the American Civil War]. The method of killing a human child—one cannot even accurately say an entirely unborn human child—proscribed by this statute is so horrible that the most clinical description of it evokes a shudder of revulsion."

Scalia did not have to wait long for *Stenberg v. Carhart* to be history. The Court's position on the validity of so-called partial-birth abortion laws changed after Justice O'Connor retired on January 31, 2006. Her replacement by Justice Samuel Alito caused another set of shifting alliances and another 5–4 abortion vote. This time Scalia was in the majority—which by this point consisted of five Catholic justices.

The 2003 federal ban on the procedure did not include an exception for maternal health—which O'Connor had said must be included to ensure that no "undue burden" is put on the pregnant woman. In passing the law, the Republican-controlled Congress, with support from about a quarter of the Democrats, had declared in special findings that the procedure was "never" necessary for the health of the mother. Congress had twice earlier tried to adopt such a ban, and twice President Bill Clinton vetoed the legislation. President George W. Bush had signed the 2003 law that came before the Court. The legislation also generated unlikely alliances. Some members of Congress who supported a basic abortion right voted for the ban. Among them were the Senate Judiciary Committee members Joseph Biden, a Delaware Democrat, and Patrick Leahy, a Vermont Democrat, both Catholics.

The statute defined the forbidden procedure as one in which a physician "deliberately and intentionally vaginally delivers a living fetus until, in the case of a head first presentation, the entire fetal head is outside the body of the mother, or, in the case of a breech presentation, any part of the fetal trunk past the navel is outside the body of the mother, for the purpose of performing an overt act that the person knows will kill the partially delivered living fetus." Again, the physician Leroy Carhart challenged the law. This time he was vigorously backed by numerous medical groups. They said that removing the fetus in one piece and causing its death when partway out could be safer for women in some circumstances because it involved fewer medical instruments that could damage the uterus and cause complications.

The justices upheld the ban in April 2007, marking the first time since the 1973 *Roe v. Wade* that the Court said governments could ban a particular abortion procedure. The decision emphasized the value of fetal life over a woman's right to end a pregnancy. Again Kennedy was in a key position, this time writing for the majority. He stressed that government "may use its voice and its regulatory authority to show its profound respect for the life within the woman." Kennedy also emphasized "the bond of love" a mother typically has for a child and said that some women regret their decision to abort.[45]

Kennedy distinguished the federal ban from the earlier Nebraska prohibition by noting that Congress had held hearings that purported to establish that "intact dilation and evacuation" (similar to the "dilation and extraction" at issue in the 2000 case) was never a medically appropriate option. Now, even though there were five votes to uphold *Roe*—Stevens, Souter, Ginsburg, Breyer, and Kennedy—there were five votes, because of Kennedy's crossover position, to allow more regulation of abortion, including a ban on a particular method.

Kennedy was joined by the Court's four other Catholics: Scalia, Thomas, and its newest members, Samuel Alito and Chief Justice John Roberts. The dissenters in *Gonzales v. Carhart* were Protestant (Stevens and Souter) and Jewish (Ginsburg and Breyer).

Given that alignment, it was easy for critics to link the decision—at least the majority's position—to a religious perspective. The *Philadelphia Inquirer* cartoonist Tony Auth, for example, drew the justices in the majority wearing bishops' miters. One of the most incendiary criticisms of the ruling came from the University of Chicago law professor Geoffrey Stone, a former dean of the law school and provost of the university. Professor Stone insisted that the Court majority had no sound legal basis for its decision to endorse the congressional findings that the procedure could "never" be best for a woman. "[T]here is a clear medical consensus that in particular circumstances intact D&E is necessary to protect the health of the woman," Stone wrote in an essay on a University of Chicago blog referring to various studies and medical school curricula. Much of his essay was reprinted in the *Chicago Tribune* in a piece entitled "Our Faith-Based Justices."[46]

Stone, who had been a colleague of Scalia's at the University of Chicago in the early 1980s, went on to say, "What, then, explains this decision? Here is a painfully awkward observation: All five justices in the majority in *Gonzales* are Catholic. The four justices who are either Protestant or Jewish all voted in accord with settled precedent. It is mortifying to have to point this out. But it is too obvious, and too telling, to ignore. Ultimately, the five justices in the majority all fell back on a common argument to justify their position. There is, they say, a compelling moral reason for the result in *Gonzales*. Because the intact D&E seems to resemble infanticide it is 'immoral' and may be prohibited even without a clear statutory exception to protect the health of the woman. By making this judgment, these justices have failed to respect the fundamental difference between religious belief and morality. To be sure, this can be an elusive distinction, but in a society that values the separation of church and state, it is fundamental."

Stone acknowledged that all Catholic justices were not, historically, steered by their religion, including William Brennan, for whom Stone was a law clerk and who had voted consistently in favor of abortion rights. Stone asserted that things were different for the five Catholics presently on the Court.

For his part, Scalia took Stone's assertions about the role Catholicism played in the decision personally. "Now, he knows that that's a damn lie," Scalia said in an interview. He then referred to the fact that Justice Kennedy, while voting to uphold the partial-birth ban, had endorsed *Roe v. Wade* in 1992. Scalia also referred to Brennan's having been at the forefront of developing constitutional protection for privacy and reproductive rights.[47]

Professor Stone, Scalia insisted, "knows that Tony Kennedy is the fifth vote supporting *Roe v. Wade*. And he knows that Bill Brennan was a Catholic and he invented the whole thing. And he knows what my judicial philosophy is and that I take neither side of that . . . That really got me mad . . . It got me so mad I will not appear at the University of Chicago until he is no longer on the faculty . . . What made it so annoying was I had been very pleased and sort of proud that Americans didn't pay any attention to that. It isn't religion that divides us anymore . . . It didn't bother anybody, but it has to bother this great liberal Geof Stone."[48]

It was true that there had been scant attention to the justices' religion when—within a span of five months—Roberts and Alito became the fourth and fifth Catholics on the bench. But Stone's blog post helped ignite renewed interest. His views generated scores of postings on his blog, including many that were critical. For example, one found Professor

Stone's commentary to reflect "the not-so-soft bigotry against Catholics and/or Catholicism that pervades the 'upper echelons' of the media and academia."[49] Yet Stone's piece also inspired other essays and news stories about the Catholicism of the majority. *The Washington Post* began an article this way: "Is it significant that the five Supreme Court justices who voted to uphold the federal ban on a controversial abortion procedure also happen to be the court's Roman Catholics?" The story went on to present dueling answers.[50] *The New York Times*'s Robin Toner observed that because of the abortion decision, debate over the influence of religion on the justices "has moved from the theoretical to the concrete."[51]

Professor Stone had not anticipated the outpouring of criticism when he made the Catholic connection in *Gonzales v. Carhart*, but he soon realized he had struck a nerve. "Scalia's reaction was completely different from what I would have anticipated when I wrote the piece," Stone said in a 2009 interview. "But it turned out his reaction was not out of the ordinary. I received all sorts of critical comments from people who identified themselves as Catholic." Stone said some audiences, even two years later and notably at Catholic schools, continued to bring up the essay when he gave speeches. Yet Scalia's response was different from others who complained. He and Stone had played poker together when Scalia was teaching at the University of Chicago, and they were friendly colleagues. Stone said he respected Scalia and would have preferred to have heard directly from him about his response to the essay.

"Scalia is, of course, right that his general view about abortion is consistent with his larger judicial philosophy," Stone said. "*Roe v. Wade* is not defensible from the standpoint of an originalist. But what made the *Carhart* case noteworthy was that the governing precedent was so clear. What caught my interest was that in a situation in which any open-minded and responsible judge would simply have gritted his teeth and followed the precedent, these five justices simply couldn't bring themselves to do so. Instead, they felt impelled to write a patently disingenuous opinion to avoid following a recent and clearly controlling decision. This wasn't the product of a conservative judicial philosophy. It was the product of something more powerful. The only plausible explanation for their behavior was that they had a deep moral revulsion to following the law in this case." Stone added that "of course I might be wrong. But I thought it was appropriate and necessary to raise the question."[52]

Testing the religious, political, or other nonjudicial inclinations of a judge was no easy task. The nature of judging dictated that a jurist's reasons for a vote were explained through law, through precedent, through references to statutes and the Constitution. No Supreme Court justice ever said he or she voted based on personal or political, let alone religious, views. Further, the five justices in the 2007 *Carhart* majority had demonstrated their general conservatism and narrow approach to individual rights in many areas never considered to be touched by religious beliefs. And Scalia, in particular, had vigorously presented an approach to constitutional decision making that had a coherence independent of any religious views. Nevertheless, chatter about the connection between religious beliefs and judicial rulings could and did emerge in mainstream discussions when the topic was abortion, about which passions ran high. And, in fact, Kennedy's comments about how a woman might feel about aborting a fetus, because of "the bond of love" for a child, gave the majority opinion a personal and emotional cast.

Some of the debate over the justices' personal religious views was fueled, in Scalia's case, by his strong and repeatedly expressed views that the Court had gone too far in separating church and state. Scalia never veered from the path he had set in his early years on the bench, when he dissented as the majority struck down a Louisiana law requiring the teaching of creation science and faculty-arranged prayer at public high school graduations. He wanted to allow more government involvement with religious activities, more government support for religion—for example, in the form of vouchers for parents to send children to parochial schools.[53]

"In no opinion that he has authored while on the Court has he found an Establishment Clause violation in a challenged law," the Stanford law professor Kathleen Sullivan observed, referring to the constitutional declaration that government "make no law respecting an establishment of religion." Sullivan contended that Scalia viewed religion as having a "relatively benign role in politics"—a view at odds with the framers' vision. Referring to his minimizing of free-exercise exemptions, for example in the 1990 peyote case, and his opinions seeking lower barriers to government involvement with religion, Sullivan asserted that "his stance reflects, at least implicitly, a specific vision of religion and religious politics. In this view, religion is assimilated into the give and take of modern political life." She argued that under his approach, "religious lobbyists might seek vouchers for religious schools in the same way that, say, farmers lobby for agricultural subsidies, or other nonprofit groups lobby for income or property tax exemptions."[54]

Scalia showed no sign of breaking that pattern as his tenure lengthened. In fact, he abandoned his usual deference for the will of the majority only when a state legislature limited aid to religion. Washington State offered tax-financed scholarships for college students but excluded individuals seeking to use the grants at religious colleges or to major in theology. When the high court majority upheld the program in 2004, Scalia dissented, separating himself from Chief Justice Rehnquist and joined only by Thomas.

Rehnquist, writing for the majority, said, "The state has merely chosen not to fund a distinct category of instruction." His decision, together with a ruling two years earlier allowing governments to give parents publicly financed "vouchers" for religious schools, essentially meant that while such "school choice" programs were constitutionally permissible, they were not constitutionally required. Scalia disagreed, insisting that a state offering scholarships for college students should not be allowed to exclude qualified religious students. "One need not delve too far into modern popular culture to perceive a trendy disdain for deep religious conviction," he wrote, echoing some of his 1996 reaction against the "worldly wise." Addressing the Washington State scholarship exemption for theology students, Scalia added, "What next? Will we deny priests and nuns their prescription-drug benefits on the ground that taxpayers' freedom of conscience forbids medicating the clergy at public expense?"[55]

One of his most controversial writings on religion came soon after, as a narrowly divided Court struck down the posting of the Ten Commandments in two Kentucky courthouses. The majority viewed the Commandments as a sacred text and insisted that local officials remain neutral toward religion.[56] To the consternation of Scalia, the more liberal justices who controlled the outcome called for increased scrutiny of the motives of local elected officials who seek to post the Ten Commandments. "The divisiveness of religion in current public life is inescapable," Justice Souter wrote for the majority. "This is no time to deny the prudence of understanding the Establishment Clause to require the government to stay neutral on religious belief, which is reserved for the conscience of the individual." Souter was joined by Justices Stevens, Ginsburg, Breyer, and the swing vote, O'Connor.

In a concurring statement touching on some of the religion-related turmoil, O'Connor said, "[T]he goal of the [Constitution's provisions on religion] is clear: to carry out the Founders' plan of preserving religious liberty to the fullest extent possible in a pluralistic society . . . [W]e have kept religion a matter for the individual conscience, not for the prosecutor or bureaucrat. At a time when we see around the world the violent consequences of the assumption of religious authority by government, Americans may count themselves fortunate: Our regard for constitutional boundaries has protected us from similar travails, while allowing private religious exercises to flourish."

In his dissent, Scalia insisted that the posting of the Ten Commandments by government officials was constitutional. He said the nation's history and the understanding of the Constitution's drafters allowed "acknowledgment of a single Creator." In such acknowledgment, he believed, the Constitution permitted the favoring of believers over nonbelievers and permitted a preference for Judeo-Christian monotheism over all other religions. When government officials give thanks to "God," Scalia wrote, joined by Chief Justice Rehnquist and Justice Thomas, "it is entirely clear from our nation's historical practices that the Establishment Clause permits this disregard of polytheists and believers in unconcerned deities, just as it permits the disregard of devout atheists." In this context, he did not believe the state was wrong to favor monotheistic religions over, for example, Hinduism and Buddhism.

The George Washington University law professor Thomas Colby expressed doubt that Scalia's decisions derived from a neutral "originalist" reading of the Constitution. He argued in a law review article that Scalia's vote to allow "government . . . to endorse Judeo-Christian monotheism" and his general support for religion in public places flowed, rather, from conservative political convictions.[57]

Scalia repeatedly insisted that his personal views, including those on religion, did not infect his decisions. "I try mightily to prevent my religious views or my political views or my philosophical views from affecting my interpretation of the laws, which is what my job is all about," Scalia said at a Pew Forum on Religion and Public Life at the University of

Chicago. At that forum, it was pointed out that Scalia did not follow Catholic teaching against the death penalty. Indeed, Scalia had said as much when he asserted that his religious views did not influence his rulings. Scalia could not resist, however, trying to score a point in the debate within the Church. He observed that Pope John Paul II's general opposition to the death penalty in "Evangelium Vitae" was not "binding teaching."

In an interview years later, Scalia cited his own religious beliefs to differentiate his approach to the Constitution from the approach of those who believed it could be interpreted through a contemporary lens to help address society's problems. "If I were an evolving constitutionalist, how could I keep my religion out of it?" he asked. "That is precisely one of the reasons I like textualism. It is an objective criterion that you can repair to, and if you find what that understanding [regarding a particular constitutional provision] was at the time, you don't have to inject your own biases and prejudices."[58]

Professor Kannar, the author of an early influential piece on Scalia's "catechism," argued that Scalia's conservative Catholicism was not unlike the religious fundamentalism that emerged in the early 1980s during the Reagan administration, which was also promoting the originalism theory of constitutional interpretation. "The analogy between a literal interpretation of the religious Bible and an 'originalist' interpretation of the civil one is not hard to make or understand," Kannar wrote. "The attitude of self-assurance toward discerning God's intent displayed by fundamentalist interpreters of the Bible bears striking similarities to the assurance displayed by many constitutional 'originalists' concerning the ability of contemporary judges to ascertain and apply the intent of the Founding generation."

More recently dubious of Scalia's insistence that his brand of originalism produces neutral rationales, Julia Vitullo-Martin ironically observed in *Commonweal* that "the sins of textualism and Catholicism are not unrelated—both reflect respect for the written word, an ordered universe, and an attachment to tradition. And both have a long contentious relationship with liberalism." Vitullo-Martin's 2003 piece in the social-political journal run by lay Catholics termed Scalia a "most strident Catholic" and, surveying the sweep of his decisions, concluded, "Is Antonin Scalia an opportunist or an originalist? Perhaps he is both."[59]

Scalia could not separate his constitutional views from the core of his identity, which was decidedly Catholic. Professor Kannar rightly asserted, "Whatever he may represent politically, Justice Scalia is also an individual in whom constitutional theory and personal identity fuse."

Scalia was a product of his immigrant background, his traditional upbringing, and his devout Catholicism. President Reagan and his team probably did not consider Scalia's Catholicism when they chose him, except as it might have suggested his views against abortion. Yet it was a very traditional Catholic Scalia who joined the Court in 1986, a jurist who only a few months before his nomination had said in a speech that legal views are "inevitably affected by moral and theological perceptions."[60] More than two decades later he would still suggest that such influences, while not determinative in rulings, were inevitable in one's overall thinking. He recalled the lasting lesson from his years with the Jesuits at Georgetown University: "[Do] not . . . separate your religious life from your intellectual life. They're not separate."[61]

TEN

"A COUNTRY I DO NOT RECOGNIZE"

On an October morning in 1995, Justice Scalia drove from his home in the leafy upscale suburb of McLean across the Potomac River into Washington and east to the Supreme Court. He was just a few days into his tenth term. Up first on the calendar would be a case that troubled him deeply. As he drove around to the back of the Court building to the underground garage, he missed the action at the front of the marble-columned building. Extra police officers were on duty, and there was a long line of people waiting to get in. The previous day, gay rights activists had demonstrated. During the night, gay men and lesbians had camped out on the marble steps in order to be at the head of the line for courtroom seats.[1]

The dispute to be heard revolved around a constitutional amendment that Colorado voters had adopted in November 1992 to stop cities from banning discrimination based on sexual orientation. Liberal enclaves in the state, such as Aspen and Boulder, had passed ordinances that protected gays from discrimination in housing, employment, and public services. Those cities were part of a national trend in liberal and urban areas to prohibit discrimination based on sexual orientation. Sponsors of the 1992 Colorado provision, known as Amendment 2, claimed that such ordinances gave unwarranted special protection to gay men and lesbians. The amendment repealed all such laws shielding gay people from discrimination and prohibited the enactment of any new laws that would offer protection.

Scalia was well-disposed toward Colorado voters' effort to prevent cities from passing ordinances to protect gay people. Homosexuals, he believed, were a politically powerful force, well financed, and skillful in claiming media attention. He scoffed at those who treated gay men and lesbians as "victims." He believed homosexuals had the ear of political leaders and were coddled by elite lawyers, who in the case now before the Court had filed briefs arguing against Colorado's antigay amendment. Scalia was particularly annoyed that the Association of American Law Schools required that law firms recruiting on their campuses sign a pledge that they were willing to hire homosexuals. In Scalia's mind, Colorado's constitutional amendment was a legitimate counter to gay activism and a means of preserving traditional sexual mores. He disagreed with a decision by the Colorado Supreme Court, now before the justices for review, that Amendment 2, intending to stop protection for gay people, violated the U.S. Constitution's equality guarantee.

A month before the Court's oral arguments Scalia had told a group at the University of Colorado in Boulder that judges should stay out of such social problems. "The question, 'What does society want?' is not a lawyer's question. It's a legislator's question," Scalia said.[2] Those challenging the antigay prohibition had a different focus, of course. They looked to judges to interpret the Constitution to shield the rights of people with unpopular causes that may not be taken up by elected legislators.

The appeal to the Supreme Court was filed by the Colorado governor Roy Romer. Yet, indicative of the many conflicts swirling around the gay rights dilemma, Romer personally opposed Amendment 2, spoke passionately against it, and was now in the awkward position of defending, on paper, the measure his state had adopted to end protections for gay men and lesbians. Going into the arguments, law clerks to the nine justices and other legal observers suspected that there were at least two other votes, with Scalia's, toward the five needed for a majority to reinstate Amendment 2. Certainly Chief Justice Rehnquist would be on Scalia's side. A consistent conservative on the bench for a quarter century, Rehnquist had voted in a 1986 case, *Bowers v. Hardwick*, to uphold state antisodomy laws that prohibited consensual homosexual conduct. That opinion had been grounded in the assertion that the country had a long history of forbidding consensual sodomy. Clarence Thomas also had proved himself an unswerving conservative, and like Scalia, he believed that too many of society's "victims" were clamoring for undeserved legal protection.

An official photograph of Antonin Scalia, Associate Justice of the Supreme Court of the United States
(Steve Petteway, Collection of the Supreme Court of the United States)

A young Scalia already exercising his Second Amendment rights at a statue on the grounds of Battle Monument, ca. 1939 (Scalia family)

Scalia's paternal family in Italy. The justice's father, Salvatore, is the rightmost boy in the front row; the young girl on the far left is Antonin's aunt Carmela. The man and woman in the rear center are his grandfather and grandmother. (Scalia family)

Scalia's parents, Salvatore Eugene Scalia and Catherine Panaro, ca. 1930
(Scalia family)

Scalia posing in 1949 in the uniform of the Order of the Arrow, an honor society for the Boy Scouts of America (Scalia family)

In the summers of his youth, Scalia would hunt with his grandfather. Here, at about ten years old, he demonstrates an early prowess with a long-barrel shotgun. (Scalia family)

Having failed the entrance exam at New York's Regis High School, his first choice, Scalia instead enrolled at Xavier Military High School in Manhattan, where he won a scholarship. He graduated in 1953. (Scalia family)

Scalia and Maureen McCarthy at their wedding, in September 1960. The couple met on a blind date at Harvard, where Scalia was pursuing his law degree. Maureen, who had initially planned to leave the date early, wound up falling for his lively sense of humor. (Scalia family)

The Scalias in 1962. Devout Catholics with an ever-growing family, both husband and wife were raised to believe "that you work hard and make your way," Maureen said. (Scalia family)

Justice Scalia and his wife surrounded by their nine children, ca. 2003. Scalia takes pride in the size of his family, crediting his wife "for raising them with very little assistance from me . . . And there's not a dullard in the bunch!" (Scalia family)

President Ronald Reagan and Antonin Scalia, June 1986. Reagan was impressed by Scalia's direct style and found a match in his deep-seated conservatism. (White House photograph)

Scalia speaking at his September 1986 investiture, after he and William Rehnquist had been sworn in to associate justice and chief justice seats. In court together, the two favored different styles; while Scalia preferred to debate and argue, Rehnquist disliked the loquaciousness of his colleagues and aspired to keep proceedings focused and fast. (White House photograph)

Peter Smith's now infamous 2006 photograph finds Scalia flicking his chin, a Sicilian gesture of debatable profanity. An editorial in the *Boston Herald*, which also published the picture, suggested that while the gesture may not have been obscene, "it's still not something you'd do to your mother." (Peter Smith, Boston University)

Herbert Block—better known by his pen name, "Herblock"—drew this 1996 political cartoon in response to Scalia's religiously charged Christian Legal Society speech. The justice contended that the country's Christian population was pitted against its secular "worldly wise," who couldn't abide belief in miracles. (Herbert Block)

Scalia, second from left, chats with Alan Greenspan, chairman of the Federal Reserve, at Secretary of Defense Donald Rumsfeld's home during a 2001 gathering for John E. Robson, president and chairman of the Export-Import Bank of the United States. (David Hume Kennerly)

Having successfully hunted this elk, Scalia—ever the sportsman—went on to mount it in his office. (Scalia family)

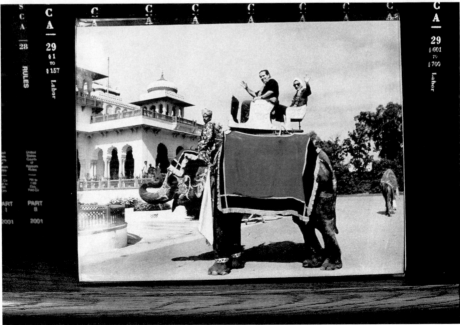

Though they have strikingly different personalities and approaches to the law, the conservative Scalia and the liberal Ruth Bader Ginsburg are longtime social friends. They attend the opera together, travel together, and celebrate each New Year's Eve together at a small dinner party. Their friendship dates to their time on a federal appellate court. Ginsburg has said that, no matter how infuriating Scalia can be to her regarding the law, he "can always make me laugh." (The Oyez Project)

The two moderate conservatives, Sandra Day O'Connor and Anthony Kennedy, had voted in prior cases against gay interests—O'Connor in the 1986 *Bowers* case and Kennedy as a lower court judge, to uphold navy regulations banning homosexuals.[3] Yet O'Connor and Kennedy both had been casting some votes on the left. The four liberal justices, based on their records, could be counted on to find Amendment 2 unconstitutional: John Paul Stevens, David Souter, Ruth Bader Ginsburg, and Stephen Breyer. All it would take was either O'Connor or Kennedy to vote on their side to make a five-justice majority.

At oral arguments, the justices faced a courtroom at capacity. Seated on one of the red upholstered benches was Richard Evans, the lead plaintiff challenging the Colorado law. Evans, an AIDS counselor in the Denver mayor's office, was one of six challengers who had come to Washington for the hearing. As the justices took their seats, Evans was overcome by the emotion of the moment. The Court was about to hear a case that went to the heart of his personal identity, an identity that he had discovered and accepted slowly, even reluctantly, two decades earlier, as a teenager.[4] Evans began to weep quietly. The woman next to him handed him her lace handkerchief.[5] From the center chair at the tall bench, Rehnquist declared, "We'll hear argument next in Number 94-1039, *Roy Romer v. Richard G. Evans*. Mr. Tymkovich."[6]

The Colorado solicitor general Timothy Tymkovich stepped to the lectern and began with the traditional formal salutation. "Mr. Chief Justice, and may it please the Court: This case involves a challenge to the authority of a state to allocate certain law-making power among its state and local governments. Colorado's Amendment 2 reserves to the state the decision of whether to extend special protections under state law on the basis of homosexual or bisexual conduct or orientation."

Tymkovich argued that Amendment 2 merely put gays in the same place as other persons in the state and ensured that they would not get special protection. The question for the justices revolved around the Fourteenth Amendment's equal protection guarantee and whether Colorado had—rather than merely taking away "special protection"—actually put homosexuals in a separate category from other residents by saying gays could not seek laws protecting them against discrimination. In short, were they now at an unconstitutional disadvantage in the political process, as the challengers and Colorado Supreme Court maintained?

About one minute into Tymkovich's argument, Justice Kennedy leaned forward to ask a question. "When we have an Equal Protection question, we measure the objective of the legislation," Kennedy said. "[H]ere, the classification [against the category of gay people] seems to be adopted for its own sake. I've never seen a case like this. Is there any precedent that you can cite to the Court where we've upheld a law such as this?" The question jarred Tymkovich, who seemed unprepared for such a doubtful reception from a potentially key justice so early in the arguments.

Kennedy's question suggested that he was not likely to use *Bowers v. Hardwick*, the case in which the Court said homosexuals did not have a constitutional right to engage in sodomy, to inform his decision on this new dispute. The question also revealed Kennedy's concern that gays had been put on unequal footing and would not be able even to seek antibias ordinances as other groups could.

Scalia knew such a line of questioning was not good for Colorado. As Tymkovich, only thirty-eight years old, struggled with Kennedy's query, Scalia offered possible parallels for Colorado's Amendment 2. "You have plenty of precedent [in] state laws that absolutely criminalize such activity, bigamy, homosexuality," Scalia told Tymkovich. To Scalia, homosexuals could not be separated from their conduct. If the 1986 *Bowers* case allowed states to criminalize consensual sodomy, why could states not then ensure that homosexuals were not given what Scalia believed was preferential treatment?

Scalia's attempt to answer Kennedy and to shape Tymkovich's argument was not unusual. While the hour-long arguments were designed to give lawyers an opportunity to put forth their best legal reasoning, the sessions also gave the justices a chance to make a case to one another. Scalia had a reputation for asking leading questions, and from his early days had been a dominating presence. Now, hearing the Colorado case, he understood that he was fighting a rising tide. As Tymkovich's thirty minutes at the lectern ran out and then Jean Dubofsky, representing Evans and the other challengers, stood up, Kennedy, and then O'Connor, another potential swing vote, asked questions that revealed their uneasiness with Colorado's measure. Scalia tried an appeal to his colleagues' regard for precedent. He asked Dubofsky, a fifty-two-year-old former state supreme court judge now in private practice, if she was asking the court to overrule the 1986 *Bowers v. Hardwick*.

"No, I am not," Dubofsky responded.

"Well, there we said that you could make homosexual conduct criminal," Scalia said. "Why can a state not take a step short of that and say, we're not going to make it criminal, but on the other hand, we certainly don't want to encourage it, and therefore we will neither have a state law giving it special protection, nor will we allow any municipalities to give it special protection . . . If you can criminalize it, surely you can take the latter step, can't you?"

"What you've done," Dubofsky replied, "is deprive people, based on their homosexual orientation, of a whole opportunity to seek protection from discrimination, which is a very different thing."

Kennedy seemed particularly receptive to Dubofsky's position.

Scalia could see defeat coming.

The justices talked next about the case a few days later in their private conference room, and the divisions from oral arguments played out. The vote was 6–3 to strike down the antigay law. Only Scalia, Rehnquist, and Thomas voted for the measure that would stop Colorado cities from shielding people based on sexual orientation. The six justices voting to strike it down were Stevens, O'Connor, Kennedy, Souter, Ginsburg, and Breyer. As the most senior justice in the majority, Stevens could decide to whom to assign the opinion. Stevens chose Kennedy. The elder justice wanted to make sure Kennedy stayed with the liberal-leaning majority. Scalia had a lot to say in dissent, and Rehnquist and Thomas agreed that he would speak best for the trio.

As the justices began writing their opinions and circulating drafts, Scalia's anger rose. Kennedy was asserting in his opinion for the majority that Amendment 2 flowed from "animus" toward gay people. It was not animus or hatred, Scalia believed, but rather the simple conviction of what was morally right and wrong. Kennedy also was making no reference to *Bowers v. Hardwick*, the Court's precedent on gay rights. Scalia seethed: How could Kennedy write an opinion that did not account for the 1986 case? In that decision, just ten years earlier, the Court had allowed homosexuality to be targeted for prosecution. To Scalia, the omission of any reference to *Bowers* revealed an intellectual dishonesty. Kennedy saw it differently. He was analyzing the case on equality grounds, not the due process privacy grounds that *Bowers* had tested.

As Scalia drafted his dissenting statement, he described the majority's

opinion as "long on emotive utterance" and "short on relevant legal citation." In laying out his legal grounds, he emphasized, true to his originalist view, that the Constitution said nothing about homosexuality, and any
questions on the subject should be left to state legislators and the usual
democratic process.

These were not new themes for Scalia. Nor was it unusual for him to
be shouting in dissent as he stood on principle. For nearly a decade as
a justice Scalia had been a loud and (largely) unheeded dissenter. The
majority had voted to affirm abortion rights and to reject school prayer as
he was left on the losing end.

Scalia was growing increasingly disenchanted about national politics,
too. In 1992 Bill Clinton had won the presidency, beating the incumbent,
George H. W. Bush. In 1993 Clinton appointed Ginsburg, a former
women's rights advocate, to the Court, to succeed Byron White. Ginsburg
was a personal friend of Scalia's but not an ally on the law. The Senate had
approved Ginsburg, the first appointee by a Democratic president since
Lyndon B. Johnson named Thurgood Marshall in 1967, by a vote of 96–3.
The following year, Clinton had appointed Stephen Breyer, a former law
professor and Boston-based U.S. court of appeals judge, to replace Harry
Blackmun. Breyer, too, won easy Senate confirmation, on a vote of 87–9.
Now, as the justices were continuing to work on the Colorado gay rights
case and the calendar turned to 1996, Clinton appeared to be on a winning
track against the Republican presidential candidate, the Kansas U.S. senator Bob Dole, and headed for reelection in November. Senator Dole was
trying to turn the federal bench into a campaign issue. He said that President Clinton's judicial appointments had set off a "crisis" in the courts and
that Clinton's reelection would undermine the judiciary with an "all-star
team of liberal leniency." Dole's effort was in vain. The character of the
federal bench, whether at the Supreme Court level or in the lower courts,
had no traction on the campaign trail or with voters in 1996.[7]

On March 11 Scalia's wife, Maureen, threw a surprise sixtieth birthday
party for her husband in the ornamental West Conference Room at the
Court. Most of Scalia's fellow justices and their spouses came. The milestone was not difficult for him. He was active, still playing squash and tennis, traveling regularly. He and Maureen had spent part of the previous
summer at a Riviera resort as a result of Hofstra University's invitation to
lecture in Nice, France. He also went to Moscow and St. Petersburg to

meet with Russian judges on a trip jointly sponsored by the United States Information Agency and a foundation at the University of Chicago Law School.[8]

Still, the frustration of his life's work on the Court was growing. In the justices' private votes in conference that spring, Scalia had lost on just about every case that mattered to him. He was in the process of writing dissents not only for *Romer v. Evans*, but also in disputes over whether a Virginia state-run military academy had to admit women and whether conversations between a psychiatrist and patient could be used at trial. As he talked with friends over pizza at A.V. Ristorante, Scalia wondered aloud about stepping down from the bench.

But he could, at least, give voice to his aggravation. His dissenting opinion in *Romer v. Evans* was beginning to take a more muscular approach than usual, not only on the law but on its social implications. His general goal for dissents was "get it on record and get it attention." This time, he was about to achieve his goal as never before.

When the opinions in the case were made public on May 20, 1996, seven months after the oral arguments, Scalia's opening sentence jolted legal observers: "The Court has mistaken a Kulturkampf for a fit of spite," he wrote, using in a positive vein the German word for "culture war." The word "Kulturkampf" originated with the German chancellor Otto von Bismarck's anti-Catholic tirade in the 1870s. But now, in the late twentieth century, the rhetoric of Patrick Buchanan and other political conservatives had brought "Kulturkampf" back in vogue. Buchanan had invoked it at the Republican National Convention in 1992 as he called on social conservatives to wage war with liberals. "We must take back our cities and take back our culture and take back our country," Buchanan had declared as he asserted that America was engaged in "a culture war, as critical to the kind of nation we will one day be as was the Cold War itself."[9]

Through his vivid rhetoric, Scalia was describing Colorado's law as less about animus or hatred of homosexuals than about efforts to "preserve traditional sexual mores against the efforts of a politically powerful minority to revise those mores through use of the laws."[10] Scalia referred to homosexuals as having "high disposable income" and "political power much greater than their numbers."[11] He lashed out at the Court for putting "the prestige of this institution behind the proposition that opposition to homosexuality is . . . reprehensible . . . The Court has no business

imposing upon all Americans the resolution favored by the elite class."
Kennedy had not used the word "reprehensible" in the majority opinion.
But his opinion did declare that "animus" toward homosexuals was not a
legitimate state purpose, and that was what Amendment 2 reflected.

For extra emphasis and to get more notice, Scalia read portions of his
dissenting statement from the bench that May morning. His voice rising as
he condemned the ruling, Scalia said the decision in *Romer v. Evans* undermined the structure of American law that he said allowed distinctions
between homosexual and heterosexual conduct. Scalia accused the Court
of signing on to the "so-called homosexual agenda." A few minutes earlier,
Kennedy had read aloud parts of his opinion, a document that would later
cause a number of gay and lesbian lawyers to weep in appreciation. Such
was the power of the competing emotions the opinions roused.

Scalia's dissent became as much a part of the story as the ruling itself.
It was excerpted in newspapers, and it ricocheted across radio airwaves. It
became the subject of editorials and letters to the editor. The tone of
Scalia's dissent, the *New Republic* wrote in an editorial, reflected "his own
fit of spite." The conservative *Weekly Standard* praised Scalia's opinion as a
"stinging critique of the questionable and dangerous logic" of the
Kennedy majority. Many other publications—some with him, most
against—quoted and editorialized on his provocative comments. People
were not just talking about the Court's decision, they were talking about
Scalia's take on it and commenting on his vitriol.[12]

His wrath seemed to reflect his frustration with his place on the Court
at that time. He conveyed the sense that the legal culture being affirmed
by the Court was leaving his views behind.

Around this time, he was alone in voting that the state-run Virginia
Military Institute should be able to keep excluding women applicants. "It
is precisely VMI's attachment to such old-fashioned concepts as manly
honor that has made it, and the system it represents, the target of those
who today succeed in abolishing public single-sex education," he wrote in
an opinion that would be released one month after *Romer v. Evans*, in
June 1996.[13]

He also was in dissent—joined only by Rehnquist—as the majority
voted that conversations between therapists and patients are privileged
and should be kept out of trials. "When is it, one must wonder, that the
psychotherapist came to play such an indispensable role in the mainte-

nance of the citizenry's mental health?" Scalia wrote as he drafted his opinion. "For most of history, men and women have worked out their difficulties by talking to . . . parents, siblings, best friends and bartenders—none of whom was awarded a privilege against testifying in court. Ask the average citizen: Would your mental health be more significantly impaired by preventing you from seeing a psychotherapist, or by preventing you from getting advice from your mom? I have little doubt what the answer would be. Yet there is no mother-child privilege."

Scalia was also finishing a strong dissent in a lower-profile case involving an independent trash hauler in Kansas whose contract was terminated when a politician he criticized won county office. In protesting the majority's ruling that the trash-hauling contractor should not have been fired, Scalia insisted that a legitimate benefit of winning political office was rewarding one's allies and disfavoring one's opponents. Then Scalia, no doubt considering all the cases he had lost during the term, including the Colorado gay rights dispute, added to his dissent in *Board of County Commissioners, Wabaunsee County, Kansas v. Umbehr*: "What secret knowledge, one must wonder, is breathed into lawyers when they become Justices of this Court, that enables them to discern that a practice which the text of the Constitution does not clearly proscribe, and which our people have regarded as constitutional for 200 years, is in fact unconstitutional? . . . Day by day, case by case, [the Court] is busy designing a Constitution for a country I do not recognize."[14] The language was powerful, the target just right. It was the perfect anthem for right-wing critics of the Supreme Court.

More than a decade later Scalia would use almost identical phrases as he referred to his father's attitude about contemporary America. The reference to his father, Salvatore Eugene, emerged as the justice was speaking in an interview about how Professor Scalia's colleagues at Brooklyn College regarded him as a man with a strict moral code. Justice Scalia said, "He would not have survived in what America has come to. He would not recognize it."[15]

In the summer of 1996, just after Scalia had denounced the "country [he did] not recognize," the retired justice Harry Blackmun sent him a note of consolation. "I know that this has not been an easy year for you," Blackmun wrote in the personal note. "But it is over with, and next October one will be rejuvenated and a new chapter will unfold. As a group or individually, we cannot get discouraged."[16] Scalia wrote back the day he received the note, in longhand: "You are right that I am more discouraged this year than I have been at the end of any of my previous nine terms up here. I am beginning to repeat myself, and I don't see much use in it any more."[17]

Looking back on that time, Scalia said years later in an interview, "It was a different era: Things were bad. We were losing all of the cases I cared about. At the end of the term . . . the hard ones, the important ones, always come then. Boom! Boom! Boom! Four of those in a row, and you're really down."[18]

Yet his dissenting arguments were forceful, his writing style compelling, his passion palpable. Scalia appeared to be doubling his efforts to articulate his conservative vision and to scold the majority for decisions he believed undermined traditional values and lacked foundation in the Constitution.[19] He was losing cases but winning a crowd beyond Washington, D.C.

One year after *Romer v. Evans* was handed down, Scalia was invited by the New York–based conservative Manhattan Institute to give its prestigious annual lecture. As he was introduced to the crowd on an unusually cold November evening at the Waldorf-Astoria hotel, Scalia received a standing ovation. When the lawyer and institute senior fellow Peter Huber introduced the justice, he noted that some people had described Scalia as "a Lear-like figure, raging on the heath against the world." Huber cheered Scalia as "a man who truly believes in something . . . who will stand for it against any opposition . . . like the Spartans at Thermopylae."[20]

Scalia ate it up, although he quipped that he might have preferred a more modest introduction because "the secret of success in life is that other people should have low expectations of you." In his address, which was regularly interrupted by applause and laughter, Scalia talked about what makes him different, how he believes the Constitution should be interpreted. "It means what it meant when it was written," he said, rejecting the alternative notion that the text should be construed to meet the needs of an evolving society. "I am now something of a dodo bird among jurists and legal scholars. You can fire a cannon in the faculty lounge of any major law school in the country and not strike an originalist."

At one point Scalia referred to the Court's opinion striking down Colorado's antigay law. He noted that Amendment 2 had blocked cities from writing laws against discrimination based on sexual orientation. "The people of Colorado . . . said that neither the state nor any of the political subdivisions of the state would add homosexuality to . . . the bases on which individuals cannot discriminate. In other words, [homosexuality] would not be made, you know, [the same in protected status as] religion, race, sex. Thou shalt not add homosexuality, that's what the [Colorado] constitutional amendment said." Then Scalia added defiantly, "My Court struck it down as unconstitutional under, I don't know, the Homosexuality Clause of the Bill of Rights. Or whatever it is." Laughter again erupted from the black-tie audience.

Scalia's willingness to talk about constitutional issues and express moral judgments in public forums outside the Court—and his ability to do it with such clarity and fervor—separated him from other justices. His fellow constitutional originalist Justice Thomas generally confined himself in public speeches to the lessons of his upbringing in Pin Point, Georgia. In his speeches, Chief Justice Rehnquist, a sometime partner in dissent, typically expounded—safely, predictably—on the history of the Court. Scalia also was willing to speak about gay rights, religion, and abortion. He provoked and inflamed. He was doing at least a dozen major speeches a year. Scalia was out there, figuratively and literally.

In the wake of *Romer v. Evans*, as he headed into his second decade on the Court, Scalia wrote opinions and speeches that increasingly were an inspiring template for right-wing politicians and conservative lawyers and law students. "He is doing this as the moral compass or the moral conscience of the court," Jay Alan Sekulow, a counsel to the conservative American Center for Law and Justice, said in the summer of 1996. Marvin Olasky of the conservative Progress and Freedom Foundation added, "There is a moral fissure running through society, and Scalia deals with it forthrightly. I find this very courageous of him." The Yale University law professor Stephen Carter, assessing Scalia from a less ideological viewpoint, said, "It is clear that he has set himself up, in effect, as saying the majority doesn't care about traditional values."[21]

Two years later, in 1998, Scalia wrote a concurring opinion (joined only by Thomas) that said the government can favor the decent over the indecent when it gives grants to projects in the arts. The case traced to a public uproar created by two National Endowment for the Arts grants

awarded in the late 1980s: one paid for a retrospective of homoerotic photographs by Robert Mapplethorpe; the other financed the work of Andres
Serrano, which included his *Piss Christ*, a photograph of a crucifix in
urine. Congress in 1990 adopted a provision dictating that the NEA take
"into consideration the general standards of decency and respect for the
diverse beliefs and values of the American public" in awarding grants.
That year the National Endowment for the Arts denied grants to four
performance artists, including Karen Finley, best known for covering her
nude body with chocolate. The four artists sued the NEA, saying the
decency standard suppressed artistic expression and violated the First
Amendment.

The Supreme Court rejected the challenge from Finley and the others
by a vote of 8–1. In an opinion written by Justice O'Connor and signed by
five other justices, the Court interpreted the provision as requiring "consideration," not an absolute test, for decency. Justice O'Connor wrote that
such considerations of decency "do not silence speakers by expressly
threatening censorship of ideas." Justice Souter was the lone dissent,
asserting that any decency standard could hurt artists whose ideas were
outside the mainstream.[22]

For his part, Scalia, joined by Thomas, thought the majority took the
wrong tack by trying to minimize the NEA screening of grants. In his concurring opinion, Scalia stressed the outrageous displays Congress was targeting and that O'Connor's majority opinion minimized. "In its laudatory
description of the accomplishments of the NEA, the Court notes with satisfaction that 'only a handful of the agency's roughly 100,000 awards have
generated formal complaints,' " Scalia wrote. "The Congress that felt it
necessary to enact [the provision at issue] evidently thought it much *more*
noteworthy that *any* money exacted from American taxpayers had been
used to produce a crucifix immersed in urine, or a display of homoerotic
photographs. It's no secret that the provision was prompted by, and
directed at, the funding of such offensive productions. Instead of banning
the funding of such productions absolutely, which I think would have
been entirely constitutional, Congress took the lesser step of requiring
them to be disfavored in the evaluation of grant applications. The Court's
opinion today renders even that lesser step a nullity." Scalia insisted sar-
castically, "It is the very business of government to favor and disfavor
points of view on innumerable subjects, which is the main reason we have

decided to elect those who run the government, rather than save money by making their posts hereditary."[23]

In 2000, when the Court considered a First Amendment dispute over whether a state could prevent the Boy Scouts of America from firing a scoutmaster who was openly gay, Scalia was an active questioner during oral arguments. The case had been brought under a New Jersey civil rights law by James Dale, a lifelong scout and troop leader, who was forced to leave the scouts when the group's leaders learned he was gay. The scouts maintained that homosexuality conflicted with its mission of training young men to be "morally straight" and "clean" and that any law that forced them to hire a homosexual compromised their message to the public and violated their freedom of association. Dale countered that the New Jersey law was aimed at discriminatory practices, not free speech or association, and that the Boy Scouts should not be exempted from the measure protecting people based on sexual orientation.

During oral arguments Scalia told Dale's lawyer Evan Wolfson, "They think that homosexuality is immoral . . . You think it does not limit the ability of the Boy Scouts to convey its message to require the Boy Scouts to have as a scoutmaster someone who embodies a contradiction of its message?" Wolfson responded that the hiring or firing of "a human being such as Mr. Dale" cannot be viewed as speech protected by the First Amendment. Scalia continued to fire questions at Wolfson, saying at one point, "You don't have to have as your raison d'etre to oppose homosexuality in order to believe that it is part of your moral code that that conduct is inappropriate, and that's the position that the Boy Scouts have taken."[24] In the end, Scalia was one of five justices who ruled that New Jersey's anti-bias law prohibiting the scouts from expelling a gay scoutmaster violated the Boy Scouts' First Amendment right of freedom of association and free speech. The Court concluded that the Boy Scouts have an expressive message against homosexuality and could not be compelled to accept gay members.[25]

The more significant second chapter of gay legal rights at the Supreme Court occurred in 2003, when the justices reconsidered the 1986 decision that allowed states to enforce sodomy laws against homosexual relations. In the 1986 *Bowers v. Hardwick* case, the Court had rejected arguments that antisodomy laws violated the constitutional right to privacy. The Court had not reconsidered this question in the case involving Colorado's Amendment 2. The new case began in Texas, when Harris County sheriff's officers, acting on a neighbor's report—falsely filed, it turned out—of a "weapons disturbance," entered a Houston apartment and discovered John Geddes Lawrence and Tyron Garner engaged in sodomy. They were arrested, held in jail overnight, and fined $200 each. Lawrence and Garner challenged the constitutionality of the antisodomy law (which criminalized both oral and anal homosexual sex) and lost in state courts. A dozen other states had laws like the Texas statute, but they were rarely enforced.

Like *Romer v. Evans* seven years earlier, the case of *Lawrence v. Texas* became a rallying point for gay rights activists and civil libertarians. The country had moved forward even further since the *Romer* case was heard in 1996. From workplace discrimination to child custody, a clear and distinct pattern was emerging. Large employers were offering benefits to same-sex partners of workers on the same basis as married workers. Lower court judges were beginning to apply the principles of equality to claims of discrimination based on sexual orientation. At the same time that Lawrence and Garner were appealing their case to the U.S. Supreme Court, the Massachusetts Supreme Judicial Court was weighing a lawsuit brought by Hillary and Julie Goodridge and five other gay and lesbian couples challenging state policy allowing only heterosexual couples to marry.

The expansion of gay legal rights reflected how themes related to homosexuality were moving from the fringe to the mainstream in American culture in the early twenty-first century. Gay elected officials were coming out of the closet in record numbers. Gay characters were becoming common on television and in movies.[26]

For the U.S. Supreme Court, the question was whether states could criminalize sexual relations between same-sex consenting adults. Texas, along with three other states (Kansas, Missouri, and Oklahoma), invoked criminal antisodomy law exclusively against same-sex couples. Nine other states had criminal sodomy laws that would apply to oral sex between heterosexual couples, too: Alabama, Florida, Idaho, Louisiana, Mississippi, North Carolina, South Carolina, Utah, and Virginia. Rarely were any of these enforced.

By a vote of 6–3 and with the exact same lineup as in *Romer v. Evans*,

the Court ruled in June 2003 that such laws prohibiting same-sex activities were unconstitutional. Justice Kennedy again wrote for the Court.
This time he more robustly validated the lives of gay men and women.
Gay men and lesbians are "entitled to respect for their private lives," he
wrote. "The state cannot demean their existence or control their destiny
by making their private sexual conduct a crime."[27]

Even from the bench, as he read parts of the opinion, Kennedy
declared outright that the ruling in *Bowers v. Hardwick* had been flat
wrong. "Bowers was not correct when it was decided, and it is not correct
today. It ought not to remain binding precedent. *Bowers v. Hardwick*
should be and now is overruled," Kennedy wrote, with none of the equivocation he had become known for in other areas of the law. At one point
he said of the 1986 case, "The sweeping references by Chief Justice Burger
to the history of Western civilization and to Judeo-Christian moral and
ethical standards did not take account of other authorities pointing in an
opposite direction." Kennedy referred specifically to foreign sources, such
as the European Court of Human Rights and a committee advising the
British Parliament in the early 1960s. Such citations to foreign law infuriated Scalia.

In his conclusion, Kennedy further cast the Constitution in terms
decidedly un-Scalian and un-originalist. "Had those who drew and ratified the Due Process Clauses of the Fifth Amendment or the Fourteenth
Amendment known the components of liberty in its manifold possibilities, they might have been more specific. They did not presume to have
this insight. They knew times can blind us to certain truths and later generations can see that laws once thought necessary and proper in fact serve
only to oppress." The *Lawrence v. Texas* decision reversed a ruling that had
hung darkly over the lives of gay men and lesbians and, far more than the
Romer v. Evans decision, went directly to how people conducted their
most intimate relationships.[28]

Justice O'Connor, the sixth vote to strike down the law, agreed that the
Texas statute should fall, but her rationale was based on the equality guarantee rather than due process. She said the Texas law was flawed because it
made oral or anal sex a crime only between same-sex, not heterosexual,
couples.[29]

Justice Scalia was even more incensed than he had been in the *Romer*
case. His dissent from the bench in *Lawrence v. Texas* was twice as long as

Kennedy's reading for the majority. He asserted that the decision was the product of a law-profession culture that has largely signed on to "the homosexual agenda."

In his written opinion, Scalia first ridiculed the fact that key justices in the majority, including Kennedy, had in 1992 upheld *Roe v. Wade*, saying it was important for stability in the law. Here, Kennedy and the others were reversing a 1986 precedent with no hesitation. "Liberty finds no refuge in a jurisprudence of doubt," Scalia wrote as he opened his opinion, quoting the first line of the three-justice opinion in *Planned Parenthood of Southeastern Pennsylvania v. Casey* upholding *Roe v. Wade*. Scalia continued: "That was the Court's sententious response, barely more than a decade ago, to those seeking to overrule *Roe v. Wade*. The Court's response today, to those who have engaged in a 17-year crusade to overrule *Bowers v. Hardwick*, is very different. The need for stability and certainty presents no barrier . . . I do not myself believe in rigid adherence to stare decisis [that is, adherence to prior Court decisions] in constitutional cases; but I do believe that we should be consistent rather than manipulative in invoking the doctrine. Today's opinions in support of reversal do not bother to distinguish—or indeed, even bother to mention—the paean to stare decisis coauthored by three members of today's majority in *Planned Parenthood v. Casey*."[30]

Picking up a theme from *Romer v. Evans*, Scalia used the same tack he had taken seven years earlier and put homosexual behavior in the same category in terms of legislative discretion as bigamy and bestiality. "The Texas statute undeniably seeks to further the belief of its citizens that certain forms of sexual behavior are 'immoral and unacceptable'—the same interest furthered by criminal laws against fornication, bigamy, adultery, adult incest, bestiality, and obscenity."

Then he noted how the Ontario Court of Appeal in Canada had earlier that very month lifted a ban on same-sex marriages. "The Court today pretends that . . . we need not fear judicial imposition of homosexual marriage, as has recently occurred in Canada (in a decision that the Canadian Government has chosen not to appeal) . . . Do not believe it." (Within a year of the *Lawrence v. Texas* decision, the Massachusetts Supreme Judicial Court, in the case of *Goodridge v. Department of Public Health*, struck down the state's gay marriage ban based on the Massachusetts constitution, not on the U.S. Constitution, and opened the door to same-sex marriages in the state.[31])

In his written dissenting opinion in *Lawrence v. Texas*, Scalia reserved his strongest condemnation for the "elitist" views that he believed undergirded the decision: "Today's opinion is the product of a Court, which is the product of a law-profession culture, that has largely signed on to the so-called homosexual agenda, by which I mean the agenda promoted by some homosexual activists directed at eliminating the moral opprobrium that has traditionally attached to homosexual conduct."

Such anger on gay rights and other moral issues had a way of undercutting his assertion of a principled approach to the law irrespective of what was at stake in the case. Using his dissent in *Lawrence v. Texas* as an example, *The New Yorker*'s Margaret Talbot wrote, "Cases in which Scalia believes that elite judges or professors are trying to dismantle the moral positions of 'the people' bring out a particular vituperativeness . . . and leave the unavoidable impression that he is speaking not only for originalism but also for his own selective notion of the vox populi."[32]

Scalia had added in his dissenting opinion in the Texas sodomy case, "Let me be clear that I have nothing against homosexuals, or any other group, promoting their agenda through normal democratic means." Yet he parted company with Thomas, who wrote a separate statement in *Lawrence v. Texas* saying that if he were a legislator, he would have voted to repeal the ban. Thomas made the point that even though, in his mind, the Constitution did not protect gay rights, the better course for state legislators was a lifting of prohibitions on consensual sodomy. That sort of line irked Scalia. He did not believe in trying to soften a position he took on the law. He believed his job was to say whether something was constitutional or not, and not to care whether he looked reasonable or not.

Scalia's intractability and high moral tone prompted the *New York Times* columnist Maureen Dowd to write, "He's so Old School, he's Old Testament, misty over the era when military institutes did not have to accept women, when elite schools did not have to make special efforts with blacks, when a gay couple in their own bedroom could be clapped in irons, when women were packed off to Our Lady of Perpetual Abstinence Home for Unwed Mothers."[33] Demonstrating that anything related to Scalia's rhetoric had an exponential effect, James Taranto of *The Wall Street Journal* weighed in the next day in defense of Scalia, saying, "Dowd completely ignores the legal argument she is taking issue with and ends up unwittingly reinforcing Scalia's point. 'Most Americans, even Republicans, have a more tolerant and happy vision of the country than Mr. Scalia and other nattering nabobs of negativism,' she claims. That may well be true—but if so, why not just change the law through the ordinary democratic process, as Scalia urged?"[34]

From an academic perch, the Yale University law professor Bruce Ackerman derided Scalia's notion that the Court had bought into the law-profession culture's homosexual agenda. "Scalia forgets that all exercises in judicial interpretation are the product of a 'law-profession culture.' Only the Court's openness to professional critique keeps it honest and distinguishes it from an organ of naked political power," Ackerman wrote. "And his claim that the Court has signed on to the 'homosexual agenda' is characteristically extreme: The majority held that the state could not throw gays into jail, not that it was required to provide civil unions, much less marriage."[35]

Scalia had warned that the Court majority was flouting public opinion. That may have been true. At the same time, however, the nation's editorial pages showed almost immediately that some of America's most prominent institutions were ready to endorse some rights for gay men and lesbians. Media on the east and west coasts praised the ruling, as did many newspapers in the center of the country, including *The Des Moines Register* and the *Chicago Tribune*. Significantly, the *Tribune*'s editorial page noted that seven years earlier it had supported Illinois's "defense of marriage act," which withheld recognition of same-sex marriages granted in other states. "That view changed," the *Tribune* editors said, adding, "it's difficult to see how same-sex marriage would undermine traditional families."[36]

In the months following the 2003 *Lawrence v. Texas* case, Scalia criticized the ruling in other venues. In a speech to the conservative Intercollegiate Studies Institute, he adopted a mocking tone as he read from Kennedy's decision striking down the antisodomy law. According to an Associated Press account, Scalia said the ruling "held to be a constitutional right what had been a criminal offense at the time of the founding and for nearly 200 years thereafter."[37]

Scalia's dissenting statements—like his appearances on the road—spoke to people beyond the Court and outside of the legal profession. His dissents were not designed to try to pick up votes from colleagues for a similar case the next time around. As David Forte wrote favorably in the *National Review* a few weeks after the *Romer v. Evans* ruling, "He speaks less to his own—the courts and the legal fraternity—and more to those in other parts of our political system. He casts up a dire warning that not only has the Supreme Court in many ways removed the Constitution from the Framers, it is also removing the democratic process from the people and their representatives. His words are on the edge of the apocalyptic: If the Republic is to stand, the Republic must take heed."[38]

Yet it was in this impassioned area of morality that Scalia made the fewest inroads. With each passing year, the nation appeared more tolerant of lesbians and gay men. Civil-union laws were proliferating, and California's highest court in time followed Massachusetts in ordering the recognition of same-sex marriage under its state constitution. (California voters reversed the result by referendum six months later and new legal battles began.[39]) Still, Scalia kept the candle burning for those on the other side. As the New York Law School professor Stephen A. Newman wrote in an essay critical of Scalia's incendiary rhetoric, "To the true believers in the movement, he is the heroic upholder of the conservative faith. The other Justices, having reached the pinnacle of the legal profession, are heroic to those in that profession; Scalia is heroic in the larger and more committed world of political activists."[40]

Scalia's dissents remained a call to arms for the conservative base, in politics and the law. Perhaps there was no greater indication of Scalia's stature than Robert Bork's significant use of one of Scalia's 1996 dissenting opinions in Bork's 2005 book about what he termed "the legal assault on American values."

Bork had been on the conservative scene before Scalia, of course. He started in private practice in 1954, when Scalia was just out of high school. Bork began teaching in 1962 at Yale Law School, where he developed his theory that judges should remain faithful to the "original" understanding of the Constitution. Eventually Bork's and Scalia's paths intertwined on the D.C. Circuit. After Bork's high-profile rejection for the Supreme Court in 1987, he left his job as a judge on the D.C. Circuit and became a prolific writer and regular commentator, arguing that America was a society in decline. In 1989 Bork wrote *The Tempting of America: The Political Seduction of the Law*. His *Slouching Toward Gomorrah: Modern Liberalism and American Decline* was published in 1996. Both were bestsellers. Then, in

2005, as Bork was editing a collection of essays for a new book, he took a page from Scalia to explain how judges were playing too great a role in society's moral dilemmas and displacing families, schools, churches, and traditional institutions. "This judicial gnosticism was described by Justice Antonin Scalia in a dissent," Bork observed as he quoted Scalia's 1996 writing in *Board of County Commissioners, Wabaunsee County, Kansas v. Umbehr*, which began, "What secret knowledge, one must wonder, is breathed into lawyers when they become Justices of this Court . . ." Bork then gave the book a title he knew would resonate, courtesy of Scalia: *A Country I Do Not Recognize.*[41]

ELEVEN

BUSH V. GORE: NOT OVER IT

At the outset, no one could have predicted that the presidential campaign between the Texas governor, George W. Bush, and Vice President Al Gore, with a hundred million ballots cast nationwide, would come down to a single vote on the Supreme Court. The case of *Bush v. Gore* would seem an aberration in the history of the Supreme Court. Yet the legal ordeal that decided the 2000 presidential election would reinforce and define the public persona of Justice Scalia. His role in the Florida dispute and his response to public criticism—even years later—would further etch the contours of his legal approach and his personality. Nearly a decade after the decision, Scalia was the justice most asked in public forums about the case, and his often-repeated admonition to "Get over it!" had the contrary effect—of tossing kindling on still-burning fires.

The Supreme Court's 5–4 vote in *Bush v. Gore* culminated a thirty-six-day controversy following the November 7, 2000, election. That final decision on December 12 shut down—decisively—ballot recounts in Florida and awarded the White House to Governor Bush. The action, taken by justices generally inclined to be deferential toward state choices, touched off widespread suspicion that the justice meted out by the Supreme Court was simply politics by a different name.

The majority, consisting of Scalia and four other appointees of Republican presidents, suggested that the situation in the country had turned desperate. They declared that they had to act quickly to end the recounts and decide the case. And they also asserted that their decision was "limited to the present circumstances," a statement that in context sounded like a compromise of the long-standing premise that the Court's business was to establish rules for all similar cases that might follow. As Justice Scalia had once said, when he puts his opinion in writing, "I have committed myself to the governing principle."[1] Many viewed *Bush v. Gore* as a breach of that commitment.

Earlier in 2000, Scalia had turned sixty-four. His ninth and youngest child, Margaret, was in her last year as a teenager, and at Amherst College. Older sons and daughters were married and rearing their own children. Maureen was busy helping her daughters and daughters-in-law with the new grandchildren. The associate justice was traveling widely, as was his practice, and the months leading up to the election were especially busy.[2] He had spent a week in Rome in early June for the National Italian American Foundation. In July he flew to London for a special meeting of the American Bar Association and separately was the honored guest at a dinner at a Grosvenor Square hotel organized by the University of London. The former prime minister Margaret Thatcher and Sir Denis Thatcher attended the dinner, as did the American legal figures Edwin Meese III and Kenneth W. Starr.[3] Starr, a former colleague of Scalia's from the U.S. Court of Appeals for the D.C. Circuit, had become well known as the special prosecutor who, in his investigation of various charges against President Bill Clinton, in 1998 uncovered Clinton's affair with the White House intern Monica Lewinsky. Clinton's two terms were nearing an end, and the ordeal that had led to the president's impeachment by the House of Representatives and subsequent acquittal by the Senate was coming to a close.

Now, in his fifteenth year on the Court, Scalia was continuing in his role as the loud dissenter. In early September 2000, when he spoke at the University of Idaho, he said that his job was often "to tell the majority to take a walk."[4] He told his audience that his originalist views sometimes conflicted with his personal convictions. He said, for example, that he did not like having to vote that the U.S. Constitution's right of free speech allowed people to express their contempt for the United States by burning a flag. He believed that the Constitution dictated that view. "Don't get me wrong," he added, repeating one of his favorite lines. "I don't like scruffy, bearded, sandal-wearing people who go around burning the United States flag."[5] This was Scalia: out there, unafraid to say what he believed, affirmatively *not* politically correct.

In the days before the November 7 election, polls showed the Democratic vice president Gore and the Republican governor Bush running neck and neck. It appeared, even up to Election Day, to be the closest presidential race in four decades.[6] Bush represented a quest for less government and, it seemed, a return to the policies of his father, George H. W. Bush, who had been president from 1989 to 1993. Gore, vice president for eight years, had a reputation as a moderate on defense and a liberal on social policy, particularly environmental protection. The contenders made the Supreme Court part of their pitches in the weeks before the election. Bush had said he wanted justices in the mold of Scalia and his fellow conservative Clarence Thomas. Gore had said he would choose only supporters of abortion rights and held up the liberals William Brennan and Thurgood Marshall as models.[7]

After the polls closed on November 7 and through the morning of November 8, neither candidate could claim the state of Florida's decisive twenty-five presidential electoral votes. The Florida Division of Elections reported on November 8 that Bush had received 2,909,135 votes and Gore 2,907,351, a margin of 1,784 votes for Bush. Because that margin of victory was less than "one-half of a percent . . . of the votes cast," a machine recount was required by Florida law. That machine recount showed Bush still winning Florida but by a smaller margin, 663 votes.[8] Gore then sought hand recounts in just four counties—ones where Democratic voters had complained widely about ballot confusion. Problems in those counties were not the kind that could be cured by machine recounts. Things were more complicated than that, as demonstrated by Palm Beach County's troublesome "butterfly ballot," which listed candidates in two columns and put the voting holes between the two, failing to clearly align the candidate name with the proper hole to be punched. The format led some Democratic voters intending to choose Gore to punch mistakenly the hole for the independent candidate Patrick Buchanan—the former Reagan adviser and conservative commentator. Even Buchanan, in a sign of the wide recognition of a problem, said that he probably picked up some Gore votes because of the confusing ballot. "My guess is I probably got some votes down there that really did not belong to me," Buchanan said on NBC's *Today* show.[9]

When the Florida election litigation began, it was difficult to believe that the nation's highest tribunal would have any role in it. The Constitution generally left election procedures to the states, even in presidential elections. Hosting family and other fellow Arizonans at a dinner in her home days after the November 7 election, Sandra Day O'Connor predicted that the dispute, which she described as "a mess" Florida officials needed to "straighten out," would never end up before the justices.[10] The conservative majority on the Supreme Court, including O'Connor, had long favored deference to the states and to state judges in particular. Justice Scalia and Chief Justice William Rehnquist were two strong proponents of such judicial restraint.

The Florida case first wended its way to the high court in late November. The Florida secretary of state, Katherine Harris, a partisan Republican elected to office in 1998 and cochair of Bush's Florida campaign, had refused to waive a November 14 state deadline for localities to turn in their ballot totals. Gore and county officials challenged that declaration. Keeping the recounts going in the four particular counties was the vice president's only hope of winning the election.

The (Democratic-dominated) Florida Supreme Court ruled against Harris, moving the deadline to November 26. Governor Bush and his supporters fought back. In the initial U.S. Supreme Court case on the Florida disputes, called *Bush v. Palm Beach County Canvassing Board*, Bush claimed that the Florida Supreme Court lacked the legal grounds to order the twelve-day extension for certifying the results of the recounts. After hearing Bush's appeal, the U.S. Supreme Court, by a 9–0 vote, rebuffed the Florida Supreme Court's decision to move the November 14 certification deadline and sent the dispute back to the state court to clarify its rationale for the extension.

"As a general rule," the Supreme Court justices observed in the December 4 decision, "this Court defers to a state court's interpretation of a state statute. But in the case of a law enacted by a state legislature applicable . . . to the selection of Presidential electors, the legislature is not acting solely under the authority given it by the people of the State, but by virtue of a direct grant of authority made under Article II." The U.S. Constitution's Article II dictated that presidential electors were to be appointed by each state "in such a manner as the legislature" directed. This was an arcane, rarely invoked provision of the Constitution, but it ended up being a core element of the Florida case as it moved along.

After the December 4 Supreme Court decision (its unanimity masking sharp divisions among justices over what was happening in Florida), Vice

President Gore began another series of legal moves for manual recounts. On November 26, even as the manual recounts in various counties continued, and while the first high court case was still pending, the Florida Elections Canvassing Commission had certified all the results of the election. Bush had been declared the winner by 357 votes. New lawsuits kept advancing against a public backdrop of twenty-four-hour cable news and Internet reports covering the political and legal wrangling over dimples, hanging chads, and other suddenly relevant ballot intricacies. As workers held up ballots to the light and squinted to determine where a chad was severed, their offices were flooded with teams of lawyers, protesters, and out-of-town rabble-rousers. In Fort Lauderdale, while members of the Broward County canvassing board reviewed hundreds of disputed ballots in a county courthouse, swarms of placard-waving GOP partisans chanted "Sore Loserman" at the opposing crowd of Gore-Lieberman supporters.[11] In Miami-Dade, when Joe Geller, the Democratic Party chair, took a sample ballot with him to show an expert witness who was planning to testify in the matter, an angry crowd surrounded him, shouting, "He stole a ballot!"[12]

Bush's forces were trying desperately to ensure that the Texas governor's lead did not drop significantly with recounts. At the same time, Gore's chance for winning public support for his legal efforts rested largely on his ability to bring his total up and narrow the margin of difference between the two candidates. The new incarnation of the legal case, now called *Bush v. Gore*, was moving quickly through state proceedings. It culminated at the Florida Supreme Court with a December 8 decision. By a 4–3 vote, the Florida Supreme Court ruled that the recounts Gore wanted could continue. The state court said the Florida Elections Canvassing Commission's certification of November 26 was flawed and noted that Miami-Dade County had failed to tabulate by hand nine thousand ballots on which the machines had failed to detect any vote for president. So the highest court in the state of Florida ordered a hand recount of so-called undervotes in dozens of counties, including Miami-Dade. Undervotes were those ballots on which no vote was registered by counting machines. The state court referred to a section of Florida law that said no vote shall be ignored "if there is a clear indication of the intent of the voter," and declared, "The clear message from this legislative policy is that every citizen's vote be counted whenever possible, whether in an election

for a local commissioner or an election for President of the United States."
The Florida court did not set a particular standard for enforcing the statutory mandate of "the intent of the voter."[13]

"Thousands of uncounted votes could obviously make a difference,"
the liberal Florida court majority wrote. "Only by examining the con-
tested ballots, which are evidence in the election context, can a meaningful and final determination in this election contest be made."

To the Bush team, this December 8 ruling violated state law giving the
canvassing commission the power to certify results, and it undermined
Article II's requirement that the presidential electors be appointed in each
state "in such manner as the legislature" dictates. Bush lawyers also
thought a violation of the Constitution's equal protection guarantee
existed, because there were no standards for the county workers directed
to determine a voter's "intent"; different counties had different ways of
evaluating ballots. They immediately appealed to the U.S. Supreme Court
and at the same time requested a stay of the recounts that the Florida
Supreme Court's December 8 ruling endorsed.

Led by Theodore Olson (a former Reagan administration lawyer, Federalist Society leading light, and longtime friend of Scalia's), the Bush
team argued that it was unconstitutional to recount votes with standards
that varied from county to county. In its December 8 ruling, the Florida
Supreme Court had provided no specifics on how to assess the "clear indication of the intent of the voter." One of the dissenting state court justices,
Charles Wells, had written, "This subjective counting is only compounded
where no standards exist or, as in this statewide contest, where there are
no statewide standards for determining voter intent by the various canvassing boards, individual judges, or multiple unknown counters who will
eventually count these ballots." Wells, who was the state court's chief justice, also accused the majority of propelling the state and country "into an
unprecedented and unnecessary constitutional crisis." Wells said the case,
going on for more than a month since the presidential election, had
reached the point at which "finality must take precedence over continued
judicial process."

Olson relied on much of Justice Wells's reasoning in his appeal and
insisted that an immediate halt to the counts was necessary to prevent a
distortion of the election results. The U.S. Supreme Court agreed, and in a
momentous order issued on Saturday, December 9—before Florida coun-

ties had completed even one full day of recounts—the Court announced it would hear arguments in Bush's appeal. Not only that, it took the remarkable step of ordering all of the Florida recounts stopped.

Under normal circumstances, it is extraordinarily difficult to persuade the Supreme Court to grant an emergency "stay" that blocks a lower court ruling from taking effect. Proponents of such action ordinarily must demonstrate that they will be "irreparably harmed" if the Court does not intervene immediately. Such "stays" are rare across the board. They are most often granted in death penalty cases when a defendant might face execution in the midst of a credible appeal if the justices do not act. Although it was not so surprising that the Court would want to hear Bush's appeal of the Florida court's legal rationale, blocking any recounts from continuing was a bolt from the blue.

That action by a bare majority constituted a decisive move against Gore. It was also a defining moment for Scalia. In the majority with him were Chief Justice Rehnquist and Justices O'Connor, Kennedy, and Thomas. But Scalia was the only one of the five to explain the rationale behind the decision to stop the recounts. That gained him a visibility that cut two ways. Scalia served the public concern and curiosity by providing an explanation. Yet his words inflamed political suspicions.

Taking it upon himself to defend the majority's action, he wrote that letting the recounts continue would threaten the "legitimacy" of Bush's election. "Count first, and rule on legality afterwards, is not a recipe for producing election results that have the public acceptance democratic stability requires," Scalia said.[14] Banging the opinion out on his personal computer, Scalia saw the case through the eyes of the Republican candidate Bush and said "the counting of votes that are of questionable legality does in my view threaten irreparable harm to [Governor Bush], and to the country, by casting a cloud upon what he claims to be the legitimacy of his election."

It was a surprising and dubious assessment of the situation: If Bush were to win the presidency through a Court judgment that the recount was unfair, it would be better to have stopped the recount outright and avoided any tally that ended up favoring Gore. It would be better if the result of a recount simply were not known. Scalia was essentially saying ignorance of the results of a recount would enhance the legitimacy of the president. This was a strange premise for a justice who went out of his way to explain the stay, presumably in the belief that candor as to its basis enhanced legitimacy.

Scalia also was willing to point out the reality that grounded the Court majority's acceptance of Bush's request for a stay. When the justices grant an emergency stay, a normal criterion is their belief that the party requesting it probably would succeed on the merits of his claim. That apparently was a factor here. "It suffices to say that the issuance of the stay suggests that a majority of the Court, while not deciding the issues presented, believe that [Governor Bush] has a substantial probability of success."

Scalia's blunt statement accompanying the Court's order to hear oral arguments on the merits of the case revealed an emphasis on Bush's ability to secure the presidency rather than on any chance Gore might have to show that he possibly won more votes in Florida. "This view makes perfect sense if the Court had already made up its mind that Bush would win the case and become president," observed the Yale University law professor Jack Balkin. "By now the ideological fissures that the high court had bravely tried to paper over [in its earlier opinion, *Bush v. Palm Beach County Canvassing Board*] had become starkly apparent."[15]

Irrespective of the true message beneath Scalia's December 9 statement, it vaulted him into the limelight. "[W]hatever happens, history will record that no member of the court played a more pivotal role than Scalia, who, by his public words and his private actions, has clearly been a driving force in the court's approach to the election," *The Washington Post* said in a front-page story two days later.[16] Although the newspaper's assertion did not fully reflect Rehnquist's leadership in the matter, it rightly captured how willing Scalia was to go public to defend what the majority did to stop the ballot counts. He was ready to put himself on the line in the bluntest terms.

Scalia actually had not intended to write anything to accompany the Court's order stopping the recounts. But he was provoked by the dissenting statement of Justice Stevens that was joined by Justices Souter, Ginsburg, and Breyer. "To stop the counting of legal votes," Stevens wrote on the morning of December 9, "the majority today departs from . . . venerable rules of judicial restraint that have guided the Court throughout its history . . . Counting every legally cast vote cannot constitute irreparable harm. On the other hand, there is a danger that a stay may cause irreparable harm to [Gore and the Democratic challengers]—and, more importantly, the public at large—because of the risk that the entry of the stay would be tantamount to a decision on the merits in favor of the applicants . . . Preventing the recount from being completed will inevitably cast a cloud on the legitimacy of the election."[17] Scalia thought otherwise and, unlike the other conservatives, simply could not hold back saying so.

The question for the justices was whether the Florida high court had violated federal law in allowing the recounts to continue. Stevens emphasized that—despite Scalia's assertion that it was likely that Bush would win—it was not clear that the Florida court had erred or that Bush had prevailed at the polls. So no grounds existed for immediately blocking the Florida court ruling, Stevens wrote—raising Scalia's ire.

Two days later, oral arguments were held on the merits of Bush's effort to shut down permanently the recounts. Again, Scalia's role was apparent, even in some of the lighter moments of the hearing. Joseph Klock, a lawyer for the Florida secretary of state, had trouble keeping the justices straight. Scalia, however, he knew. At one point Klock addressed a question from Justice Stevens by first beginning, "Well, Justice Brennan." Klock immediately realized his mistake; Brennan had retired a decade earlier and died in 1997. "I'm sorry," Klock said. "That's why they tell you not to do that."[18] He was referring to warnings he had received to avoid calling the justices by name.

But then it happened again. "Justice Breyer, what I'm saying is . . ." Klock began as he answered a question from Souter.

"I'm Justice Souter. You'd better cut that out," Souter said good-naturedly.

Then Justice Scalia entered: "Mr. Klock. I'm Scalia."

"Yes, sir . . . It will be hard to forget," Klock replied, as spectators tittered. When it was Olson's time at the lectern, he told the justices that the Florida court improperly changed statutory deadlines in violation of Article II and authorized ballot recounts that lacked standards, breaching the Fourteenth Amendment's guarantee of equal protection of the law. Up next was David Boies, representing Vice President Gore, who defended the state court ruling as fully within Florida law and the Constitution.

Boies, a prominent, seemingly peerless Wall Street litigator with such clients as the New York Yankees owner, George Steinbrenner, was just coming off his successful representation of the Justice Department in its major antitrust case against Microsoft. He appeared at the top of his game—except for now. Along with spectators in the courtroom, he could feel the justices' resistance as he urged them to defer to the state court and allow the recounts to resume under the state court's "intent of the voter" standard. Boies said that administrative personnel would understand that standard as they examined punch cards and other ballots.

Scalia had given Klock a hard time, but he saved his severest scrutiny for Boies. At one point Scalia asserted that "it was clear that Broward and Palm Beach Counties had applied different criteria to dimpled ballots. One of them was counting all dimpled ballots, the other one plainly was not." Questioning how Florida would allow different standards for different counties, Scalia said, "That's just not rational."

Boies countered, first, that Broward County results were not relevant at trial and that the relevant comparison of Miami-Dade and Palm Beach recount standards had passed muster. He said there was no evidence in the record that there were significant differing standards for recounts in those two counties. He added that county workers in any polling place would be able figure out the actual intention of a particular voter. County workers routinely were allowed to adopt their own standards, and the Court's past cases suggested that localities received wide latitude in counting votes.

Boies knew this was uncharted terrain for the Court because—despite the tenor of the questions—it had not previously held that differences among localities in how votes were qualified and tabulated constituted a violation of the guarantee that voters be treated equally. It had never ruled that states must establish certain standards for reviewing ballots, whether they be handwritten on paper, electronic, or the infamous machine punch cards that produced "hanging chads"—partially perforated squares or circles next to a candidate's name. "Bush's argument, if accepted and applied generally, would massively expand the reach of the [Constitution's] Equal Protection Clause," Boies later observed.[19] One narrower aspect of Bush's argument, however, presented a novel question: Could a state allow itself use of different interpretations of the identical physical ballot by different people operating under its auspices? As it turned out, seven justices thought this was a problem.

When Olson returned to the lectern in rebuttal, he picked up again on the justices' concerns about equal protection of the law. "There is no question, based upon this record, that there are different standards from county to county." He dismissed questions related to the fact that balloting regulations necessarily vary among counties simply because of differences in the ballots themselves, from punch cards to optically scanned versions. "Certainly the standard should be that similarly situated voters and similarly situated ballots ought to be evaluated by comparable standards," he said.

The emphasis on the equal protection guarantee troubled conservatives listening to the arguments. Over the years, and especially during the Earl Warren era, that provision of the Fourteenth Amendment had become synonymous with judicial activism as the Court invoked it to strike down state measures the Court deemed unfair to racial minorities and the politically disenfranchised. In a *National Review* online column after the oral arguments, the American Enterprise Institute's Michael Greve wrote derisively that "whacking the states with the all-purpose Fourteenth Amendment club is what the Supreme Court does for a living." Capturing the dilemma at hand for conservatives, however, Greve added, "Even [Olson], however, will take an equal-protection victory—and fight the battle over judicial imperialism another day. So should the rest of us."

It is difficult to overstate how much Scalia had tried to rein in the Court's use of the equal protection guarantee and how much the Rehnquist Court had been defined by its federalism decisions safeguarding state authority. Given this pronounced trend, the emerging rationales of the majority in *Bush v Gore* were startling.

That was particularly so for Scalia. When he was the lone dissent in 1996 in support of Virginia Military Institute's all-male admissions policy, for example, he had rejected the notion that the equal protection guarantee required women to be admitted to the state school. "[I]n my view the function of this Court is to preserve our society's values regarding (among other things) equal protection, not to revise them," he wrote. "[I]t is my view that when a practice not expressly prohibited by the text of the Bill of Rights bears the endorsement of a long tradition of open, widespread, and unchallenged use that dates back to the beginning of the Republic, we have no proper basis for striking it down."[20]

More broadly, there had been a long-standing effort by Rehnquist, Scalia, O'Connor, Kennedy, and Thomas to prevent what they maintained were federal intrusions on state and local affairs.[21] The Rehnquist Court's signature was defending states' authority and sovereignty. Now, in *Bush v. Gore*, the five conservatives were taking the opposite tack and enhancing federal power. Their ruling was issued the day after the oral arguments. Available to the press and public shortly after 10:00 p.m., as uplink television trucks surrounded the columned building and hundreds of reporters awaited word, the thirteen-page opinion was distributed by public information officers rather than the justices themselves. The Court did not take the bench to hand it down.

The majority declared that the allowed standards for counting ballots could vary too widely to be fair. It held that a standard based on the "intent of the voter" was too vague to meet requirements of the Equal Protection Clause of the Fourteenth Amendment. "The Florida Supreme Court has ordered that the intent of the voter be discerned from such ballots," the majority wrote about ballot cards that were distinguished by hanging chads or mere indentations. "The recount mechanisms implemented in response to the decisions of the Florida Supreme Court do not satisfy the minimum requirement for non-arbitrary treatment of voters necessary to secure the fundamental right. Florida's basic command for the count of legally cast votes is to consider the 'intent of the voter.' This is unobjectionable as an abstract proposition and a starting principle. The problem inheres in the absence of specific standards to ensure equal application."

Justices Souter and Breyer reached a similar conclusion. But where they vigorously dissented—they signed not a word of the majority's opinion—was in what to do with the equal protection problem. The majority said it could not return the dispute to the Florida Supreme Court for more precise, uniform standards because of the December 12 national deadline for establishing a state's presidential electors. Justices Souter and Breyer (as well as Stevens and Ginsburg) objected that the deadline was not so hard-and-fast.

Under federal law, December 12 was the "safe harbor" deadline that automatically protected a state's presidential electors from challenge by Congress. There was some debate over the importance of the December 12 date, and even if courts had not acted by December 12, many legal analysts said it was unlikely that Congress would have intervened immediately. In fact, nothing in federal law required that a state's presidential electors be named until the date set for the electors to meet and cast their votes, which was December 18 on the 2000 election calendar.

Finally, the five-justice majority declared, "our consideration is limited to the present circumstances, for the problem of equal protection in election processes generally presents many complexities." That undercut the traditional principle that rulings of a Court should endure.

The opinion was issued per curiam, or "by the court," rather than publicly authored by one particular justice. Behind the scenes, it had been largely written by Justices Kennedy and O'Connor, the two moderate conservatives. To make it a majority opinion, Rehnquist, Scalia, and Thomas signed on. Scalia's signature on such an interpretation of the Constitution's equal protection guarantee seemed a marked departure from his usual course, suggesting that despite protestations of restraint and consistency, he would sometimes vote against his general legal principles. His stance in *Bush v. Gore*—that a Court decision could be good for one case only—also appeared deeply inconsistent with his assertion of the need for clear and enduring rules.

Perhaps there was a tacit acceptance of that in the separate rationale Scalia offered up—a rationale that failed to garner a majority of votes. Scalia, along with Thomas, joined Chief Justice Rehnquist in a concurring statement in *Bush v. Gore* related to the Article II presidential electors provision. The trio said that the recount ordered by the Florida Supreme Court, especially of "undervotes," flouted the Florida legislature. They also said that the Florida legislature had sought to give the state's electors the benefit of the December 12 "safe harbor" against later challenge to its electors on the floor of Congress. The three justices contended the Florida Supreme Court had usurped the authority of the state legislature and violated the standard of Article II. Justices O'Connor and Kennedy, the two swing-vote conservatives who clinched the victory of Bush over Gore, did not accept that rationale.

The four dissenting justices who had protested the order stopping the recounts on December 9 had even stronger words this time around. Stevens, who had turned eighty in 2000 and was the most senior member of the left, said the majority decision called into question the Court's impartiality, the coin of its own legitimacy. "Although we may never know with complete certainty the identity of the winner of this year's Presidential election," Stevens wrote, "the identity of the loser is perfectly clear. It is the Nation's confidence in the judge as an impartial guardian of the rule of law."

He objected to the fact that the three justices, including Scalia, had relied on Article II to reject the Florida Supreme Court's view of Florida law. He noted that when questions arise over the meaning of a state law, the Court traditionally has accepted the interpretation of a state's highest court. "Neither Section 5 [of the Fourteenth Amendment] nor Article II grants federal judges any special authority to substitute their views for those of the state judiciary on matters of state law," Stevens wrote. He asserted that the Florida Supreme Court made no substantive change in Florida electoral law. "Its decisions were rooted in long-established precedent and were consistent with the relevant statutory provisions, taken as a whole. It did what courts do—it decided the case before it in light of the legislature's intent to leave no legally cast vote uncounted."

Stevens also disagreed with the majority's equal protection ruling. He said it should be left to state election personnel to decide how to determine the "intent of the voter" standard, and he asserted, "We have never before called into question the substantive standard by which a State determines that a vote has been legally cast." Unlike Souter and Breyer, Stevens, along with Ginsburg, had no quarrel with the recount procedures and believed that the Florida Supreme Court should be upheld outright.

Writing a separate dissenting statement, Souter said the justices should have stayed out of the Florida matter. "If this Court had allowed the State to follow the course indicated by the opinions of its own Supreme Court, it is entirely possible that there would ultimately have been no issue requiring our review, and political tension could have worked itself out in the Congress," he wrote, citing the procedures in federal law covering the counting of electoral votes.

Souter's reference to "political tension" was a reminder that the conservative justices, particularly Scalia, had on prior occasions warned that the Court should avoid political skirmishes. In 1992 Scalia had memorably complained that the majority was inflaming political passions when it reaffirmed abortion rights. "The Imperial Judiciary lives," Scalia had written in *Planned Parenthood of Southeastern Pennsylvania v. Casey*, as he accused the majority of acting beyond the "modest role envisioned for [judges] by the Founders."

Justice Souter, along with Justice Breyer, was seriously troubled by the lack of any uniform standards for evaluating the punch card and other ballot types. But they disagreed that recounts should be barred. They wanted to return the case to Florida courts to set uniform standards, and they objected to December 12 as a firm deadline. They said any recounts could be finished by the date set for the meeting of electors, December 18.[22]

In her dissenting opinion, which focused on the three-justice concurrence based on Article II, Justice Ginsburg highlighted the Court's usual respect for state court interpretations of state law. "Rarely has this Court rejected outright an interpretation of state law by a state high court . . . The extraordinary setting of this case has obscured the ordinary principle that dictates its proper resolution: Federal Courts defer to state high courts' interpretations of their state's own law. This principle reflects the core of federalism, on which all agree."

Ginsburg then quoted from an essay Justice O'Connor had written for the *William and Mary Law Review* the year before she joined the high court: "There is no reason to assume that state court judges cannot and will not provide a 'hospitable forum' in litigating federal constitutional questions." Ginsburg was not the sort of justice who liked to throw colleagues' words back in their faces. And, in fact, Ginsburg was using O'Connor's past writing to answer the Rehnquist concurrence—which O'Connor did not join—rather than the majority opinion, which O'Connor did. Nevertheless, Ginsburg's opinion showed how angry the result reached by the majority had made her, how hypocritical she found it. Her message: observe the federalism you have long been demanding over these past years.

Ginsburg did pull her punches in one significant regard. During the drafting process Scalia likened some of her words to those of the Reverend Al Sharpton. A black minister from Brooklyn, Sharpton had often been accused of race-baiting, most notoriously when a black teenager, Tawana Brawley, falsely claimed in 1987 that she had been raped by a group of white men. In the Florida case, as Jeffrey Toobin reported in his book *Too Close to Call*, Justice Ginsburg had referred to press reports about balloting problems that disproportionately affected black voters and caused their ballots in majority black precincts to be discarded at higher rates than in nonblack areas. She cited the reports as she observed that if there was any equal protection violation in Florida, it was more likely caused by local and state authorities than by the Florida Supreme Court. When Scalia saw Ginsburg's references to "potential racial discrimination," Toobin wrote, Scalia "wrote a memorandum accusing her of using the

Supreme Court to engage in 'Al Sharpton tactics' about the election. Scalia's memo, like so many Republican thrusts over the previous thirty-five days, posed a dilemma for Ginsburg. Should she fire back with equal fury and engage her adversary at the same rhetorical temperature, or should she take the high road and tone down the confrontation? . . . She removed the reference to race from her opinion."[23]

The fourth and final dissenter, Breyer, the most junior justice, also wrote a separate statement. He declared that the majority had risked "a self-inflicted wound—a wound that may harm not just the Court, but the Nation."[24]

The public criticism of the decision was unprecedented. Tens of thousands of people wrote to the justices to complain. The ruling became the subject of scores of law review articles. Any assessment of the Rehnquist Court was implicitly or explicitly framed in terms of the ruling. The decision seemed to contradict much of what the Court had stood for in the fourteen years since Rehnquist took over in 1986. The Court had earned a decidedly un-activist reputation. It was known for its restrained, legalistic approach. It was not known for a self-consciously loud voice or one that would exacerbate the politics of the day. Even as it invalidated affirmative action and other race-based policies; even as it trimmed abortion rights; even as it opened the door to gay rights, it did so in terms that were narrow, or in any event less than absolute, sometimes even tentative. It was known for a "minimalism," in the words of the then University of Chicago law professor Cass Sunstein. Even as the Court reined in Congress's power in a series of decisions favoring the states, the Court only modestly affected overall federal statutory power.[25]

Yet here were the conservative fivesome who set the tone of the bench, who had consistently favored states' rights and advocated judicial restraint, suddenly adopting an intrusive view of equal protection. The message seemed to be that they found the stakes simply too high to follow their usual course. The signal heard by some, which these justices would not have wanted to send, was that they would do all that was required to ensure a Bush victory. The criticism ran the ideological spectrum, but liberals, predictably, were more angered. Many law professors found the decision hard to reconcile with the Court's past track record and concluded that the majority acted out of partisan political motives. "The Bush outcome was not a product of conservative Justices' political ideologies," wrote the University of Virginia's Michael Klarman. "[T]hese Justices' oft-professed commitment to federalism and to judicial restraint logically should have led them to the opposite result. Rather, the Bush outcome was a product of these Justices' partisan political preference for George W. Bush."[26]

Northwestern University's Garry Wills wrote in *The New York Times*, "Conservatives who have been slow to apply Fourteenth Amendment guarantees were quick to bring them into a whole new area . . . The imperative of electing Bush made the majority on the Court neglect its own favorite doctrines of states' rights, federalism, localism, judicial restraint and 'originalism' (the adopters of the Fourteenth Amendment surely had no notion they were outlawing county authority to conduct recounts)." Referring to a Miami demonstrator who had carried a sign saying GOD MADE BUSH PRESIDENT, Wills then targeted Scalia. The demonstrator, Wills wrote, "was speaking for many more sophisticated people. Decked out in fancier phrases, in fact, that would not be a position very far from Antonin Scalia's."[27]

Even law professors sympathetic to Bush's legal position were troubled that the Court so fully displaced the authority of Florida judges. Michael McConnell, then a University of Utah law professor, said it would have been better, after finding an equal protection violation, to have sent the case back to Florida courts to see if they could establish standards and to see what the results would be for the ultimate December 18 deadline. McConnell (who would turn out to be one of Bush's first choices for a prestigious appeals court post) said that allowing a recount to go on might have instilled more confidence in the Supreme Court's decision. As it was, McConnell observed in an essay in *The Wall Street Journal* on December 14, 2000, "The court did not have the resolution to declare that no recount was necessary, or the patience to declare that a proper recount should proceed. That means, unfortunately, that Mr. Bush will take office under conditions of continued uncertainty. I do not think that part of the decision did him, or the nation, a favor."[28]

As Scalia traveled the country for his usual speaking engagements, he defended the Court's action. He said the country had become "a fool in the eyes of the world," that the Court was forced to bring an end to the chaos. That theme became a constant, as did his refrain to law students and others seeking an explanation: "Get over it!"

"You forget what was going on at the time," he protested when PBS's Charlie Rose brought it up eight years later in an interview. "We were the laughing stock of the world. The world's greatest democracy couldn't conduct an election. We didn't know who our next president was going to be. The lengthy transition that has become standard, when you change from one president to another, could not begin, because you didn't know who the president was going to be. It was becoming a very serious problem."[29]

As he had said in other interviews, Scalia asserted that he would have preferred to base the decision on Article II rather than signing on to the rationale involving the equal protection guarantee. But that view did not draw the majority.

Scalia was accused of hypocrisy regarding the equal protection rationale, which for years he had wished to narrow and in *Bush v. Gore* expanded. But he also faced some criticism because of his voiced adherence to originalism. The concurring statement he signed with Rehnquist and Thomas offered no evidence that the framers of Article II intended to bolster the role of state legislatures in the selection of presidential electors and to limit the role of state judges in interpreting that law, as Scalia had voted in the Florida case.[30]

Some critics had also accused Scalia of potential conflicts of interest. In a column titled "Supreme Travesty of Justice," the *Washington Post* columnist Mary McGrory speculated right after the decision that "Justice Scalia would like to become chief justice," and she said he "might as well have been wearing a Bush button on his robes." Richard K. Neumann, Jr., writing in the *Georgetown Journal of Legal Ethics* three years later, observed that when Bush was campaigning for president, he pointed to Scalia and Thomas as models for his future Court appointments. Neumann said that because of Scalia's possible "ambition" to be chief justice, there was "an appearance of partiality" toward the candidate more likely to elevate him to the center chair. Neumann and other law professors further noted that Scalia's two eldest sons, Eugene and John, were lawyers associated with the Bush side of the case. Eugene Scalia, a partner of Gibson, Dunn and Crutcher, Theodore Olson's home firm, agreed not to share in any fees derived from the case. John Scalia had accepted a job with Greenberg Traurig, a Miami firm that was also representing Bush, but had not yet started.[31]

No party to the case formally asked Scalia to remove himself from the matter. The justices made recusal decisions on an individual basis, and opinions in press reports were mixed about whether Scalia or any of the other justices with political connections should have sat out the case.[32] Scalia later said that he believed his eldest son, Eugene, became a victim of partisan dissatisfaction with the ruling. After he took office, Bush nominated Eugene in 2001 to be solicitor for the Department of Labor. Senate Democrats blocked his nomination as they denounced him for his writings that questioned studies of ergonomics and worker fatigue. Bush ended up giving Eugene Scalia a two-year recess appointment in January 2002, which did not require Senate confirmation but offered only a limited tenure. Asked years later whether he felt his eldest son was scapegoated, Justice Scalia said, "Oh, yeah, of course . . . It was a shame. I felt bad." Scalia was accustomed to getting himself into hot water, not his children.[33] In a later interview, speaking broadly about some of the problems his adult children have faced because of him, Justice Scalia said, "Gene, I'm sure, didn't get his appointment as solicitor of labor in part because of his name."[34]

Even after Bush's reelection in 2004, Bush v. Gore did not fade from public consciousness. Perhaps it was the nation's dissatisfaction with Bush's handling of the wars in Iraq and Afghanistan or other matters, but questions of his legitimacy as president continued to smolder. The subject kept dogging Justice Scalia, too. People were always bringing him back to 2000. When he showed up on college campuses, there would be protest signs about Bush v. Gore. When he gave interviews years later, the case inevitably came up. In 2008, when Bush was practically done with his second term, the Court's actions in Bush v. Gore constituted the most predictable subject of questions from reporters for Scalia. "Gee, I really don't want to get into this," he said at one point in an April 2008 session with Lesley Stahl of CBS's 60 Minutes. "Get over it. It's so old by now."[35]

A few weeks later, when Brian Lamb of C-SPAN raised Bush v. Gore, Scalia was similarly impatient, although more elaborative of his reasons. Lamb, who had become an institution in America with the Cable Satellite Public Affairs Network, had known Scalia since he first came to town to work in the Nixon administration. When Scalia was the newly appointed general counsel to the White House Office of Telecommunications Policy, Lamb was the communications director. They became friends, and Lamb was godfather to Matthew Scalia, who was born in May 1973 while Scalia and Lamb were both working for Nixon. During the 2008 interview related to Scalia's book *Making Your Case*, Lamb indirectly raised the subject of *Bush v. Gore*, and Scalia became immediately and fiercely defensive.

"[W]e didn't go looking for trouble," Scalia told Lamb. "The Court didn't uninvited leap into this electoral dispute. It was before the courts because Mr. Gore had brought it before the courts. He wanted the courts to decide the election, and when the matter came to us, it was simply a question whether the last word was going to be the Florida Supreme Court or the United States Supreme Court as to who would win the presidential election. When one of the parties to the cases said the Florida Supreme Court violated the federal Constitution, what were we supposed to do, turn the case down as being not important enough? Hardly."[36]

Yet, although Gore had filed the lawsuits that went to the Supreme Court, Governor Bush was the first to bring a case to try to stop the recounts. Further, the Supreme Court had hardly intervened in all national dilemmas and crises. Ultimately, the Constitution gave Congress authority over electoral votes, and the Florida controversy could have been left to the legislative branch.

Scalia then told Lamb, "Anyway, as everyone knows, in the first election, it would have come out the same way had the Court not intervened, because the press did an extensive study of each of the counties in Florida, and had the votes . . . Had they been counted the way Mr. Gore wanted, he would still have lost."

There was some truth to that. *The Wall Street Journal*, *The New York Times*, and other newspapers undertook comprehensive reviews of the Florida ballots and generally concluded that Bush still would have won if the ballot recounts had been allowed to continue. Yet the groups also found that more Floridians actually had intended to vote for Gore, who had captured the popular vote in the 2000 election.[37] A separate *USA Today / Miami Herald /* Knight Ridder review found that voter mistakes by thousands of Democratic voters—errors that legally disqualified their ballots—probably cost Al Gore 15,000 to 25,000 votes, which would have been enough to change the outcome. Among the problems that caused the gap were errors by voters, confusing instructions, and flawed machine counts.[38]

In his interview with Lamb, after Scalia had run down his litany of reasons for why the Court ruled the way it did, he again said, "So, you know. Get over it, Brian."

It was so classically Scalia: the confident assertion that comes across as a public brush-off, the unwillingness to give any ground. The other side within the Court, while not as brash, not as public, was similarly dug in. Even as many as nine years out, when Justice Stevens was asked to respond to Scalia's constant admonition of "Get over it," Stevens grimaced and said, "No comment."[39]

Scalia's words and actions suggested that he believed he knew better than anyone else how a case should be regarded. He appeared to have a hard time seeing a situation from where anyone else sat. Scalia would live with the reputation of the Court's ruling in *Bush v. Gore.* "I take most of the heat for that case," Scalia said ruefully with a hint in his voice that he thinks that just is not fair.[40]

TWELVE

"QUACK, QUACK"

———————

As he was planning his annual duck-hunting trip to Louisiana in 2003, Justice Scalia arranged for Vice President Dick Cheney to join him. Scalia's friend Wallace Carline, whose game reserve was the site of the annual hunt, admired Cheney, and Scalia was pleased to bring the two men together. So on the foggy, lightly rainy morning of January 5, 2004, Scalia boarded Air Force Two with Cheney for the flight from Washington, D.C., to southern Louisiana. Joining them was Scalia's son-in-law Britt Courtney, married to his daughter Catherine and an enthusiastic hunter who had previously taken the trip with Scalia, and the justice's second-eldest son, John, on the hunt for the first time.[1]

The Supreme Court was in its traditional winter break. The justices had heard cases in mid-December and would not be back on the bench for another week. The arguments scheduled for early 2004 would be difficult. The calendar included cases arising from President Bush's "enemy combatant" designation of men picked up by U.S. forces in Afghanistan and elsewhere and held without charges. These were the first cases of their kind to come to the Court since the September 11, 2001, attacks that killed three thousand Americans. Al Qaeda terrorists had crashed jets into the World Trade Center towers, the Pentagon, and a field in rural Pennsylvania.

Also on the Supreme Court calendar was a dispute that involved Vice President Cheney, concerning an energy task force he presided over in the early days of George W. Bush's presidency. The final report of the National Energy Policy Development Group, as it was officially known, contained several recommendations that strongly favored the energy industry, including the opening of the Arctic National Wildlife Refuge for oil drilling. Critics of the recommendations had complained in the summer of 2001 that the task force had excluded environmentalists and sought advice only from energy executives. They also maintained that outsiders from the oil, coal, gas, and other energy industries had transformed the task force into an advisory panel subject to the Federal Advisory Committee Act. Such advisory committees were required to make their membership "fairly balanced" in views and to hold open meetings. Judicial Watch, a conservative watchdog organization, and the Sierra Club, a liberal environmentalist group, sued to get documents from the task force related to the participants at the meetings and the extent of their participation.

The Bush administration claimed it had a right to keep the documents confidential, which heightened public concerns about the secret influence of wealthy business interests on national energy policy. A federal district court judge had ordered Cheney to release the papers related to private citizens' participation in the energy task force. Cheney appealed. The U.S. Court of Appeals for the D.C. Circuit said it lacked jurisdiction to review the preliminary order to release the papers, essentially endorsing the district court order. Now the case was before the Supreme Court.

In the weeks before their duck-hunting trip, Scalia and Cheney had socialized a couple of times. They had dined together with Secretary of Defense Donald Rumsfeld, another alumnus of the Ford administration, at a restaurant on Maryland's Eastern Shore, where Cheney and Rumsfeld owned homes.[2] Then Scalia, along with other justices and prominent officials, had attended the vice president's annual Christmas party at his home at the Naval Observatory on December 11.[3]

It was the next day, December 12, when the justices formally looked at the Bush administration's appeal in the dispute over Cheney's task force documents. Theodore Olson, who had represented Bush in the historic Florida election case and was subsequently appointed to be U.S. solicitor general, had argued that the Court should take Cheney's appeal because the lower court order for documents intruded on executive branch power. The Court voted in its private conference to hear Cheney's case. Its order was made public the following Monday, December 15, and oral arguments set for the spring.

When Air Force Two landed on January 5 in the southern Louisiana town of Patterson, Wallace Carline was waiting. Carline, who owned an oil-rig services company, drove Cheney, Scalia, and the others to a dock, where they took a boat to his hunting camp. They were joined by a few of Carline's business friends eager to rub shoulders with the vice president and Supreme Court justice. Over the next two days, Scalia, Cheney, and the others hunted and fished together. They slept in rooms of two or three. Cheney had his own quarters. All in all, the hunting of mallards and teal was good, not great. Scalia had seen better years.[4]

Vice President Cheney flew back to Washington on Wednesday, January 7. Scalia stayed until Friday. On his return to the Court, he began preparing for oral arguments in the first cases of 2004. Soon, however, he was distracted by news stories about his vacation with Cheney. Just as Scalia was leaving town, *The Daily Review* in Morgan City, Louisiana, had written about his recreational trip with Cheney and others. The story quoted the local sheriff as saying that Carline did not want residents to know about his celebrity guests until after they had left the camp. That story was immediately picked up by the Associated Press. About a week later, on January 17, the *Los Angeles Times* ran its own story about the hunting expedition with a new focus on Cheney's being a party to a Supreme Court case. It was then that the crucial question of why Scalia had vacationed with a Court litigant hit the national spotlight. Within days, government watchdog and investigative journalism groups, including the Washington-based Center for Public Integrity, were questioning whether Scalia could be impartial in the dispute over the task force's closed records.[5]

The Democratic U.S. senators Patrick Leahy of Vermont and Joseph Lieberman of Connecticut wrote a strongly worded letter to Chief Justice Rehnquist inquiring about the Court's ethics rules.[6] Regarding Scalia's vacation with Cheney, they said in their January 22 letter, "Coming just three weeks after the Supreme Court [accepted] a case in which the Vice President is a principal party, this trip raises questions. When a sitting judge, poised to hear a case involving a particular litigant, goes on a vacation with that litigant, reasonable people will question whether that judge can be a fair and impartial adjudicator." Leahy, who was the ranking Democrat on the Senate Judiciary Committee, and Lieberman, the ranking Democrat on the Governmental Affairs Committee, added that, "while judges should not be isolated from the society in which they live, they must take special care that their extra-judicial activities do not create a conflict with their judicial duties, give rise to an appearance of impropriety, or create a reason for questioning their impartiality."

Scalia had just taken an exclusive vacation with the vice president of the United States. How could the public, the senators were asking, believe Scalia would regard his pal Cheney in the same way he would regard Cheney's legal challengers?

In response four days later, Chief Justice Rehnquist said that individual justices were able to decide for themselves whether conflicts of interest existed. "There is no formal procedure for court review of the decision of a justice in an individual case," Rehnquist wrote in the letter addressed to Leahy. "This is because it has long been settled that each justice must decide such a question for himself." Rehnquist also chided the senators for suggesting that Scalia disqualify himself. "[A]nyone at all is free to criticize the action of a Justice—as to recusal or as to the merits—after the case has been decided," the chief justice wrote. "But I think that any suggestion by you or Senator Lieberman as to why a Justice should recuse himself in a pending case is ill considered." Rehnquist, partly because of his personal experience in such matters, had long believed that each justice should decide for him or herself whether to sit out a case.[7]

Rehnquist's response prompted the Democratic U.S. representatives Henry Waxman, of California, and John Conyers, Jr., of Michigan, to fire off a separate letter to the chief justice. They asked him to consider whether the Supreme Court should develop a formal procedure for reviewing the recusal decisions of justices.[8] The last time a majority of the justices had addressed the recusal subject was 1993, when seven of them, including Scalia, signed a statement asserting they would disqualify themselves from cases when relatives were representing a party to a case. In that statement, they also observed that "needless recusal deprives the litigants of the nine justices to which they are entitled,"[9] a theme Scalia would strike through the Cheney duck-hunting storm.

Federal law on the matter was open-ended. Dating to the 1974 post-Watergate reforms, the statute governing recusals dictated that "any justice, judge, or magistrate judge of the United States shall disqualify himself in any proceeding in which his impartiality might reasonably be questioned."[10] Scalia believed that his actions with Cheney did not violate that 1974 mandate. "I do not think my impartiality could reasonably be challenged," Scalia had written in response to an early query by the *Los Angeles Times* reporter David Savage.[11]

Scalia compared the trip to being invited to the White House. "Social contacts with high-level executive officials (including cabinet officers) have never been thought improper for judges who may have before them cases in which those people are involved in their official capacity, as opposed to their personal capacity." Scalia noted that Supreme Court justices often were invited to dine at the White House, even when cases involving presidential actions were pending.[12]

Scalia also wrote in his letter to the *Los Angeles Times* that "[e]ven though the duck hunting was lousy (our host said that in 35 years of hunting on this lease he had never seen so few ducks), I did come back with a few ducks, which tasted swell." That quip made Scalia a magnet for criticism of the sort that his "Get over it" line from *Bush v. Gore* engendered. When *The Washington Post* editorialized against Scalia's involvement in the Cheney case because of the duck-hunting vacation, it added, "Mr. Scalia . . . came back with a big appearance problem, one that— judging from his jesting comments on the matter—he does not appreciate."[13]

Scalia's colleagues were supporting him in their fashion. Justice Ruth Bader Ginsburg was asked about the matter when she spoke at a Rotary Club event in Honolulu. She declined to answer a question about whether Scalia should sit on the upcoming case. Instead, she chose to compliment the hunting skills of her longtime friend. She said a deer Scalia once killed had made for a mouthwatering meal at one of their family New Year's Eve dinners. "Justice Scalia has been more successful at deer hunting than he has at duck hunting," Ginsburg said as her audience laughed.[14]

A few days later, on February 10, Scalia spoke before six hundred people at Amherst College in Massachusetts. It was a long-scheduled commitment that drew more campus and press attention because of the Cheney matter. When a student asked about that case, Scalia repeated some of the points he made to the *Los Angeles Times*. "It did not involve a lawsuit against Dick Cheney as a private individual," Scalia said. "This was a government issue. It's acceptable practice to socialize with executive branch officials when there are not personal claims against them. That's all I'm going to say for now. Quack, quack."[15]

Reporters in the audience wondered if they had heard right. "Quack,

quack"? At least one correspondent called the Supreme Court's public information office, prompting a staffer there to telephone Scalia to ask whether he indeed had quacked. Yes, Scalia had said "quack quack," but he was merely mimicking the protesters outside the auditorium who were wearing feathers. One demonstrator carried a sign that said LET'S GO HUNTING. Others wore black armbands in protest.

Separately, some Amherst professors made their opposition to Scalia's presence on campus known by publicly boycotting his speech. The professors' actions provoked Meg Scalia, the youngest of the justice's children, to write a spirited letter to the editor of the campus paper. Meg had graduated from Amherst two years earlier, in 2002. "I don't know when it became acceptable to refuse to listen to another's viewpoints," she wrote, suggesting that the professors' decision not to show up to hear her father's speech was "the adult version of covering your ears and yelling, 'I'm not listening! I'm not listening!' "[16]

The youngest Scalia continued, "My father, who is one of the most conservative figures in government, chose to send me to Amherst to be taught by some of the greatest minds in the country . . . Would a man who is opposed to the 'liberal ideals of constructive disagreement and debate' send his daughter to a school well known for its liberal leanings? Absolutely not."

Justice Scalia read the letter when it appeared in the Amherst campus newspaper. "I was proud of the fact that she nailed exactly the right argument, exactly the argument that would shame these people," he said. "Instead of grousing, 'why couldn't you be nice to my father'—it's BOOM!"[17]

In an interview years later, Meg Scalia said that she wrote the letter as a way to "vent." "This was *my* college," she said, recalling her anger at what she considered a self-indulgent act by the professors. "I was appalled at what they did." As an undergraduate at Amherst and then as a graduate student at the University of Virginia, she added that she had become accustomed to hearing from liberals who wanted to convey their scorn for her father. Some "looked at me as if I was the devil," she said. To the really nasty comments about her father, her standard brush-off was: "I'll tell him at dinner next week."[18]

By late February, virtually every major paper in the country had editorialized against Scalia's participation in the Cheney case because of the shared hunting trip.[19] *Newsday* wrote that "Scalia's reputation and the court's credibility are on the line." The more conservative, Rupert Murdoch–owned *New York Post* said, "To find Democrats and other liberal types with their sights set squarely on Scalia is hardly surprising—his pointed eloquent opinions annoy them no end. This time Scalia was asking for it."[20]

Cartoonists and comics were having a field day. Tony Auth of *The Philadelphia Inquirer* drew a cartoon captioned "Cheney and Scalia on the Hunt" in which the pair was in a boat marked "Undisclosed Location" and the bubble over Dick Cheney's head said, "Ahh, Nino . . . Shooting ducks, Nailing Democrats . . . Life is good." Dana Summers of the *Orlando Sentinel* drew Cheney shooting at Lady Justice, with the grinning Scalia looking on. The comic host Jay Leno quipped on *The Tonight Show* that when Cheney visited the White House, "Security made him empty his pockets and out fell Justice Antonin Scalia."[21]

Using some of those comic examples, the Sierra Club, one of the two parties opposite Cheney and the other defendants in the Supreme Court case, filed a formal request on February 23 asking Scalia to take himself off the case. "Because the American public, as reflected in the nation's newspaper editorials, has unanimously concluded that there is an appearance of favoritism," the Sierra Club argued, "any objective observer would be compelled to conclude that Justice Scalia's impartiality has been questioned." Written by the lawyer Alan Morrison, the filing argued that the case presented more than the typical social contact between a justice and an executive branch official. Recusal was necessary to restore public confidence in the Court's handling of the case, it said. The Sierra Club, whose request was not joined by Judicial Watch (the other plaintiff), relied on the 1974 law that said "a justice [or] judge . . . of the United States shall disqualify himself in any proceeding in which his impartiality might reasonably be questioned."[22]

Scalia could not believe the grief he was getting. The Sierra Club noted in its filing that no newspaper had editorialized in support of him. He could feel sentiment among his Court colleagues shifting, too. In the beginning, he believed their attitude was "Oh, there's nothing to it." That view was being replaced by embarrassment and concern. At their private meetings on pending cases, his colleagues began asking about the appearance of impropriety. Sandra Day O'Connor and Anthony Kennedy were particularly worried. John Paul Stevens did not like that Scalia went on the trip with Cheney, but Stevens believed the ordeal was more complicated than simply whether Scalia should have vacationed with the vice president. Stevens worried about an attempt to use the media to manipulate him off the case.

Scalia was annoyed and upset at his colleagues' wavering support. If they felt that way, he thought, why did they not tell him at the outset?

"I remember talking to him about the Cheney thing," recalled Leonard Leo, the executive vice president of the Federalist Society and a longtime Scalia friend. "He felt very strongly about his own ethical integrity. He took it very personally. They [the other justices] were all . . . instead of just sort of unflinchingly backing him up, they were like, 'Ah, maybe you shouldn't have done that. We know you're a good man.' . . . So I think he felt like he was put out there alone."[23]

In the cloistered center of the Court, Scalia's obvious hurt feelings prompted O'Connor to write him a personal note. In essence, she said, You have to do what you need to do. She added that she would back him no matter what he decided. The note provided some warmth in a relationship that was often cool. Scalia was not going to sit out the case, and he was glad he would have O'Connor's support in that choice.

He held to his original position. Didn't people realize that throughout history, justices were often close friends with the president or other senior administration officials? And any money he saved in the free air flight down to Louisiana on Air Force Two was spent on the expense of a one-way fare back home. On March 18 Scalia laid out those thoughts and other rationales. In a twenty-one-page public response to the Sierra Club's request that he step out of the case, he wagged his finger at those who tried to shame him. "If it is reasonable to think that a Supreme Court justice can be bought so cheap, the nation is in deeper trouble than I had imagined," he wrote, characteristically letting his intense feelings show. "Since I do not believe my impartiality can reasonably be questioned, I do not think it would be proper for me to recuse."

Scalia provided a detailed chronology of the trip to Louisiana and said, "The vice president and I were never in the same blind, and never discussed the case." Scalia noted that friendship alone could be ground for recusal but said that would be the situation only when "the personal fortune or the personal freedom of the friend is at issue."[24]

Cheney had not been acting in a personal capacity but as a government official when he declined to turn over the records sought by Judicial Watch and the Sierra Club. Yet arguably Cheney would be concerned about his reputation or any negative consequences toward him for his actions in his official role. Scalia acknowledged the point and responded: "To be sure, there could be political consequences from the disclosure of the fact (if it be so) that the vice president favored business interests, and especially a sector of the business with which he was formerly connected. But political consequences are not my concern." So Scalia realized that if the documents showed that Cheney, a former chief executive officer of Halliburton Corporation, had improperly favored his old friends in the energy business, it would undermine the integrity of the vice president and his task force. Scalia minimized the outcome of such a revelation.

Mocking that sentiment and recalling the December 2000 *Bush v. Gore* ruling, the *New York Times* columnist Maureen Dowd, one of his regular critics, wrote, " 'Political consequences are not my concern,' says the justice. Unless, of course, it's about picking the president of the United States."[25]

Scalia had rejected Alan Morrison's argument that press opinions helped prove that Scalia's impartiality could be reasonably questioned. Scalia believed the reaction of a "press . . . eager to find foot-faults" was not necessarily reasonable. He simply did not see the press as a reliable surrogate for the public, a fair-minded watchdog of corruption. Scalia's sentiment recalled his 1990 speech addressing what he believed was the inadequacy of news media coverage of the law. His maxim that "by and large, no news is good news" was taking on new meaning in his latest controversy.[26]

The deeper message of Scalia's response to the Sierra Club revealed the value of power networks and the clubby atmosphere that pervaded Washington. "Many justices have reached this Court precisely because they were friends of the incumbent president or other senior officials," Scalia wrote in the memorandum spurning the Sierra Club request. Scalia noted that Justice Harlan F. Stone had played lawn games with members of the Hoover administration outside the White House, that Chief Justice Fred Vinson had played poker with President Truman, that Justice John Marshall Harlan and his wife sang hymns at the White House with President Rutherford B. Hayes, and that Justice Byron White, appointed by President John F. Kennedy, had skied in Colorado with Attorney General Robert F. Kennedy. "A rule that required members of this Court to remove themselves from cases in which the official actions of friends were at issue would be utterly disabling," Scalia wrote.

That was probably true. Yet Scalia's explanation, that who you know has always been important in Washington, fed his critics' point about how Cheney's task force dispute arose in the first place. The Sierra Club and other environmentalists asserted that the energy policy favored oil industry officials because the panel had given inordinate influence to friends of Cheney and Bush, such as the Enron Corporation CEO Kenneth Lay, who had been invited to participate in the task force and whom Bush called "Kenny Boy." The Federal Advisory Committee Act was designed precisely to counteract the negative effect of officials' inclination to play favorites. Yet here was Scalia saying that's how Washington works: many of us are sitting on this Court "precisely because" of presidential friendships. Scalia seemed unaware of the irony of the situation and how it was only feeding public indignation.

It was not the first time that he heard public calls for his disqualification on a case involving hunting buddies. Two years earlier, in 2002, Scalia played a role in a dispute involving the Mississippi congressional district of the U.S. representative Chip Pickering. Scalia was a friend of Pickering and his father, the U.S. district judge Charles W. Pickering, and had gone turkey hunting with them. The state of Mississippi had merged Pickering's district with one held by the Democratic congressman Ronnie Shows, an action taken because of a state population decline in the 2000 census and the subsequent need to reduce the number of Mississippi U.S. House districts from five to four. The Bush Justice Department had intervened in the drawing of new boundaries in a way that reduced the black Democratic population in the district and boosted white Republican precincts. Mississippi Democrats made an emergency appeal to the U.S. Supreme Court in a crucial phase of the redistricting dispute. The matter went to Justice Scalia, who oversaw emergency filings from that southern region. Scalia rejected the appeal. *The Clarion-Ledger* of Jackson wrote an editorial in February 2002 that said, "The Supreme Court justice has not only visited Mississippi to turkey hunt with the elder Pickering, but when Chip Pickering was sworn in to Congress, Scalia presided with Judge Pickering administering the oath. Small world, isn't it? Or . . . It's the 'or' that should send up red flags. Justice Scalia should have recused himself from [the redistricting case] decision."[27] Pickering defeated Shows the following November.

Scalia was aware that conflicts of interest could arise for a judge and had thought out his position two decades earlier. During his appeals court confirmation hearings at the Senate Judiciary Committee in 1982, Scalia addressed the question of when he should sit out a case. "As far as my own personal soul search is concerned," he had said, "I would disqualify myself in any case in which I believed my connection with one of the litigants or any other circumstances would cause my judgment to be distorted in favor of or against one of the parties. I would furthermore disqualify myself if a situation arose in which, even though my judgment would not be distorted, a reasonable person would believe that my judgment would be distorted. That does not mean anybody in the world, but a reasonable person."[28]

Scalia had previously abided by his statements. As an appeals court judge, he had taken himself out of AT&T cases for a period of time because he had been a legal consultant to AT&T during his years as a law professor. He had advised the company in its antitrust dispute with MCI Communications and earned $25,800 in 1982. After three years, he sat on an AT&T case unrelated to his consulting that centered on a relatively minor procedural interpretation of a Federal Communications Commission rule. Scalia wrote an opinion against the company.[29]

His participation in that dispute was raised at the 1986 Senate confirmation hearing when Scalia was being considered for the Supreme Court. Senators, including Patrick Leahy, asked him why he did not sit out longer than three years on AT&T cases. Scalia said he thought three years "would be more than enough to eliminate any appearance of impropriety" and noted that he had checked with the D.C. Circuit chief judge Spottswood Robinson on the matter. Leahy seemed satisfied with Scalia's answer in 1986 and voted for the nominee.

Now Senator Leahy was infuriated by the justice's refusal to sit out the Cheney case. Over the years, Leahy—whose mother was Italian American—and Scalia had become social acquaintances. They mingled at annual dinners sponsored by the National Italian American Foundation, at the residences of Italian ambassadors, and at other black-tie evenings celebrating Italian art and music. Now, however, their differences were playing out in not-so-chummy terms. "It is unfortunate that Justice Scalia does not appreciate how his private vacation with Vice President Cheney . . . creates an appearance of impropriety in the minds of reasonable people," Leahy said immediately after Scalia issued his March 18 memorandum. "Instead of strengthening public confidence in our court system, Justice Scalia's decision risks undermining it. Such nearsightedness on a matter so basic to public trust in the independent judiciary is as puzzling to the American people as it is harmful to the court."[30] Leahy said he did not care about the details of the trip and who was in which duck blind. "To many, the very fact that this vacation weekend happened while this decision [in the Cheney task force dispute] was pending is enough to make the situation quack like a duck."

When the case was heard a month later, on April 27, 2004, Scalia was at his usual place along the mahogany bench. It was the second case of the morning. When the justices took a brief break between the cases, Scalia momentarily stood up, as if he might leave. But he was stretching himself in the brief interlude. He had no intention of leaving for the Cheney case.

Beyond the question of Scalia's participation, the dispute was eliciting considerable press and public attention for the myriad substantive issues it raised. At the core was the question of favoritism for oil executives such as Kenneth Lay, whose Enron Corporation had subsequently collapsed under the weight of wrongdoing. Also inciting interest was how much the energy task force's situation recalled the Ford administration years, when Cheney (and Scalia) argued for strong regard of executive privilege and fended off congressional scrutiny of White House inner workings.

When Cheney was first sued over the task force documents, he told a reporter that he wanted to preserve the confidentiality of executive branch activities. "If you're a student of politics and the presidency, it's a very important issue. It ought to be resolved in a court, unless you're willing to compromise on a basic fundamental principle, which we're not." It would later emerge that during this time, Cheney's office was involved in a multitude of secret executive branch endeavors, including a domestic eavesdropping program in response to the September 11 terrorist attacks.[31]

At the Supreme Court, the question was not whether there had been an improper relationship between Cheney and any private advisers to the energy task force, let alone any question of the relationship between Scalia and Cheney. Rather, the question was whether the Bush-Cheney administration had grounds for appealing the lower court order that they had to reveal names of private citizens the energy panel consulted. Administration lawyers were arguing that any release of the documents related to the vice president's work would violate the constitutional separation of powers and regard for executive privilege.

"The Constitution explicitly commits to the President's discretion the authority to obtain the opinions of subordinates and to formulate recommendations for legislation," the U.S. solicitor general Theodore Olson told the justices. "Congress may neither intrude on the President's ability to perform these functions, nor authorize private litigants to use the courts to do so." Olson, who earlier had worked in the Reagan administration and believed in strong executive powers, argued that forcing release of the task force documents "violates the Constitution in the context of this case [and] intrudes on the president's 'core functions' of seeking advice and developing legislation."[32]

When it was his turn at the lectern, Alan Morrison, representing the Sierra Club, disputed the constitutional arguments and noted that the administration acknowledged "that there were substantial numbers of meetings between outside people and the task force. The question is what happened at those meetings, and that's why we seek discovery"—that is, the production of documents and interviews with participants. Reminding the justices that the environmental group was trying to determine who attended the task force meetings and what access they had to draft reports and recommendations, Morrison said, "I do not think that the government has any right to withhold that kind of information in this kind of case."

Paul Orfanedes, representing Judicial Watch, told the justices that Cheney had met with Lay, among other energy executives, to generate recommendations. To that, Scalia retorted, "What does that prove? They talked to a lot of people, got a lot of advice, but does that make them de facto members of the committee?"

"Well," Orfanedes responded, "that's the question that we are seeking to answer through our discovery . . . These are not mere unsupported allegations."

In the end, the Supreme Court ruled by a 7–2 vote not to force Cheney to make public the internal membership documents from the 2001 energy task force. Even two of the more liberal justices, Stevens and Breyer, were concerned about the separation-of-powers dilemma the case presented. The majority did not rule on the merits. Rather, the justices returned the case to the D.C. Circuit, saying that panel had failed to consider the "weighty separation-of-powers issue" raised by the dispute over the executive branch documents. The Supreme Court termed the district judge's order requiring production of task force materials "overly broad," yet the Court suggested that it would not find the task force completely shielded from all pretrial discovery. Writing for the majority, Justice Kennedy stressed constitutional protections for executive privilege and said "the need for information for use in civil cases, while far from negligible, does not share the urgency or significance of [a] criminal subpoena."[33]

Scalia voted with Justice Kennedy's majority view, returning the case for further proceedings. Scalia also joined Justice Thomas in a separate opinion that would have fully protected the Cheney task force from turning over any documents. None of the justices in the majority, nor the two dissenters, Ginsburg and Souter, referred to the Scalia-Cheney friendship.

The challenge by the Sierra Club and Judicial Watch dissolved a year later when the U.S. Court of Appeals for the District of Columbia Circuit dismissed the lawsuit against Cheney. "In making decisions on personnel and policy, and in formulating legislative proposals, the President must be free to seek confidential information from many sources, both inside the government and outside," wrote Judge A. Raymond Randolph for the D.C. Circuit. With none of the other D.C. Circuit judges who heard the case dissenting, Randolph wrote that a committee such as the National Energy Policy Development Group should be considered wholly made up of federal officials, and beyond the reach of the Federal Advisory Committee Act, if no outsiders held a vote or veto power over committee decisions. "Neither Judicial Watch nor the Sierra Club explicitly claimed that any non-federal individual had a vote on the NEPDG or had a veto over its decisions," Randolph noted.[34]

When it was all over, Scalia's participation in the Cheney case was far from determinative, and irrespective of the parties involved, he tended to favor strong executive authority. Yet the controversy added to the public persona of this outspoken justice. It swelled the weight of examples that showed Scalia scoffing at public opinion and mocking news media scrutiny. These episodes exposed him to regular questions about whether his off-bench statements were prejudicing his on-the-bench impartiality.

Other justices went out of their way to make it appear as if they had no political alliances. The former justice Lewis Powell famously refrained from voting in presidential elections. Others were generally guarded when they picked up a microphone before law students, professors, and other audiences, and tried not to convey personal allegiances or views on how the Court had ruled. Chief Justice Rehnquist, partisan to the core, nonetheless would rarely offer audiences more than a straightforward litany of the facts of a case and how the majority ruled. Rehnquist would keep his views on the wisdom of the ruling to himself. Scalia, on the other hand, got it all off his chest. "Part of my charm is telling people what they don't like to hear," he said. He was defiantly successful.

When he was asked about the duck-hunting incident two years later at the University of Connecticut Law School in Hartford, he said, "For Pete's sake, if you can't trust your Supreme Court justice more than that, get a life . . . I think the proudest thing I have done on the bench is not allow myself to be chased off that case."[35]

Scalia later elaborated in an interview: "It's the thing I've done here that required the most character. You can be proud about intellectual accomplishments . . . But you know that quote of my father's . . . 'Brains are like muscles . . .' ['you can hire them by the hour. The only thing that's not for sale is character.'] . . . That [staying on the case] took some guts."[36]

Scalia's combativeness defined his public personality. It was as if he never lost what his aunt Lenora Panaro called "*capo tosta*," the bullheadedness. "You couldn't dissuade him," she said. "He knew what he wanted—even when he was little."[37]

Many of his most notorious outbursts recorded in press accounts occurred in the 2000s, perhaps as part of the lingering scrutiny after *Bush v. Gore*, perhaps because of the Internet age and the instantaneous communication of his bold posture. In one instance he found it necessary to yield to a request that he take himself out of a case because of what he had said in a speech.

A year before the duck-hunting incident with Cheney, Scalia had spoken at an outdoor Religious Freedom Day ceremony organized by the Knights of Columbus in Fredericksburg, Virginia. As he had on other occasions celebrating religion, Scalia first recounted an experience from September 11, 2001, when he was in Rome at an international conference of judges. He recalled that attendees, most of whom were European, watched President Bush's televised address to the nation that night. Scalia noted that Bush's address ended, as presidential addresses often do, with Bush saying, "God bless America." That prompted one European judge to tell Scalia, "How I wish that the head of state of my country, at a similar time of national tragedy and distress, could conclude his address with 'God bless.' "[38]

Scalia recounted the story many times as a lesson in the value of Americans' willingness to praise God in public places. But as he spoke in Fredericksburg, dressed in overcoat and wool cap against the winter cold, Scalia added a new footnote as he endorsed keeping "God [in] the public forum and political life." Scalia referred to a decision a few months earlier by the U.S. Court of Appeals for the Ninth Circuit stating that public school teachers' leading the recitation of the Pledge of Allegiance to the flag, with its "under God" language, violated the freedom of religion of atheist children and atheist parents.

Scalia suggested that the appeals court decision was misguided. "The new constitutional philosophy says if those who decide the law think it would be a good idea to get religion out of the public forum," he continued, "then it will be exterminated from the public forum through judicial fiat." Scalia concluded by telling his audience, "On this day, when we're celebrating our constitutional heritage, I urge you to be faithful to that heritage—to impose on our fellow citizens only the restrictions that are there in the Constitution, not invent new ones." His implication was that the Ninth Circuit court had carved out a religious right where none was deserved.[39]

The dispute over the Pledge of Allegiance had started with Michael Newdow, an atheist in Sacramento who argued that recitation of the words "under God" in the pledge harmed him and his daughter. Every morning when his daughter's classmates stood up, faced the flag, placed their hands over their hearts, and pledged to one "nation under God," he contended, they were sending the message that Newdow's atheism was wrong.

In September 2003, as the Supreme Court was considering whether to review the Ninth Circuit ruling, Newdow asked Scalia to take himself out of the matter because of the justice's comments in Fredericksburg.[40] Newdow noted that the Ninth Circuit's decision, which came at the fulcrum of patriotism and politics, had generated great criticism. "A firestorm of controversy arose when the opinion was first released," Newdow wrote in his request for Scalia's recusal. "This reaction was clearly the result of the religious aspects of this case, and the value theistic Americans place upon the worship of God. The associated passions—though understandable—are the very reason we have an Establishment Clause, and, perhaps in this arena more than any other, it is essential that the judiciary present a neutral front."[41]

Newdow emphasized that Scalia had made his disapproving comments at an event sponsored by the Knights of Columbus, which had ardently supported the formal addition of the words "under God" to the pledge in 1954. Newdow, a lawyer who represented himself in the case, said he was not challenging Scalia's right to speak out on important legal matters, but rather his decision to voice a conclusion on a pending case before reading the briefs or hearing oral arguments.

The next month, when the Court agreed to consider whether the recitation of the pledge was an official endorsement of religion—as Newdow claimed and the Ninth Circuit ruled—and also whether Newdow had "standing" to bring the lawsuit, Scalia revealed that he would not hear the case. His decision was announced in a brief note that accompanied the Court's taking of the pledge dispute. It said only that Justice Scalia "took no part" in the consideration of the case.[42]

The 2004 Pledge of Allegiance controversy was one of the most closely watched tests of the line between church and state. In the end, however, the justices did not reach the merits of the constitutional question. The majority found that Newdow lacked legal standing to sue, because he did not have custody of his daughter. The Court majority described the recitation of the pledge as "a patriotic exercise designed to foster national unity and pride in [the] principles" it invokes, but declined to resolve Newdow's arguments about how it might violate his religious rights.[43]

Shortly before Scalia's Fredericksburg remarks, he had addressed the topic of physician-assisted suicide to a law school audience in Portland, Oregon, in a way that turned into another sideshow—although that time in a lower court proceeding on an Oregon law and in a less publicized episode. Voters in Oregon had passed in 1994, and affirmed in 1997, a law that allowed patients to obtain lethal medication when physicians had certified they had less than six months to live. The "right to die" law, the first of its kind in the nation, had taken effect in 1997. In 2001 Bush's attorney general John Ashcroft had issued a directive intended to block the law. He sought to use his power under the Controlled Substances Act to cancel the authority of any physician who participated in the Oregon law to write prescriptions. Oregon officials and groups that endorsed physician-assisted suicide—a process that used federally controlled substances—sued the federal government.

As that lawsuit was pending, Scalia happened to present a wide-ranging talk at Lewis and Clark College in Portland. Scalia explained in the 2002 speech his "originalist thinking" and rejected the notion of a "living Constitution."[44]

"You want a right to abortion . . . persuade your fellow citizens it's a good idea and pass a law." Then he added, "You want the right to die? The Constitution said nothing about it." He said that should be put to a vote. A woman in the audience said, "We did, sir."

"That's right and that's fine," Scalia responded. "You don't hear me complaining about Oregon's law." Scalia's comments prompted the U.S. district court judge Robert Jones, hearing the Ashcroft case, to take the unusual step of asking lawyers from both sides to respond to Scalia's comments. Jones ended up rejecting Ashcroft's intervention and validated the Oregon law. On appeal, the U.S. Court of Appeals for the Ninth Circuit affirmed that decision.[45]

When the matter came before the U.S. Supreme Court years later, neither party sought Scalia's recusal in the case. Interestingly, when his vote was on the line, Scalia did not endorse the Oregon voters' action. The question for resolution was not whether the Constitution itself either created a right to physician-assisted suicide or prohibited states from creating such a right, but whether Ashcroft had properly invoked his authority under the Controlled Substances Act to block Oregon's law. On that question, Scalia dissented from the six-justice majority opinion that found, as the lower courts had, that Attorney General Ashcroft lacked the legal authority to preclude the "right to die" law.

In some respects, it was a surprising vote. Scalia had joined the Court's earlier federalism opinions requiring more than an interest in a matter of social policy (guns, violence against women, for example) to justify federal action. Yet in the Oregon case he said federal authority could be invoked based on public morality: "From an early time in our national history, the Federal Government has used its enumerated powers, such as its power to regulate interstate commerce, for the purpose of protecting public morality—for example, by banning the interstate shipment of lottery tickets, or the interstate transport of women for immoral purposes."[46]

Scalia argued with the notions that physician-assisted suicide involved essentially medical judgments and that Congress did not intend to make the attorney general responsible for such judgments. He said the attorney general's judgment in the assisted-suicide dispute "no more depends upon a 'quintessentially medical judgment' than does the legitimacy of polygamy or eugenic infanticide."

Scalia's views were not unlike John Ashcroft's. As a Republican senator from Missouri, Ashcroft in 1997 had urged then Attorney General Janet Reno to find that the Oregon measure violated federal law. A strong advocate of "faith-based" programs and a hero to the Christian Coalition, Ashcroft believed assisted suicide to be morally wrong. Under other circumstances, Ashcroft, like Scalia for that matter, tended to want a freer rein for state authority and less intervention from Washington. When Ashcroft became attorney general under George W. Bush, his office declared that "assisting suicide is not a legitimate medical purpose" for dispensing drugs.

The Supreme Court majority that ruled in favor of Oregon found politics at the core of Ashcroft's directive. In the opinion by Justice Kennedy, the Court noted that in the late 1990s Ashcroft was among the members of Congress who had tried to undermine Oregon's law through pressure on Attorney General Reno and also through a failed attempt at legislation. Kennedy detailed how Ashcroft, once he was appointed by Bush to be attorney general, issued a directive against the Oregon law "without consulting Oregon or apparently anyone outside his department." If the directive had stood, the Kennedy majority said, it would have meant a "radical shift" of state power to the federal government. Scalia, who in other circumstances might have agreed with such federalism interests, differed this time around. His positions appeared contradictory and opened him up to criticism that he was voting moral, rather than legal, interests.[47]

To such criticism, Scalia said in an interview, "The regulation of commerce to achieve what the federal government considers to be moral aims goes back a long way."[48]

In the spring of 2004 Scalia accepted a request channeled through a friend and occasional hunting partner, the U.S. District Court judge Charles Pickering, to speak at a Presbyterian Christian School in Hattiesburg, Mississippi. Scalia combined the speech with an appearance at the nearby William Carey College, a private Baptist school. At both events Scalia had run-ins with the media that would, again, bring his off-bench behavior headlines and reveal his rocky relationship with the press.

At the close of Scalia's speech at William Carey College, the college president, Larry Kennedy, told reporters that they could attend a scheduled reception with Scalia.[49] The justice felt blindsided by the announcement because he did not typically meet with reporters at his speaking engagements. As he and Kennedy were heading toward the reception, they crossed the path of a cameraman for WDAM, Hattiesburg Channel 7. "He was filming the justice and everybody walking behind him," recalled Deputy U.S. Marshal Melanie Rube. "Justice Scalia looked like he got angry. He walked over, kind of threw his notebook down, and said something to the President of the College. I'm not sure what it was but I know it involved telling the media to go away or telling the cameraman to go away."[50] Kennedy spoke to the cameraman, who then packed up and left. The Associated Press reporter Denise Grones also witnessed the incident and recalled, "I heard him say something along the lines of he didn't like the media and he didn't know why we were there. He was not going to speak to us."[51]

That reinforced to Deputy Marshal Rube the idea that Scalia had definite views about how journalists should be treated at Scalia events and caused her to take action a few hours later when Scalia began speaking in the Presbyterian Christian School gym about his favorite topic, originalism. The Associated Press reporter Grones and the *Hattiesburg American* reporter Antoinette Konz were taping the speech, as was routine for their coverage. Grones had found Scalia's earlier speech at William Carey College heavy going and had chatted with Konz about the difficulty of translating jurisprudential theory to average readers.

As the reporters were trying to listen to the justice and take notes, Deputy Marshal Rube approached them and demanded that they stop their tape recorders and erase their tapes. "I sat down beside [Grones]," Rube recalled. "I picked up the digital recorder that was now between the two of us and I asked her was she recording and she said, yes. And I said

I'm sorry, ma'am, it's the Justice's policy that he not be recorded and I'm going to have to ask you to turn this off and erase it. She did not want to erase it." When Grones said she needed the recorder to make sure the quotes in her story were accurate, Rube said, "I'm sorry. I'm not trying to make your job any more difficult, but it is his standing policy not to be recorded." Rube pushed a button on the recorder to stop the recording and confiscated the tape. She then demanded Konz's tape.

The reporters, both of whom were relatively new in the profession, were shocked at the treatment they received. When they returned to their respective news offices, their editors immediately protested to the marshal's office. They also published stories about the marshal's seizing their tapes and the fact that Scalia might have ordered it. The national media quickly focused on whether a jurist responsible for upholding the Constitution was responsible for a confiscation of reporters' tapes at a public event.[52]

The U.S. representative Barney Frank, a Democrat from Massachusetts on the House Judiciary Committee, was among the public officials and media representatives who wrote to Attorney General Ashcroft, Chief Justice Rehnquist, and Justice Scalia, trying to find out why the news reporters were censored. "Justice Scalia of course has the right to make whatever speeches he wishes to make," Frank wrote. "But I am deeply troubled by the notion that he not only has the right to demand that no record be made of these speeches, even when they are given in public forums, but that he may use federal law enforcement officials to carry out his wishes . . . Since we depend on the Supreme Court to defend our freedoms, including freedom of expression, and freedom of the press, the notion that a law enforcement official would, on behalf of a Supreme Court Justice, interfere with those freedoms is a very grave matter."[53]

The whole episode recalled an incident a year earlier, in March 2003, when Scalia received the Citadel of Free Speech Award from the City Club of Cleveland and barred television and radio reporters from covering his speech. He refused to allow C-SPAN, run by his old friend Brian Lamb, into the event. In another incident seven years earlier in Los Angeles, officers accompanying Scalia at an appearance at a downtown hotel tried to seize the tape recorder of the *Los Angeles Times* reporter Henry Weinstein. He refused to turn it over and quickly left the event.[54]

As media outrage over the Hattiesburg incident spiraled, Scalia insisted he did not intend for newspaper reporters to have to give up their tapes. "I am writing to extend my apology for what occurred during my talk at Presbyterian Christian School in Hattiesburg last Wednesday," Scalia wrote on April 9, 2004, to the *Hattiesburg American* reporter Konz. "As I understand it from press reports, a United States Marshal erased, or caused you to erase, the tape recorder that you were using for the purpose of assuring the accuracy of your press report. I imagine that is an upsetting and indeed enraging experience, and I want you to know how it happened.

"What happened in Hattiesburg is this: It had been announced at my talk earlier that day, at William Carey College, that video or audio recording was not permitted. [This was Scalia's long-standing prohibition.] That announcement was not repeated at the high school, but the marshals believed (with good reason) that the same policy was in effect. Indeed, perhaps they thought the announcement had been made.

"I abhor as much as any American the prospect of a law enforcement officer seizing a reporter's notes or recording. The marshals were doing what they believed to be their job, and the fault was mine in not assuring that the ground rules had been clarified. (To tell the truth, even if they had been clarified and some reporter had broken them, I would not have wanted the tape erased.) I have learned my lesson (at your expense), and shall certainly be more careful in the future. Indeed, in the future I will make it clear that recording for use of the print media is no problem at all."[55]

Scalia also responded on April 9 to a letter he had received from Lucy A. Dalglish, of the Reporters Committee for Freedom of the Press, referring to her "well justified concern over the incident at Presbyterian Christian School in Hattiesburg."

"You are correct that the action was not taken at my direction," Scalia wrote. "I was as upset as you were. I have written to the reporters involved, extending my apology and undertaking to revise my policy so as to permit recording for use of the print media. (That policy will, as you say, promote accurate reporting . . .)"[56]

The news organizations' complaints, along with those from federal officials such as Representative Frank, triggered investigations by the Department of Justice and its U.S. Marshals Service. Debra Sanderson, a senior inspector with Judicial Security who was on duty with Rube the day of Scalia's Hattiesburg appearance, testified to Scalia's policy (prior to the Hattiesburg incident) of not permitting his speeches to be recorded for any purpose. Sanderson said from the start that his chambers or Court police had told her "he did not want his speeches recorded. And then when I picked him up at the airport [on at least one occasion] I asked him that again and he said he doesn't allow any taping of his speeches."[57]

Sanderson also echoed what Deputy Marshal Rube and the Associated Press reporter Grones said about Scalia's being upset to discover that reporters had been invited to the reception at the William Carey College event. Recounted Sanderson, Scalia was "very noticeably upset, and he told Dr. Kennedy that, and he threw his folder down and said, he was just about ready to leave. But when they, the press, left, he was okay and he greeted people."

Sanderson talked with Scalia the day after the incident as she accompanied him to the airport. She called his attention to a newspaper story about the confiscation of the tapes. "I said, 'Justice, did you see this article in the paper?' And he said, 'No, but I saw it on TV.' And I said, 'Well I thought I was doing what you wanted me to do. You don't want your speech recorded.' And he made the comment, 'Well I just don't want to be on the radio or TV. I don't care if the newspaper wants to record it.' And I didn't say anything, but I thought: how do you distinguish it? The newspaper records it. Why couldn't the radio or the TV get it? But I didn't say that. I said okay. That was it and he told me not to worry about it and that was our conversation."

After a Department of Justice investigation, officials decided not to pursue any criminal matters regarding the incident. The U.S. Marshals Service general counsel also reviewed the allegations and found no violations.

Scalia was surprised at the uproar and press attention. The incident betrayed not only his deep lack of trust in the press but also his misunderstanding of its work. Back in 1990 he had spoken at a Pepperdine University event about how the general press was not competent to cover legal affairs. But he had received so much journalistic criticism, he said, that he never presented the speech again. "I never gave it again because it got— the press got, you know . . ." he began in an interview nearly twenty years later, and then his voice trailed off. "The press is very thin-skinned whether you know this or not. They can dish it out but they can't take it, and they were so upset by this talk."[58]

•

The out-of-Court Scalia could not be separated from his black-robe persona, and he was more than a legal provocateur. In breaking from the usual decorum for a jurist, he was increasing his following. Rarely did Scalia pick up a pen or stand at a lectern that he did not draw an audience on the Internet, over the airwaves, and on cable. His singeing opinions made him a celebrity and generated a cult following on Internet sites created in the mid-2000s. He was becoming the most-quoted member of the contemporary Court in casebooks and in law review articles. His off-the-bench personality was a constant source of curiosity for the media, as well as for late-night comedians.

His notoriety was not without some cost. For his critics, his bluster would become more remarkable than his intellect. "Widely advertised as exceptionally smart, he sometimes does and says things that are extraordinarily stupid," wrote the liberal commentator Joe Conason in 2006 in *The New York Observer*.[59]

A few years later, Stanley Pottinger, a former colleague from the Ford administration who had become a writer, asked Scalia in a television interview about the difference between how he was perceived and who he really was. Scalia briefly looked down, narrowed his eyes, then said, "I do know that I am sometimes surprised at . . . you know . . . the expressed vehemence of . . . almost antagonism.

"You know," Scalia added, "I'm not that nasty a fellow." And then he laughed, a little nervously but mostly looking very self-satisfied as the camera rolled.[60]

THIRTEEN

THE CENTER CHAIR

When in the fall of 2004 Chief Justice William Rehnquist fell ill with thyroid cancer, his condition set off months of conjecture over his potential replacement. Antonin Scalia's name was at the center of the speculation. On the Supreme Court for eighteen years, Scalia had become the intellectual leader of legal conservatives. Law students and professors—the like-minded but even many who disagreed with him—devoured his legal opinions. Of the nine sitting justices, he was most often the subject of academic law review articles. He had a celebrity quality that drew standing-room-only crowds to his appearances on college campuses. And he was held up as a model justice by President George W. Bush, who would be the one deciding on a new chief justice if Rehnquist retired.

Yet Scalia was also the Court's contrarian. The speculation on Rehnquist's replacement turned on the question: Could a justice whose views of the Constitution harked back two centuries, who often used sharp language in criticizing other justices' opinions, and who routinely lost the votes of his colleagues become chief justice of the United States? Within the decorous chambers, Scalia was notorious for pushing away other justices at critical points in the decision-making process. In a close case, when he was barely holding on to a majority, he could not resist brash comments that might alienate a key vote. When he was in dissent, he did not go quietly. On critical points of law he declared that his colleagues' opinions "cannot be taken seriously"; were "beyond the absurd"; and should be considered "nothing short of preposterous."[1] In June 2004, a few months before Rehnquist revealed the cancer, the Court ruled that the execution of mentally retarded convicts violated the Eighth Amendment prohibition on cruel and unusual punishment. Scalia, in dissent, blasted the majority: "Seldom has an opinion of this Court rested so obviously upon nothing but the personal views of its members."[2]

As Rehnquist's illness progressed, Scalia began drafting a similarly angry dissent in another death penalty case. This one tested whether defendants who committed their crimes before they were eighteen years old should, like the mentally retarded, be outside the reach of capital punishment. A majority of the justices was about to so hold. In a dissenting opinion that would be joined by Rehnquist and Justice Thomas, Scalia again contended that the majority was simply asserting its own moral judgment and, regarding the culpability of juveniles, "picking and choosing among social data." He declared, "[T]his is no way to run a legal system."[3]

Around this time, Justice Ruth Bader Ginsburg said of Scalia, "I love him. But sometimes I'd like to strangle him." Justice John Paul Stevens, the eldest member of the bench, added separately, "I think everybody respects Nino's wonderful writing ability and his style and all the rest. But everybody on the Court from time to time has thought he was unwise to take such an extreme position, both in tone and in the position."[4]

Stevens, who expressed fondness for Scalia even when Scalia was at his most rhetorically overdramatic, later elaborated, "If he thinks a position is totally indefensible, he'll say so. And sometimes I think his rhetoric is stronger than what is justified or what is actually persuasive. He's got to have the last word. But is it really worth it?"[5]

By early 2005 Rehnquist was still undergoing aggressive chemotherapy for the thyroid cancer, and there was no indication that his health was improving. When the Court first disclosed Rehnquist's cancer and the need for a tracheotomy on October 25, 2004, its news release had said, "He is expected to be on the Bench when the Court reconvenes on Monday, November 1."[6] When November came, Rehnquist issued another statement, saying simply that he was continuing to recuperate at home. "According to my doctors," he wrote, "my plan to return to the office today was too optimistic. I am continuing to take radiation and chemotherapy treatments on an outpatient basis."[7]

Rehnquist did not return for December cases. Editorial writers at newspapers started to question whether the chief justice was up to the job.[8] But then on January 20, 2005, Inauguration Day for President George W. Bush's second term, Rehnquist appeared before a national television audience to swear in the president. Using a cane, walking with care down blue and red carpeted steps at the Capitol's West Front, the eighty-year-old chief justice made his way to the inaugural platform. He wore his black robe with the distinctive four gold stripes on each sleeve that he had whimsically applied a decade earlier to mimic a character in Gilbert and Sullivan's *Iolanthe*.[9] At his neck, a scarf concealed the incision for the tracheotomy tube. As Rehnquist administered the oath of office to Bush, his voice was weak. Whether he would last another term, or be able to complete the current one, was even more in doubt.

Rehnquist, first appointed by Nixon in January 1972, had been chief justice for nearly nineteen years, since 1986, the same year Scalia joined the Court. Rehnquist had presided over a remarkable shift in the law. The son of a wholesale paper salesman and a homemaker in a first-generation Swedish American home, Rehnquist had spent his early years on the Supreme Court bench on the fringe, a lone dissenter. He faced regular criticism in the news media for his hard-line decisions. He shrugged it off, once saying, "If you're bothered by what the press says about you, you're just not cut out for this job."[10]

By the early 2000s, Rehnquist, joined by like-minded conservatives, had comfortably found himself in the majority and having his say. Many of his earlier dissenting opinions were now views held by a majority of the Court. He had prevailed, for example, to enhance state authority in the face of control by Washington, to allow more public support for religion, and to curtail protracted death penalty appeals. The Court had changed with the addition of more justices on the right wing. The national scene, as well, had become more conservative.

Through the years, Rehnquist—unlike Scalia—had become more apt to compromise and go along even if he did not subscribe 100 percent to a colleague's rationale. Rarely did Rehnquist set out his differing views in a concurring statement. Scalia, on the other hand, was far more likely to make even his slightest disagreements known. The professor James Staab observed in *The Political Thought of Justice Antonin Scalia* that Scalia wrote more concurring opinions than any of his colleagues.[11]

Rehnquist, also unlike Scalia, had long ago given up the law school speaking circuit. The chief justice did not wrestle Scalia for the public mantle of legal conservatism. Rehnquist was intelligent and wry but hardly had his younger colleague's magnetism at a microphone.

Scalia thought Rehnquist compromised too much on his conservatism. The younger justice made that clear in a 2000 dispute testing whether the Warren Court landmark *Miranda v. Arizona* should be overturned. That 1966 decision had led to the well-known mandatory police warnings that a person under arrest has the right to remain silent, that anything he says can be used against him, and that he has a right to have an attorney present and, if he cannot afford one, a lawyer will be appointed. The question for the justices in 2000 was whether Congress had lifted the warnings requirement when it passed a law in 1968 that said confessions that were given voluntarily could be used at trial even when defendants had not been read their rights. That statute, intended at the time as a rebuke to the Warren Court, had never been enforced. But the Richmond-based U.S. Court of Appeals for the Fourth Circuit revived the 1968 law in a 1999 case involving a Maryland bank robbery suspect, Charles Thomas Dickerson, when it said a voluntary confession could be used although police had not read Dickerson his rights.[12]

Rehnquist had criticized *Miranda v. Arizona* in earlier cases as constitutionally unnecessary and had voted for decisions that narrowed its scope. But in the new dispute in 2000, the chief justice led a seven-justice majority in a decision reaffirming the landmark and emphasizing the Court's own power to spurn Congress's rejection of a ruling. "We hold that *Miranda*, being a constitutional decision of this Court, may not be in effect overruled by an Act of Congress, and we decline to overrule *Miranda* ourselves," Rehnquist wrote, joined by all of his colleagues but Scalia and Thomas. Rehnquist's opinion acknowledged that the majority in 2000 might not have agreed with *Miranda*'s reasoning and the resulting rule, but said that principles regarding respect for precedent "weigh heavily against overruling it now." He noted that the Miranda warnings, a staple of TV cop shows, had become embedded in police practice and the national culture.[13]

In a no-holds-barred dissenting opinion, Scalia declared Rehnquist's rationale unprincipled, an unwarranted restriction on law enforcement, and lacking true constitutional grounding. Scalia scoffed at the idea that the Court should look at *Miranda*'s special place in American culture. "As far as I am aware, the public is not under the illusion that we are infallible," Scalia wrote, and went on to declare in high metaphorical mode, "Today's judgment converts *Miranda* from a milestone of judicial over-reaching into the very Cheops' Pyramid (or perhaps the Sphinx would be a better analogue) of judicial arrogance."

Democrats were divided over the idea of a possible Scalia elevation to be chief justice. The Center for American Progress, a liberal think tank established by former aides to President Clinton, put out materials attempting to counter any momentum among Bush's aides to elevate Scalia. The group criticized his lone dissent in the Virginia Military Institute case, where he disagreed with the Court's ruling that the state-run academy had to admit women. His votes in death penalty and other prison cases were also targeted.[14]

Some on the left thought a Chief Justice Scalia might actually drive away votes from fellow conservatives. "He won't be very effective," the Northwestern University law professor Steven Lubet wrote in early 2005. "Some chief justices, such as Earl Warren, have been masterful coalition builders, persuading colleagues to join them in landmark rulings. That sort of leadership can occasionally change the direction of the entire court, but it requires political skills that Scalia has never displayed."[15] Certainly, coalition building was not Scalia's strength. Socially, Scalia could work a group. And in fact, until Rehnquist became ill and could not handle the cigarette and cigar smoke of the evening, Scalia was at Rehnquist's side during their regular poker game. On the law, however, Scalia was decidedly a solo operator. If someone joined him, it was on his terms.

Yet the Senate minority leader, Harry Reid, a Democrat from Nevada, said in an interview on NBC's *Meet the Press* that although he disagreed with Scalia on legal issues, he would support him to be chief justice because he is "one smart guy." Reid suggested also that Scalia's "ethics problems" arising from not disqualifying himself from his hunting pal Vice President Dick Cheney's case could be a hindrance.[16]

Any offer of the chief justice position was, of course, in President Bush's hands. And the president was saying nothing. Administration aides were careful to avoid public speculation because of uncertainty over whether Chief Justice Rehnquist would actually retire. Behind the scenes they were also thinking about, most substantively, what they would want from a new chief justice in terms of decisions and endurance.

As a preliminary matter, the sixty-nine-year-old Scalia would be an unusual nomination for a GOP administration. Since Reagan's time, GOP presidents had demonstrated that they wanted young nominees whose legacies would span many decades. Rehnquist had been sixty-one when Reagan elevated him to be chief justice in 1986, but no other GOP Supreme Court appointee since Reagan took office had been older than fifty-one at the time of the nomination.[17]

When Scalia was asked about his interest in the job, he scoffed dismissively. "Where do people get such an idea?" He criticized reports that said he would want the job. He referred to his age and noted Republican presidents' tendency to turn to younger candidates for the Court. Still, he privately did not rule out that it could happen. "It would be unusual for someone who's been on the Court as long as he has to not think about becoming chief justice," the former education secretary William Bennett, a former Scalia poker buddy, told the Associated Press. "He's not going to campaign for it, but he's well-qualified. He's a leader."[18]

Scalia changed his behavior just enough to make other observers believe he might be campaigning for the elevation. The man who had shunned cameras and caused U.S. marshals to confiscate reporters' tapes appeared suddenly to be on "a charm offensive . . . stepping, squinting and blinking, into the public glare," wrote *The Washington Post*'s Dana Milbank.[19]

Margaret Talbot observed in *The New Yorker* in the spring of 2005, "Lately, it seems that Justice Scalia is campaigning for the job of Chief Justice. Just last year, he was so averse to press coverage that he allowed federal marshals to seize the tape recorders of two reporters who attended one of his speeches." Talbot, who predicted that if Scalia were nominated, "he would probably be approved," opened a wide-ranging profile on Scalia with an apt metaphor: "Lining up to hear a Supreme Court Justice speak is more like lining up for a rock concert than you might think. This is especially true if the speech is on a college campus and the speaker in question is Justice Antonin Scalia . . . Scalia is the most likely to offer the jurisprudential equivalent of smashing a guitar on stage."[20]

Students, conservatives and liberals, came out in droves for him. Once, when Scalia was greeting students after a speech at Louisiana State University, a young man told the justice, "I've named my pet fish after you."

"Oh, you've named him 'Nino,' " the justice said, referring to his well-known nickname.

"No," the young man said. "I've named him 'Justice Scalia.' "

Overhearing the conversation, a law professor asked the student, "Do you have other fish named after the other justices?"

"No," he said. "Justice Scalia ate all the others."[21]

Rock star, larger than life—however he was regarded—Scalia suddenly was ubiquitous. The year 2005 had begun with Scalia consenting to be covered by C-SPAN at an American University forum with Justice Breyer, who was at the time writing a book, *Active Liberty*, to counter Scalia's originalist legal approach. The subject of their debate was whether foreign court rulings should be used in U.S. Supreme Court decisions. On stage in upholstered armchairs at the campus in Washington, D.C., Scalia engaged in a lively debate with Breyer. "We don't have the same moral and legal framework as the rest of the world, and never have," said Scalia, who had become the strongest voice on the Court against looking to foreign rulings for guidance on American cases. "If you told the framers of the Constitution that [what] we're after is to do something that will be just like Europe, they would have been appalled. And if you read the Federalist Papers, it's full of, you know, statements that make very clear they don't have a whole lot of respect for many of the rules of European countries."[22]

Supreme Court justices increasingly had been referring to foreign law, but not without public controversy or congressional criticism. In the 2003 case of *Lawrence v. Texas*, when the majority struck down state sodomy bans, the majority noted that the European Court of Human Rights had affirmed the right of homosexual adults to engage in sexual conduct. A year earlier, when the majority barred the execution of mentally retarded convicts, it noted that "within the world community" such executions are "overwhelmingly disapproved." Breyer, who was in the majority on both of those rulings, told the American University audience that it was important to open "your eyes to things that are going on elsewhere." He did not consider foreign decisions "determinative," but "simply, from time to time, relevant."

Scalia countered, "I'm not preventing you from reading these cases. Just don't put it in your opinions."

Two months after the American University appearance, in March 2005, Scalia permitted the filming of a talk he gave at the Woodrow Wilson International Center for Scholars in Washington. Reporting on the Wilson Center appearance in the context of Rehnquist's illness and possible retirement, *The Washington Post*'s Milbank speculated, "[I]t might be shrewd for Scalia to be pursuing a bit of image polishing in advance of a hypothetical confirmation hearing."

In that speech Scalia returned to his favorite topic, the original meaning, as he saw it, of the Constitution. "This is such a minority position in modern academia and in modern legal circles that on occasion I'm asked when I give a talk like this a question from the back of the room: 'Justice Scalia, when did you first become an originalist?'—as though it is some kind of weird affliction that seizes some people—'When did you start eating human flesh?' " Scalia asserted, as usual, that the Constitution was no longer being interpreted to embody the choices the framers (of the 1787 Constitution and its amendments) made. He argued that modern judges should return to the eighteenth-century world (or that of later amendments) as they try to understand how the text applies to cases.

Referring to his regular dissenting role and invoking another choice line, he said, "My most important function on the Supreme Court is to tell the majority to take a walk." At the Wilson Center, Scalia reprised, too, his criticism of the Court's 1996 decision in *Romer v. Evans*, in which the justices struck down a Colorado constitutional amendment that tried to block cities from protecting homosexuals. Recounted Scalia, "And the Supreme Court said, 'Yes, it is unconstitutional.' On the basis of—I don't know, the Sexual Preference Clause of the Bill of Rights, presumably. And the liberals loved it, and the conservatives gnashed their teeth." In his writing and at a lectern, Scalia enthralled audiences with his cadence.

The following month, on April 21, 2005, Scalia was back on television. He joined Justices Breyer and O'Connor at the National Archives in Washington, D.C. With the C-SPAN cameras running and the NBC *Meet the Press* anchor Tim Russert moderating, the three justices engaged in conversation about the law and court customs. Scalia referred to political wrangling between President George W. Bush and the Senate over lower court nominations, and contended judges themselves had politicized the bench. "I think what is going on is unprecedented in the difficulty of getting judicial nominations confirmed. I was nominated almost 20 years ago. I was known to be conservative in my policy views, but I was known to be a good lawyer, an honest man, and somebody who could be fair and write an intelligent opinion. I was confirmed unanimously by the Senate," he said. "Now, something very fundamental has changed. What we originalists . . . have been saying . . . for a long time is that you cannot adopt a theory that the Constitution is evolving and the Supreme Court will tell you what it means from age to age. You cannot do that without causing the Supreme Court to become a very political institution."[23]

All told, over a series of weeks in the spring of 2005 Scalia brought his substantive views to the public in many more televised events than he had ever allowed in the prior decade. Whether there was true momentum among Bush insiders for a Chief Justice Scalia seemed irrelevant as the media drumbeat continued. In May 2005 *The Christian Science Monitor* ran a front-page story that began, "Of all the possible candidates mentioned . . . none seems more primed for all-out warfare in the Senate confirmation process than Antonin Scalia."[24]

A few weeks later, on June 12, 2005, Thomas Goldstein, an appellate lawyer in Washington and founder of a popular Supreme Court blog, wrote on his SCOTUSblog: "I now think that I may have underestimated the possibility that the President will elevate Justice Scalia. Obviously, conservatives have the greatest confidence in and admiration for Justice Scalia's jurisprudence. And as I said before, he is perhaps the most eloquent proponent of the originalist construction of the Constitution that the Administration favors. Democrats may have very considerable trouble preventing his confirmation—more than I thought in writing my previous post."[25]

Around this time, as Scalia was ascending on the national scene, his crusade for an originalist construction of the Constitution was bearing fruit in two particular areas of criminal law—and not in the familiar conservative ways. It was the result of groundwork Scalia had laid in dissents in earlier cases and of an unusual alliance of justices cutting across the common liberal-conservative divide. In these areas, Scalia could write significant *majority* opinions—not merely provocative *dissenting* views. No matter how much the latter circulated among lawyers and law professors, the former became the real law of the land.

One area involved the role of judges and juries in criminal sentencing. Scalia believed that any element of a crime that was used to boost a sentence must be determined by a jury beyond a reasonable doubt. That element, such as use of a weapon in the commission of a crime, could not be ascertained only by a judge. Scalia's view flew in the face of modern sentencing laws, including the U.S. Sentencing Guidelines, which allowed judges to increase—or decrease—a defendant's sentence on the basis of their own findings and without jury consideration.

Scalia first expounded his position on the constitutionally protected role of juries, compared to judges, in the 1998 case of a man who had been deported and then reentered the United States illegally, Hugo Roman Almendarez-Torres. The case tested whether a judge, rather than a jury, could determine that a defendant was a repeat offender, which would then make him eligible for a longer sentence. Federal prosecutors asked the judge to boost Almendarez-Torres's sentence for unlawful entry based on their assertion that he had a record of aggravated felonies. The judge obliged, and Almendarez-Torres received twenty years rather than the maximum of only two years for unlawful entry into the United States.

In Almendarez-Torres's appeal, the question for the Supreme Court was whether a fact that substantially increased the maximum permissible punishment for a crime (here, the record of aggravated felonies) could be determined by the sentencing judge rather than being found beyond a reasonable doubt by a jury. By a 5–4 vote, the Court had permitted the sentence increase without a jury finding. Writing for the Court, Justice Breyer noted some ambiguity in past cases but said, "At most, petitioner might read all these cases, taken together, for the broad proposition that *sometimes* the Constitution does require (though sometimes it does not require) the state to treat a sentencing factor as an element. But we do not see how they can help petitioner more than that."[26] Justice Breyer, whose approach to constitutionally based decisions often involved case-specific consideration of multiple facts, also had been one of the major architects of the U.S. Sentencing Commission system that the judge-jury issue would throw into doubt.

Dissenting, Scalia, joined by the liberals Stevens, Souter, and Ginsburg, wrote, "[I]t is genuinely doubtful whether the Constitution permits a judge (rather than a jury) to determine by a mere preponderance of the evidence (rather than beyond a reasonable doubt) a fact that increases the maximum penalty to which a criminal defendant is subject." Unable to resist a put-down, Scalia referred to the "feebleness" of the majority's rationale and said, "Whatever else one may say about today's opinion, there is no doubt that it has brought to this area of the law more confusion than clarification."

A major reversal came two years later, when Scalia's dissenting opinion formed the grounds for a majority in a similar case. Justice Stevens crafted the majority in the new case of *Apprendi v. New Jersey*, by relying heavily on Scalia's 1998 opinion and picking up Justice Thomas's crucial fifth vote. Thomas wrote a concurring opinion in *Apprendi v. New Jersey* that said he had erred in the Almendarez-Torres dispute.

In this case, Charles Apprendi, who was white, had pleaded guilty in 1995 to unlawful firearms possession after firing several bullets into the home of a black family. The maximum sentence for the firearms offense was ten years. But the sentencing judge, relying on New Jersey's hate-crime law, had determined that Apprendi was motivated by racial bias and added two more years to the firearms penalty, for a total of twelve years. Taking Apprendi's side, the Stevens majority ruled that any fact that increases the penalty for a crime beyond the prescribed statutory maximum must be submitted to a jury and proved beyond a reasonable doubt. He said the Sixth Amendment barred judges from doing the kind of fact-finding that occurred in Apprendi's case.[27]

Scalia signed Stevens's opinion and then wrote separately, in part to criticize Justice Breyer's dissenting opinion. Breyer, joined at the time by Rehnquist, had argued for greater judicial discretion on sentencing factors and an overall pragmatic approach to sentencing. Retorted Scalia, "Justice Breyer proceeds on the all-too-common assumption that the Constitution means what we think it ought to mean. It does not; it means what it says. And the guarantee that '[i]n all criminal prosecutions the accused shall enjoy the right to . . . trial, by an impartial jury' has no intelligible content unless it means that all the facts which must exist in order to subject the defendant to a legally prescribed punishment *must* be found by the jury."

Justice O'Connor was the most outraged of the four dissenters in *Apprendi v. New Jersey*. She predicted that the decision would be a "water-shed" that would lead to a rollback of reforms in federal and state systems intended to equalize sentences based on objective factors. Such systems generally favored equality over individualized discretion, even at the cost of a new harshness. They standardized prison time to ensure that wealthy and well-connected defendants did not get off easier than the poor and disenfranchised—while also producing a rigidity that led many judges and others to criticize the approach as compelling the imposition of sentences that seemed too severe in particular cases. These systems gave judges a role in determining numerous statutory facts that could make a sentence go up or down. The logic of *Apprendi v. New Jersey* ran counter to this overall approach. "In one bold stroke the Court today casts aside our traditional cautious approach and instead embraces a universal and seemingly bright-line rule limiting the power of Congress and state legislatures to define criminal offenses and the sentences that follow," she wrote, joined by her three fellow dissenters, Rehnquist, Breyer, and Kennedy.[28]

Years later Scalia said in an interview that he had felt the winds blowing his way beginning with the four votes in the 1998 *Almendarez-Torres* case. "I led the charge," he said. When he was able to come within a single vote of a majority, he allowed, "I was optimistic" for the next case.[29]

The more senior Justice Stevens, who authored the *Apprendi* decision, grinned when he heard of Scalia's "led the charge" remark, suggested that was not how he saw it, but also said he did not want to quibble with Scalia's view of who was in charge. "If that's the way he assesses it, that's okay," Stevens said. "I'm happy to have him think he led the charge. He's committed."[30]

Over the next five years, the same 5–4 split from Apprendi's case reinforced the jury rule in an array of criminal sentencing disputes. In a 2004 case, Scalia wrote a decision striking down state rules that set standard prison terms for various crimes but directed judges to make findings about facts, such as the drugs or guns involved, that could increase the sentence. That new case from Washington State involved Ralph Blakely, who had pleaded guilty to second-degree kidnapping after abducting his estranged wife at gunpoint. Blakely faced a maximum of fifty-three months in prison under Washington law, but the judge concluded, as permitted under state law, that Blakely had acted with "deliberate cruelty" and gave him a ninety-month term.

"Our commitment to *Apprendi* in this context reflects not just respect for long-standing precedent, but the need to give intelligible content to the right of jury trial," Scalia wrote. "That right is no mere procedural formality, but a fundamental reservation of power in our constitutional structure."[31] And, as it happened, the reservation of power was to the group of citizens convened as a jury. That necessarily limited the power of judges over vital matters touching individuals' lives, which reflected Scalia's suspicion of broad judicial power under the Constitution. Scalia

himself drew the connection: "Just as suffrage ensures the people's ultimate control in the legislative and executive branches, jury trial is meant
to ensure their control in the judiciary."[32]

Writing for the dissenters, O'Connor said, "The consequences of
today's decision will be as far reaching as they are disturbing." She noted
that the federal sentencing system and many states, like Washington, gave
judges the leeway to go beyond established guidelines or rules, depending
upon an individual's case. Reading part of her dissenting opinion from
the Court's mahogany bench, O'Connor recalled her opposition to the
2000 *Apprendi* ruling and said, "What I have feared most has now come to
pass. Over twenty years of sentencing reform are all but lost, and tens of
thousands of criminal judgments are in jeopardy." She predicted that the
U.S. Sentencing Guidelines, established two decades earlier, would fall
next. She was right.

The U.S. Sentencing Guidelines, which were actually rules, were the
product of a sentencing reform law passed by Congress in 1984 after years
of hearings on how to make sentences fairer and ensure that race, wealth,
or other impermissible factors did not enter the equation. The 1984
statute established the U.S. Sentencing Commission, which (with then
Judge Breyer as a commissioner and leading voice) devised an elaborate
grid system that accounted for a range of federal offenses and respective
prison time calculations. The guidelines were generally binding, but a
judge could depart from them for certain aggravating or mitigating circumstances. For example, if a judge determined that a defendant was a
ringleader in a drug deal or trafficked in a particularly large amount of
drugs, the sentence had to be boosted—without a jury first finding
beyond a reasonable doubt his ringleader status or the amount of drugs
involved. A judge also could determine that a defendant aided federal
agents in trying to solve a related crime and should be given credit for his
assistance.

Less than two years after O'Connor's warning in the *Blakely* case, the
justices, with Scalia's vote, invalidated the U.S. Sentencing Guidelines as a
violation of the Sixth Amendment jury right. A separate narrow majority,
with Justice Ginsburg as the key vote, allowed them to stay in place to
"guide" judges setting sentences.[33] Scalia was not happy with the compromise that kept the rules as guidelines alive, yet he was satisfied with the
overall turn of events.

"It was, frankly, a great disappointment to me that Americans were so out of touch with that important guarantee," he said. "State after state was adopting this stuff and sending people away for an additional ten extra years . . . [even when] the judge didn't even find it beyond a reasonable doubt . . . If the jury guarantee means anything, it means you don't serve any time in jail unless the fact that is the predicate for that sentence has been found by a jury.[34]

"It was less my own love for the jury," he continued, "because frankly, I'm not sure I'm nuts about the jury—at least the jury as it has been altered by an evolutionary court." He then detoured into a separate complaint that related to the jury: "The jury did not used to be a 'cross section' of the community, which is what the opinions of this court, and actually the Warren Court era, require it to be. It used to be responsible citizens of the area—and you used to find in the old English records that it was the same people who were jurors over and over again . . . When I was young, New York used to have blue-ribbon juries. If you had a complicated antitrust case, you would get people who had gone to college, studied economics, so you were not dealing with trying to explain these difficult economic concepts to people who couldn't understand them. And that was held unconstitutional." Returning to his favoring of juries over judges in sentencing, he said, "So, it's not because I'm in love with the jury necessarily. It's because I'm in love with the Constitution."

Scalia had similar success among his colleagues to win a bright-line rule on the Constitution's guarantee that defendants may confront their accusers. The Sixth Amendment's confrontation clause provides that "in all criminal prosecutions, the accused shall enjoy the right . . . to be confronted with the witnesses against him."

Again, Scalia first laid down his marker in a dissenting opinion. The 1990 case of *Maryland v. Craig* centered on a Howard County woman who was charged with the sexual abuse of a six-year-old girl who attended the kindergarten and prekindergarten center the woman operated. Prosecutors sought to invoke a Maryland law that allowed a judge to hear the testimony of a child witness through a one-way closed-circuit television. The child cannot see the defendant under the procedure, but the defendant and lawyer are able to watch and raise objections. The majority, in an opinion by Justice O'Connor, ruled that the Sixth Amendment does not categorically prohibit such a plan for child testimony in an abuse case. She said Court precedent allowed the preference for face-to-face confrontation at trial to give way to public policy considerations and the necessities of a case. O'Connor found it significant that Maryland's procedure preserved major elements of the confrontation right: "The child witness must be competent to testify and must testify under oath; the defendant retains full opportunity for contemporaneous cross-examination; and the judge, jury, and defendant are able to view (albeit by video monitor) the demeanor (and body) of the witness as he or she testifies."[35]

Writing for the four dissenters, Scalia said, "Seldom has this Court failed so conspicuously to sustain a categorical guarantee of the Constitution against the tide of prevailing current opinion. The Sixth Amendment provides, with unmistakable clarity, that '[i]n all criminal prosecutions, the accused shall enjoy the right . . . to be confronted with the witnesses against him.' The purpose of enshrining this protection in the Constitution was to assure that none of the many policy interests from time to time pursued by statutory law could overcome a defendant's right to face his or her accusers in court."[36] Here Scalia was insisting that new policy assessments, even to protect child victims of abuse, could not revise the constitutional meaning.

More than a decade later Scalia effectively won the day on the issue. The 2004 case arose from an altercation between Michael and Sylvia Crawford and Kenneth Lee at Lee's apartment. Sylvia had told her husband, Michael, that Lee had earlier tried to rape her. Michael Crawford stabbed Lee in the torso and claimed to police that he acted in self-defense. In an interview with police on the night of the stabbing, police had asked Sylvia whether she saw anything in Lee's hands as Michael came at him with a knife. She said no. Prosecutors charged Michael Crawford with assault and attempted murder and played a tape recording of Sylvia's statement to the police as evidence that the stabbing was not in self-defense. She did not testify at trial, based on the marital privilege that generally bars a spouse from testifying without the other spouse's consent. The trial judge allowed the recording in, without her testimony or the chance that her statement could be subject to cross-examination. Crawford was convicted of assault. The trial court and the Washington Supreme Court, hearing Crawford's appeal, found the statement worth an exception to the usual hearsay rule and right of confrontation because, given all the other facts of the case, it was "trustworthy."[37]

On Crawford's appeal, Scalia won a narrow majority for a rule that allowed no such exceptions based on reliability. Applying an originalist interpretation, Scalia wrote, "Our cases have . . . remained faithful to the Framers' understanding: Testimonial statements of witnesses absent from trial have been admitted only where the declarant is unavailable, and only where the defendant has had a prior opportunity to cross-examine . . . Dispensing with confrontation because testimony is obviously reliable is akin to dispensing with a jury trial because a defendant is obviously guilty. That is not what the Sixth Amendment prescribes."[38]

These cases demonstrated an originalist consistency for a justice who was not personally inclined to want to give criminal defendants a break. Even if he did not favor the consequences, he sought to be true to his view of the meaning of the drafters of the Bill of Rights. "When people ask me what opinions I'm most proud of," Scalia said in an interview, "I say, well, opinions that count the most are majority opinions, and that [*Crawford v. Washington*] is one of the ones I'm most proud of—bringing the Confrontation Clause back to what the people thought it meant when they adopted it."[39] This was not an area of the law that drew headlines, yet it mattered on the ground for prosecutors and defendants at trial. It was an area where Scalia could prevail and make a difference. Critics said the changes wrought by the *Crawford* line of cases made prosecutions in domestic violence and child abuse more difficult. But for Scalia, who focused on the right to confrontation as it was adopted in 1791, such contemporary consequences were not relevant.

It was just a year after that *Crawford* decision, from which Rehnquist dissented, that the chief justice's ill health was so apparent that Court watchers presumed a retirement announcement was imminent. Rehnquist made it to June 2005, the end of the 2004–2005 term, without any announcement. His battle with thyroid cancer had left his body frail, and as he announced on Monday, June 27, 2005, that the term was ending for the summer, his voice was raspy, his breathing labored. The following Friday, July 1, 2005, Justice O'Connor dropped her bombshell. She was going to retire to take care of her husband, John, who had Alzheimer's disease. O'Connor had been ambivalent about the retirement decision and had been waiting to see what Rehnquist, her longtime friend from Stanford Law School and Phoenix civic life, would do. Justices usually do not want to cause two vacancies in a single year, because of the chance that the politically charged confirmation process could delay the appointment of a new justice and result in one, even two, lingering vacancies.

When O'Connor learned from Rehnquist that he did not intend to retire, she felt surer that it was time for her to step down. Her husband had been coming with her to chambers each day, but it was becoming clear that he needed full-time care and she needed more flexibility with her schedule. O'Connor asked the marshal of the Court, Pamela Talkin, to let the White House know on Friday, July 1, that a letter would be coming that morning from a justice. O'Connor never told Talkin what was in the letter that she was turning over to her a few days early, for safekeeping, but she knew that Talkin understood what was about to happen. On July 1, Talkin reached the White House counsel Harriet Miers and told her she would be delivering a letter. A police officer drove Talkin over in a small sedan—rather than one of the Court's official cars—so she would not be detected. The White House made the news public that morning.[40]

When Scalia heard the news on his car radio that Friday, he said he almost drove off the road. Like most everyone else close to O'Connor, he had not seen it coming. It had been a well-known secret that John O'Connor suffered from Alzheimer's disease, but Justice O'Connor seemed to be handling his deteriorating condition. The truth was that the pioneering justice who exuded a "can-do" attitude simply could not handle the demands of her job on the nation's highest court and the decline of her husband of fifty-three years. So a few months short of her twenty-fifth anniversary as a justice and at the relatively young age of seventy-four, the nation's first woman justice decided to retire.

In terms of Scalia's future, a change at the Court now would be all about an associate justice's seat, not the center chair of the chief justice.

To succeed O'Connor, President Bush settled on John Roberts, a former administration lawyer and private appellate attorney who had been on the U.S. Court of Appeals for the District of Columbia Circuit for two years. Roberts, age fifty and a graduate of Harvard College and Harvard Law School, had a reputation for steadiness. His rulings on the D.C. Circuit were measured and largely uncontroversial. Yet he was chosen by a president who held up Scalia and Thomas as models. Although more temperate in his opinions than Scalia, Roberts nevertheless had established himself early in his career as a movement conservative.

As a lawyer in the Reagan and the first Bush administrations, Roberts had argued for the reversal of *Roe v. Wade* and had been actively involved in efforts to curtail affirmative action, busing, and other programs intended to favor racial minorities. He recommended in early 1982 that the White House take an "aggressive stance" against pending congressional legislation to strengthen the 1965 Voting Rights Act. Then, as deputy solicitor general, he argued against Federal Communications Commission programs that favored blacks and other minorities who wished to increase their ownership of broadcast licenses.[41]

Yet Roberts had worked in private practice for about a decade, representing an array of clients, and had argued thirty-nine cases before the Supreme Court, earning a stellar reputation as an appellate advocate.[42] The reaction by Senate Republicans was effusive, and while many Senate Democrats expressed some caution about his record, they sent no signals about a potential filibuster or real opposition.[43]

On TV's *The Daily Show*, the mock news host Jon Stewart interviewed the University of Southern California law professor and political pundit Susan Estrich about the Roberts selection. "He's nicer than Scalia," Estrich said. "More pleasant."

"Nicer than Scalia?" Stewart responded. "Aren't we *all* nicer than Scalia."[44] When Scalia heard about the exchange, he was dumbfounded. Why did he have that reputation? Wasn't he pleasant?

John Roberts had been in the national spotlight for about six weeks when the man for whom he had been a Supreme Court law clerk died. Rehnquist lost his battle with thyroid cancer on September 3, 2005. Two days later, President Bush withdrew Roberts's nomination for O'Connor's impending vacancy and announced that he wanted to make Roberts chief justice of the United States. Roberts's early weeks in the spotlight had positioned him perfectly. His stature had risen, and he no longer seemed so junior to other appeals court judges who had been on the Bush short list for a chief justice opening, such as the U.S. appeals court judge J. Harvie Wilkinson of the Richmond-based U.S. Court of Appeals for the Fourth Circuit.

In just a few weeks the momentum for Scalia had faded. Onstage was someone nearly twenty years younger, with far more potential to extend President Bush's legacy. Scalia tried not to be disappointed. He had worked hard not to even think about the possibility of elevation as he

watched Rehnquist become sicker and sicker over the months. In an interview years later he said of the possibility that he might have been chief
justice, "That would have been a great honor. But it was so unrealistic. It
was not something to think about . . . Just on age alone. It was ridiculous.
I would advise them against doing that." Because he knew that it was such
a long shot, he had tried to push it from his mind at the time. "You don't
really think enough about it to know if you feel bad."[45]

The new media interest in Scalia and comparisons of him and Roberts
did not disappear in the fall of 2005. In September, as the hearings for
John Roberts were beginning, *BusinessWeek* said of Scalia, "His age, combined with his combative personality, a raft of controversial opinions, and
the messy realities confronting a politically weakened President, conspired
against him . . . For many movement conservatives, Scalia's thunderous
orations and incendiary writings from the bench made him the ideal
Chief Justice to press the campaign for limited government and traditional values. But in the end, the combative Scalia left the path open for
Roberts, a man with seemingly no rough edges."[46] Scalia was certainly a
man with rough edges. Yet even if he had been a more diplomatic sort,
there was no getting around the fact that Scalia in 2005 was one year shy
of his seventieth birthday. Why would the White House gamble on him
when it could get a younger model—and someone who was more like
Scalia than it appeared at first blush?

Roberts was approved by the Senate on a vote of 78–22 on September 29, just in time for the traditional first Monday in October opening of
the Court's annual term.[47]

For Justice O'Connor's seat, President Bush chose the U.S. appeals court
judge Samuel Alito, a lawyer in the Reagan and first Bush administrations
and a fifteen-year veteran of the Philadelphia-based U.S. Court of Appeals
for the Third Circuit. After he withdrew Roberts for the O'Connor seat,
Bush had nominated the White House counsel Miers to succeed O'Connor, but Miers pulled out after criticism from such prominent conservatives as Robert Bork, who called her a disaster on every level. Alito, who
went to Princeton and earned his law degree at Yale, easily satisfied Bork
and other conservatives but drew great liberal opposition. He was
approved by the narrow Senate vote of 58–42.

Alito, who exuded a shy steadiness, joked later about the difficulty of the confirmation process. Speaking at a November 2006 Federalist Society convention, he recalled "the travails" of the confirmation process and said that even afterward, he hated to go by the Senate Hart Office Building, where his hearings had been held. "I cross to the other side of the street," he said. "I quicken my step until I'm well past the building."[48]

Alito then went on, as he spoke to the Federalist Society audience honoring Scalia's twenty years on the Supreme Court, to praise Scalia for enriching "the personal and the intellectual life of the Court."

"I must complain, however, that he did lead me astray in one thing," said Alito, revealing a wry, self-deprecating humor. "He was confirmed in the Senate by 98–0. I always thought that any Italian-American circuit judge who was born in Trenton, N.J., and was nominated for the Supreme Court would get a similar reception. It didn't quite turn out that way. But what's 40 votes?"

Alito had first become aware of Scalia's writing through Scalia's late 1970s essay attacking the D.C. Circuit for its ruling in the Vermont Yankee case—which had come to stand for judicial activism in the area of federal nuclear power regulation. That was the same essay and topic of related Scalia lectures that introduced Ruth Bader Ginsburg to him. Alito, who admired Scalia's writings for their dazzle and subscribed to a similar originalist approach, took ethnic offense, however, at the nickname of "Sc'Alito" that some commentators gave him as he was mentioned for possible elevation to the high court.[49]

What Scalia lost in the turn of events—if there ever was a chance for his elevation—he gained in two strong votes from like-minded conservative movement judges. They had hitched their hopes to Reagan's promise of a different legal world. Roberts, especially, had considered him an inspiration in the 1980s.

It was fitting that Roberts's first major speech after becoming chief justice in the fall of 2005 was at the Ronald Reagan Library in Simi Valley, California. His March 2006 presentation was charmingly self-effacing yet also offered insights into his commitment to the Reagan agenda. Roberts recalled his first day in the White House counsel's office in 1982, when he received a telephone call. "It was the White House operator. [She asked,] 'Could I hold for the president?'"

"Well, yes, I could," Roberts told his audience with a grin. "Then, I think I did what most people do when they get a call from the president. I stood up. A few minutes went by . . . I sat down." (He waited, and waited, and then he heard muffled laughter in the hall from his new colleagues.) "It dawned on me what was going on . . . They had a betting pool for how long I would stay on hold . . . Whoever had the 15–20 minute slot won the money."[50]

Roberts told the standing-room-only crowd at the Reagan Library that he had been persuaded to join the Justice Department a year earlier after hearing President Reagan's first inaugural speech, which Roberts termed "a call to action" and which was famous for Reagan's assertion that "government is not the solution, it is the problem."

"I felt he was speaking to me," Roberts said.

Around the time Roberts was preparing for that appearance at the Reagan Library in California in early 2006, he was working with Justice Scalia on several important cases that would reveal their parallel thinking. The new chief justice had agreed with a Scalia opinion for the Court that the U.S. Army Corps of Engineers had overstepped its authority to regulate environmentally fragile wetlands. Roberts penned a separate statement that the corps "chose to adhere to its essentially boundless view of the scope of its power." In another case, Roberts, again banding with Scalia, wrote a caustic dissenting opinion to a decision that said police may not enter a home to conduct a search if one resident gives permission but the other says no. The decision in a Georgia cocaine case said that if police search a home after being invited in by, for example, the wife, over the protests of the husband, any evidence found cannot be used against the husband. Roberts said the majority misread the constitutional protection against unreasonable police searches and described its tone as "overwrought." In his dissenting opinion, joined by Scalia, Roberts wrote, "The rule the majority fashions does not implement the high office of the Fourth Amendment to protect privacy, but instead provides protection on a random and happenstance basis, protecting, for example, a co-occupant who happens to be at the front door when the other occupant consents to a search, but not one napping or watching television in the next room."[51]

Separately, when the Court majority said that a Tennessee death row inmate could get a new hearing to challenge his murder conviction partly because of new DNA evidence, Roberts chided the majority for second-guessing a lower court judge who found the evidence unpersuasive. The

Court majority's decision allowed Paul Gregory House, who was con-victed of murdering a neighbor in 1985, to go before a federal judge to assert that his trial was constitutionally flawed. Based on evidence from House that included DNA testing and new witness testimony, the justices in the majority determined that jurors would not have found him guilty beyond a reasonable doubt.[52] In his dissenting opinion, joined by Scalia and Thomas, Chief Justice Roberts said he doubted House's story and referred to the fact that House had told officials that he received scratches and bruises from tearing down a building, and from a cat, not from the victim. "Scratches from a cat, indeed," Roberts wrote, striking a derisive chord not unlike Scalia's.[53] (Three years later, in May 2009, prosecutors dropped all charges against House, saying crucial DNA evidence brought forth after conviction did not match House. He had spent more than two decades on death row.)

Earlier during their first weeks together, Roberts had signed Scalia's dissenting opinion that protested a Court majority decision that said Ore-gon could enforce a law allowing physician-assisted suicides, despite a directive against such medical involvement by Attorney General Ashcroft. Scalia wrote that Congress properly could have wanted the attorney gen-eral to make a judgment in this area. The legitimacy of assisted suicide, he wrote, joined by Roberts and Thomas, "rests, not on 'science' or 'medi-cine,' but on a naked value judgment."[54]

Overall, in many of the tightest cases that could be considered ideolog-ical litmus tests in Roberts's first term on the Court, he voted more with Scalia than with any other justice. Noting that Roberts voted with Scalia 95 percent of the time and Alito joined Scalia about 90 percent of the time, the American University law professor and Supreme Court chroni-cler Herman Schwartz wrote in *The Nation*: "Having been elevated to the pinnacle of their profession because of their ideological purity and relia-bility, why should they change?"[55]

Although Scalia had not grasped the gold ring, he had been joined by a chief justice and associate justice whose legal reasoning and judicial style owed much to his influence. At the end of their second term together, 2006–2007, Roberts showed that he could take control of the bench in a way that had eluded his predecessor, Rehnquist. Roberts and the four other conservatives (Scalia, Kennedy, Thomas, and Alito) formed a major-ity to change the law on abortion rights, race, religion, and student speech rights.[56] Of the nineteen cases that broke along ideological lines, the five prevailed in thirteen of them. "It is not often in the law that so few have so quickly changed so much," an angry Breyer wrote. The Harvard University law professor Richard Fallon observed, "We're seeing the Court in the image Ronald Reagan dreamed of. It is sort of poetic that Chief Justice Roberts is someone who long ago was inspired by Reagan."[57]

Long ago Roberts was directed by Scalia, too. Roberts, like many young conservatives in Washington in the early 1980s, was roused by Scalia's writing and the rigor of his intellect. Surveying the appeals courts as part of his job as a young Reagan administration lawyer, Roberts had categorized Scalia as one of the three or four most revered appellate judges, even before Scalia had been on the D.C. Circuit a full year. At that time, when Roberts himself was resisting the prevailing liberalism, he thought that Scalia's contrary message might just go somewhere.

FOURTEEN

SHOWMAN OF THE BENCH

On a cold, slate gray February morning, the case of Hedrick Humphries, who was suing the Cracker Barrel restaurant chain for racial discrimination, came before the Supreme Court. A tall fifty-nine-year-old African American, Humphries had long worked for restaurants in the Chicago area, following the model of his father, who had managed delis on the South Side. In 1999 Humphries had become an associate manager at the Cracker Barrel in Bradley, Illinois. For his first two years, his reviews were exceptional, and he received merit raises.[1] When a new head manager came in, things changed. The new boss said all African Americans were "drunk or high on drugs" and that "all Mexicans have a bunch of kids." He began issuing disciplinary reports on Humphries, who, in turn, claimed his boss was prejudiced. Humphries reported the remarks and other racially tinged incidents to a Cracker Barrel district manager. Humphries was fired.[2]

He sued Cracker Barrel for firing him in retaliation for his charges of racial bias. Humphries sued under Section 1981 of the Civil Rights Act of 1866, a Reconstruction-era law considered the first significant civil rights legislation passed by Congress. The act insisted that blacks must have the same rights to contract as whites.[3] As Humphries was pressing his complaint in lower courts, Cracker Barrel, a nationwide chain of moderately priced southern-style restaurants, was defending itself against several other race and sex bias claims. In one, the U.S. Justice Department charged that the restaurant had allowed white servers to refuse to wait on black customers and had segregated customer seating by race.[4]

In his personal claim, Humphries asserted that while Cracker Barrel said he was fired for failing to lock a safe, no one had interviewed him or investigated the alleged incident.[5] He said he was really let go because he had complained about how blacks were mistreated. Cracker Barrel said the claims lacked merit and also insisted that the portion of the 1866 civil rights law Humphries invoked, commonly known as Section 1981, did not cover claims of retaliation, only acts of discrimination in the first instance.[6] Addressing those arguments in a 2007 ruling, a panel of the Chicago-based U.S. Court of Appeals for the Seventh Circuit had sided with Humphries by a 2–1 vote.[7] The appeals court noted that the Supreme Court in a 1969 case had referred to the "broad and sweeping nature of the protection . . . [of] the Civil Rights Act of 1866." The appeals court said the law prohibited discrimination in all facets of the job, including when a worker faced retaliation for bias complaints. If it did not, the judges said, "it would create perverse incentives for the employer to fire complainants as quickly as possible to thereby limit (or entirely avoid) damages under Section 1981." The judges noted that this is not an insignificant issue, because Section 1981 remedies often had more teeth than those allowed under Title VII of the 1964 Civil Rights Act, a separate law commonly invoked in discrimination lawsuits. The appeals court's bottom line was that the law would be meaningless if an employer could fire a black man for attempting to enforce his rights under the civil rights law.

The ruling was signed by Judges Ann Claire Williams and Richard Posner, neither of whom had a reputation for liberal interpretation of statutes.[8] The third judge on the panel, Frank Easterbrook, said that the majority was ignoring "a sea change" in how the Supreme Court was interpreting civil rights statutes—a prescient point that would be evident in the oral arguments at the Supreme Court, where Justice Scalia took a leading role.

Cracker Barrel's lawyer, Michael Hawkins, had an argument that directly appealed to the justice known for narrowly reading the scope of civil rights statutes: Section 1981 simply does not refer to a cause of action for retaliation.

"You have to look to the text," Hawkins, a tall man with gray hair, told the justices.

When Justice Breyer pressed Hawkins, Scalia interjected: "Mr. Hawkins, don't we have a whole line of recent cases [in] which we say we have set our face against implying causes of action?"

"Yes," Hawkins said.

"A whole bunch of recent cases saying we're not going to do that anymore," Scalia continued.

"Yes, Your Honor," Hawkins said.

"We used to do it, but we said we're not going to do it anymore."

"That's correct, Your Honor," Hawkins said.

"So why don't you invoke those?" Scalia asked, eager to help Hawkins make his argument.

Scalia's reference—"we used to do it"—was to an era when the Court under Chief Justice Earl Warren, and even under the Nixon appointee Chief Justice Warren Burger, broadly read federal laws to let people bring their grievances to court. One of Scalia's most enduring notions was that society's problems were better solved in the nation's legislatures by popularly elected officials, and not by appointed judges. It was one of the many themes he vigorously reinforced during oral arguments. Scalia's approach to these public hearings echoed his approach to opinion writing, which was full-throated and aggressive. At the same time, he could cut through the legal jargon like no one else and frame the case in engaging, real-world terms.

As the Cracker Barrel arguments showed, Scalia had an unequaled presence on the bench. His questions were challenging, sometimes audacious. He played to the audience with jokes and put-downs. He could be a showman, a streetwise guy, and a pulverizer—as aggressive an advocate as any of the lawyers who stood at the lectern to make their cases. This was all very much a part of Scalia's persona and contributed to the attention he drew.

For nearly twenty years he had been alone in such a forceful approach. The 2005 appointment of John Roberts as chief justice presented him with a partner of sorts in oral arguments. Although Roberts was not the showman Scalia was, they both believed that if they were going to dismiss an argument, they had to do it decisively. They sometimes reinforced each other's points and finished each other's sentences.[9]

During the Cracker Barrel appeal, Chief Justice Roberts buttressed Scalia's line of questioning at several turns. Roberts referred to the prior period of Court analysis as the "freewheeling approach to statutory interpretation." In unison, they made clear that they opposed reading rights into statutes that Congress had not specifically delineated, and they suggested by their questions that they were ready to curtail the reach of Section 1981.

Next up at the lectern, after the Cracker Barrel lawyer Hawkins, was Cynthia Hyndman, representing Humphries. She insisted that Cracker Barrel was "basically asking this Court to allow an employer to be able to fire an employee who" sued to enforce his rights under the Civil Rights Act of 1866.

"Take the example of a person who complains that he was not promoted because of his race in violation of Section 1981," continued Hyndman, in dark-rimmed glasses. "His employer fires him for making that complaint. If he did not have protection under Section 1981 against retaliation, he would never have the opportunity to remedy that discriminatory promotion."

"That's a good argument to Congress," Scalia responded. "Congress should enact a retaliatory provision. But the statute says what it says, and what it says is that there has to be discrimination on the basis of race. And firing somebody for—in retaliation for making a complaint is not firing him on the basis of race."

Yet, Hyndman pointed out, in a 2005 case, *Jackson v. Birmingham Board of Education*, the Court had ruled that a federal law prohibiting sex bias in education inherently covered people who faced reprisals for complaining about bias. That case involved the male coach of a girls' high school basketball team in Birmingham, Alabama. He had sued the Birmingham Board of Education under Title IX of the Education Amendments of 1972, claiming that the board retaliated against him for complaining about sex discrimination in the high school's athletic program. Like Section 1981, the 1972 law had no explicit language about "retaliation" claims. Justice Sandra Day O'Connor, who cast the decisive vote in the 2005 case and wrote the opinion, said that retaliation against a person because he had complained about bias is a form of bias itself. In short, discrimination and retaliation were not separate wrongs.

O'Connor's opinion for the majority in *Jackson v. Birmingham Board of Education* rested largely on a 1969 decision in which the justices had broadly interpreted the 1866 Civil Rights Act. "So it follows here," Hyndman said, "under Section 1981 if someone makes a complaint about race discrimination and they are retaliated against they are being discriminated against on the basis of race." The Seventh Circuit had similarly interpreted *Jackson v. Birmingham Board of Education* to cover Humphries's case.

"Well, you can say that," Scalia retorted to Hyndman, "but it doesn't make any sense."

"Well, that's what the Court held in *Jackson*, Your Honor," she said.

"It didn't make any sense then, either," Scalia shot back to general laughter.

The third and final lawyer to take a turn at the Supreme Court lectern this cold morning was the U.S. solicitor general, Paul Clement. He represented the Justice Department, which was siding with Humphries. Clement said the Court's past rulings should lead the justices to read the Civil Rights Act provision expansively.

"The Court has already inferred a private right of action under Section 1981," said Clement, dressed in the traditional gray morning coat and tails of the government's top advocate at the Court. "So the question before the Court now is simply the scope of the basic guarantee in Section 1981 and particularly whether it prohibits retaliation against someone who exercised their undoubted right to complain about racial discrimination in the contractual process."

"It's a little more complicated than that," Scalia responded, continuing to dominate the questioning. "We inferred that cause of action in the bad old days, when we were inferring causes of action all over the place."

Yes, Clement acknowledged, the justices had narrowed their approach to antibias law to limit lawsuits filed by workers. But, Clement insisted, in recent years—not the "bad old days"—the Court had allowed employees to sue for various grievances under civil rights statutes even when the particular wrong was not spelled out in the law's text.

Scalia, who seemed to be confused about the dates of some of the cases under discussion, wisecracked, "When do you think the bad old days ended?"

In the same vein, Clement responded, "The bad old days ended when you got on the Court, Mr. Justice Scalia."[10]

As other justices chuckled knowingly, the man himself leaned back in his chair and rolled with laughter.

Taking center stage, Scalia was seizing the discussion and forcing a response to his position. Yet the moment, like so many others that showed

Scalia passionate, animated, in full color, necessarily raised the question: To what end? Did his domination of oral arguments turn a case in his favor? What did it get him? Hedrick Humphries's dispute with Cracker Barrel, when it was decided several months later, would answer a piece of that larger question.

It was difficult to overstate the contrast between Scalia and the atmosphere of restraint that permeated the Supreme Court's majestic courtroom. Braided gold ties held back crimson velvet drapes. Two U.S. flags positioned on each side of the mahogany bench hung perfectly still. Police officers walked slowly through the spectator section ready to shush any whisperer. If someone dared drape an arm over the back of a chair, a police officer tapped him on the shoulder to indicate disapproval. At ten o'clock each morning, when the justices processed into the courtroom, a marshal in muted gray morning coat and striped trousers admonished all "to draw near and give their attention, for the Court is now sitting."

It all contributed to the jarring nature of Scalia's behavior. Amid the reserved lexicon of the law, he used phrases like "idiotic" and "gollywoggle."[11] His behavior on the bench was different enough from that of his colleagues that it became the subject of news stories and law reviews. In an empirical study of oral arguments, the University of Kansas social psychologist Lawrence S. Wrightsman observed of Scalia, "Over a set of oral arguments, he asks more questions and makes more comments than any other justice, he communicates a sense of urgency on the bench, and his style is forever forceful (many advocates see him as overbearing)."[12]

Wrightsman noted in a 2008 book that Scalia embodied the tendencies of what social psychologists called "extraversion," which included traits such as being talkative, a show-off, bossy, and adventurous. Explaining the "adventurous" description, Wrightsman noted that in 2005 Scalia took twenty-four trips to legal conferences, including in Australia, Ireland, Turkey, and Italy. " 'Show-off' is not too extreme," Wrightsman wrote, referring to Scalia's playing a bit part in an opera production. With his friend and fellow opera lover Justice Ginsburg, Scalia had appeared in white powdered wig and eighteenth-century costume as an "extra" in the Washington National Opera's 1994 production of Richard Strauss's *Ariadne auf Naxos*.

Scalia only reluctantly accepted the assertion that his approach in oral arguments was demonstrably different. "I don't think it's true that I am the most talkative," he said in an interview. "If you take the time of oral argument, it is certainly Steve [Breyer]. My questions tend to be short and to the point, not long and hypothetical. And have you ever heard Ruth [Bader Ginsburg] excoriate somebody who is arguing a civil procedure case? She can be really tough."[13]

Presented with a few of his attention-drawing moments that knocked spectators back in their red upholstered chairs, Scalia allowed, "Why does the argument have to be dull, for God's sake?" Yet his initial protestations were a reminder that he often could not hear himself as others heard him. He had such an ear for language, but it seemed he was deaf to when his own words might be dominating the debate. Or, alternatively, he simply did not care.

To some extent Scalia's behavior on the bench was just an exaggerated form of what other justices were trying to do with their own queries—argue with each other, something that occurred surprisingly little off the bench. Mostly, however, Scalia's frequent and sharp interventions seemed the result of an irresistible impulse. His appetite for debate was so strong that he could hardly stop himself from entering the fray. When he heard counsel give confused arguments, or arguments he thought wrong, he jumped in. When he heard a question from a colleague go unanswered, he leaped too. Some of this was because time was short and, he believed, could not be wasted by bad argumentation. Some of it seemed to show him to be the schoolboy who knew the answer and blurted it out, now without the need to raise his hand for permission.

Scalia's activity regularly incited news commentary. *Slate* magazine's Dahlia Lithwick, who chronicled oral arguments in an online column, wrote, "He comes in like a medieval knight, girded for battle. He knows what the law is. He knows what the opinion should say. And he uses the hour allocated for argument to bludgeon his brethren into agreement. Usually this is sort of fun and charming. But it's starting to affect the other justices."[14] Lithwick referred to the apparent frustration of other justices about getting a word in edgewise as she reported on the case of *Nevada Department of Human Resources v. Hibbs*. It was a 2003 dispute, just a few years before Roberts and Alito, who succeeded Rehnquist, joined the bench.

The case revolved around the validity of a provision in the federal Family and Medical Leave Act that allowed state employees who had been denied the requisite twelve-week leave to care for a sick relative to sue their state employers. The question was whether Congress, in passing the act, was addressing pervasive sex discrimination and exercising its Fourteenth Amendment power to enforce the constitutional guarantee of equality, in which case it could lift states' usual immunity from lawsuits. If, on the other hand, Congress was merely enacting a neutral piece of labor legislation, the state could not be sued for money in federal court. William Hibbs had been fired from his job as a Nevada state social worker after he took time off to care for his wife following a car accident. Hibbs sued the state of Nevada for denying him the family leave required under law. Lower courts had allowed his case to proceed, but Nevada officials appealed.

First up at the Court's lectern was the Nevada deputy attorney general, Paul Taggart, who contended that the Family and Medical Leave Act was "everyday economic legislation, a national labor standard, not antidiscrimination legislation." He said it was not different from a minimum wage rule. Some justices expressed skepticism about Taggart's position and noted that the law's proponents had contended it was consistent with the Fourteenth Amendment's Equal Protection Clause.[15]

Scalia interrupted Taggart's answer and asserted that the proper understanding was that Congress had written a law "in conformance" with the Constitution's Equal Protection Clause, "not to enforce" it.

"We agree with that position, Justice Scalia," Taggart responded.

Justice Breyer asked Taggart, "If you imagined the state employers had been shown to discriminate against women in hiring, wouldn't Congress have a lot of leeway in choosing the remedy for that discrimination, and wouldn't this statute be part of that remedy?"

"I don't want to agree with you a hundred percent," Taggart responded hesitantly.

"According to your brief," Scalia interjected, "you agree zero percent."

Scalia so took over the hour-long session that at one point Justice Souter began to ask a question but then realized he was interrupting Taggart. "I'm sorry," Souter said. "I was trying to get another question in before Justice Scalia."

Near the end, with Assistant Attorney General Viet Dinh at the lectern defending the Family Leave Act on behalf of the federal government, Justice Stevens began a question by saying, "Justice Scalia should probably ask this question but—"

Without missing a beat, Scalia cracked, "Pass it to me."

Even as Scalia entered his seventies, he remained energetic on the bench. He was a "terrier," as one of his fellow justices described him. To Scalia, oral argument sessions were not a forum for pleasantries. "You try to give the counsel the best opportunity to respond to the difficulty that you have with his position on a certain point. If his first response doesn't do it, you say, 'No, try again.' To just let him make a response that doesn't hit the target, and then to sit back? No. You have to pursue it. You have to press it, to see if there is indeed a response that he has."[16]

Toward that end, Scalia appreciated the addition of Roberts. Together, they created a one-two punch that had not existed when Rehnquist was chief justice. As Professor Wrightsman observed, "While William Rehnquist was Chief Justice he asked some questions, but not as many as any other judge except the silent Justice Thomas. In contrast, Chief Justice Roberts has taken a more active role in the questioning. In the 24 oral arguments during the October 2006 term that led to 5-to-4 splits, he asked more questions than any other justice except Scalia."[17]

From his years of appellate advocacy, for the government and then in private practice, Roberts was an astute player during arguments. Like Scalia, he asked questions in rapid-fire succession, although usually with a less combative tone of voice. Roberts and Scalia often took up the mantle for the executive branch, where they had both spent their formative legal years. Overall, together, they made Court sessions more aggressive.[18]

In one 2007 argument Roberts and Scalia were in lockstep scrutinizing a lawyer for an Arizona death row inmate who argued that the convict's trial counsel had violated his right to effective assistance of counsel because he had failed to present crucial evidence that might have led the jury to give him life in prison rather than death.[19] The U.S. Court of Appeals for the Ninth Circuit had agreed and ordered a new hearing. Now the defendant's appellate lawyer asked the justices to reject Arizona officials' appeal. Together, Scalia and Roberts posed nearly twenty questions to the defendant's lawyer, suspicious of the claim of ineffective assistance of counsel, before any of the other seven justices got a word in. In the end, the justices ruled 5–4, with Scalia and Roberts in the majority, to reinstate the death sentence in the case.[20]

In addition to challenging a lawyer's main points, Scalia said that his goal during oral arguments was to get across his own position to his colleagues: "The other thing you do in any questioning [is] . . . convey to the other justices what your thinking on the case is."[21] This was all part of his process of persuasion, and other justices did it to varying degrees. But more than any of his colleagues, Scalia hammered on his personal emphases—for example, in the Cracker Barrel case, to try to narrow the grounds for bias lawsuits. It was all part of a larger, louder effort to get out a message that generally ran counter to where the Court had been. Scalia tried to make his points wherever he had an audience, over and over.

Scalia frequently used oral argument sessions to target the use of legislative history, such as congressional committee reports and floor speeches, as a way to determine the scope of a statute. He believed that judges trying to interpret a statute's meaning should look at its words and not delve into committee reports that purported to explain the bill's intentions. This had been the common practice of statutory interpretation for decades, although Scalia had been making progress in stopping reliance on such reports, which he regarded as unreliable. In a 2008 article addressing the "Scalia effect" on legislative history, the law professors James Brudney and Corey Ditslear found that, "[f]aced with his outspoken opposition . . . some justices seem to have concluded, even if subconsciously, that invoking legislative history . . . was not worth the risk of losing support for one's majority opinion or inviting a sharply-worded concurrence" from Scalia. Yet the authors, whose article stemmed from analysis of scores of workplace-law cases, also found that Scalia's resistance to legislative history used by the liberals on the Court did not extend with equal force to opinions written by his conservative colleagues. "Scalia seems prepared to give these conservative colleagues more of a free ride: he is [as] likely to join their majorities, or vote for their results, when they rely on legislative history as when they do not."[22]

In his book on Supreme Court advocacy, the appellate specialist David Frederick referred to an exchange between Scalia and the Washington lawyer Kenneth Geller over the use of such legislative history. "It is impossible to capture in writing the aggressive manner in which Justice Scalia immediately challenged Geller's invocation of the legislative history," Frederick wrote, "as though an advocate is not permitted to cite the most supportive material simply because it does not comport with a justice's judicial philosophy." Frederick noted that Geller reminded Scalia that when an advocate answers a question from the bench, he is speaking to the full Court, not to only one justice.[23]

In oral arguments in a 2006 dispute over the scope of the Individuals with Disabilities Education Act, a question arose over whether to rely on a conference report from the House of Representatives leading up to passage of the act. The House report called for a broad reading of a provision regarding the reimbursement of costs for parents who prevail in an IDEA action requiring a school district to pay the private school tuition of a disabled child who cannot be served in public schools. In the case before the justices, *Arlington Central School District Board of Education v. Murphy*, parents sought reimbursement for the cost of an educational consultant who helped them in the IDEA proceeding.[24]

"I just wonder why don't we look and see what [members of Congress] intended, since they told us," Justice Breyer said at one point during the hearing. "In the conference report, they say the conferees intend the phrase, 'attorneys' fees as part of costs,' to include reasonable expenses and fees of expert witnesses and the reasonable cost of any test or evaluation which is found to be necessary for the preparation of a parent or guardian's case in the action or proceeding. So why are we metaphysically trying to guess what Congress intended when they told us what they intended?"

Raymond Kuntz, the lawyer for the school district in southern New York protesting the paying of expert fees, responded that such an open-ended reimbursement was not delineated in the IDEA statute.

Following up on Breyer's reference to a conference report, Scalia asked the lawyer, "Was this language in the Senate conference report?"

"No," Kuntz answered. To which Scalia, satisfied, remarked, "Well, that's only half the Congress, isn't it?"

Later, Scalia said to the lawyer for the parents who were seeking reimbursement, "When the President signed it, did he also have the conference report in front of him? . . . He had the statute in front of him, didn't he?"

"What I am suggesting," David Vladeck, the parents' lawyer, countered, "is that the Court's role, as I understand it, is to be the faithful agent of Congress, and if the expectation of Members of Congress is that language in committee reports will garner respect from the Court, it is hard to then change the rules on Congress." Vladeck contended that members of Congress noted in the conference report and other legislative history that the word "costs" in the IDEA should be given broad meaning to ensure that parents are fully compensated when they have to fight school boards for the appropriate education for a needy child.

"The reason one does not use legislative history," Scalia responded, "if one does not use it, as I don't—is not because Congress doesn't expect it to be used, but because Congress does not have the power to delegate to one of its committees the content of its statutes. The Constitution provides that legislation will be passed by two houses and signed by the President, and the problem with legislative history, for those of us who have a problem with it, is this amounts to a delegation by Congress. It's not a matter of what Congress expected. I don't care what Congress expected. It can't do it."

The limits on Congress had been a longtime subject for Scalia. Since his time in the Ford administration testifying before congressional committees, he had found some of Congress's methods sloppy at best and constitutionally intrusive at worst. Regarding the larger question of whether Congress has been faithful to the Constitution, Scalia declared in one speech, "My court is fond of saying that acts of Congress come to the court with the presumption of constitutionality. But if Congress is going to take the attitude that it will do anything it can get away with and let the Supreme Court worry about the Constitution . . . then perhaps that presumption is unwarranted."[25]

During oral arguments, many of the justices tried to bolster one side of the case over another. Scalia simply did it with more force and consistency. "If you want to abandon [a line of reasoning] that's fine with me, but . . ." Scalia said at one point in another case, to laughter, his voice trailing off and suggesting that was not the wisest course. When the lawyer said he was "uncomfortable" with the concept Scalia was pressing, Scalia rejoined, "I don't care if you're uncomfortable with it" and continued to steer the lawyer in the direction he thought better.[26]

In his research, Professor Wrightsman found that Scalia, more than other justices, asked more "concession-eliciting" questions, beginning with "Surely you'd agree" or "Surely you'd concede." In a case from Georgia testing the constitutionality of a state law that required candidates for state public office to submit to drug testing, Scalia so commandeered the argument of the former candidate challenging the drug testing, who happened to be representing himself, that Chief Justice Rehnquist said at one point, "I think he's capable of answering himself."[27]

Seasoned advocates were pounded as much as novices. Scalia relentlessly challenged the former U.S. solicitor general Seth Waxman during a 2007 case testing the constitutional rights of prisoners at the U.S. naval base at Guantánamo Bay, Cuba. Scalia asked Waxman for prior cases that would support his position. "Do you have a single case in the 200 years of our country or, for that matter, in the five centuries of the English empire in which habeas [corpus] was granted to an alien in a territory that was not under the sovereign control of either the United States or England?"[28]

As Waxman offered examples, Scalia knocked them down on an array of grounds. "It's totally irrelevant," Scalia said at one point.

After a while a frustrated Waxman said, "I'll take one more chance, Justice Scalia."

"Okay, try them. I mean, line them up."

Spectators laughed. In a heavy-going hearing, when the phrase "habeas" was uttered ninety-four times, Scalia readily lapsed into such colloquialisms. In fact, Scalia, more often than not, brought an argument down to everyman's language. As in his written opinions, his hypothetical questions were alive. A spectator could *see* what he was talking about, which, again, helped him convey his message and his argument. In a case involving the rights to treasure from a sunken ship, he began a question, "Suppose I drop a silver dollar down a grate, and I try to bring it up with a piece of gum on a stick and I can't do it, and I shrug my shoulders and walk off because I have not gotten it, and then somebody comes up and lifts up the grate and gets my silver dollar. Is that his silver dollar?" Years later, in a dispute over a Freedom of Information Act request, Scalia said to a lawyer, "Counsel, you have just described for us a thousand-headed monster of litigation, and your proposal for a solution is to cut off one eyebrow."[29]

In the same manner, Scalia cut through the euphemisms of the day. That happened at one point during oral arguments in an appeal by the Arthur Andersen accounting firm, defending the "document retention" policies related to its work for the Enron Energy Services company, which collapsed in a tangle of fraud and bookkeeping schemes. "We all know that what are euphemistically termed 'record-retention programs' are, in fact, record-destruction programs," Scalia said, "and that one of the purposes of the destruction is to eliminate from the files information that private individuals can use for lawsuits and that Government investigators can use for investigations. And there has been nothing unlawful about having such a program, even if one of your purposes is not to leave lying around in the file stuff that can be used against you by either the government or a private individual."[30]

His effort to eschew jargon could sometimes border on insensitivity. In one case he was impatient with a lawyer representing a special education student whose mother challenged a school's policy of letting students grade one another's tests. The mother, Kristja Falvo, said the practice, which involved the calling out of grades to a teacher, caused humiliation particularly for her son, a "special education" student who was mainstreamed into regular classes. She sued the Owasso Independent School District in Oklahoma under the 1974 Family Education Rights and Privacy Act. The question was whether homework and classroom quizzes should be considered "educational records" subject to the privacy protections of the law.

When Falvo's lawyer was before the justices, Scalia observed that the record said the boy was in speech therapy for, in Scalia's terms, "only" forty-five minutes a week. He suggested that the lawyer was exaggerating the boy's disability.

"He was slow at reading," the lawyer said.

"Well, how does speech therapy help that?" Scalia shot back. "What does he have—a stutter? I suggest you not paint your client as more sympathetic than he is."[31]

Scalia did not shy from invoking stereotypes. That was evident in the case of Reymundo Toledo-Flores, whose case tested whether a state law conviction for simple cocaine possession could be considered an "aggravated drug trafficking felony" for purposes of deportation. Federal immigration law required legal permanent residents (green-card holders) who were convicted of an aggravated felony to be deported without an opportunity for appeal.[32]

A key issue in the case involving Toledo-Flores, from Mexico, who was convicted in Texas of possession of cocaine, was whether his challenge might be moot because he already had been deported to Mexico for entering the United States illegally. Toledo-Flores's lawyer argued that the case was not moot, because under part of his conditions of "supervised release" in Mexico, Toledo-Flores had to observe certain rules, including abstaining from alcohol. Scalia interjected, "Nobody thinks your client is really, you know, abstaining from tequila down in Mexico because he is on supervised release in the United States."[33]

The clichéd reference to a tequila-drinking Mexican jarred some journalists and other Court watchers.[34] *Slate*'s Lithwick referred to "Scalia's deliberate carelessness with language, his sense that he is somehow above the sorts of linguistic delicacy the rest of us expect in our dealings with others. Indeed, he seems to think it's his obligation to be ever more reckless with his words, perhaps because he's about the only guy left who faces no consequences for his rhetorical body-slams."[35]

It was true. Scalia's remarks were often the subject of commentary, yet they did not seem to cost him beyond rounds of publicity, which he did not appear to mind. He shrugged and said he got used to it. In a 2008 appearance at Chicago's Union League Club, Scalia was asked whether "freedom of speech is under assault by political correctness." He answered, "It's not under assault. It takes courage not to be politically correct. If you're a coward, that's your fault."[36]

He elaborated later in an interview regarding his remarks on the bench: "I like to put the point concisely and colorfully, if possible . . . I didn't have to say 'tequila drinking,' but it's a nice touch, I think."[37]

Some of what he said was for exaggerated effect, to be sure. And if he were not such a verbal stylist, he might be called more to account. But he was a showman in the spirit of his grandfather Pasquale. In 2005 the Boston University law professor Jay Wexler tracked oral argument transcripts to see when the court reporter noted "laughter" after a justice's remarks and concluded, "Justice Scalia won the competition by a landslide, instigating 77 laughing episodes."[38] *The New York Times* ran a front-page story on the Wexler study, with its own fitting headline: SO, A GUY WALKS UP TO THE BAR, AND SCALIA SAYS . . ."[39] The social psychologist Wrightsman did a similar tabulation for the following term and found that Scalia generated sixty-four indications of "laughter" in the seventy-eight oral arguments. Justice Breyer was the only justice who came close to that total, with forty-nine "laughter" incidents.[40]

None of the liberal justices, including Breyer, spoke with anything near the verbal swagger of Scalia. As Scalia observed, Breyer tended to ask lengthy, intricate questions that recalled his years in academia. Justice Stevens, the most senior of the liberal justices, was the careful gentleman even when he was ready to level someone. "May I ask what might be an awfully elementary question?" he would begin.

Justice Ginsburg often tried to undercut her friend's ideologically incompatible line of reasoning. Yet she worked her knife subtly. In the 2007 case of *Danforth v. Minnesota*, as Scalia was pummeling a state pub-

lic defender at the lectern, Ginsburg interjected, "That issue is not a necessary part of your case at all, is it?" Later, when she raised an argument that
would help the defendant's case, Scalia quickly made an effort to discount
it. During the same Minnesota case, when the lawyer for the state was
at the lectern, Scalia jumped in after a question from Justice Breyer
and began telling the lawyer how he should answer the question. "You
wouldn't want to say that," Scalia began, as he expounded on his own view
of the state's constitutional argument. Before the lawyer could respond,
Chief Justice Roberts made a joke that took note of the fact that Scalia was
not asking questions as much as providing answers.[41]

"I think you're handling these questions very well," Roberts quipped as
spectators laughed. Ginsburg—in all seriousness—remarked of Scalia's
elaboration on what he believed the state of Minnesota's argument should
be, "That was not a question addressed to you." She was referring to the
fact that Scalia's remark was no question at all. In an interview, Ginsburg
acknowledged that she found Scalia sometimes "irritating." Yet, she said, "I
have always enjoyed Nino. No matter how overworked and tired I feel, he
can always say things that make me laugh."[42]

Souter, the fourth liberal, sat to Scalia's left by order of alternating seniority and sometimes acted as a foil to him. The two were a study in personal contrasts. Souter was a lifelong bachelor who lived alone in a small
apartment in an out-of-the-way section of Washington, D.C. Where Scalia
loved the social scene in Washington and eagerly traveled in the United
States and abroad during any Court recess, Souter slipped into his Volkswagen Jetta and drove back to his native New Hampshire as soon as the
term was in recess each summer.

They often played off each other, as in a Maryland case about whether
police officers had a right to order passengers out of a vehicle that officers
had stopped because of the driver's apparently unlawful activity. The justices questioned whether a hard-and-fast rule should exist, allowing passengers to be detained. Souter began a hypothetical query: "Let's assume
that the bright-line rule allowed nothing more than requiring the passenger to get out of the car so that if the passenger then said, 'I've had enough
of this, I'm leaving,' the passenger, so far as the bright-line rule is concerned, would be allowed to go?"

Scalia interjected, "In fact, the passenger says, 'Thank goodness. This
guy was speeding. I am so glad to get out of this car. Let me catch the
nearest cab and go.' "

Rejoined Souter, "You can see what Justice Scalia's passengers tend to feel like."[43]

Later in their tenure together, in a more serious dispute over the imposition of the death penalty, Scalia and Souter momentarily ignored the lawyer at the lectern and conducted their own colloquy of sorts. The case of *Kansas v. Marsh* tested the constitutionality of a Kansas law that required a convicted murderer to be sentenced to death if jurors found that the aggravating circumstances of the crime, such as the brutality toward the victim, were of a weight equal to the mitigating factors, such as the defendant's own troubled childhood. Michael Lee Marsh had shot, stabbed, and slashed the throat of Marry Ane Pusch. He then set the home on fire, burning to death Pusch's toddler daughter.

Marsh was challenging the Kansas death penalty law as a violation of the Eighth Amendment's requirement of individual capital sentencing. His lawyer argued in a written brief that when a jury is in equipoise on the aggravating and mitigating factors of a case, it has not been able to conclude that the defendant uniquely warrants the death penalty. That was just the kind of argument that made the case difficult for some of the justices. To Souter, it seemed the jury was being put in the position of saying, "We're on the fence, but execute anyway."

Scalia responded during the oral argument: "Surely, it's a reasoned moral response to say, 'We have found these horrible aggravating factors in this murder . . . There are these terrible aggravating factors. Three of them, we found. And we further find that there is no mitigating evidence to outweigh those aggravating factors.' That seems to me a perfectly valid moral response."[44]

"That is correct, Justice Scalia," the Kansas attorney general Phill Kline said.

"But that is not our case, is it?" Souter quickly noted. "Because our case is not, 'We don't find that the mitigators outweigh.' Our case is, 'We find the mitigators of equal weight.' That's why you get to equipoise. It's not a question of the failure of mitigators to predominate."

"No," Scalia said.

Souter came right back, saying that "what poses the problem" is that the mitigating elements can be equal to the aggravating, and still require a death sentence.

"But it seems to me that to be equal in weight," Scalia said, "is not to predominate. And that's all the jury is saying." He added, "The people of

Kansas think that the aggravators that they have specified are serious enough that unless there is something to overcome them, the death penalty is appropriate."

When the case was decided, Scalia's view prevailed—but not necessarily because of Scalia. The other four justices in the majority (Roberts, Kennedy, Thomas, Alito) had indicated by their prior votes in capital punishment cases and their questions at oral arguments that they were inclined toward the state's position. Alito, a former federal prosecutor, cast the critical fifth vote.

Yet the oral arguments in *Kansas v. Marsh* were an important piece in how Scalia expressed his message. When the case was resolved, he signed the Court opinion written by Justice Thomas that said to meet the Eighth Amendment requirement of individualized sentencing, it was enough that the jury had the opportunity to consider all relevant mitigating evidence. Then Scalia wrote separately, provoked by a dissenting opinion of Souter's that called the Kansas law "morally absurd" and said that "tolerat[ing] this moral irrationality defies decades of precedent aimed at eliminating freakish capital sentencing in the United States." Souter also admonished that advances in DNA testing and recent exonerations for death row inmates should make the Court warier of capital sentencing.

Scalia particularly objected to Souter's reference to the risks in the capital punishment system. "Like other human institutions, courts and juries are not perfect," Scalia wrote in his concurrence. "One cannot have a system of criminal punishment without accepting the possibility that someone will be punished mistakenly. That is a truism, not a revelation. But with regard to the punishment of death in the current American system, that possibility has been reduced to an insignificant minimum. This explains why those ideologically driven to ferret out and proclaim a mistaken modern execution have not a single verifiable case to point to, whereas it is easy as pie to identify plainly guilty murderers who have been set free. The American people have determined that the good to be derived from capital punishment—in deterrence, and perhaps most of all in the meting out of condign justice for horrible crimes—outweighs the risk of error."

Scalia continued his reproach: "It is no proper part of the business of this Court, or any of its Justices, to second-guess that judgment, much less to impugn it before the world, and less still to frustrate it by imposing judicially invented obstacles to its execution."

Scalia's assertion that the chance someone would be wrongly executed "has been reduced to an insignificant minimum" recalled his earlier comments that death penalty cases, for him, simply were not close calls. "[I]n my 15 years on the bench," he said at a 2002 conference at the University of Chicago sponsored by the Pew Forum on Religion and Public Life, "I can only think of one case when I thought there was a little doubt as to the substantive guilt. The vast majority of issues that are appealed involve foot faults during the course of the prosecution—evidence was admitted that shouldn't have been admitted and so forth. But the case where there is serious doubt about whether this is really the person that did it is enormously rare . . . [I]t is not a problem I have to wrestle with."

E. J. Dionne, Jr., a *Washington Post* columnist and Brookings Institution fellow moderating the conference, asked Scalia, "What happened in that one case?"

"I think the Court ultimately concluded that there was nothing to the objection," Scalia answered. "But that was the only one where I think it even worth inquiring into."[45]

Scalia used a multitude of forums, including oral arguments and speeches to groups, to make his case. He gained widespread media attention, an audience among academics, and a following among law students and lawyers. It did not necessarily gain him votes on the Court. In fact, in some situations, notably when Justice O'Connor was on the bench, his harangues could have the opposite effect.[46]

Still, in recent years, Scalia had come closer to winning a majority—simply because of the changed Court membership. For nearly two decades, when Scalia and O'Connor served together, Scalia typically had to worry about whether he could win the votes of the centrist conservatives O'Connor and Kennedy. Since Alito's succession of O'Connor, only Kennedy was a regular swing vote. That was no small matter on a Court where five votes made a majority. Alito and Roberts, closer to Scalia's brand of originalism than Rehnquist, both improved Scalia's win-loss record.[47]

Yet he could not count on the new justices automatically seeing the law his way—which was fully demonstrated in the Cracker Barrel case begun by Hedrick Humphries. In the end, a majority of the justices, including Roberts and Alito, voted to find that the civil rights law known as Section 1981 covered the kind of retaliation that Humphries claimed. Only two justices dissented from the ruling, Scalia and Thomas.[48]

Justice Breyer, who wrote the decision in the Cracker Barrel case, referred to a pattern of decisions dating to 1969 that had interpreted antibias laws to cover retaliation. He also highlighted O'Connor's 2005 decision in which the Court ruled that a federal law that prohibited sex bias in education inherently covered people who faced reprisals for complaining about bias. Breyer said there was a "considerable burden upon those who would seek a different interpretation that would necessarily unsettle many Court precedents." Roberts and Alito, who did not write separately, plainly agreed. Despite Roberts's statement that the Court precedents represented a "freewheeling approach to statutory construction," he felt bound by them.

In their dissent, Scalia and Thomas said the Court's decision had no foundation in the text of Section 1981. "Retaliation is not discrimination based on race," Thomas wrote in an opinion joined by Scalia. "When an individual is subjected to reprisal because he has complained about racial discrimination, the injury he suffers is not on account of his race; rather, it is the result of his conduct."

Undercutting any persuasive effect of that view was the fact that the Bush administration and numerous U.S. appeals courts were of the opposite mind, saying Section 1981, in fact, covered retaliation. Such countervailing weight was similarly present in the case several years earlier of William Hibbs involving the Family and Medical Leave Act. The Court, siding with the federal government, ruled 6–3 to allow state workers such as Hibbs to sue and recover money damages for their employers' violations of the Family and Medical Leave Act. Scalia dissented, joined only by Thomas and Kennedy.[49]

The lesson of those cases was that Scalia's position often was too extreme to win a majority, no matter how hard he argued. In a separate matter, all of his conservative colleagues agreed in the Individuals with Disabilities Education Act case regarding reimbursements. Over the dissenting views of Stevens, Souter, and Breyer, the Court ruled that the IDEA did not authorize reimbursement for expert fees.[50] Justice Ginsburg joined the bottom-line judgment of Scalia and the other conservatives to find that parents who won an IDEA challenge could not be compensated for a consultant's costs. Justice Ginsburg wrote a separate opinion because she differed in the rationale that supported the judgment.

No demonstrated pattern of success, or failure, resulted from Scalia's tactics at oral arguments—within the Court, that is. Beyond the marble walls, his way of constantly calling attention to his views could not be discounted. He was persistent, vigilant, and clear. Lawyers knew and debated his lines of reasoning. His presence filled the courtroom. He was a captivating force that was not going away.

An episode capturing that Scalia phenomenon occurred early in Roberts's tenure as chief justice. Scalia had taken the lead on two significant disputes that were both announced on the morning of June 19, 2006. In the first, the Court interpreted the breadth of Clean Water Act coverage for endangered wetlands. The question was when federal regulators could prevent development (and its potential discharge of pollutants) on wetlands that were far from, though indirectly connected to, rivers and other navigable waters. In its ruling, the Court reversed a decision that favored the U.S. Army Corps of Engineers. The Court said that two Michigan developers deserved another chance to obtain permits to build on ecologically fragile marshy lands. The Court, however, put forth three competing rationales that took a half hour to explain from the bench.

The morning began with Scalia announcing the judgment favoring the developers and reading an opinion, signed by Roberts, Thomas, and Alito, that would have stripped protections from many areas covered by the 1972 Clean Water Act. Scalia described the lands in question as mere "transitory puddles." Then Justice Kennedy, who had agreed with Scalia's bottom-line judgment allowing the developers a new hearing, said he disagreed with Scalia's standard and went on to articulate a test more favorable to environmental interests. Kennedy said the corps should be able to protect wetlands as long as they were ecologically connected to—and ultimately could affect pollution in—rivers, lakes, and other navigable waters. Kennedy also said that evidence in the paired cases suggested that the wetlands at issue had the sufficient "nexus" to navigable waters to justify denial of the permits. Speaking next from the bench was Justice Stevens, who had been joined by Souter, Ginsburg, and Breyer against the developers. Stevens said the Scalia view could jeopardize the quality of the nation's waterways. He said Scalia's opinion should not dictate the standard in lower courts, because Kennedy—the key fifth vote reversing the lower courts—had rejected that in favor of an easier test for regulation.

After the quarrelsome set of opinions from *Rapanos v. United States* and *Carabell v. U.S. Army Corps of Engineers* had been read, Chief Justice Roberts said that a second pair of cases, *Davis v. Washington* and *Hammon v. Indiana*, would be announced. Those cases related to the constitutional guarantee that defendants be able to confront witnesses against them, a right that had been bolstered by Scalia's 2004 breakthrough decision in *Crawford v. Washington*.

With that handoff from the chief justice, Scalia looked up at spectators and, before he began reading his opinion, said, "It's me again." The courtroom broke up.[51]

FIFTEEN

POWER IN A TIME OF TERRORISM

Three days before he would turn seventy years old, Justice Scalia was back at the University of Fribourg in Switzerland, where he had spent a semester on an exchange program as an undergraduate at Georgetown University. He was there to give a speech on the workings of the U.S. legal system, and he was ready to expound, as usual, on the importance of the Constitution's original meaning. His student trip to Switzerland five decades earlier had whetted his curiosity about foreign cultures and had begun a pattern of his seizing opportunities for travel abroad.[1] As a justice, Scalia visited and spoke in foreign countries more than any of his colleagues.[2] He was energized by the trips and thought nothing of flying for eight hours, spending two nights overseas, and flying home. At the same time, while he was as active as ever, his upcoming seventieth birthday weighed on him. He was beginning to feel his age, complaining more to his wife about aches and pains, trying—and failing—finally to quit smoking. His tennis game was becoming less about shuffling back and forth to get the ball and more one of standing and hoping the ball would come right to him. At the Court, Scalia was now the third-eldest justice, behind John Paul Stevens, about to turn eighty-six in April 2006, and Ruth Bader Ginsburg, who would celebrate her seventy-third birthday that March 15, four days after Scalia hit age seventy on March 11. When he returned from Switzerland, Scalia and Ginsburg would share a glass of wine with their colleagues, as had long been the tradition among the justices to honor birthdays.

After his standard speech to the university audience, Scalia took questions, which immediately revealed that this campus—like others in West-ern Europe—was enraged about the George W. Bush administration's detention and interrogation policies and possible human rights violations in its "war on terror." The U.S. military was deep into wars in Afghanistan and Iraq, and Americans were growing increasingly impatient with both.[3] Controversy also swirled around U.S. practices related to hundreds of for-eign fighters picked up on the battlefield, designated as "enemy combat-ants," and transferred to the U.S. naval base at Guantánamo Bay, Cuba, for detention and interrogation. Someone in the audience asked Scalia about the rights of detainees captured by the U.S. military.

"War is war," he said, "and it has never been the case that when you captured a combatant you have to give them a jury trial in your civil courts. Give me a break." Scalia insisted that if someone was captured "by my Army on a battlefield," he should remain in a military setting such as Guantánamo and not be transferred to regular civilian courts. Then Scalia referred to one of his sons, Matthew, who was an army officer who had served in Iraq with the First Armored Division. "I had a son on that bat-tlefield and they were shooting at my son, and I'm not about to give this man who was captured in a war a full jury trial. I mean it's crazy."[4]

The statements were high-voltage Scalia. At an earlier time, his remarks to a single audience overseas might have been heard only by that audience. But the Internet and round-the-clock news programs quickly propelled Scalia's words around the globe. Some critics questioned his timing in speaking publicly on the subject of foreign detainees. The Supreme Court was scheduled a few weeks later in March to hear the case of Salid Ahmed Hamdan, a Yemeni who allegedly served as a bodyguard and driver for Osama bin Laden and was being held at the Guantánamo prison. Hamdan had been charged with conspiracy to commit terrorism and was to be prosecuted before a military commission. His lawyers were arguing that the military commissions, established by a Bush executive order in November 2001 without the approval of Congress, violated the Geneva Conventions and the Uniform Code of Military Justice. President Bush had said at the time he ordered the special commissions that terror suspects simply did not deserve the rights afforded in usual courts-martial or civilian trials. Under his order, for example, a detainee need not be present for his trial or have access to the evidence against him. The presid-ing officer could allow evidence obtained through torture, and in the end no court might hear an appeal from, or conduct a full review of, a commission decision.

When *Newsweek* magazine, the first to report Scalia's remarks in Switzerland, posted an article on its website about Scalia on March 26, it questioned whether he should sit on the case. Other news media quickly picked up the story, and the next day a group of five retired U.S. generals and admirals, who had filed a "friend of the court" brief siding with Hamdan, submitted a request asking that Scalia disqualify himself from the Hamdan appeal. They said Scalia's statements compromised an expectation of judicial impartiality.

The Washington lawyer David Remes, representing the five retired officers, wrote in a letter to the Supreme Court clerk William Suter that Scalia's remarks "give rise to the unfortunate appearance that even before the briefing in this case was completed, the Justice had made up his mind about the merits. The Justice's remarks also give rise to the unfortunate appearance that the Justice may bring to this case a personal animus toward [Hamdan] and those similarly situated arising from the military service of the Justice's son in Iraq. In a case that is fundamentally about fair process, it is especially important that this Court's own process be perceived to be fair."[5]

For the full Supreme Court, the *Hamdan* case offered the most difficult dilemma to date in assessing the balance between asserted executive power and the justices' own jurisdiction. It tested the president's ability to imprison terrorist suspects without the usual rights constituting due process of law, against the permanent post–September 11 backdrop of American worries about another terrorist attack as well as devotion to the Constitution. By 2006, also, American opposition to the war in Iraq was rising drastically, as was worldwide denunciation of the Bush administration's treatment of detainees.

In that vein, the *Hamdan* case also arose amid an increasing drumbeat of complaints about the administration's quest for unchecked authority. Vice President Dick Cheney, Scalia's old friend from the Ford years, was playing a leading role in assertions of executive power regarding antiterrorism moves. Cheney said in a 2002 CNN interview that during his thirty-five years in Washington, "there's been a constant, steady erosion of the prerogatives and the power of the Oval Office . . . previous instances where presidents have given up, if you will, important principles."[6]

Beyond the political tensions of the day, more important for Scalia, the terrorism-related cases at the Supreme Court brought together numerous strands of his well-defined approach to the law: his broad view of executive branch power; his originalist take on the right of prisoners (whether they be U.S. citizens or, alternatively, foreigners) to make their case in American courts; and his view of how congressional statutes should be interpreted. The cases also held a personal dimension, as Scalia suggested at the University of Fribourg, related to his son Matthew, the seventh of his nine children. Matthew had graduated from the U.S. Military Academy at West Point in 1995 and set himself on a career in the army.

All of Scalia's children were pursuing their own callings and raising large families. The grandchildren were coming, at least one a year. In rapid succession, Scalia and his wife had ten, fifteen, and then twenty grandchildren. As the decade wore on, they were nearing thirty grandchildren—despite three of the nine children being unmarried and childless. Ann, the eldest, who had worked in marketing, was raising five children in the Chicago suburbs; Eugene and John, the next two, were still building up their legal practices at prominent law firms in the greater Washington, D.C., area and watching their broods grow; Catherine, the next, had worked in library science and was home with six children; next in line, Mary, a Bryn Mawr graduate whose classmates had worn black armbands in protest when her father attended her graduation, was rearing her six; Paul, who was just before Matthew in the birth order, was a parish priest in Virginia; Christopher was unmarried, too, and working on a Ph.D. in English at the University of Wisconsin; Margaret, the youngest, who had defended her father at Amherst, was also unmarried and beginning a Ph.D. program in cognitive psychology at the University of Virginia.

In October 2004, soon after Matthew's tour in Iraq had ended and about a year and a half before his father's reference to him at the University of Fribourg, Matthew had written a piece for *Legal Times* about some of his wartime experiences: "Our mission was twofold: Defeat remnants of the old regime, while assisting the Iraqi people in rebuilding their country. Each unit had specific sites that required constant protection from looters or insurgents. My company maintained a force at all times at an electrical station and a United Nations food distribution warehouse . . . On a typical day, scores of people came to our gate complaining of the lack of electricity, reporting crimes, or telling us where we might find Saddam."[7]

Justice Scalia did not think Matthew's service prejudiced him against a detainee in a case, and in a later interview he rejected out of hand the suggestion from the retired officers' letter. "That's like saying people who don't have any children over there are biased the other way," Scalia said. "That's ridiculous."[8] He insisted that his remarks in Switzerland were general and removed from the specifics of Hamdan's case. Hamdan was not requesting a civilian jury trial—the subject of Scalia's comments. The precise legal question his case raised centered on the validity of the military commission procedures. "It was not the same issue that was involved in the case," Scalia said. "Just because I think defendants are on the wrong side of one issue doesn't mean I think they are on the wrong side of all issues." Scalia added that his son brought the war closer to home. "The fact that he was there for fourteen months made me more concerned about the Iraq experience than many Americans," he said. "To have someone over there always makes it more personal."[9]

Hamdan's lawyer, the Georgetown University law professor Neal Katyal, did not think Scalia's recusal was necessary. According to a report at the time in *Vanity Fair* magazine, he was even perturbed by the move of the retired generals and admirals. "This is outrageous!" he said. "What do those generals think they are doing? I was furious that they were so irresponsible. I deeply admire and trust Justice Scalia. We disagree on many things, but it would have been the height of arrogance for me, a litigant, to tell him what to do."[10]

Scalia's remarks this time around did not generate the kind of critical press attention he had endured during the Cheney duck-hunting episode. Yet some news organizations editorialized against his speaking out on detainee matters. *The Philadelphia Inquirer* wrote, "To be sure, Scalia didn't specifically name Salim Ahmed Hamdan . . . To a layman's ear, though, it sure sounded like Scalia had taken a stand on a critical legal issue in a case he was just about to hear."[11] *The New York Times*'s editorial against Scalia was topped by a headline that left no doubt about its assessment: THE OVER-THE-TOP JUSTICE. The piece, referring to Scalia's University of Fribourg remarks, asserted that "Justice Scalia seemed to prejudge key issues in a momentous case involving the rights of Gitmo detainees."[12]

Scalia typically brushed off such editorials or questions about whether his off-the-bench statements tainted his on-the-bench decisions. On occasion, however, he would refer inquiring reporters to an attitude he had expressed in a 2002 case, *Republican Party of Minnesota v. White*. "A judge's lack of predisposition regarding the relevant legal issues in a case has never been thought a necessary component of equal justice, and with good reason," Scalia wrote in the Court majority's opinion striking down a Minnesota prohibition on judicial candidates' speaking out. "For one thing, it is virtually impossible to find a judge who does not have preconceptions about the law . . . Indeed, even if it were possible to select judges who did not have preconceived views on legal issues, it would hardly be desirable to do so."[13]

Such sentiment reinforced the notion that Scalia felt no compunction to hold back. And, as would be seen in the series of cases arising from U.S. antiterrorism efforts after September 11, Scalia had intense views and did not shy from expressing what he thought—from the bench, in his writing, or on the road. At every juncture he would find audiences—both receptive and critical—for his passionate speeches, whether on detainee rights, emerging controversies over torture, or even in defense of the fictional federal agent and terrorist tracker Jack Bauer on the TV drama *24*.

The *Hamdan* case, especially, would find Scalia in a fury. But before the Hamdan matter, there had been a preliminary set of important cases. In these 2004 decisions, Scalia demonstrated that he drew a sharp line between the rights of U.S. citizens detained on U.S. soil and foreign prisoners at Guantánamo, which he considered outside the sovereignty of the United States.

Yaser Hamdi, an American citizen who was born in Louisiana and grew up in Saudi Arabia, had been captured with Taliban fighters on an Afghan battlefield in late 2001 and detained by the U.S. military as an "enemy combatant." He was eventually transferred to a brig in Charleston, South Carolina, and held in solitary confinement. He sought a writ of habeas corpus on the ground that his confinement was unlawful. Hamdi had lost in a lower U.S. appeals court, and the Bush administration, fighting Hamdi's appeal, had urged the justices to rule that the government could hold a combatant—even a U.S. citizen—indefinitely, without charges. Administration lawyers urged the Court not to second-guess a "quintessentially military judgment" to imprison someone as an enemy combatant.[14]

Largely rejecting that view, Justice O'Connor wrote an opinion for a plurality of four justices (and joined by Justice Thomas in the bottom-line judgment) that allowed detention but only after an individual had gotten a hearing before a judge. As a preliminary matter, O'Connor said that a congressional resolution that authorized "all necessary and appropriate force" after the September 11 terrorist hijackings gave the president power to hold Hamdi.[15] Justice O'Connor then added several conditions to the administration's ability to detain a U.S. citizen suspected of terrorism. She said he must be told the factual basis for his designation as an enemy combatant and be allowed to rebut the charges before a neutral judge or other decision maker. In a sharp rebuke to the administration, O'Connor then wrote, "We have long . . . made clear that a state of war is not a blank check for the President when it comes to the rights of the Nation's citizens . . . Whatever power the United States Constitution envisions for the executive in its exchanges with other nations or with enemy organizations in times of conflict, it most assuredly envisions a role for all three branches when individual liberties are at stake."[16] That attitude about the role of all three branches would be a defining element of the Court's future rulings in this area of the law.

Scalia, along with Stevens, Souter, and Ginsburg, dissented on varying grounds from the part of O'Connor's judgment that found that the American citizen Hamdi could be held without charges and a trial. While Souter and Ginsburg homed in on the lack of statutory authority for detention, Scalia and Stevens contended that U.S. citizens could never be indefinitely detained as enemy combatants unless Congress formally suspended the writ of habeas corpus. "[A]s critical as the government's interest may be in detaining those who actually pose an immediate threat to the national security of the United States, during ongoing international conflict," Scalia wrote in his opinion joined by Stevens, "history and common sense teach us that an unchecked system of detention carries the potential to become a means for oppression for others who do not present that sort of threat."

Scalia also had a familiar gripe with O'Connor's attempt to provide guidance to the administration for the minimum procedures needed for a citizen terrorist suspect. Her pragmatism had constantly vexed him and prompted some of his most derisive rhetoric. "There is a certain harmony of approach in the plurality's making up for Congress's failure to invoke the Suspension Clause and its making up for the Executive's failure to apply what it says are needed procedures—an approach that reflects what might be called a Mr. Fix-it Mentality," Scalia wrote. "The plurality seems to view it as its mission to Make Everything Come Out Right, rather than merely to decree the consequences, as far as individual rights are concerned, of the other two branches' actions and omissions."

O'Connor's brand of pragmatic judging was anathema to him. Considerations of how next to handle Hamdi's case should be left to the political branches, he believed. But for O'Connor and those who signed her opinion, the best course was to sketch out the minimum requirements for a citizen detainee. Assessing the options for this early test of handling a detainee, the Harvard Law professors Richard Fallon and Daniel Meltzer agreed, writing in a law review article, "Had the Court simply ordered Hamdi's release, executive officials could have rearrested him immediately and then put a new procedural scheme into place. Were that second scheme also found deficient, the government could have repeated the exercise as often as necessary until it developed an acceptable set of procedures. That scenario would have disserved both the government and Yaser Hamdi. Instead, the Court appropriately assumed a responsibility to apprise the President and Congress of what the Constitution minimally requires, while leaving the political branches considerable room for maneuver."[17]

On the same day that the Hamdi ruling was issued in 2004, the Court by a 6–3 vote dealt a more serious blow to the Bush administration's antiterrorism-related practices. This time, Scalia favored the Bush position. He dissented from a Court decision by Stevens that said foreigners captured in Afghanistan and elsewhere and detained at the Guantánamo naval base should be allowed to challenge their detention in petitions for habeas corpus. That case of *Rasul v. Bush* had been brought by the families of twelve Kuwaiti and two Australian prisoners. The prisoners had been captured during U.S. military battles against Al Qaeda and the Taliban in Afghanistan and elsewhere.

The Guantánamo prisoners contended that they were innocent of any terrorism and had been captured by bounty hunters who then turned them over to the U.S. military for rewards. The administration had chosen Guantánamo as a site for terrorism-related prisoners in large measure because it assumed it would be considered outside the jurisdiction of federal courts. Bush lawyers had relied on a post–World War II case, *Johnson v. Eisentrager*, for the premise that foreigners captured and kept outside of the country did not have access to U.S. courts. In that 1950 decision, the Supreme Court had rejected an appeal from German nationals who had been captured by U.S. troops during World War II in China, tried by a military tribunal, then held in occupied Germany. Bush administration lawyers had argued that the Guantánamo prison was similar to the U.S.-run prison in Germany in the *Eisentrager* case. But Stevens, writing in *Rasul v. Bush*, found the comparison inapt. The Guantánamo detainees, Stevens wrote, "are not nationals of countries at war with the United States, and they deny that they have engaged in or plotted acts of aggression against the United States; they have never been afforded access to any tribunal, much less charged with and convicted of wrongdoing; and for more than two years they have been imprisoned in territory over which the United States exercises exclusive jurisdiction and control."[18]

Stevens was joined by Justices O'Connor, Souter, Ginsburg, and Breyer in his opinion. Justice Kennedy joined in the judgment favoring the Guantánamo detainees. Dissenting were Chief Justice Rehnquist and Justices Scalia and Thomas. Writing for that trio, Scalia said the Bush administration had been ambushed by a new interpretation of U.S. sovereignty. "Today, the Court springs a trap on the Executive, subjecting Guantánamo Bay to the oversight of the federal courts even though it has never before been thought to be within their jurisdiction—and thus making it a foolish place to have housed alien wartime detainees . . . The commander in chief and his subordinates had every reason to expect that the internment of combatants at Guantánamo Bay would not have the consequence of bringing the cumbersome machinery of our domestic courts into military affairs."

Scalia's reference to the "cumbersome machinery" of the nation's courts was a reminder of his long-held stance that judges should play a limited role in society, especially in this case involving military matters. His comments in the 2004 *Rasul v. Bush* case made clear his idea that foreign detainees had limited rights in U.S. courts and arguably presaged what he would say at the University of Fribourg about lack of rights for foreigners captured on the battlefield.

Scalia's notions about executive power in antiterrorism policy would be more broadly revealed as the justices took up the case of *Hamdan v. Rumsfeld* three weeks after he returned from Switzerland. Unlike the ear-

lier cases of *Hamdi* and *Rasul*, which dealt with narrow, preliminary matters of presidential authority and the jurisdiction of federal courts over
Guantánamo prisoners, the *Hamdan* controversy was a fundamental challenge to the underpinning of Bush's legal system for dealing with terrorist
suspects. It would also offer more of a showdown between the Bush-
Cheney view of presidential power and that of the Court majority.

Cheney had spent much of his time in Washington in executive branch
service and, since his early days with Nixon, was concerned with what he
viewed as unjust infringements on executive authority. He became a key
player in the initial drafting of Bush's terrorist detention and interrogation policy and worked hard to shield it from challenge in the courts.[19]
Some political scientists and historians claimed that not since the Watergate era had there been such a power grab by the executive, and they
chalked up a good part of that grab to Vice President Cheney. The Dickinson College political science professor Andrew Rudalevige wrote in a 2006
article in *Presidential Studies Quarterly,* "It is George W. Bush's presidency
that provides the clearest—because most openly claimed and aggressively
argued—case study of presidential unilateralism in the post-Watergate
era."[20] The U.S. representative Jane Harman, a California Democrat who
was the ranking member of the House Intelligence Committee, told *The
New Yorker's* Jane Mayer, who had written extensively on Bush antiterrorism policy, that Cheney and his top aide were still fighting Watergate.
"They're focused on restoring the Nixon Presidency," she said. "They've
persuaded themselves that, following Nixon, things went all wrong."[21]

In 2006 newspapers and television were offering regular allegations of
domestic wiretapping and revelations about administration policy that
might have authorized treatment of detainees that many would consider
to be torture. It appeared, at the least, that some officials had fostered an
atmosphere in which military guards felt free to engage in unauthorized
abuse of detainees. The first reports of prisoner abuse at Iraq's Abu Ghraib
prison had emerged just as the high Court was hearing the 2004 cases of
Hamdi and *Rasul*. The full scope of that abuse was revealed in later
months, at the same time that the news media reported allegations of
abuse at the Guantánamo prison and details of executive branch efforts to
permit what Cheney called "robust interrogation" of "high value" terrorist
suspects.[22] An August 2002 Department of Justice memorandum that
Cheney's staff helped shepherd dictated that any effort to apply federal

anti-torture law "in a manner that interferes with the President's direction of such core war matters as detention and interrogation of enemy combatants thus would be unconstitutional." The Georgetown University law professor David Cole, writing in the *New York Review of Books* about Bush's effort to make his powers as commander in chief overriding, referred to the torture memo and contended, "[T]here is little to distinguish the current administration's view from that famously espoused by Richard Nixon when asked to justify his authorization of illegal, warrantless wiretapping of Americans during the Vietnam War: 'When the President does it, that means it is not illegal.'"[23]

Such were the tensions that contributed to the highly charged atmosphere at the Court when the oral arguments in *Hamdan v. Rumsfeld* were held on March 28, 2006. Scalia was on the bench, having batted away the request that he disqualify himself. Next to Scalia, however, the black leather chair was empty. Chief Justice Roberts disqualified himself because he had ruled in the *Hamdan* case a year earlier as a judge on the U.S. Court of Appeals for the D.C. Circuit. Roberts had sided with the Bush administration against Hamdan. The D.C. Circuit's decision had been announced just four days before Bush revealed his choice of Roberts for the Supreme Court in July 2005.

A month after the Court had agreed to review that D.C. Circuit decision and hear Hamdan's claim, Congress had passed a law that prevented Guantánamo prisoners from challenging the constitutionality of their confinement before U.S. judges. The Detainee Treatment Act, which passed on December 30, 2005, had been largely a response to the justices' earlier ruling in *Rasul v. Bush* and was an effort to ensure that prisoners at the naval base on the southeastern coast of Cuba could not take their cases to federal judges. An overriding question was whether the new law applied to prisoners already at Guantánamo and challenging their detention when it was adopted.

As oral arguments began over the validity of special commissions to try terrorist suspects, Scalia jumped in first to challenge Neal Katyal's reliance on statements and reports by members of Congress that would indicate that Hamdan's case and others pending at the time the Detainee Treatment Act took effect could still proceed. Katyal insisted that based on the act's history, it could apply only prospectively, not to prisoners like Hamdan who had earlier filed a petition challenging the military commissioners themselves. Katyal told the justices that the administration was seeking "fundamentally open-ended authority" and seizing a "presidential blank check," an echo of Justice O'Connor's opinion in the *Hamdi* case.[24]

Just as familiar as Scalia's early attack on the legislative history was the ideological split that emerged. Justices Stevens, Kennedy, Souter, Ginsburg, and Breyer expressed serious concerns about the military trial procedures that would affect Hamdan. Those five justices also were especially challenging to the Bush administration argument that the Court had been suddenly deprived of jurisdiction in the case by the December 2005 act. On the other side, Scalia and Alito voiced strong sympathy for the administration's effort to protect national security and control how any terrorist suspect is tried. "You acknowledge the existence of things called commissions, or do you?" Scalia asked Katyal at one point.

"We do," he responded. "Absolutely."

"What is the use of them if they have to follow all of the procedures required by the UCMJ?" Scalia asked, referring to the Uniform Code of Military Justice. "I mean, I thought that the whole object was to have a different procedure."

That went to the heart of Katyal's case on behalf of Hamdan. Katyal was not saying the Department of Defense could not use military commissions. He was saying that they had to adopt standard procedures that would guarantee, for example, that a detainee could attend the proceeding and then be able to appeal a determination to an independent court.

Some of the tensest moments of the special ninety-minute hearing came when the U.S. solicitor general, Paul Clement, stood at the lectern to argue that the executive branch had broad authority to define the crimes of war heard by a military commission, and that Congress had stripped the high Court of power to hear any petition for a writ of habeas corpus from Hamdan or any other Guantánamo detainee. For centuries in the Anglo-American tradition, prisoners generally could seek a writ of habeas corpus to challenge their imprisonment. It was such a fundamental idea that when the Constitution was written, the framers included a provision, the "suspension clause," which said that Congress could suspend the right of habeas only for "rebellion or invasion."

Justice Stevens, a former navy officer who was the last World War II veteran on the high Court, tried to pin down Clement on his assertion that Congress had not specifically suspended the writ, but that the "exigencies of 9/11" had had such an effect.

"My view would be if Congress sort of stumbles upon suspension of the writ, but the preconditions are still satisfied, that would be constitutionally valid," Clement said.

Justice Souter sharply questioned why Congress would not have been clearer on whether all claims from Guantánamo detainees were suddenly off-limits for federal judges. He challenged Clement's argument that Congress could limit the jurisdiction over habeas corpus without specifically suspending the writ.

Speaking loudly and showing uncommon anger, Souter said, "Isn't there a pretty good argument that suspension of the writ of habeas corpus is just about the most stupendously significant act that the Congress of the United States can take and therefore we ought to be at least a little slow to accept your argument that it can be done from pure inadvertence?"

Clement barely had begun to answer Justice Souter when Souter interrupted him and said, "You are leaving us with the position of the United States that the Congress may validly suspend it inadvertently. Is that really your position?"

Clement again began to respond: "I think at least if you're talking about the extension of the writ to enemy combatants . . . held outside . . . the territory of the United States—" Souter interrupted him again: "Now wait a minute! The writ is the writ. There are not two writs of habeas corpus, for some cases and for other cases. The rights that may be asserted, the rights that may be vindicated, will vary with the circumstances, but jurisdiction over habeas corpus is jurisdiction over habeas corpus."

Following up on some of Souter's questions, Ginsburg said, "It is an extraordinary act, I think, to withdraw jurisdiction from this Court in a pending case." She noted that the justices had announced in November 2005, a month before the Detainee Treatment Act was passed, that they would hear Hamdan's case. She was suggesting that it would be best to read the act as not having so usurped the role of the courts.

Three months after the oral arguments, the Court announced its ruling in what would be the most momentous fight to date over presidential power in the war on terrorism. Entering through the crimson drapes at 10:00 a.m. sharp on June 29, 2006, Scalia and the eight other justices took their places along the bench. It was the last day of the 2005–2006 annual term. For such a significant judgment day, the courtroom was strangely empty. There were no oral arguments on the calendar to draw sightseers. It was a rare Thursday sitting, required by the justices' desire to finish the last cases before a traditional end-of-June deadline. A handful of lawyers, including Katyal, sat in wooden chairs in the bar section. Solicitor General Clement was at the front of the room at a rectangular table close to the bench, awaiting the decision. A sprinkling of tourists occupied the red upholstered benches in the spectator rows.

The reporters' benches, off to the justices' right, however, were at capacity for a potentially historic case. Also filled were the special seats to the justices' left, which were reserved for their guests. Chief Justice Roberts's wife, Jane, had come in for this last day of her husband's first term on the Court. She entered the courtroom with Maureen Scalia.

When Justice Stevens announced that he had the majority opinion in the *Hamdan* case, observers knew immediately that the Bush administration had lost. As the next half hour would show, it was no faint loss. Reading from a stack of papers before him, Stevens said that Bush's plan to prosecute Guantánamo detainees in special tribunals, rather than in regular civilian or military courts, needed authorization from Congress and had not been independently justified by military necessity. In those circumstances, Stevens said, the tribunal plan violated the Geneva Conventions and exceeded the president's constitutional authority. The military commission system ordered by Bush in November 2001 failed to provide for a "regularly constituted court," as required by Article 3 of the Geneva Conventions, and anyway, Stevens said, its procedures fell short of those required under the Conventions and the Uniform Code of Military Justice for use by courts-martial.[25] Common Article 3 banned cruel treatment and torture of detainees, and concerning tribunals, it prohibited "the passing of sentences and carrying out of executions without previous judgment pronounced by a regularly constituted court affording all the judicial guarantees which are recognized as indispensable by civilized peoples." The Bush administration had argued from the start that the Geneva Conventions did not apply to "enemy combatants."

In a flat midwestern twang, but with the authority of a military veteran, Stevens detailed the lack of procedural safeguards in Bush's plan, including that accused detainees would not be allowed to see all the evidence against them or be able to challenge some witnesses' accounts or statements obtained through coercion or, at worst, torture.

Stevens rejected Bush's assertion that there was "inherent executive authority" to act alone in matters of national security. A key flaw of the tribunal plan was that the president had not sought congressional approval. Rebuffing an administration argument, Stevens said that a resolution passed by Congress shortly after the September 11 attacks authorizing the use of military force did not cover Bush's blueprint for the tribunals. More significantly for the Court's own power, Stevens also declared that the Detainee Treatment Act passed in December 2005, which eliminated federal judges' habeas corpus authority over Guantánamo disputes, did not apply to cases, such as Hamdan's, that were already in the courts. Citing senators' comments during the floor debate of the DTA, Stevens said, "The drafting history makes clear" that such a substantial change in the law is not to be applied retroactively. Scalia shifted in his black leather chair, visibly annoyed by this last comment referring to the legislative history.

The silver-haired Stevens told courtroom spectators that his full written opinion stretched over seventy-three pages. It was joined by Souter, Ginsburg, Breyer, and—for the most part—Kennedy. When Stevens was finished, the other justices looked over at Scalia, who pulled in his chair and neatened the stack of pages in his hands by tapping them on the desk. As was his way, Scalia opened with a wisecrack, saying his dissent was "a mere twenty-four pages." Scalia, his still-black hair combed straight back, declared that the majority had rejected Bush's tribunal arrangement for "the flimsiest of reasons." He claimed that the Detainee Treatment Act prevented the Court from ruling on the merits of any habeas corpus case from Guantánamo, and he mocked the majority's use of transcripts from the Senate debate on the act to interpret the applicability of the law. "With regard to the floor statements," Scalia said in his written opinion, "at least the Court shows some semblance of seemly shame, tucking away its reference to them in a half-hearted footnote. Not so for its reliance on the DTA's drafting history, which is displayed prominently. I have explained elsewhere that such drafting history is no more legitimate or reliable an indicator of the objective meaning of a statute than any other form of legislative history."

Scalia had long believed judges should be bound by the pure words of the law, not by the interpretations stated before enactment by committees or members of Congress. This student of a classical education added in his written opinion that it was a "fantasy" to think that "Senate floor speeches are attended (like the Philippics of Demosthenes) by throngs of eager listeners, instead of being delivered (like Demosthenes' practice sessions on the beach) alone into vast emptiness."

And equally true to form, as Scalia invoked Demosthenes, he also referred with comic effect to the "fig leaf" of legislative history the majority used. Scalia said of the Detainee Treatment Act, which became law on December 30, 2005, "It unambiguously provides that, as of that date, 'no court, justice, or judge shall have jurisdiction to hear or consider an application for a writ of habeas corpus filed by or on behalf of an alien detained by the Department of Defense at Guantánamo Bay, Cuba.' " He went on to reject the Stevens majority's explanation of why then pending cases were not covered, which was driven by a powerful commitment to preserving the judicial role, a commitment Scalia did not share in this situation.

When he turned to the military commissions themselves, he framed the issue in language reminiscent of his strong views at the University of Fribourg related to those who would shoot at U.S. troops, citing "the murderous conspiracy that slaughtered thousands" on September 11. Addressing the fundamental struggle between the executive and the judiciary, Scalia said the majority was wrong not to defer to Bush. The president was responsible, Scalia said, his voice rising in indignation, for "punishment of the mass-murdering terrorists of September 11." He believed that the administration could establish a special category of prisoners—military prisoners, of foreign nationality, captured in an area of battle and held outside the U.S. border.

Joined in his written dissent by Thomas and Alito, Scalia condemned what he deemed the Court's encroachment on the president's authority as commander in chief. "[T]he President has determined that 'To protect the United States and its citizens, and for the effective conduct of military operations and prevention of terrorist attacks, it is necessary for individuals subject to this order . . . to be detained, and, when tried, to be tried for violations of the laws of war and other applicable laws by military tribunals.' It is not clear where the Court derives the authority—or the audacity—to contradict this determination." The majority insisted, however, even within those confines involving the commander in chief's power, on preserving the Court's role and curtailed the president in light of statutes and treaties.

Especially defensive about attitudes toward the military, Scalia protested Stevens's suggestion in the majority opinion that Bush's commission plan could have made the executive branch vulnerable to military influence. "We do not live under a military junta," he added in a footnote. "It is a disservice to both those in the Armed Forces and the President to suggest that the President is subject to the undue control of the military." It also irked Scalia that the majority seemed to have an eye toward foreign reactions. As he so strongly articulated in Eighth Amendment death penalty cases around this time, Scalia believed the internationalist perspective wrongheaded and loathed the idea that the Court was worried about what "the world" would think about the United States.[26]

The drama of the morning was heightened by the stony silence of Chief Justice Roberts, whose earlier action on the case, which favored the administration, prevented him from acting this time around. Yet if Roberts had been able to join Scalia's side now, it would have given Scalia a fourth but not crucial fifth vote.

Immediately after the decision was issued, the former U.S. solicitor general Walter Dellinger called Hamdan v. Rumsfeld "the most important decision on presidential power ever." Even as he reconsidered the next day whether to pull back on such a bold claim, Dellinger ranked the case with United States v. Nixon, which had required the president to turn over the Watergate tapes, and to Youngstown Sheet and Tube Co. v. Sawyer, which required President Truman to relinquish steel mills he had seized during the Korean War. "The further back you stand, the more significant it appears," Dellinger said in a Slate magazine online commentary. "Up close, it's a case about Mr. Hamdan, or maybe about Hamdan and a dozen others . . . But that is not what Hamdan is really about. Hamdan is about whether the president can refuse to comply with the" law.[27]

In fact, the decision struck the core of the Bush administration system for holding foreign terrorism suspects and, more generally, the president's authority in war-related matters and international obligations. That was why Scalia's indignation was so palpable. His views on executive branch authority were not his alone among the dissenters, but he had believed in expansive presidential authority longer than the others, and he was readier to declare it in the most uncompromising terms.

The dispute took Scalia back to his Ford years, where issues of executive power played out in a highly charged and polarizing atmosphere among the branches. Both Nixon and Bush were reviled by the left. Both were subject to cries of an "imperial presidency." Both saw another branch trying to check its executive authority. In the late 1970s it was Congress. Now it was the Court.

Further, the decision in *Hamdan* was viewed as a particular rebuke to Scalia's Ford administration colleague Cheney because the vice president and his top lawyer, David Addington, had worked closely on the tribunal order. "The court's decision, in *Hamdan v. Rumsfeld*, was widely seen as a calamity for Cheney's war plan against al-Qaeda," wrote Barton Gellman and Jo Becker in a *Washington Post* series on Cheney's use of vice presidential power. When Hamdan was eventually tried in a military commission, the administration had another setback. The former driver for bin Laden was convicted of one terrorism-related charge but acquitted of a more serious conspiracy allegation. He was released from Guantánamo in November 2008 and sent home to Yemen.[28]

Scalia had stayed in touch with Cheney and continued to socialize with him.[29] None of these legal cases, however, came up in their conversations, Scalia said. Asked in an interview whether he talked to Cheney about any terrorism-related matters, Scalia said, "Oh my, no. He wouldn't think of it. Listen, I say this to foreign groups when they come here, and I don't think they believe me, because in most of their cultures, it would be incredible: In twenty-seven years of being a federal judge in Washington, I have never once been approached by a member of either house of Congress or by someone in the executive branch, about a pending case. Never once. Because they know it is impermissible and because they know that I would recuse myself and put the contact into the file."[30]

Scalia insisted he had no hardened predisposition in these cases, and in fact referred to his Hamdi decision against the Bush administration as proof that he was calling them, based on his originalist approach, as he got them. Yet Scalia seemed to find it easier to identify with the administration's interests. He could readily put himself in the shoes of those fighting terrorism rather than those foreigners in orange jumpsuits held behind razor wire without charges. A year after the *Hamdan* case, his attitude was revealed in a moment of levity as he defended the extreme tactics of TV's fictional counterterrorism agent Jack Bauer. Scalia was participating in an international judicial conference in Ottawa when the discussion turned to torture and Scalia said there should be no absolute rule against it. As the Toronto *Globe and Mail* reported, a Canadian judge said in passing, "Thankfully, security agencies in all our countries do not subscribe to the mantra 'What would Jack Bauer do?' "

To which Scalia responded, "Jack Bauer saved Los Angeles . . . He saved hundreds of thousands of lives." He apparently was referring to Agent Bauer's rough interrogation tactics in saving California from a terrorist nuclear attack in an early season of *24*. "Are you going to convict Jack Bauer?" Scalia reportedly asked as he challenged his fellow judges. "Say that criminal law is against him? You have the right to a jury trial? Is any jury going to convict Jack Bauer? I don't think so. So the question is really whether we believe in these absolutes. And ought we believe in these absolutes?"[31]

Scalia, in a later interview, said he was fixated on the television drama. "I don't know about the current season," he gushed, "but, boy, those early seasons—I'd be up to two o'clock, because you're at the end of one [episode], and you'd say, 'No, I've got to see the next.' "[32]

In a more serious discussion a few months after the Ottawa conference, Scalia specifically addressed constitutional protections against torture—or, for him, the limits on such protections. In an interview with BBC Radio 4's *Law in Action*, Scalia said some physical torture might be constitutionally permissible to gain information about an imminent threat such as a ticking bomb. "It would be absurd to say that you . . . couldn't do that," Scalia said. "And once you acknowledge that, we're into a different game. How close does the threat have to be? And how severe can the infliction of pain be? I don't think these are easy questions at all, in either direction. But I certainly know you can't come in smugly and with great self-satisfaction and say, 'Oh, it's torture, and therefore it's no good.' You would not apply that in some real-life situations. It may not be a ticking bomb in Los Angeles but it may be where is this group that we know is plotting some very painful action against the United States."

Scalia's reference to someone coming in "smugly and with great self-satisfaction" was an echo of past condemnation of critics. He had a way of portraying people who held views counter to his as haughty, self-righteous know-it-alls—which, ironically, was sometimes how he was perceived.

In the interview with the BBC in February 2008 Scalia said the U.S. Constitution's ban on cruel and unusual punishment "is referring to punishment for crime," not actions in the course of interrogations. He was trying to draw a line between what was constitutionally permissible and what was not. But true to his way, once he got into the discussion, he would not pull his punches. Asked later about his comments seeming to endorse aggressive interrogations, Scalia insisted that he had been lured, unsuspectingly, into controversy by the BBC interviewer. "He led me into that by a constitutional question," Scalia said. "My main response was that [interrogation torture] is not punishment at all. Maybe it [torture] shouldn't be done. But if it's wrong, it's not wrong because it violates the cruel and unusual punishment clause of the Constitution, which relates to punishment for crime."[33]

Editorial writers and cartoonists criticized Scalia as endorsing torture. "Much of the press is hostile to my message," he said, later complaining that he was often a target for media criticism because of his generally conservative views. "They place whatever I do, quite often, in the worst light."[34] But Scalia was unmatched, at the Court at least, for constantly venturing into troubled territory, whether with a Sicilian chin flick at a photographer or a defense of torture to a London correspondent. The Associated Press reported two months later that Justice Breyer obliquely took issue with Scalia's remarks on torture at a Washington gathering of the Anti-Defamation League. Breyer spoke approvingly of a long-standing Israeli court decision that outlawed torture.[35]

By mid-2008 President Bush, the Congress, and the Supreme Court had engaged in a series of moves over the rights of Guantánamo detainees that had escalated to the fundamental question of whether the Constitution covered at all the foreigners held at the U.S. naval base. In earlier opinions, the Court majority appeared to be trying to balance its protection of individual rights with the government's efforts to avert another terrorist attack. Yet the Court also had revealed impatience with the administration's quest to keep foreign detainees' cases away from federal judges.

The new dispute in 2008 traced to two of the Court's earlier rulings, the 2004 *Rasul v. Bush* and the 2006 *Hamdan v. Rumsfeld*. After *Rasul*, Lakhdar Boumediene, an Algerian who was arrested in Bosnia in 2001 in connection with a suspected plot to attack the U.S. embassy in Sarajevo, filed a habeas petition challenging his detention at Guantánamo. He was joined by more than thirty other detainees, some of whom had begun their challenges before the *Rasul* decision in 2004. As the cases slowly worked through the system, they ran up against the Detainee Treatment Act, which Congress passed in 2005 to overturn *Rasul* and ensure that "no court, justice, or judge shall have jurisdiction to hear or consider . . . an application for a writ of habeas corpus" filed by a Guantánamo prisoner. The cases of Boumediene and other detainees also were essentially intercepted by Congress's passage of the Military Commissions Act in 2006, which, after the *Hamdan* ruling, authorized the military tribunals and said no court could hear *any* challenge to a foreign detainee's case.

The prisoners claimed that the 2006 Military Commissions Act, which attempted finally to close the door on all habeas petitions, was unconstitutional. The U.S. Court of Appeals for the District of Columbia Circuit rejected that argument and ruled that the Military Commissions Act properly stripped federal courts of all jurisdiction over the detainees. Initially, when the *Boumediene* detainees appealed to the Court, the justices, over the dissent of three of the nine justices (Souter, Ginsburg, and Breyer), spurned the petitions. However, two key justices who joined in rejecting the appeals (Stevens and Kennedy) said the issues raised by the cases were important and signaled that they would be watching developments at the base. Two months later, after public reports about flaws in military proceedings at Guantánamo, Stevens and Kennedy decided the time was right to intervene. A Court majority announced it had taken the unusual step of reconsidering the previously spurned petitions and would set oral arguments in the case.

Unlike the statutory issues of *Rasul* and *Hamdan*, the case of *Boumediene v. Bush* went to the core of the Constitution and the Great Writ. The question was not whether the habeas statute reached Guantánamo, or congressional authorization of the military commissions, but whether the Constitution itself guaranteed a detainee review of a claim that he was not in fact a terrorist and not being rightly imprisoned.

In the end, the justices ruled against the administration's (and now Congress's) attempt to keep detainees away from federal judges. It was the third rebuke of the Bush administration on Guantánamo policies. Kennedy, casting the key fifth vote and writing for the majority, said that foreign prisoners held at the U.S.-controlled base in Cuba were entitled to a hearing in federal court and not merely a military screening to determine whether they were enemy combatants. Kennedy acknowledged the executive branch's interest in policies that protected national security at a time of terrorist threats, yet he stressed that "the laws and Constitution are designed to survive, and remain in force, in extraordinary times."[36]

As Kennedy read portions of his seventy-page opinion from the bench on June 12, 2008, he observed that many of the Guantánamo prisoners had been held for six years without review of their claims. "Their access to the writ is a necessity," he said, looking out into the marble courtroom. After emphasizing that the habeas privilege was one of the few safeguards of liberty detailed in the Constitution, Kennedy addressed the Guantánamo screening procedures devised by the administration and Congress. He pointed to several flaws, including a detainee's limited ability to challenge the facts against him and to put into the record his own version of events. He added that "the political branches" may not "switch the Constitution on or off at will." Kennedy's opinion was signed by the others from the *Hamdan* majority: Stevens, Souter, Ginsburg, and Breyer.

Their message was clear. A majority was not going to relinquish judicial authority to hear all challenges from detainees, even those at a base that the federal government had wanted to be beyond such jurisdiction.

Dissenting were Roberts, Scalia, Thomas, and Alito. From the bench that June morning, Scalia read at length from his dissent for the foursome. He said the majority was wrongly usurping the "mandate of the political branches" in the Guantánamo-related statutes crafted by Congress and signed by Bush. He said that judges "simply have no competency to second-guess" military officials on which of the foreigners picked up on the battlefield should be imprisoned.

With references to terrorist acts back a quarter century, Scalia opened his written opinion by stating, "I think it appropriate to begin with a description of the disastrous consequences of what the Court has done today. America is at war with radical Islamists. The enemy began by killing Americans and American allies abroad: 241 at the marine barracks in Lebanon, 19 at the Khobar Towers in Dhahran, 224 at our embassies in Dar es Salaam and Nairobi, and 17 on the USS Cole in Yemen. On September 11, 2001, the enemy brought the battle to American soil, killing 2,749 at the Twin Towers in New York City, 184 at the Pentagon in Washington, D.C., and 40 in Pennsylvania. It has threatened further attacks against our homeland; one need only walk about buttressed and barricaded Washington, or board a plane anywhere in the country, to know that the threat is a serious one. Our Armed Forces are now in the field against the enemy, in Afghanistan and Iraq. Last week, 13 of our countrymen in arms were killed."

His son Matthew was back in the United States on a new assignment,[37] and Scalia gave a nod to "some 190,000 of our men and women . . . now fighting." Then he resorted to what the New York University law professor Ronald Dworkin termed his "usual splenetic flamboyance."[38] Wrote Scalia: "The game of bait-and-switch that today's opinion plays upon the Nation's Commander in Chief will make the war harder on us. It will almost certainly cause more Americans to be killed."

Dworkin had a point about Scalia's heated rhetoric. Scalia wrote with a recriminatory tone that often undercut his effectiveness. He was hyperbolic and almost entirely dismissive of arguments from the other side. Writing for the majority, Justice Kennedy had acknowledged worries about another terrorist attack and the executive's ability to prepare for it, yet he said, "Liberty and security can be reconciled; and in our system they are reconciled within the framework of the law." Scalia was not going to suggest in any way that this was a close call, that the other side had points at least to acknowledge. "What drives today's decision," he said, "is neither the meaning of the Suspension Clause, nor the principles of our precedents, but rather an inflated notion of judicial supremacy."

When pressed a year later about this controversial assertion that people would die because of the ruling, Scalia said it was "obvious, inevitable."

"If you let loose, because of more rigid procedural requirements, dangerous people who are going to go back to the field, you are undoubtedly placing lives at risk. Undoubtedly."[39]

SIXTEEN

"YOU GET ONE SHOT"

His desk is messy with papers, books, and the Marlboro Lights he cannot give up. He often smokes when he writes, he says, that's the problem. At the computer behind him on June 24, 2008, he has been finishing an opinion that culminates decades of arguments for his originalist approach to the Constitution. He is writing a decision for the majority that will declare for the first time that the Second Amendment contains an individual right to bear arms. It will strike down a Washington, D.C., handgun prohibition and overturn decades of received law. This will be a victory for Scalia and for his interpretive method.

Now age seventy-two and in his twenty-second term on the Court, Scalia is finding new influence among his colleagues, and the firearms case reflects that. He is on the road more, too, continuing to draw standing-room-only crowds. Along with his stock speech on originalism, he is promoting a new book, *Making Your Case*. Written with Bryan A. Garner, a legal writing specialist, it is about crafting persuasive briefs and presenting effective oral arguments. For publicity, Scalia has done television interviews with Lesley Stahl of CBS's *60 Minutes*, Charlie Rose of PBS, and Brian Lamb of C-SPAN. In April, just as these book-related interviews were revving up, he received a "lifetime achievement" award at the Georgetown University Law Center. He said he was beginning to feel like a doddering movie has-been. "It's usually given to an over-the-hill Hollywood actor, you know," he says now in an interview. "He stumbles up to the stage for a lifetime achievement award. I hope I haven't reached that stage yet."[1]

The ruling on the Second Amendment demonstrates that he may be at the peak of his legal influence, rather than over the hill. There is something climactic in this guns case, which will be the Supreme Court's first definitive interpretation of the Second Amendment. The short text of the amendment says: "A well regulated militia, being necessary to the security of a free state, the right of the people to keep and bear arms shall not be infringed." The dispute calls into question the original understanding of the Constitution's framers, and this is where Scalia lives. He believes deeply in the result, which will say that the Second Amendment encompasses an individual's right to keep handguns in the home for self protection. Right now in his chambers, he is trying not to get riled by the dissenting justices' complaints about his opinion. Speaking through Justice John Paul Stevens, they are arguing that Scalia lacks evidence and that his opinion is a "strained" and "unpersuasive" interpretation of the text of the amendment. And in a separate dissenting opinion, Justice Stephen Breyer, who advocates a more contemporary reading of the Constitution and wrote a book in 2005 countering Scalia's philosophy, is stressing that the Washington, D.C., ordinance has the legitimate purpose of saving lives and that the high Court need not return to the framers' era to determine the validity of the ordinance.[2]

Scalia has fired back, but in a way that will keep him his majority. That, in itself, is difficult for the man who is used to responding in incendiary terms. The four other conservative justices (John Roberts, Anthony Kennedy, Clarence Thomas, and Samuel Alito) are sticking with him, in their own belief that the constitutional "right . . . to keep and bear arms" refers to an individual right, not one for a state militia, such as contemporary National Guard units, as lower federal courts generally have held.

A component of this case of *District of Columbia v. Heller* is personal for Scalia, too. Since his days as a boy hunting rabbits with his grandfather on Long Island, Scalia has enjoyed guns for recreation. In high school at Xavier, he learned to shoot with precision. Now into his seventies, he still goes game hunting. "It is a sport that I very much enjoy," he will say later in another interview. "It gets me outside of the Beltway, gets me into the woods, far away from all this stuff . . . [Hunting] gives you an objective for . . . getting there in darkness and watching the woods gradually lighten up, or being knee deep in cold water in the marshes and watching the rosy sunrise. It's wonderful."[3]

As he extols the beauty of the rural outdoors, he explains that he prefers hunting turkey (known for their cunning) over other game. "It is more proactive. You're not just waiting. There's something wonderful about hearing them. Have you ever heard a turkey gobble? It's a very strange sound, like a wooden rattle. [You] hear that far away and then make sounds like a hen to induce [the turkey] to come closer and closer. Finally, he sticks his head up over a log, and you have to take your shot, or else you've lost him. Turkeys are very wily creatures. They have superb eyesight and they're very cautious. You get one shot. If you miss, the whole day's ruined."

Scalia goes on to lament that hunting has become an increasingly exclusive sport. "High schools used to have marksman contests," he says. "There used to be firearm safety programs . . . If hunting dies out, that's the end of it. If it becomes a sport for the aristocracy, for the few who can have hunting preserves and hunting clubs, you're going to have a different social culture."

Two years earlier, as the Second Amendment case was nearing the Court, Scalia told a convention of the National Wild Turkey Federation that he hoped America's hunting culture would prevail and that people would have greater regard for recreational firearm use. "The hunting culture, of course, begins with a culture that does not have a hostile attitude toward firearms," Scalia said in the 2006 address to the Wild Turkey Federation at a convention hall in Nashville. He urged the audience to help end the stereotype of guns being used only for evil ends. "The attitude of people associating guns with nothing but crime, that is what has to be changed," Justice Scalia said, according to a report in the *Tennessean* newspaper. "I grew up at a time when people were not afraid of people with firearms . . . I used to travel on the subway from Queens to Manhattan with a rifle. Could you imagine doing that today in New York City?"[4]

Justice Thomas, Scalia's fellow originalist and a solid vote for Scalia in *District of Columbia v. Heller*, is decidedly not in this for the gun rights, or even the thrill of breaking new legal ground. "I'm not a gun person," Thomas said, emphasizing how despite their similar approaches to the law, he and Scalia are markedly different men. "Do I get high about this case or that case? No. I do my job. And he loves killing unarmed animals. I don't. He loves opera. I prefer blues or jazz. We're different. I'm a [Nebraska] Cornhuskers fan. I don't think he even watches sports. We're just different. We happen to be going in the same direction in the same cases, so we run into each other a lot."[5]

On the other hand, the newest justice, Alito, who is not as closely aligned with Scalia on the law,[6] finds the opportunity to reach back into the Second Amendment history exhilarating. Of the challenge of interpreting the original meaning, he will say in a later interview, "I love it."[7]

In the firearms dispute from Washington, D.C., Dick Anthony Heller, a security guard stationed at a federal building, wanted to keep a handgun in his home for self-defense, which would have violated the city prohibition tracing to 1976. Heller and other gun owners had been enlisted by libertarian lawyers at the Washington-based Cato Institute looking for a test of the prevailing legal wisdom on the Second Amendment.[8] The last time the Supreme Court had taken up a case on the subject was in 1939. Ruling in that dispute, *United States v. Miller*, the Court had presumed (but did not rule definitively) that the "right" to bear arms was not an individual one, rather one for the state militia. In the decades since, lower court judges who had reviewed the question had largely interpreted *Miller* to mean that no individual gun right existed. That ran contrary to the assertions of such gun rights advocates as the National Rifle Association. The former chief justice Warren Burger had responded to the groups' arguments by saying on PBS's *The MacNeil/Lehrer NewsHour* in 1991 that the Second Amendment "has been the subject of one of the greatest pieces of fraud, I repeat the word 'fraud,' on the American public by special interest groups that I have ever seen in my lifetime." Burger insisted that the "right to bear arms" belonged to the states and complained that the National Rifle Association was wrongly promoting the opposite view.[9]

When the U.S. Court of Appeals for the District of Columbia Circuit in 2007 reviewed the handgun ban of the nation's capital, the court departed from that legal trend and ruled that the prohibition violated the Second Amendment. The D.C. Circuit decision was written by Scalia's old friend and fellow conservative Laurence Silberman. Throwing out the handgun ban, Judge Silberman said the Second Amendment "protects an individual right to keep and bear arms . . . for such activities as hunting and self-defense."[10]

As the Washington, D.C., appeal headed to the high Court, the dispute captured the attention of the public, and it became clear that the notion of an individual right to bear arms already was ingrained in American society. One poll taken a month before the justices were to hear the case found that nearly three out of four Americans—73 percent—believed the Second Amendment spelled out an individual right to own a firearm.

Barack Obama and Hillary Clinton, then competing for the Democratic presidential nomination, promoted their support for Second Amendment individual rights in their campaigns.[11]

In the end, Justice Scalia's opinion for the Court, released on June 26, 2009, the last day of the 2008–2009 term, supported that popular view. The decision, covering sixty-four pages, was signed in full by Roberts, Kennedy, Thomas, and Alito. No one had peeled off in a concurrence, as often happened with a Scalia opinion in a momentous case. Scalia was pleased, yet in the decorum of the high Court, said Justice Thomas, "He never walked around saying that. He didn't high-five anyone."[12]

At the heart of Scalia's decision for the Court were an analysis of the connection between the Second Amendment's first and second clauses and an interpretation of the word "militia." Scalia minimized the first clause referring to "a well regulated militia, being necessary to the security of a free state," and accentuated the second clause referring to "the right of the people." Further, Scalia wrote, in the eighteenth century, "militia" covered all able-bodied males acting for the common defense, not just a state-organized military group. "The conception of the militia at the time of the Second Amendment's ratification was the body of all citizens capable of military service, who would bring the sorts of lawful weapons that they possessed at home to militia duty." That meant, he said, there was a broad right to guns for individuals.[13]

Scalia characterized the 1939 *Miller* decision, involving the federal convictions of two men caught transporting an unregistered short-barreled shotgun, as narrowly confined to types of weapons that were not covered by the Second Amendment. He insisted that case could be read to reinforce the Court's holding in the Washington, D.C., case. He said *Miller* suggested that the amendment conferred an individual right to keep and bear arms—the opposite of what dissenting justices asserted and the opposite of what "hundreds of judges have relied on," according to Justice Stevens, in the decades since the *Miller* case.[14]

Scalia offered a major caveat: "[N]othing in our opinion should be taken to cast doubt on the longstanding prohibitions on the possession of firearms by felons and the mentally ill, or laws forbidding the carrying of firearms in sensitive places such as schools and government buildings, or laws imposing conditions and qualifications on the commercial sale of arms." Scalia acknowledged that the majority was leaving many unanswered questions regarding individual gun regulations beyond Washington, D.C., but said, "since this case represents this Court's first in-depth examination of the Second Amendment, one should not expect it to clarify the entire field." Such sentiment went against his usual distaste for case-by-case decision-making. It also immediately spawned scores of lawsuits testing the breadth of the right to bear arms, including whether the Second Amendment coverage for the federal enclave of Washington, D.C., extended to the states.[15]

Dissenting with Stevens and Breyer were Justice David Souter and Justice Ruth Bader Ginsburg. This reflected the ideological split of recent years: conservatives in the majority, liberals in the dissent. Writing the leading dissenting statement, Stevens said the amendment's purpose was exclusively directed toward the military and not intended to "enshrine [a] common-law right of self-defense in the Constitution." He rejected Scalia's distinction between the first two clauses, and in applying his own historical analysis, Stevens contended that the framers believed that without the Second Amendment, the Constitution's Article I provision authorizing Congress to organize and call into service the militia would also allow Congress to disarm them. "Until today," Stevens wrote, "it has been understood that legislatures may regulate the civilian use and misuse of firearms so long as they do not interfere with the preservation of a well-regulated militia. The Court's announcement . . . upsets that settled understanding, but leaves for future cases the formidable task of defining the scope of permissible regulations."[16]

Unlike Stevens, who engaged Scalia in historical terms, Breyer, in his separate dissenting opinion, concentrated on the intentions of the Washington, D.C., city council and said, "the District's regulation, which focuses upon the presence of handguns in high-crime urban areas, represents a permissible legislative response to a serious, indeed life-threatening, problem."[17]

Liberals beyond the courtroom denounced Scalia's majority opinion, too. That was to be expected. But vigorous criticism also came from two prominent judges associated with strands of conservatism. The Chicago-based U.S. Court of Appeals judge Richard Posner, who had often presented himself as a legal pragmatist, termed the Scalia opinion "questionable in both method and result." He said it was "evidence that the Supreme Court, in deciding constitutional cases, exercises a freewheeling discretion strongly flavored with ideology." Writing in *The New Republic*, Posner contended that a true "originalist" method would have yielded the opposite result. He said the two clauses of the amendment supported each other to dictate that men who served in state militias would be allowed to possess weapons for that purpose. "The federal government could regulate them [militia] but not disarm them," Posner explained, endorsing Stevens's dissenting view.[18]

More bitingly, Judge Posner deemed Scalia's interpretation "faux originalism" and insisted, "true originalism licenses loose construction . . . especially . . . for interpreting a constitutional provision ratified more than two centuries ago, dealing with a subject that has been transformed in the intervening period by social and technological change, including urbanization and a revolution in warfare and weaponry." Directing criticism at Scalia personally, Posner said, "Scalia and his staff labored mightily to produce a long opinion (the majority opinion is almost 25,000 words long) that would convince, or perhaps just overwhelm, the doubters. The range of historical references in the majority opinion is breathtaking, but it is not evidence of disinterested historical inquiry. It is evidence of the ability of well-staffed courts to produce snow jobs."[19]

Posner, a prolific commentator who is a longtime critic of Scalia's originalism, is skilled at such attention-getting affronts. The justice usually regards Posner's missives as attempts to show himself to be smarter than everyone else. A more substantively devastating assessment of the *Heller* majority opinion came from Judge J. Harvie Wilkinson, a veteran of the Richmond-based U.S. Court of Appeals for the Fourth Circuit. An old friend of Scalia, Wilkinson only two years earlier had hosted with Scalia an engagement dinner for their mutual friend Ted Olson and his fiancée at the sumptuous Inn at Little Washington in rural Virginia. Wilkinson was now hitting Scalia where he lived. Wilkinson compared *District of Columbia v. Heller* to *Roe v. Wade*—the decision that Scalia has endlessly attacked for its legal methodology. "[E]ach represents a rejection of neutral principles that counseled restraint and deference to others regardless of the issues involved," Wilkinson asserted in an essay for the *Virginia Law Review*, terming the 1973 *Roe* and 2008 *Heller* acts of "judicial aggrandizement; a transfer of power to judges from the political branches of government—and thus, ultimately, from the people themselves."[20]

In the minds of its critics, of course, *Roe* has long exemplified judicial activism, and it spawned the conservative legal movement that helped carry Scalia to the federal bench. To use it against Scalia was the unkindest cut and reflected Wilkinson's not-so-subtle arguments of hypocrisy in Scalia's methods. Not only that, Wilkinson invoked another case Scalia loves to hate, *Romer v. Evans*, in which Scalia dissented from the majority's support for gay rights in a Colorado dispute. "As Justice Scalia has argued, the Court 'has no business imposing upon all Americans the resolution favored by the elite class from which the Members of [the Court] are selected,' " Wilkinson wrote. His point was that in *Heller*, the Supreme Court had—as Scalia contended of *Roe* and *Romer*—taken an issue that deeply divided the nation and usurped the popular will and legislative choices.

Scalia could not abide such comparisons. *Heller* was not like *Roe* or *Romer*, he believed, because—to his mind—constitutional provisions supported the outcome. Scalia also felt he had answered everything a critic could raise, point by point. "I took satisfaction in doing it right," Scalia said. "Nothing could take away from that." Further, the kick of delving into a nearly unexamined portion of the Constitution endured. "It's like being John Marshall for a little tiny portion of the Constitution," he said months after the decision was handed down.[21]

Still, criticism from such judges as Wilkinson and Posner—both of whom were appointed to the bench by Reagan during the counterrevolution—demonstrated how Scalia could be attacked for seeing what he wanted to see in the Constitution, and not what was necessarily there. Scalia and some other adherents of originalism cast the method as the purest form of constitutional interpretation. They say they are strictly bound by the legal understanding of the Constitution's terms at the time of drafting and ratification. But is that so? Isn't that approach as subjective as others? Justice Breyer has observed that the framers did not say what factors judges should take into account when they interpret the Constitution; when putting highly general words into the Constitution, the framers did not lay down a historical-understanding methodology of interpretation, or indeed any particular methodology of interpretation, leaving that up to future judges. Breyer also rejected the notion that those who do not adhere to originalism, and instead look at the consequences of decision-making in a contemporary context, necessarily open the door to subjectivity. "[U]nder their approach important safeguards of objectivity remain," Breyer wrote in his counterstatement to Scalia, *Active Liberty.* "For one thing, a judge who emphasizes consequences, no less than any other, is aware of the legal precedents, rules, standards, practices, and institutional understanding that a decision will affect."[22]

Even Justice Alito, who considers himself an originalist, has observed, "To say that you're an originalist doesn't really decide the case. Original- ism gives you a principle to apply. Very often, particularly in areas where things have changed so much, identifying the principle doesn't really decide the case." Notably, Alito differed with Scalia on two cases keyed to the Sixth Amendment: he diverged on what the Constitution dictated about judges' power in criminal sentencing, and again on the reach of defendants' right to be confronted by the witnesses against them.[23]

Some critics beyond the Court said originalism aligns too neatly with the personal values of its proponents. As Christopher Eisgruber, public affairs professor and provost at Princeton University, wrote, "It is hard to believe that the analysis is being driven by a disinterested analysis of his- torical intentions, rather than by judges' values . . . What happens instead is that originalist judges (or law professors) recite a lot of facts about the framers and then announce a legal conclusion remarkably consistent with their own views."[24] Through his originalism, Scalia indeed found no abor- tion rights, found no room for school prayer and public aid to parochial schools, and yet found strict prohibitions on affirmative action and vari- ous legislative rules for election campaign activities. Running counter to arguments that his originalism is in sync with political conservatism, how- ever, was Scalia's reading of the Constitution to expand the rights of crim- inal defendants in particular areas, such as the confrontation of witnesses.

As Scalia's own reputation demonstrates, originalism and its pro- ponents stand for more than the simple resolution of individual court cases. "[O]riginalism's enormous influence has come less as a theory of jurisprudence than as a highly persuasive political ideology that inspires passionate political engagement," observed the Indiana University law professor Dawn Johnsen in *Constitutional Commentary.* "The right uses both originalism and abortion to far greater political advantage than pub- lic opinion polls would predict, including to impugn the constitutional fidelity of 'nonoriginalists' and supporters of *Roe v. Wade.*"[25]

It is indeed true that this is one of those arcane areas of the law that plays out politically and could have great consequences in American life.

Scalia had changed the terms of the debate at the Court, in law schools, and in professional legal analyses. For better or worse, with successes and failures, with praise and criticism, this was his. Less than a year after the Second Amendment ruling, Edward Lazarus, a former law clerk to Justice Blackmun and a legal commentator, wrote in *Time* magazine that while Kennedy is the "most powerful justice" by virtue of his swing vote position on the Court, Scalia is the most influential. "He has made respectable a mode of conservative constitutional interpretation—'originalism'—that would likely be moribund without him," Lazarus wrote.[26]

As his public persona swelled, Scalia continued to have a wider influence on the law through alliances with the new conservative majority. With a separate coalition that cut across ideological lines, he persisted in transforming the breadth of the Sixth Amendment. On the same day he announced the majority decision in the Washington, D.C., guns case, Scalia delivered a majority opinion that expanded his 2004 majority opinion in *Crawford v. Washington*, regarding the right of defendants to be "confronted by the witnesses against them." The *Crawford* decision had forbidden introduction at trial of an earlier statement a wife had made about her husband's attack on another man, unless the wife took the stand to be cross-examined. (The husband was claiming self-defense and the wife had earlier said that the man had no weapon. She declined to testify against her husband.)[27] In the new case, Scalia declared that a California murder convict should get a new trial because his jury heard statements made earlier by the victim, his ex-girlfriend, that should have been excluded under the Sixth Amendment confrontation right. Dwayne Giles claimed he shot his girlfriend in self-defense. Prosecutors introduced evidence at trial of the woman's earlier account to police about his attacks. Giles said the testimony should have been excluded. He claimed his Sixth Amendment right barred testimony from anyone who could not be called to the stand and cross-examined. Prosecutors, in return, argued that Giles forfeited his confrontation right by killing the woman. In the Court's opinion reversing a lower court decision and siding with Giles, Scalia wrote that such a view infringed the Constitution. He said it did not matter that officials were trying to end domestic violence, which he termed "an intolerable offense" that state legislatures rightly try to fight. "[F]or that serious crime, as for others, abridging the constitutional rights of criminal defendants is not in the state's arsenal," he wrote.[28]

The following year, in 2009, Scalia pulled together the same majority to extend the right of confrontation to seemingly routine forensic reports—among them, blood and ballistic reports—prepared for use in prosecution. By a 5–4 vote in the case of *Melendez-Diaz v. Massachusetts*, the Court ruled that the Sixth Amendment gives defendants the right to cross-examine the preparer of such reports. The forensic findings could no longer automatically be introduced at trial in written form, Scalia said; the preparer must affirmatively present the findings in live testimony, unless the defendant agrees otherwise. With Scalia were Stevens, Souter, Thomas, and Ginsburg. When the lead dissenter, Justice Kennedy, wrote that the majority was sweeping away ninety years of precedent and the standard practices of at least thirty-five states, Scalia responded by proceeding to try to demonstrate in detail "the falsity of the dissent's opening alarum."[29]

As the years passed, Scalia did not mute his rhetoric. "Nino, in my view, sometimes does go overboard," Justice Ginsburg said, considering his writing over the decades. "It would be better if he dropped things like: 'This opinion is not to be taken seriously.' He might have been more influential here if he did that. We went back and forth in VMI [a 1996 case]. I understood him and didn't take offense. But other people, [Harry] Blackmun is one, [Sandra Day] O'Connor is another, might have found his one-liners insulting."[30]

A prime example of his tone was heard in a 2008 dispute over the lethal injection method for executions, when he mockingly rebuked Stevens for declaring that he had come to oppose the death penalty as cruel and unusual punishment. A seven-justice majority—which included both Scalia and Stevens—had rejected arguments that a commonly used three-drug lethal injection method caused excruciating pain, thus violating the Eighth Amendment ban on cruel and unusual punishment. Writing for the majority, Chief Justice Roberts had said that the fact that "an execution method may result in pain, either by accident or as an inescapable consequence of death, does not establish the sort of objectively intolerable risk of harm that qualifies as cruel and unusual." Roberts said the Kentucky prisoners who challenged the lethal injection method failed to show a sufficient risk of pain from the improper administration of the injection protocol.[31] Roberts was joined in full by Kennedy and Alito. Justices Thomas and Scalia signed a separate opinion, written by Thomas, saying they believed a method of execution would violate the Eighth Amendment only if it were deliberately designed to inflict pain.

Justices Stevens and Breyer concurred in the bottom-line judgment but also had differing rationales.[32] For his part, Stevens then cautioned that a case might still be made against the three-drug protocol. "Instead of ending the controversy," Stevens continued, "I am now convinced that this case will generate debate not only about the constitutionality of the three-drug protocol . . . but also about the justification for the death penalty itself." Then Stevens, the eldest and longest-serving justice among his sitting colleagues, concluded that he no longer considered the death penalty constitutional. "The time for a dispassionate, impartial comparison of the enormous costs that death penalty litigation imposes on society with the benefits that it produces has surely arrived," he wrote in the case of *Baze v. Rees*. "I have relied on my own experience in reaching the conclusion that the imposition of the death penalty represents 'the pointless and needless extinction of life with only marginal contributions to any discernible social or public purposes. A penalty with such negligible returns to the state [is] patently excessive and cruel and unusual punishment violative of the Eighth Amendment.' "[33]

Scalia could not let Stevens's personal remarks go unanswered: "What prompts Justice Stevens to repudiate his prior view and to adopt the astounding position that a criminal sanction expressly mentioned in the Constitution violates the Constitution?" he wrote, joined only by Thomas. "Purer expression cannot be found of the principle of rule by judicial fiat . . . This . . . conclusion is insupportable as an interpretation of the Constitution, which generally leaves it to democratically elected legislatures rather than courts to decide what makes significant contribution to social or public purposes."[34]

Yet, during his tenure, Scalia has applied varying standards for when judges should defer to a legislature. He certainly believes it important to defer to state choices on the death penalty and other issues of social morality such as abortion and gay rights. But he did not accept deference based on legislative choices, as for example, in the Washington, D.C., guns case. In the same vein, he has long opposed reliance on legislative choices related to racial policies as, for example, with affirmative action.

His critics also accused him of inconsistency in another respect during these years in the late 2000s. As much as Scalia could give it out, he had limits on what he could take. At a 2009 Florida event a college student asked Scalia why the justices refused to allow cameras into their courtroom for oral arguments despite being open enough to go on the road to promote their books. At the moment, Scalia was out publicizing *Making Your Case*. Hearing the student's question, Scalia retorted, "That's a nasty, impolite question," according to a *South Florida Sun-Sentinel* report widely picked up by other media.[35] A week later, when asked in an interview why he felt the need to reprimand the twenty-year-old student, Scalia said, "I do not mind difficult questions. The part of any appearance I enjoy the most is the Q-and-A. But hers was not just a hard question. It was intentionally nasty [and] calculated to embarrass. I'm doing her a favor to answer her question. I shouldn't have to put up with her abuse."[36]

So there he was, at a luncheon sponsored by the Palm Beach County Bar Association, 750 people at tables before him, letting a college student get under his skin. Scalia may be one of life's large characters—but he could still be distracted by life's smaller slights. And, unlike other public figures who stew in silence when insulted, he could still erupt in the most public ways: throwing down a notebook in Hattiesburg, flicking his chin in Boston.

Barack Obama, who won the presidency in November 2008, invoked Scalia's name during his campaign for the White House. "We can't have more justices like Clarence Thomas and Antonin Scalia," the Democratic candidate declared, and within just a few months of taking office, he had the opportunity to show what kind of justice he did want. David Souter, a New Hampshire native and lifelong bachelor who had never adapted to the ways of Washington, decided to step down. Souter was turned off by the town's zero-sum politicking and impersonal cocktail-party rituals. A few weeks before his retirement announcement, the erudite justice had said that one of the great disappointments of Court work is that he could not engage in his usual reading for enjoyment. When the term started each October, he said, "I undergo an annual intellectual lobotomy." Souter had been looking for an opportunity to leave the bench, and a new Democratic president who would appoint a liberal successor presented that occasion.

President Obama made the historic choice of the New York–based U.S. Court of Appeals judge Sonia Sotomayor, fifty-four years old at the time and of Puerto Rican heritage. The choice would give the nation's highest court its first Hispanic voice and second female perspective among the sitting justices. Just a few weeks earlier, in spring 2009, Justice Ginsburg—at this point the only woman on the bench—had spoken in an interview about the cost of the male-dominated Court. Ginsburg said she believes there are real, although not entirely obvious, consequences in the Court's internal decision-making as well as the image projected during oral arguments. "You know the line that Sandra [Day O'Connor] and I keep repeating . . . that 'at the end of the day, a wise old man and a wise old woman reach the same judgment'? But there are perceptions that we have because we are women. We can be sensitive to things that are said in draft opinions that [justices] are not aware can be offensive. It's a subtle influence."

"It's seldom in the outcome," Justice Ginsburg said, then added, "It is sometimes in the outcome." Yet the "worst part," she said, is the image a lone woman among the nine projects: that a woman on a top court is the exception. "Young women are going to think, 'Can I really aspire to that kind of post?' "[37]

President Obama apparently believed such lack of women significant enough to address and interviewed only female candidates for the Souter vacancy. As his final choice stood next to him at the White House on the morning of May 26, 2009, Obama called Sotomayor an "inspiring woman who I believe will make a great justice." Sotomayor was raised in a housing project in the Bronx. Her father had died when she was only nine. Still, she'd gone on to win a scholarship to Princeton and attended Yale Law School. Her career over three decades included tenure as a New York prosecutor, corporate litigator, and trial judge (appointed by the first President Bush in 1992) before becoming an appeals court judge (elevated by President Clinton in 1998). While Sotomayor has the depth of legal experience necessary for the high Court, Obama declared, she had also been "tested by obstacles and hardships" and brought the common touch he had sought in a nominee.[38]

In Sotomayor's remarks, televised live to a national audience, she said, "My heart today is bursting with gratitude. I stand on the shoulders of countless people." She then gave more of the credit for her rise not to a legal mentor or one of her teachers but to her mother. "I have often said that I am all I am because of her, and that I am only half the woman she is," Sotomayor said of her mother, Celina, who worked six days a week as a nurse to support her small family.

Some of the initial public criticism of Sotomayor arose from anonymous reports by lawyers in the *Almanac of the Federal Judiciary* describing her as a "terror on the bench," "temperamental," and "overly aggressive."[39] Senator Lindsey Graham, a Republican from South Carolina, said those reviews were a concern to him. "I don't like bully judges."[40] In a segment on the subject, the NPR Supreme Court correspondent Nina Totenberg compared Sotomayor's bench style to that of Scalia and Roberts and concluded, "If Sonia Sotomayor sometimes dominates oral argument at her court, if she is feisty, even pushy, then she should fit right in at the U.S. Supreme Court."[41]

In other corners of conservatism, a separate criticism arose—that she was deeply committed to affirmative action and would rule for her own people. That was shot down by defenders who countered that the first Latina nominee was a victim of inaccurate and rancid stereotyping.[42] When he was nominated in 1991, Justice Thomas experienced some of this same stereotyping. When asked in an interview before Sotomayor's hearings whether he had sympathy for her, Thomas focused on the fact that many of her liberal supporters had been his critics. "I don't know her," he said. "I had dinner with her once. She was nice to me . . . I've always found it fascinating that people get upset with me because they think that because I'm black I have to have a particular point of view. But the people who have presumed that about me cannot now object if the same thing happens to Sotomayor. You see what I'm saying? A bigot cannot yell too loudly about bigotry."[43]

Scalia had kept up with the nomination speculation in May and predicted to friends that President Obama would go with Sotomayor over the handful of other highly credentialed women whose names were circulating in media reports. His view was that presidents wanted some "first" for their legacy. As it happened, Scalia's name was constantly invoked during this period by legal analysts and political commentators, senators, and even President Obama. Liberals were hoping President Obama would choose someone who could counter Scalia's argumentative force on the court.[44] In another vein, *The New York Times*'s Adam Liptak wrote that while the retiring Souter was known as a careful judge, "he was never good material for newspaper columnists looking for scraps of color. For that, you want to keep up with Justice Antonin Scalia."[45]

President Obama, despite his previously voiced criticism of Scalia, praised him for his persuasive writing. In an interview with C-SPAN a few days before he announced the Sotomayor nomination, Obama said, "Justice Scalia is a terrific writer and makes really interesting arguments."[46]

In fact, Scalia has a way of dominating, even when he is losing. One of the marquee cases of the 2008–2009 term arose from a West Virginia saga with facts that read like a John Grisham novel: A small-town resident claimed he had been wronged by a big corporation and won a multimillion-dollar award after a lengthy jury trial. Then the corporation's top executive contributed enough money to a judicial election to get a new judge on the state supreme court. The newly elected judge cast the key vote that favored the big corporation and reversed the verdict. [47]

In the real-life West Virginia case, Judge Brent Benjamin had denied requests to take himself off a case that involved a businessman who had contributed $3 million to the race. Don Blankenship, CEO of A. T. Massey Coal, gave far more than any other donor to ensure the Republican Benjamin's election over the Democratic incumbent. Once on the bench, Benjamin cast the deciding vote to ensure that a $50 million fraud verdict against Massey Coal was reversed.

Hugh Caperton, of Harman Mining, had won the verdict after a lengthy trial. As he listened to the West Virginia Supreme Court justices hear the case, he remembered "looking up at a judge who had just gotten $3 million . . . to be elected and thinking, 'How in the world is this fair?' " Caperton had been run out of business by his coal rival, Massey, a decade earlier.

Benjamin said the money that helped get him elected was spent independently of his own campaign. Explaining in an opinion why he did not pull out of the case, Benjamin said he had no personal relationship with any of the parties or a financial stake in the outcome. For his part, Blankenship said he was not so much trying to get Benjamin elected as trying to defeat the incumbent whom he considered antibusiness and bad for the state.

The question before the Court, regarding when constitutional due process of law required a judge to disqualify himself or herself, put the justices on relatively undefined terrain. State judicial codes varied on standards for recusal, although many, like West Virginia, left it to the discretion of the judge. It had been decades since the Court directly examined the issue of when the federal Constitution might actually require judges to sit out a case. Through the years, and in a myriad of contexts, the justices had resisted rules that permitted a litigant to manipulate a judge off a case. And when Scalia happened to get caught up in controversy over his duck hunting with Vice President Dick Cheney, Scalia argued—in a line that was quoted by Judge Benjamin when he declined to step out of the Massey dispute: "The decision whether a judge's impartiality can 'reasonably be questioned' is to be made in light of the facts as they existed, and not as they were surmised or reported."[48]

Caperton was represented in his appeal by the ubiquitous Ted Olson, who told the justices that the $3 million Blankenship spent supporting Brent Benjamin's campaign while pursuing an appeal of his case created a constitutionally unacceptable appearance of impropriety.

During oral arguments Scalia and Roberts monopolized half of Olson's allotted time. Perhaps they knew that they were headed for the losing side and were desperately trying to convince Kennedy, anybody, of their view. Roberts and Scalia believed the justices should not try to set a rule for state judge recusals in these situations. Roberts presented a variety of scenarios in which trade groups made campaign contributions, and he questioned whether a judge would have to sit out any case involving those groups. Scalia asked why, under Olson's proposed standard, he would not have had to disqualify himself from cases involving President Reagan, the man who appointed him.

Olson said there was a difference between a life-tenured appointment and the situation when a benefactor has contributed millions to help elect an individual who would have an opportunity to rule on his case. Scalia shot back, "You've been around Washington a long time. How far do you think gratitude goes in the general political world?"[49]

Three months later, the Court ruled in a 5–4 vote for Caperton and against Massey Coal. Justice Kennedy, joining the liberals, wrote in the Court's opinion that a judge must sit out a case when "a serious risk of actual bias" arises because "a person with a personal stake in a particular case had a significant and disproportionate influence" in getting the judge on the bench to hear the case. The Kennedy majority emphasized the importance of public confidence in the courts and objective criteria to avoid the appearance of bias. Dissenting justices, including Scalia, asserted that the majority's standard was too vague. Chief Justice Roberts, writing for that foursome, listed forty questions raised by the majority opinion, including "How do we determine whether a given [campaign] expenditure is 'disproportionate'? Disproportionate to what?"[50]

Scalia wrote a separate dissenting opinion voicing concerns about the potential for frivolous litigation: "What above all else is eroding public confidence in the nation's judicial system is the perception that litigation is just a game, that the party with the most resourceful lawyer can play it to win, that our seemingly interminable legal proceedings are wonderfully self-perpetuating but incapable of delivering real-world justice." Then, with a stylish resort to allusion, his typical derision, and a broader complaint about the limited role of judges, Scalia concluded, "A Talmudic maxim instructs with respect to the Scripture: 'Turn it over, and turn it over, for all is therein.' Divinely inspired text may contain the answers to all earthly questions, but the due process clause most assuredly does not. The Court today continues its quixotic quest to right all wrongs and repair all imperfections through the Constitution."[51]

It was a sour loss, and another reminder of the fact that much of Scalia's influence depends on how Justice Kennedy votes. Yet, overall, Kennedy is likelier to side with conservatives than liberals, giving Scalia a greater shot at a majority opinion and leading to his writing a greater percentage of high-profile decisions in the 2008–2009 term than ever. His opinion in one case reinstated a federal ban on isolated expletives (the "s-word" and "f-word," as Scalia termed them) in broadcast radio and television. The case arose from outbursts by Cher and Nicole Richie at televised awards ceremonies. "Even isolated utterances can be made in pandering . . . vulgar and shocking manners, and can constitute harmful first blows to children," Scalia wrote in the decision joined by Roberts, Kennedy, Thomas, and Alito.[52]

As the calendar turned to summer in 2009, Scalia's eldest grandchild was getting ready to go to college for the first time and another was expected—the thirtieth for him and Maureen. In a TV interview to promote *Making Your Case*, Scalia had told his old friend Brian Lamb that "it was not easy" financially supporting their brood of nine. "My wife is . . . very parsimonious—also very well organized. Matthew went to West Point. That saved us college tuition for him. Three of the others went to state colleges. We don't do graduate school. We do college. Graduate school they have to scramble on their own, although we have helped a little bit. . . . When I first became a judge, I could not have hacked it, except that I taught on the side and made some additional income from teaching. Anyway, they're all out of college now, and it's a great relief to have that burden off your shoulders."[53]

He and Maureen traveled together to various judicial conferences, including to Ireland in the summer of 2008 and Brazil in the spring of 2009. There were increasing variations on "lifetime achievement" awards. And the long-view assessments that had begun in earnest when Scalia passed his twentieth anniversary continued, most echoing the sentiments offered at a 2007 celebration for Scalia given by Elena Kagan, the Harvard Law dean who went on to become the U.S. solicitor general in 2009. "His views on textualism and originalism, his views on the role of judges in our society, on the practice of judging, have really transformed the terms of legal debate in this country," she declared. "He is the justice who has had the most important impact over the years on how we think and talk about law."[54]

At the same time, Scalia's stable of critics was more entrenched, too. Barney Frank, an openly gay member of the U.S. House of Representatives from Massachusetts, called Scalia a "homophobe" in a 2009 interview. Regarding whether the Constitution would protect same-sex marriages, Frank told a reporter from a gay news website, "I wouldn't want it to go to the United States Supreme Court now because that homophobe Antonin Scalia has too many votes on this current court."[55] Scalia had no public response.

The justices who are most ideologically opposed to Scalia's views— Ginsburg, Stevens, Breyer—regard him as a potent force with staying power. "He is in tune with many of the current generation of law students," Ginsburg said. "When I was teaching in law schools and when I was going to law school, more students tended to be more left than right of center. That was true in the sixties and even into the seventies. In the eighties and nineties, the conservative movement that was practically nonexistent blossomed. Students now put 'Federalist Society' on their résumés." Stevens, who has served with Scalia the longest, added that, "He's made a huge difference, some of it constructive, some of it unfortunate."[56]

Just before the 2008–2009 Court term began, Scalia moved into new chambers. The offices had long been occupied by Justice Stevens, who, a year earlier, had moved to another set of chambers. Scalia brought in a new burl walnut desk and mounted the mammoth head of an elk he had shot while hunting in Colorado in 2004. The elk was so heavy that Scalia and his companion hunters had trouble hauling the carcass onto a truck. Now the huge head with handsome six-by-six rack protrudes from the wall across from his desk—an imposing presence.

Scalia transferred chambers because of an ongoing section-by-section renovation of the Court building. "When they started the renovation, I had thought, 'Oh boy, I'll get Sandra's chambers, which are beautiful. A great view.'" (The retired Justice O'Connor's old chambers in the northwest corner of the building looked out toward the Capitol.) "But I didn't think [about how] John had to move somewhere first," Scalia continued. "Once he moved there, he wasn't going to move back. That was the same with me. Once I move in here, I'm not going to move back again."[57]

As Scalia says this, he leans back from his shiny, now uncluttered desk. He is wearing a crisp white shirt with the usual French cuffs. In 2009, after almost a quarter century on the Court, nothing seems worn out about him. With good health, Scalia could be on the bench for another decade.

When it is pointed out he has been in the majority more and getting the opportunity to write more significant opinions for the Court, Scalia brushes it off. "The wins." He sighs. "The wins: Damn few."[58]

He is not entirely satisfied. Even when he is with the majority—which he was to a surprising extent in the 2008–2009 term, just behind the key vote, Kennedy—Scalia can be frustrated if the majority opinion fails to go as far as he wants or does not bring his themes to the fore. That was evident in a dispute over a decision by officials in New Haven, Connecticut, to throw out the results of a firefighter promotion test because whites outscored racial minorities. In an opinion by Kennedy, the conservative fivesome ruled for the white firefighters who had challenged the city's action as a violation of Title VII of the 1964 Civil Rights Act's bar on discriminatory treatment. New Haven officials had said that, after seeing the lopsided results, they worried the test was flawed and that they would be sued by minorities for having a practice that caused a discriminatory impact, which is also forbidden under Title VII. The Court ruled that the city lacked the required "strong basis in evidence" that it would be liable in lawsuits from black and Hispanic firefighters disproportionately hurt by the tests. "The city turned a blind eye to evidence supporting the exams' validity," Kennedy wrote.[59]

Scalia penned a concurring statement to observe that the case "merely postpones the evil day on which the Court will have to confront the question: Whether, or to what extent, are the disparate-impact provisions of Title VII of the Civil Rights Act of 1964 consistent with the Constitution's guarantee of equal protection? The question is not an easy one . . . But if the Federal Government is prohibited from discriminating on the basis of race, then surely it is also prohibited from enacting laws mandating that third parties—e.g., employers, whether private, State, or municipal—discriminate on the basis of race," by taking steps to avoid a disparate impact against minorities.

The Supreme Court is likely never to go as far as Scalia wants on racial policies. And in an equally explosive area of the law, he will likely never see the overturning of *Roe v. Wade*—Kennedy would block that. Scalia is also likely to continue on the losing side of gay rights, courtesy of Kennedy. Yet, in upcoming years, Scalia could help bring about more mingling of church and state and less government regulation of campaign financing—again, because of votes by Kennedy and fellow conservatives.[60] Scalia will also certainly continue to nourish his originalist constitutional theory and bring it to wider audiences.

Win or lose, Scalia remains energized. Justice Breyer has often referred to the "physical energy" and "intellectual rigor" Scalia brings to the task.[61] And Thomas observes, "He puts on his music and gets his computer ready. It's like he's conducting a symphony . . . with majority opinions, and dissents, too."[62]

Scalia might be at the apex of his influence. With conservatives holding the balance of power, and still being among the younger members of the nine, these final years of the first decade of the twenty-first century might offer Scalia his best ever opportunity to prevail. This could be his best shot.

NOTES

PROLOGUE
1. Antonin Scalia, address to Federalist Society annual convention, November 22, 2008, Mayflower Hotel, Washington, D.C. Justice Scalia began by reading sections of a standard speech on his originalist method of constitutional interpretation. He had given this stock speech to dozens of audiences in the United States and abroad, including at the Woodrow Wilson International Center for Scholars in Washington, D.C., in 2005, and at the University of Fribourg in Switzerland in 2006.
2. In addition to the Second Amendment decision, *District of Columbia v. Heller*, 554 U.S._ (2008), Scalia referred to his Supreme Court opinions based on an originalist reading of the Constitution's Sixth Amendment right to confront an accuser, for example, in *Crawford v. Washington*, 541 U.S. 36 (2004).
3. The lower court ruling reviewed by the justices in the 2008 case arose from a rare interpretation of the Second Amendment as containing an individual right to bear arms: *Parker v. District of Columbia*, 478 F.3d 370 (D.C. Cir. 2007). That lower court decision was written by the U.S. Court of Appeals judge Laurence Silberman, a recurring figure in Justice Scalia's professional life.
4. Ronald Reagan (1981–89), George H. W. Bush (1989–93), George W. Bush (2001–09).
5. Federalist Society annual dinner, Marriott Wardman Park, November 16, 2006.
6. Antonin Scalia, "Originalism: The Lesser Evil," *University of Cincinnati Law Review* 57 (1989): 849.
7. The liberal justice David Souter announced on May 1, 2009, that he would retire in the summer. Other justices most likely to retire would be the older liberal justices John Paul Stevens, born in 1920, and Ruth Bader Ginsburg, born in 1933.
8. See, for example, Hannelore Sudermann, "Scalia Explains his Style: U.S. Supreme Court Justice Says He Sticks to the Original Intent of the U.S. Constitution," *Spokesman Review*, September 8, 2000.
9. *Gonzales v. Raich*, 545 U.S. 1 (2005): Justices O'Connor and Thomas wrote separate dissenting opinions; *United States v. Lopez*, 514 U.S. 549 (1995).

1. A PLACE IN THE AMERICAN STORY

1. "River Begins to Rise: Flood Fears Revived," Trenton *State Gazette*, March 12, 1936; "City Hit by Storm: More Rain Today," *New York Times*, March 12, 1936; "8 Dead as Flood Sweeps Seaboard: Jersey Is Hard Hit," *New York Times*, March 13, 1936.

2. Catherine was born on November 7, 1905, while the family was still in New York on Barrow Street.

3. Steel cables from Trenton were used to build the great Brooklyn Bridge, which opened in 1883.

4. Pasquale would occasionally return home even after he had taken up with another woman. Justice Scalia said he believed he was a teenager when he first met Pasquale.

5. Declarations of Intention signed by Antonino Scalia on February 3, 1921, and Samuel Eugene Scalia December 24, 1923; Petitions for Naturalization by Antonino Scalia and Samuel Eugene Scalia filed February 11, 1926. U.S. Immigration and Naturalization Service, New Jersey Department of State, Division of Archives and Records Management.

6. Ibid.

7. Trenton City directories. Trentonian Room, Trenton Public Library.

8. Author interview with Eugene Scalia, June 8, 2007.

9. Author interview with Antonin Scalia, January 28, 2008.

10. *Brooklyn College Bulletin*, 1944–45. Brooklyn College, Archives and Special Collections Division.

11. U.S. Census 1930, Population Schedule, New Jersey Department of State, Division of Archives and Record Management.

12. "Italian Fellowships Go to 8 at Columbia," *New York Times*, May 17, 1934.

13. Author interviews with Antonin Scalia, November 16 and 26, 2007.

14. Author interviews with Lenora Panaro, November 29, 2007, and September 11, 2008.

15. Author interview with Antonin Scalia, November 16, 2007.

16. Brooklyn College Yearbook 1948–49, Brooklyn College, Archives and Special Collections Division; "Brooklyn College to Start Classes: Mayor Will Speak Tomorrow as 10,000 Undergraduates Flock to New Campus," *New York Times*, October 17, 1937.

17. "S. Eugene Scalia," personal tribute by Joseph F. DeSimone, October 2, 1989. Brooklyn College, Archives and Special Collections Division.

18. Author interview with Antonin Scalia, May 1, 2008.

19. Mangione and Morreale, *La Storia*, 129, 138.

20. Ibid., 301.

21. Antonin Scalia, address to National Italian American Foundation luncheon, Rayburn House Office Building, May 18, 2006.

22. Antonin Scalia, "The Disease as Cure: 'In Order to Get Beyond Racism, We Must First Take Account of Race,' " *Washington University Law Quarterly* (1979): 147–57; Antonin Scalia, address to National Italian American Foundation luncheon, Rayburn House Office Building, May 18, 2006.

23. Barzini, *The Italians*, 107.

24. Antonin Scalia, "Tribute to Emerson G. Spies," *Virginia Law Review* 77, no. 3 (1991): 427. Author interview with Antonin Scalia, August 26, 2008.

25. Carmela and Frank eventually settled in Williston Park on Long Island.

26. Author interview with Eugene Scalia, June 8, 2007.

27. Senior High School of Trenton yearbook, 1923. Trentonian Room, Trenton Public Library.
28. Justice Scalia took questions from Thomas Jefferson High School (Virginia) students on April 9, 2008; the event was televised on C-SPAN.
29. Brian Lamb interview with Antonin Scalia, May 4, 2008, televised on C-SPAN.
30. Justice Scalia appearance December 5, 2006, at a joint meeting of the American Constitution Society and Federalist Society, Washington Capital Hilton, Washington, D.C.
31. Cited in feature story on Antonin Scalia in the Columbus Citizens Foundation report of the 2005 Columbus Week Celebrations; Edmund Burke, *Reflections on the Revolution in France*, edited by J.G.A. Pocock (Indianapolis: Hackett, 1987), 41.
32. Author interview with Antonin Scalia, January 28, 2008.
33. Nicholas G. Katsarelas, "Nominee: The Little 'Nino' of Trenton's Italian Neighborhood," Associated Press, June 18, 1986.
34. Author interview with Arthur Gajarsa, July 27, 2007.
35. Author interview with Lenora Panaro, September 11, 2008.
36. Author interview with Eugene Scalia, June 8, 2007.
37. Author interview with Antonin Scalia, January 28, 2008.
38. Author interview with Antonin Scalia, February 9, 2009.
39. *Xavier Reflections on 150 Years* (New York: The College of St. Francis Xavier, 1997); additional information provided by Joe Gorski, the Xavier vice president for advancement and alumni relations.
40. *Xavier Reflections on 150 Years*, 158.
41. The Xavier Institute of Industrial Relations operated from the late 1930s to the late 1950s.
42. *Xavier: Reflections on 150 Years*, 150.
43. "Presenting," profile of Antonin Scalia, *Review*, November 7, 1952.
44. Ibid. Justice Scalia could not remember how he was chosen for the *Mind Your Manners* television show, but he recalled being able stay overnight at the Algonquin Hotel and being slipped a wad of money from the organizers.
45. Author interview with Antonin Scalia, January 28, 2008.
46. Antonin Scalia, "Economic Affairs as Human Affairs," *Cato Journal* 3 (Winter 1985): 703.
47. "Girls Debate Boys on Election Issues," *New York Times*, October 20, 1952.
48. For history of Princeton's selective admissions process, see, for example, Karabel, *The Chosen*.
49. Author interviews with Antonin Scalia, January 28, 2008, and June 24, 2008.
50. Author interview with Lenora Panaro, November 29, 2007.
51. Author interview with Antonin Scalia, January 28, 2008.
52. DeSimone recollection. Brooklyn College, Archives and Special Collections Division.
53. "McCarthy Wins Senior Favor: Named Outstanding American," *The Hoya*, May 13, 1954.
54. "Georgetown at Fribourg," 1956 *Ye Domesday Booke* (Georgetown University's yearbook).
55. Author interview with Antonin Scalia, January 28, 2008.
56. Scalia speech reprinted in *Georgetown College Journal* 86 (1957–58). Georgetown Library Special Collections and Archive Department.
57. Cicero, *De Legibus*, Book 1, vol. VI, 18. Translations from Harvard Law Library

website: www.law.harvard.edu/library/about/history/reading-room-ceiling-quotations
.html.
58. Psalm 129. Translation from Harvard Law Library website.
59. Justinian, *Digest*, Book 1, Title 3, 17. Translation from Harvard Law Library website.
60. Antonin Scalia, "A Tribute to Chief Judge Richard Arnold," *Arkansas Law Review* 58
(2005): 541.
61. From the *Harvard Law Record*: "Thurmond Claims Rights Act Product of Practical
Politics," December 12, 1958; "Mrs. Roosevelt Discusses Conditions in Soviet Union,"
March 13, 1958; "Bohemians Beware! Beatniks Are Here," April 9, 1959.
62. Frank I. Michelman, "*Anastasoff* and Remembrance," *Arkansas Law Review* 58 (2005):
558.
63. Professor Wechsler's Oliver Wendell Holmes lecture was delivered on April 7, 1959;
reprinted in *Harvard Law Review* (1959): 19; also reported by Anthony Lewis, "Law
Expert Puts Principles First," *New York Times*, April 8, 1959. Decades later, Scalia said
in interviews with the author that he did not attend the Wechsler lecture.
64. Michelman, "*Anastasoff* and Remembrance," 558.
65. Author interview with Frank Michelman, February 18, 2009.
66. Author interview with Antonin Scalia, June 24, 2008.
67. Author interview with James Lynn, September 28, 2007.
68. Ibid.
69. Author interview with Antonin Scalia, November 16, 2007.
70. Author interview with Maureen Scalia, December 4, 2008.
71. Maureen Scalia had one sibling, an older brother, who attended Middlebury College.
72. Author interviews with Maureen Scalia, December 4, 2008, and February 20, 2009.
73. Justice Scalia said he did not apply for a judicial clerkship at the Supreme Court or
anywhere else. "Why would I apply for a judicial clerkship?" he said in an interview
with the author. "I had a Sheldon [Fellowship], this wonderful year traveling around
with my new bride."
74. Author interview with Antonin Scalia, August 26, 2008.
75. Commencement address, University of Dayton School of Law, delivered May 1984.
76. John C. Jeffries, Jr., "Tribute," *New York University Annual Survey of American Law*
(2006): 11.

2. IN THE TURBULENCE OF WATERGATE
1. Inside accounts of days leading up to and immediately following Nixon's resignation
from the Ford archives and numerous books including Woodward and Bernstein, *The
Final Days*, and Hartmann, *Palace Politics*.
2. Laurence Silberman to Bob Silberman, December 5, 1973. Laurence Silberman Papers,
Hoover Institution.
3. Author interview with Maureen Scalia, December 4, 2008; author interview with
Antonin Scalia, February 9, 2009.
4. Explaining why he sought the assistant attorney general job for the Office of Legal
Counsel, Scalia added, "OLC was just too attractive a job for a legal intellectual."
5. Anthony Ripley, "Federal Grand Jury Indicts 7 Nixon Aides on Charges of Conspiracy
on Watergate," *New York Times*, March 2, 1974.
6. Alexander Butterfield, former assistant to Haldeman, had revealed the existence of the

White House taping system ten months earlier, prompting then special prosecutor Cox to begin subpoenaing the recordings of presidential conversations. On May 20, 1974, during the week Scalia had his first interview for the assistant attorney general job, the U.S. district judge John Sirica refused a White House motion to reject Jaworski's subpoena for the tapes.

7. Laurence Silberman to Bob Silberman, December 5, 1973. Laurence Silberman Papers. Hoover Institution.

8. Carroll Kilpatrick, "Nixon Forces Firing of Cox: Richardson, Ruckelshaus Quit," *New York Times*, October 21, 1973. Bork later said he carried out Nixon's order to try to bring some order to the chaos generated by Nixon and to prevent "massive resignations from the top levels of the Department of Justice."

9. Author interview with Laurence Silberman, January 18, 2007.

10. Dixon was a law professor at Washington University in St. Louis. He died in 1980.

11. Author interview with Laurence Silberman, January 18, 2007.

12. Scalia had been at the Administrative Conference since September 1972; he worked for the Office of Telecommunications Policy from 1971 to 1972.

13. Adam Bernstein, "Clay Whitehead, 69, Changed TV Landscape," *Washington Post*, July 29, 2008; Dennis Hevesi, "Clay T. Whitehead, Guide of Policy That Helped Cable TV, Is Dead at 69," *New York Times*, July 31, 2008; for commentary on the context of the political battles in the Office of Telecommunications Policy, see Eric Mink, "For the Hard Right, Control of the Government Is Not Enough," *St. Louis Post-Dispatch*, May 19, 2005.

14. Memos from the Public Broadcasting Policy Base: www.current.org/pbpb/nixon/nixon71.html.

15. Hartmann, *Palace Politics*, 165; Woodward and Bernstein, *Final Days*, 214–15.

16. The elder Rose introduced Scalia to his son Jonathan. Scalia had been recruited to the law firm by Jim Lynn, who had become Nixon's secretary of Housing and Urban Development (HUD) and was now, as Scalia was seeking a job in the Justice Department, moving on to Ford's economic team.

17. Author interview with Antonin Scalia, November 16, 2007.

18. Author interview with Antonin Scalia, June 24, 2008.

19. Transcript of testimony from witnesses before the Senate Judiciary Committee hearing on Antonin Scalia's nomination for Supreme Court, August 6, 1986.

20. Author interview with Jonathan Rose, February 8, 2007.

21. Silberman daily meeting log, March 1–May 10, 1974. Laurence Silberman Papers, Hoover Institution.

22. Author interview with Laurence Silberman, January 18, 2007.

23. Author interview with Jonathan Rose, February 8, 2007.

24. Silberman watched the *United States v. Nixon* arguments at the Supreme Court and afterward went to lunch with Solicitor General Robert Bork and their respective wives at the nearby Monocle restaurant. Silberman daily meeting log, May 13–July 12, 1974. Laurence Silberman Papers, Hoover Institution.

25. Anthony Lewis, "Earl Warren, 83, Who Led High Court in Time of Vast Social Change, Is Dead," *New York Times*, July 10, 1974.

26. Details of the funeral from the program "Funeral of the Honorable Earl Warren"; details of arrangements for his body to lie in repose at the Supreme Court from a July 10, 1974, press release issued by the Court. Lewis F. Powell, Jr. Archive, Washington and Lee University.

27. *United States v. Nixon*, 418 U.S. 683 (1974); Justice Rehnquist did not participate because of his earlier connection to Nixon administration parties in the case.

28. John Herbers, "Nixon Admits Ordering Halt on Watergate Inquiry," *New York Times*, August 6, 1974.

29. Author interview with Antonin Scalia, November 26, 2007.

30. Author interview with Maureen Scalia, December 4, 2008.

31. Author interview with Antonin Scalia, January 28, 2008.

32. Author interview with Eugene Scalia, June 29, 2007: "My parents were a little stricter than other parents in terms of what we could wear. It took a long time for them to accept our wearing blue jeans to school. We'd say, 'Everybody's wearing blue jeans.' And they'd say, 'Why would you want to be like everybody else?'" Separately, Justice Scalia said he did not send his children to the parochial schools because his northern Virginia school district offered a first-rate no-cost education.

33. Author interview with Antonin Scalia, January 28, 2008.

34. Philip Buchen, "Memorandum for the White House Staff," October 30, 1974, reiterating earlier precautions about securing files. Gerald R. Ford Library.

35. Benton Becker to Philip Buchen, August 13, 1974, internal parentheses omitted; July 18, 1973, was a crucial date because that is when John Ehrlichman and H. R. Haldeman resigned and the White House counsel John Dean was fired. Gerald R. Ford Library.

36. Barry Roth, "Memorandum for the Record," October 1, 1974. Gerald R. Ford Library.

37. Donald Rumsfeld to Philip Buchen, September 29, 1974. Gerald R. Ford Library.

38. Benton Becker to Philip Buchen, "He [Nixon] is the legal owner of all records from his administration including, but not limited to, tapes," Becker wrote. Gerald R. Ford Library.

39. Jerry Jones, "Memorandum for the White House Staff," August 9, 1974. Gerald R. Ford Library.

40. GSA's Sampson to Arthur L. Fox II and Reuben B. Robertson III of Public Citizen Litigation Group, responding to their August 14, 1974, letter questioning the assumption that the president owns all his personal papers. Gerald R. Ford Library.

41. President Ford to William Saxbe, August 22, 1974, Gerald R. Ford Library. Ford's request happened to be officially transmitted on the day Scalia was confirmed for the assistant attorney general spot. Ford asked Attorney General William Saxbe for a legal opinion concerning papers and other historical materials retained by the White House during Nixon's administration: "Some such materials were left in the Executive Office Building or in the White House at the time of former President Nixon's departure; others had previously been deposited with the Administrator of General Services. I would like your advice concerning ownership of these materials and the obligations of the government with respect to subpoenas or court orders issued against the government or its officials pertaining to them." Laurence Silberman recounted in an interview with the author, "I called Nino. I said, 'We need a legal opinion on this. I suspect the papers belong to the president, but I haven't looked at it. You've got to look at it quickly.'"

42. Author interview with James Wilderotter, July 29, 2007.

43. Author interview with Antonin Scalia, November 16, 2008.

44. Scalia circulated a first draft to Assistant Attorney General Carla Hills on September 3, 1974. Carla Anderson Hills Papers, Hoover Institution.

45. Hartmann, *Palace Politics*, 258.

46. Gerald Ford pardon statement, September 8, 1974. Gerald R. Ford Library.

47. President Ford signed the Presidential Recordings and Materials Preservation Act December 19, 1974.

48. Philip Buchen to President Ford, August 13, 1974. Gerald R. Ford Library.

49. Antonin Scalia testimony at "Hearings Before a Subcommittee on Government Operations," House of Representatives, May 10, 1973; see also Martin Arnold, "Congress, the Press and Federal Agencies Are Taking Sides for Battle Over Government's Right to Secrecy," *New York Times*, November 15, 1974.

50. Information on Scalia's role in the administration's opposition to the Freedom of Information Act amendments from author interviews, Gerald R. Ford Library documents, and from the National Security Archive at George Washington University, which has collected materials related to the act and made them available to journalists.

51. John S. Warner, CIA general counsel, memo for the files, September 26, 1974: "Mr. Scalia brought up a new subject: he asked our views on possible veto of the Freedom of Information Act amendments, H.R. 12471. I informed him that OMB had polled us the day before by telephone, and I had indicated the Agency took a very strong position that this bill, if approved by Congress, should be vetoed. Mr. Scalia stated that, if we wanted to have any impact, we should move quickly to make our views known directly to the President. He indicated that neither State nor Defense would be recommending veto. Later in the day Mr. Scalia telephoned urging us to contact The White House, specifically Geoffrey C. Shepard, Associate Director. I contacted Mr. Shepard and stated our position. He indicated that, in their papers to go forward to the President, they had anticipated this would be our position, but appreciated our call and felt sending a letter to the President would be helpful."

52. Donald Rumsfeld was a longtime friend of Gerald Ford's, whom he helped win the House minority leadership post in 1965.

53. Hartmann, *Palace Politics*, 283.

54. Mann, *Rise of the Vulcans*, 12.

55. Asked about opposition to FOIA amendments, Scalia told the author in a January 28, 2008, interview, "I might have prepared stuff for Larry [Silberman]. I just don't remember."

56. Antonin Scalia memorandum for Phil Areeda, with attachments, November 13, 1974, Gerald R. Ford Library. Scalia's memo had continued, "Based upon a combination of assumptions which involve substantial elements of judgment but are considered to be within realistic limits, the costs of administering the Act with the amendments vetoed by President Ford could reasonably be anticipated to run as high as approximately a half-billion dollars a year, with a saving of up to about $100,000,000 a year through the changes requested by the President."

57. The House of Representatives voted 371–31 on November 20, 1974, to override President Ford's veto of amendments to the 1966 Freedom of Information Act. The Senate voted 65–27 to override the veto the following day, on November 21, 1974.

58. Quoted in Scott Shane, "For Some, Spying Controversy Recalls a Past Drama," *New York Times*, February 6, 2006. A few years earlier Cheney had said, "I have repeatedly seen an erosion of the powers and the ability of the president . . . to do his job. We are weaker today as an institution because of the unwise compromises that have been

made over the last 30 to 35 years." Quoted in Bob Woodward and Dan Balz, " 'We Will Rally the World': Bush and his Advisors Set Objectives but Struggled with How to Achieve Them," *Washington Post*, January 28, 2002.

59. Antonin Scalia testimony at "Freedom of Information Act" hearing, Senate Committee on the Judiciary Subcommittee on the Constitution, November 12, 1981. The following year, Scalia said in an interview with *U.S. News & World Report*, "The Freedom of Information Act—or, more specifically, the 1974 amendments to the act—came out of an era of exuberant, single-minded pursuit of individual objectives. We are now discovering that such tunnel-vision zeal—whether directed toward the environment or automobile safety or freedom of information—is indulged at excessive cost to other important objectives." "Interview with Antonin Scalia, professor of law, University of Chicago: Cut Access to Government Data? Yes, Government Files Shouldn't 'Become the World's Largest Free Reference Service,'" *U.S. News & World Report*, January 18, 1982.

60. Scalia, Testimony at "Freedom of Information Act" hearing.

3. WITNESS FOR THE EXECUTIVE

1. Edmund Muskie and Antonin Scalia remarks from an "Executive Privilege—Secrecy in Government" transcript of hearings before the Subcommittee on Government Operations, U.S. Senate, beginning September 29, 1975.

2. Ibid.

3. Antonin Scalia testimony, "Executive Privilege—Secrecy in Government" transcript of October 23, 1975, session.

4. Nicholas M. Horrock, "Ford Aides Seek to Modify Laws on Spying Method," *New York Times*, October 15, 1975; Nicholas M. Horrock, "Senate Unit Sets Hearings on NSA," *New York Times*, October 24, 1975.

5. The Church Committee was formally known as the United States Senate Select Committee to Study Governmental Operations with Respect to Intelligence Activities. It met in 1975 and 1976 and issued a series of fourteen reports.

6. Author interview with Antonin Scalia, November 26, 2007; Charlie Savage, *Takeover*, 30.

7. Antonin Scalia testimony and House members' comments from transcript of House Select Committee on Intelligence hearing, November 20, 1975.

8. Author interview with Maureen Scalia, December 4, 2008.

9. David E. Rosenbaum, "House Committee Drops Charge Against Kissinger," *New York Times*, December 11, 1975.

10. *Branzburg v. Hayes*, 408 U.S. 665 (1972).

11. "Newsmen's Privilege," transcript of hearing conducted by House Judiciary Subcommittee on Courts, Civil Liberties, and the Administration of Justice, April 23, 1975.

12. Ibid.

13. During the two-and-a-half-year period covering mid-1970 through early 1973, according to Scalia, the Justice Department approved subpoenas for thirteen reporters. See "Newsmen's Shield Bill Snagged Again," *New York Times*, April 24, 1975.

14. The legislation died in committee and would be periodically resurrected through the late 2000s.

15. Memorandum of Justice Scalia in *Cheney, Vice President of the United States v. United States District Court for the District of Columbia*, No. 03-475, March 18, 2004; Scalia

rejected a motion that he disqualify himself in a case related to Vice President Cheney because he had gone duck hunting with him.

16. John Herbers, "Executive Branch Is Now Many Blooming Twigs," *New York Times*, March 2, 1975.

17. Blackmun's Court papers were made public at the Library of Congress in 2004, a decade after he retired and five years after his death.

18. Antonin Scalia, remembrance, "In Memoriam: Edward H. Levi (1912–2000)," *University of Chicago Law Review* (2000): 983.

19. Ibid.

20. Author interview with Antonin Scalia, May 1, 2008.

21. "Assail Guffey Act as Near Kin to NRA," *New York Times*, March 12, 1936; see also "Court Room Is Crowded," *New York Times*, March 12, 1936.

22. *Carter v. Carter Coal Co.*, 298 U.S. 238 (1936).

23. The Railroad Retirement Act established a pension system for rail workers financed by the railroads. The act was invalidated in *Railroad Retirement Board v. Alton Railroad Co.*, 295 U.S. 330 (1935); other FDR initiatives were struck down in *Schechter Poultry Corp. v. United States*, 295 U.S. 495 (1935) and *Humphrey's Executor v. United States*, 295 U.S. 602 (1935).

24. *Morehead v. New York ex rel. Tipaldo*, 298 U.S. 587 (1936). Regarding the New York wage law, intended to help working women and children, the Court said, "The state is without power . . . to prohibit change or nullify contracts between employers and adult women workers as to the amount of wages to be paid."

25. Kennedy, *Freedom from Fear*, 331. Roosevelt uncharacteristically underestimated "popular devotion to the Court's traditional role," Kennedy wrote. "He also miscalculated badly his choice of tactics and timing. From the moment of its unveiling, his Court plan stirred a nest of furies."

26. Justice Owen Roberts's vote in the Washington State case—a switch from his position in the similar New York dispute—had been cast in a private conference with his colleagues nearly two months before Roosevelt's unveiling of his Court-packing plan. Yet Roberts's move was widely called "the switch in time that saved nine." That popular rendering probably reflected the fact that, although Roosevelt had not yet proposed his drastic "Court-packing" measure, his dissatisfaction was well known and pressure on the Court from various political and legal quarters had been building.

27. At the time of his retirement, Justice Douglas had served for longer than any other justice in history.

28. Letter from Byron White to Warren Burger, October 20, 1975. Lewis F. Powell, Jr. Archive, Washington and Lee University.

29. William O. Douglas letter to President Ford, November 12, 1975. Lewis F. Powell, Jr. Archive, Washington and Lee University.

30. See Milton Viorst, "Bill Douglas Has Never Stopped Fighting the Bullies of Yakima: Douglas Under Fire," *New York Times Magazine*, June 14, 1970; Marjorie Hunter, "House Panel Votes Against Impeaching Douglas," *New York Times*, December 4, 1970.

31. Antonin Scalia, remembrance, "In Memoriam: Edward H. Levi (1912–2000)," 983.

32. Edward Levi to President Ford, November 10, 1975. Gerald R. Ford Library.

33. Ibid.

34. Author interview with Antonin Scalia, November 16, 2007; author interview with Justice John Paul Stevens, March 6, 2009.

35. Edward Levi to President Ford, November 10, 1975. Gerald R. Ford Library.

36. "Memorandum for Max Friedersdorf," November 22, 1975. Gerald R. Ford Library.
37. Max Friedersdorf to President Ford, November 28, 1975. Gerald R. Ford Library.
38. Robert D. McFadden, "The President's Choice: John Paul Stevens," *New York Times*, November 29, 1975.
39. Dick Cheney to Jim Connor, December 9, 1975. Gerald R. Ford Library.
40. *Alfred Dunhill of London v. Cuba*, 425 U.S. 682 (1976); Blackmun notes from oral arguments heard in case on January 19, 1976. Harry A. Blackmun Papers, Library of Congress.
41. Buchanan, *Right from the Beginning*, 326.
42. Author interview with Antonin Scalia, January 28, 2008.
43. "Re: Executive Privilege," undated memorandum from Assistant Attorney General Scalia, Office of Legal Counsel. Gerald R. Ford Library.

4. MEETING OF THE MINDS

1. "An Imperial Judiciary: Fact or Myth?" edited transcript of forum sponsored by the American Enterprise Institute for Public Policy Research, Washington, D.C., December 12, 1978.
2. *Regulation* magazine took a skeptical view of government regulation.
3. Arthur Ciervo, "Profiles: Antonin Scalia," *Georgetown Today*, September 1975, 16.
4. Author interview with Antonin Scalia, May 1, 2008. In an April 1, 1986, interview with Brian Lamb on C-SPAN, Scalia had complained that too many students sought to go to law school "to save the world."
5. Robert Bolt, *A Man for All Seasons* (London: Heinemann, 1960), 39.
6. Author interview with Antonin Scalia, June 24, 2008.
7. Arthur Ciervo, "Profiles," 16.
8. "An Imperial Judiciary: Fact or Myth?" transcript.
9. Ibid.
10. It was widely reported at the time of the April 5, 1976, attack that Landsmark, who was a Yale law graduate working for the Contractors Association of Boston, was impaled by the flagpole, but he said it did not hit him. "Boston Appointee Felt Racism's Pain," *New York Times*, October 23, 1988.
11. *Roe v. Wade*, 410 U.S. 113 (1973).
12. Antonin Scalia testimony at "Tuition Tax Credits" hearing, Senate Committee on Finance Hearing, June 3, 1981; related testimony at "Oversight on Private Schools" hearing, House Committee on Education and Labor Subcommittee on Elementary, Secondary, and Vocational Education, May 13, 1981.
13. Ibid.
14. Author interview with Antonin Scalia, May 1, 2008.
15. Antonin Scalia, "The Disease as Cure: 'In Order to Get Beyond Racism We Must First Take Account of Race,'" *Washington University Law Quarterly* (1979): 147.
16. See, for example, *United Steelworkers of America v. Weber*, 443 U.S. 193 (1979); *Regents of the University of California v. Bakke*, 438 U.S. 265 (1978).
17. Antonin Scalia, "The Disease as Cure," 147.
18. *Congressional Quarterly Weekly Report* 38 (1980): 2046.
19. Meese, *With Reagan*, 315–16.
20. Smith, *Law and Justice in the Reagan Administration*, 57.
21. Ibid.

22. Justice Scalia referred to the deanship interview in a 2005 speech at Washington and Lee, joking that after nearly twenty years as a justice, "I don't know how it would have turned out." Calvin R. Trice, "Scalia Gives Lecture at W&L," *Richmond Times Dispatch*, April 16, 2005.

23. See also Timothy B. Clark, "Substance over Process," *National Journal*, January 3, 1981, noting that Scalia, a visiting professor at Stanford Law School, argued that one of the administration's first tasks should be to work toward amendments to various agencies' statutory charters to reduce regulation.

24. Judge Scalia's 1982 financial disclosure form, the first he submitted as a judge on the D.C. Circuit, showed his prior salary for part of the year at the University of Chicago at $32,972 and his American Enterprise Institute editing and consulting fees at $15,000. Various other consulting contracts, including $25,800 from AT&T, totaled about $50,000 for the reporting period. Financial Disclosure Form, stamped May 19, 1983, Ronald Reagan Library.

25. Oaks became a member of the Quorum of the Twelve and was ordained an apostle in 1984.

26. "I almost could have flipped a coin to make the choice," Smith wrote afterward. "It was that close." Smith, *Law & Justice in the Reagan Administration*, 23.

27. Author interview with Antonin Scalia, November 26, 2007.

28. Frank D. Stella to President Reagan, July 21, 1981: "I am writing to respectfully urge your serious consideration of Mr. Antonin Scalia for appointment to the U.S. Court of Appeals for the District of Columbia Circuit." Ronald Reagan Library.

29. Author interview with Steven Calabresi, June 10, 2008.

30. Author interview with Lee Liberman Otis, August 9, 2007; author interview with Steven Calabresi, June 10, 2008.

31. Steven Calabresi's father, Paul, Guido's older brother, had taught at the Yale School of Medicine, then became a founding faculty member of the medical school at Brown University.

32. Author interview with Lee Liberman Otis, August 9, 2007.

33. Author interview with Antonin Scalia, May 9, 2008.

34. Ibid.

35. Author interview with David McIntosh, February 5, 2007.

36. Mark Holmes, "Federalists Invade Yale," *The Phoenix*, May 10, 1982.

37. Author interview with Steven Calabresi, June 10, 2008.

38. See, for example, "Federal Judge Assails Supreme Court Rulings," *New York Times*, April 27, 1982.

39. Ibid.; also Holmes, "Federalists Invade Yale."

40. Theodore Olson remarks at Federalist Society's 25th Anniversary Gala, Union Station, Washington, D.C., November 15, 2007.

41. Jerry M. Landay, "The Federalist Society: The Conservative Cabal That's Transforming American Law," *Washington Monthly*, March 2000.

42. Teles, *The Rise of the Conservative Legal Movement*, 150, 179.

43. Ibid., 141.

44. Justice Scalia speech to Federalist Society's 25th Anniversary Gala, Union Station, Washington, D.C., November 15, 2007.

45. Ralph Winter, the first Federalist Society faculty adviser at Yale, was appointed by Reagan to the U.S. Court of Appeals for the Second Circuit in December 1981.

46. Steven Calabresi would become a law clerk to Robert Bork, then a special assistant to

Attorney General Meese at the Justice Department, then a law clerk to Antonin Scalia on the Supreme Court, then a Northwestern law professor. Lee Liberman Otis would become a law clerk to Judge Scalia on the D.C. Circuit, a special assistant at the Justice Department, a law clerk to Justice Scalia on the Supreme Court, then general counsel at the Department of Energy. She returned to the Federalist Society in 2007 as a senior vice president. David McIntosh would become special assistant to Attorney General Meese, then return to Indiana and run for the U.S. House of Representatives, where he served from 1995 to 2001. Spencer Abraham, the Federalist Society connection at Harvard, eventually became a U.S. senator from Michigan from 1995 to 2001 and then served in the George W. Bush administration as secretary of energy.
47. Author interviews with Antonin Scalia, November 26, 2007, and February 9, 2009.

5. RELENTLESS IN DISSENT
1. The D.C. Circuit typically hears cases with three-judge panels. It sits "en banc" when a matter warrants a hearing by the full court.
2. Thomas, *The Man to See*, 443.
3. *New York Times v. Sullivan*, 376 U.S. 254 (1964).
4. A trial judge had determined that Tavoulareas was a "public figure" in the controversy, so that under the Supreme Court's *New York Times v. Sullivan*, the jury would have to assess the dispute under the "actual malice" standard. That is, jurors had to look at whether the *Post* published in knowing or reckless disregard of the truth of its story.
5. *Tavoulareas v. Piro*, 759 F.2d 90 (D.C. Cir. 1985).
6. Ibid.
7. Author interview with David Kendall, December 22, 2008.
8. Williams had not argued the *Post*'s case in earlier proceedings, but for his longtime client and old friend Ben Bradlee, editor of *The Washington Post*, Williams wanted to be in this match.
9. David Lauter, "Two Masters Compete for Appellate Votes," *National Law Journal*, October 21, 1985; additional descriptions of case background and oral arguments from Thomas, *The Man to See*, 438–44.
10. Lauter, "Two Masters Compete for Appellate Votes."
11. Martin Tolchin, "Appeal of Verdict Against Washington Post Is Heard," *New York Times*, October 4, 1985; Lauter, "Two Masters Compete for Appellate Votes." Separately, Walsh was representing Hammer DeRoburt, the president of the tiny South Pacific republic of Nauru.
12. *Natural Resources Defense Council v. Nuclear Regulatory Commission*, 547 F.2d 633 (D.C. Cir. 1976). Supreme Court reversal is at *Vermont Yankee Nuclear Power Corp. v. NRDC*, 435 U.S. 519 (1978).
13. Antonin Scalia, "Vermont Yankee: The APA, the D.C. Circuit, and the Supreme Court," *Supreme Court Review* (1978): 345.
14. *Motor Vehicles Manufacturer's Association v. State Farm Insurance*, 463 U.S. 29 (1983); *State Farm Mutual Automobile Insurance Co. v. Department of Transportation*, 680 F.2d 206 (D.C. Cir. 1982).
15. Stuart Taylor, Jr., "A Time of Transition for No. 2 Court," *New York Times*, September 8, 1982.
16. "Jurist in Racial Dispute: James Skelly Wright," *New York Times*, November 16, 1960;

Peter Braestrup, "Wright Is Named to Appeals Court," *New York Times*, December 16, 1961.

17. "Promoting Justice," *New York Times*, March 30, 1978.

18. Philip Taubman, "Milton Kronheim's, Where the Justices Adjourn for Lunch," *New York Times*, July 15, 1979.

19. Bork, *The Tempting of America*, 147.

20. When Wright stepped down in early 1986, it provided an opening for Reagan's seventh of eight total nominees and his first-time majority of appointees on the powerful Circuit. *The New York Times* noted the transformed bench in an article that said, "In the annals of the Federal judiciary, this will go down as a historic week." Philip Shenon, "Shift Gives Reagan D.C. Circuit Majority," *New York Times*, May 24, 1986.

21. Author interview with Mickey Knox, Judge Bazelon's widow, June 13, 2007.

22. Author interview with Ruth Bader Ginsburg, March 29, 2007.

23. Robert Bork had been part of the New Year's Eve celebrations but stopped coming; his 1987 Supreme Court rejection made relations in the group somewhat awkward.

24. Joan Biskupic, "Justices Strike a Balance: Pals Ginsburg, Scalia Ring in the New Year, Then Duke It Out in Court," *USA Today*, December 26, 2007.

25. Author interview with Brian Lamb, February 15, 2007.

26. D.C. Circuit judge Scalia during an April 1, 1986, interview with Brian Lamb on C-SPAN.

27. Author interview with Michael Brody, September 21, 2007.

28. Author interview with E. Joshua Rosenkranz, October 23, 2007.

29. Author interview with Michael Brody, March 6, 2009.

30. Ruth Marcus and Susan Schmidt, "Scalia Tenacious After Staking Out a Position. Supreme Court Nominee's Views Attuned to Reagan Era Conservative Philosophy," *Washington Post*, June 22, 1986.

31. Antonin Scalia memo April 2, 1984. J. Skelly Wright Papers, Library of Congress.

32. Author interview with Patricia Wald, September 5, 2007; also Patricia M. Wald, speech introducing Antonin Scalia at 1988 Judicial Conference for the District of Columbia Circuit, Williamsburg, Virginia, May 23, 1988.

33. "Antonin Scalia," fourteen-page undated memo prepared by Lee Liberman and other Justice Department lawyers as part of Supreme Court selection process. Ronald Reagan Library.

34. See *Synar v. United States*, 626 F. Supp. 1374 (D.D.C. 1986). Scalia was the lead author of the opinion by a special three-judge court invalidating the law popularly known as the Gramm-Rudman-Hollings Act, which set annual maximum deficit and federal spending amounts to try to eliminate the federal budget deficit.

35. See, for example, *Steele v. Federal Communications Commission*, 770 F.2d 1192 (D.C. Cir. 1985). The case involved the 1984 FCC award of an FM license to the woman applicant Dale Bell for a station on St. Simon's Island, Georgia. In the challenge brought by the rejected applicant James Steele, the 2–1 majority, which included Scalia, said the FCC was engaging in the "most simplistic kind of ethnic stereotyping."

36. *Ollman v. Evans*, 750 F.2d 970 (D.C. Cir. 1984).

37. Pearlstine, *Off the Record*, episode recounted by Dahlia Lithwick, "Target Practice: Justice Scalia Sets His Sights on *New York Times Co. v. Sullivan*," *Slate*, July 17, 2007. Asked about Pearlstine's remark that Scalia wanted to reverse the case, Scalia said he held out no hope. "There's not a snowball's chance in hell of reversing that. I'm critical of it

because if there's anything that is counter to originalism, it's that. The Court made up a new libel law." Author interview with Antonin Scalia, February 18, 2009.

38. Scalia dissenting in *Center for Auto Safety v. National Highway Traffic Safety Administration*, 793 F.2d 1322 (D.C. Cir. 1986). He also dissented from a D.C. Circuit ruling that allowed consumers, represented by the Community Nutrition Institute, to challenge milk regulations that raised prices on reconstituted milk made from dry milk powder and water. *Community Nutrition Institute v. Block*, 698 F.2d 1239 (D.C. Cir. 1983). The U.S. Supreme Court reversed the D.C. Circuit in the case, saying the 1937 law at issue allowed only "handlers" who process raw agricultural commodities to sue. *Block v. Community Nutrition Institute*, 467 U.S. 340 (1984).

39. Author interview with Steven Calabresi, June 10, 2008.

40. *Chaney v. Heckler*, 718 F.2d 1174 (D.C. Cir. 1984).

41. "Antonin Scalia," fourteen-page undated memo prepared by Lee Liberman and other Justice Department lawyers as part of Supreme Court selection process. Ronald Reagan Library.

42. Scalia dissenting in *Community for Creative Non-Violence v. Watt*, 703 F.2d 586 (D.C. Cir. 1983). Judges Bork and MacKinnon were in the majority.

43. *Hirschey v. FERC*, 777 F.2d 1 (D.C. Cir. 1985).

44. Antonin Scalia, speech on the use of legislative history, delivered between fall 1985 and spring 1986 at various law schools. Signed copy obtained from the University of Chicago Law Library.

45. *Block v. Community Nutrition Institute*, 467 U.S. 340 (1984), 749 F.2d 50 (D.C. Cir. 1984).

46. Author interview with Antonin Scalia, August 26, 2008.

47. Author interview with Arthur Gajarsa, July 27, 2007.

48. Author interview with Thomas Susman, April 23, 2007. Susman, who worked in the Kennedy and Johnson administrations, said of Scalia, "He had come out of the Nixon administration unscathed. He was so smart and so open and likable. It couldn't be that he was so closed-minded and rigid in his thinking. I wouldn't admit of that criticism of him. History has proved me wrong. But he has remained a good friend."

49. Author interview with Arthur Gajarsa, July 27, 2007.

50. William Safire, "Free Speech v. Scalia," *New York Times*, April 29, 1985.

51. *Tavoulareas v. Piro*, 817 F.2d 762 (D.C. Cir. 1987).

52. Transcript, "Hearings Before the Committee on the Judiciary, United States Senate, 99th Congress, 2nd Session, on the Nomination of Judge Antonin Scalia to be Associate Justice of the Supreme Court of the United States," August 5–6, 1986, Washington, D.C., U.S. Government Printing Office.

53. Antonin Scalia to George MacKinnon, August 26, 1986. George E. MacKinnon Papers, Minnesota Historical Society.

54. Scalia also wrote in his August 26, 1986, memorandum to MacKinnon, "Tyler's contemporaneous explanation of the meaning of the article he had written is powerful evidence that the article is best understood as implying that Mobil's entry into the arrangement [with the companies that hired Peter Tavoulareas] was prompted by William Tavoulareas's nepotistic intent; it is virtually dispositive evidence that the article could reasonably be so understood. Nevertheless, the en banc majority concludes that Tyler's memo is 'of no probative value.' Moreover, even if we agreed with the majority that Tyler's memo was ambiguous (and we do not), it was for the jury to resolve that ambiguity."

55. George MacKinnon to Antonin Scalia, November 7, 1986. George E. MacKinnon Papers, Minnesota Historical Society.

6. "I HAVE NO AGENDA"
1. Quotations from Strom Thurmond and other senators, and from Antonin Scalia, from transcript, "Hearings Before the Committee on the Judiciary, United States Senate, 99th Congress, 2nd Session, on the Nomination of Judge Antonin Scalia to be Associate Justice of the Supreme Court of the United States," August 5–6, 1986. Washington, D.C., U.S. Government Printing Office. Regarding systematic screening, see, for example, Patrick Buchanan memo to chief of staff Donald Regan, July 10, 1985, Ronald Reagan Library; Haynes Johnson, "Restoring Balance to the Scales of Justice," *Washington Post*, October 20, 1985; Stuart Taylor, Jr., "Scalia's Views, Stylishly Expressed, Line Up with Reagan's," *New York Times*, July 14, 1986; Stuart Taylor, Jr., "Has Reagan Got the Court He Wants?" *New York Times*, June 22, 1986.
2. *Congressional Quarterly 1986 Almanac* (Washington, D.C.: Congressional Quarterly Press, 1986), 71–72. Stuart Taylor, Jr., "Senate Opens Rehnquist Hearing, and the Lines of Battle Are Drawn," *New York Times*, July 30, 1986; Stuart Taylor, Jr., "Rehnquist Says He Didn't Deter Voters in 60's," *New York Times*, July 31, 1986.
3. George Lardner, Jr., and Al Kamen, "Rehnquist Hearings Leave Question of Veracity," *Washington Post*, August 10, 1986.
4. Statement of Senator Alan K. Simpson, hearing, August 5, 1986.
5. Senate Floor Debate on the Nomination of Justice William Rehnquist to be Chief Justice of the United States, September 11, 1986, *Congressional Record*. For additional context on longstanding complaints against Rehnquist arising from his work on the Jackson memo and poll activities in Phoenix, see John A. Jenkins, "The Partisan," *New York Times Magazine*, March 3, 1985.
6. *Congressional Record*, Senate Floor Debate on the Nomination of Judge William Rehnquist to be Supreme Court Justice of the United States, September 11, 1986; also Lardner and Kamen, "Rehnquist Hearings Leave Questions of Veracity."
7. Rehnquist was confirmed in the end, but with more "nay" votes than any other previous successful nominee in a century, 65–33.
8. Edwin Meese III, address to the American Bar Association annual meeting, July 9, 1985, Sheraton Washington Hotel, Washington, D.C. Meese referred to this approach as a "jurisprudence of original intention."
9. Meese, a former Alameda County, California, prosecutor who had come to Washington with Reagan in 1981, also warned that the contemporary Court was nearing "a drift back toward the radical egalitarianism and expansive civil libertarianism of the [Earl] Warren Court." See also Stuart Taylor, Jr., "Meese, in Bar Group Speech, Criticizes High Court," *New York Times*, July 10, 1985. Meese's views from his book *With Reagan*.
10. *Wallace v. Jaffree*, 472 U.S. 38 (1985), decided by a 6–3 vote. Stevens wrote the opinion; Burger, Rehnquist, and White dissented. *Aguilar v. Felton*, 473 U.S. 402 (1985), decided by a 5–4 vote. Brennan wrote the opinion; Burger, White, Rehnquist, and O'Connor dissented.
11. The *New York Times* columnist Anthony Lewis called Meese's address "the most radical document to come from a legal officer of the United States in generations." Anthony Lewis, "Mr. Meese's Freedom," *New York Times*, September 30, 1985.

12. William J. Brennan, Jr., "The Constitution of the United States: Contemporary Ratification," Symposium, Georgetown University, Washington, D.C., October 12, 1985; Haynes Johnson, "Restoring Balance to the Scales of Justice," *Washington Post*, October 20, 1985; Burt Solomon, "Meese Sets Ambitious Agenda That Challenges Fundamental Legal Beliefs," *National Journal*, November 23, 1985.

13. Amicus curiae brief in *Thornburgh v. American College of Obstetricians and Gynecologists*, No. 84-495.

14. Caroline Rand Herron and Michael Wright, "Senate Panel Blocks Job for Reynolds," *New York Times*, June 30, 1985.

15. Ibid.

16. Author interview with Edwin Meese, December 3, 2007.

17. Author interview with Lee Liberman Otis, August 9, 2007.

18. Robert Bork, "Neutral Principles and Some First Amendment Problems," *Indiana Law Journal* 47 (1971): 1.

19. Stephen J. Adler, "Live Wire on the DC Circuit," *American Lawyer*, March 1985.

20. Wallison, *Ronald Reagan*, 151–53; and Peter J. Wallison, "Memorandum for the File," August 29, 1986, Ronald Reagan Library.

21. James Reston, "The New Hatchet Man," *New York Times*, June 19, 1985.

22. Patrick Buchanan, "Memorandum for the Chief of Staff," July 10, 1985. Ronald Reagan Library.

23. Adler, "Live Wire on the DC Circuit."

24. Frank D. Stella and Ambassador John A. Volpe, National Italian American Foundation, to Reagan, February 2, 1984, Ronald Reagan Library; William Denis Fugazy, Coalition of Italo-American Associations, letter to Reagan, March 20, 1985, Ronald Reagan Library.

25. For example, Thomas Patrick Melady, the president of Sacred Heart University in Bridgeport, Connecticut, wrote to Patrick Buchanan: "American Catholics number around 29–30 percent of the population but have had little or no presence on the U.S. Supreme Court. [Brennan was Catholic but as a supporter of abortion rights had been criticized by Church leaders.] I urge that every consideration be given to correcting this situation if a first class candidate can be found." Melady continued, "I believe that such a person exists," and he gave Scalia's credentials. Thomas Patrick Melady to Patrick Buchanan, August 5, 1985, Ronald Reagan Library.

26. John Roberts to Fred Fielding, April 19, 1983. Roberts said of the proposed intermediate court, "The new court will assuredly not represent the President's judicial philosophy and will have the authority to reverse decisions from courts to which the president has been able to make several appointments that do reflect his judicial philosophy." The proposal for the intermediate court died in Congress. Ronald Reagan Library.

27. "Antonin Scalia," fourteen-page undated memo prepared by Lee Liberman and other Justice Department lawyers as part of Supreme Court selection process. Ronald Reagan Library.

28. Author interview with Edwin Meese, December 3, 2007.

29. Author interview with Antonin Scalia, November 26, 2008.

30. Ibid.

31. Regan, *For the Record*, 333.

32. Wallison, *Ronald Reagan*, 151–53; author interview with Peter Wallison, May 11, 2006.

33. Peter J. Wallison, "Memorandum for the File," August 29, 1986, Ronald Reagan Library.

34. Burger to Powell with Powell notation on letter, June 17, 1986. Lewis F. Powell, Jr. Archives, Washington and Lee University.

35. Author interview with Peter Wallison, May 11, 2006.

36. All quotations are from Senate Judiciary Committee hearing transcript.

37. Antonin Scalia, "The Freedom of Information Act Has No Clothes," *Regulation*, March/April 1982.

38. William Safire, "El Nino's Current," *New York Times*, June 20, 1986.

39. Scalia dissenting in the libel case of *Ollman v. Evans*, 750 F.2d 970 (D.C. Cir. 1984).

40. "Antonin Scalia," fourteen-page undated memo prepared by Lee Liberman and other Justice Department lawyers as part of Supreme Court selection process, Ronald Reagan Library. Scalia had long acknowledged his opposition to *New York Times v. Sullivan*.

41. Transcript of confirmation hearing on the nomination of Antonin Scalia to the U.S. Court of Appeals for the District of Columbia Circuit, Senate Judiciary Committee, August 4, 1982.

42. "Antonin Scalia," fourteen-page undated memo prepared by Lee Liberman and other Justice Department lawyers as part of Supreme Court selection process. Ronald Reagan Library.

43. Phil Gailey, "President Denounces Abortion as 'Murder,' " *New York Times*, June 24, 1986, recounting transcript from *Los Angeles Times* session with President Reagan that was released by the White House.

44. Lee Liberman and other Justice Department lawyers who prepared the report on Scalia presumed he opposed the constitutional right to abortion.

45. Author interview with Laurence Silberman, January 18, 2007.

46. "The Legal Order," by Antonin Scalia, part of a Symposium on Equality and the Law, the 1985 Federalist Society national meeting, printed in the *Harvard Journal of Law & Public Policy* 9, no. 1 (1986).

47. The school board policy had emerged from a collective bargaining deal between the teachers' union and the school board and was intended to increase the percentage of black faculty and provide more black role models for minority students. The case had been brought by eight white teachers who were laid off.

48. Justice O'Connor concurring, *Wygant v. Jackson Board of Education*, 467 U.S. 267 (1986).

49. Transcript, "Hearings Before the Committee on the Judiciary, United States Senate, 99th Congress, 2nd Session, on the Nomination of Judge Antonin Scalia to be Associate Justice of the Supreme Court of the United States," August 5–6, 1986, Washington, D.C., U.S. Government Printing Office.

50. Antonin Scalia, "The Disease as Cure: 'In Order to Get Beyond Racism We Must First Take Account of Race,' " *Washington University Law Quarterly* (1979): 147.

51. Specter, *Passion for Truth*, 318.

52. Ibid.

53. Author interview with Antonin Scalia, November 26, 2007.

54. Benjamin Weiser and Al Kamen, "How Scalia Faced Ethics Issue," *Washington Post*, June 22, 1986.

55. Schwartz, *Packing the Courts*, 51, citing the Rehnquist nomination battle and a June 1986 controversy and narrow vote for Daniel Manion to be a judge on the U.S. Court of Appeals for the Seventh Circuit.

56. President Reagan, "Remarks on the Resignation of Supreme Court Chief Justice Warren E. Burger and the Nominations of William H. Rehnquist to be Chief Justice and Antonin Scalia to Be an Associate Justice," June 17, 1986.

57. Antonin Scalia to Harry Blackmun, September 5, 1986. Harry A. Blackmun files. Library of Congress.

58. The two absent senators on September 17, 1986, were the Republicans Barry Goldwater and Jake Garn, who previously said they supported Scalia.

59. Joseph Biden, *Congressional Record*, September 17, 1986. Biden made a similar comment during the Senate Judiciary Committee vote on Scalia. "I was encouraged by Judge Scalia's statement that he does not have an agenda of cases he is seeking to overturn . . . I do not find him significantly more conservative than Chief Justice Burger." Howard Kurtz, "Senate Panel Approves Rehnquist, 13 to 5; Judiciary Committee Unanimously Endorses Scalia for High Court," *Washington Post*, August 15, 1986.

60. Transcript of Senate Judiciary Committee hearing on the nomination for Ruth Bader Ginsburg to be associate justice of the Supreme Court, July 22, 1993.

7. "IS ANYBODY LISTENING?"

1. Author interviews with Antonin Scalia and Eugene Scalia; chronology of Catherine and Salvatore Eugene's deaths also related by Lenora Panaro; see also *New York Times* obituary of Salvatore Eugene Scalia, January 7, 1986.

2. Author interview with Antonin Scalia, January 28, 2008.

3. Falcone was assassinated in 1992 in a Mafia car bombing.

4. Author interview with Antonin Scalia, November 16, 2007.

5. During the Wednesday business, the justices voted on the cases heard in oral arguments on Monday and Tuesday. On Friday they voted on the Wednesday oral arguments and also took up pending petitions to decide which cases to grant review.

6. Rehnquist was the most junior justice from 1972 to 1975; when Stevens joined, in 1975, Rehnquist moved up one seat; when O'Connor joined, in 1981, Rehnquist moved up one other and remained third to the last to speak until his elevation to chief justice.

7. Rehnquist to Powell, January 18, 1985. Lewis F. Powell, Jr. Archives, Washington and Lee University.

8. Ibid.

9. Rehnquist was appointed on the same day as Lewis Powell but, for purposes of seniority, came after him.

10. Fred Barbash, "Rehnquist's and GOP Platform's Voices in Close Harmony," *Washington Post*, September 2, 1980.

11. Cited in numerous sources, including Horwitz, *The Warren Court and the Pursuit of Justice*, vii; Brennan's first use of the "essential dignity" phrase is often traced to a 1987 speech in Jerusalem; see "Brennan Praises Israel's Protection of Civil Liberties," Associated Press, December 22, 1987.

12. Irons, *Brennan vs. Rehnquist*, 327.

13. Antonin Scalia, statement on the April 15, 2002, death of Byron White.

14. *Thornburgh v. American College of Obstetricians and Gynecologists*, 476 U.S. 747 (1986).

15. Scalia to Blackmun, August 31, 1991. Harry A. Blackmun Papers, Library of Congress.

16. Nan Rehnquist note to Jo Powell, August 2, 1986. Lewis F. Powell, Jr. Archive, Washington and Lee University.

17. Powell letter to his children and their families, November 5, 1986. Lewis F. Powell, Jr. Archive, Washington and Lee University.

18. Jeffries, *Justice Lewis F. Powell, Jr.*

19. Linda Greenhouse, "The Law: At the Bar; Name-Calling in the Supreme Court: When the Justices Vent Their Spleen, Is There a Social Cost?" *New York Times*, July 28, 1989.

20. Scalia "Memorandum to the Conference," September 24, 1986. Lewis F. Powell, Jr. Archive, Washington and Lee University.

21. Author interview with Lee Liberman Otis, August 9, 2007.

22. Author interview with Laurence Silberman, January 18, 2007.

23. See, for context of Justice O'Connor's emerging influence in the mid-1980s, Biskupic, *Sandra Day O'Connor*, 157–82.

24. *United States v. Dunn*, 480 U.S. 294 (1987). Scalia to White, February 23, 1987. Lewis F. Powell, Jr. Archive, Washington and Lee University.

25. *California Federal Savings & Loan Assn. v. Guerra*, 479 U.S. 272 (1987); Scalia wrote Marshall on November 4, 1986, with several requests for changes. Lewis F. Powell, Jr. Archive, Washington and Lee University.

26. *Thompson v. Thompson*, 484 U.S. 174 (1988). Scalia to Marshall, November 17, 1987; Marshall to Scalia, November 18, 1987. Lewis F. Powell, Jr. Archive, Washington and Lee University.

27. *Bowen v. Massachusetts*, 487 U.S. 879 (1988); Brennan to Scalia, June 3, 1988; Scalia to the Conference, June 22, 1988; Brennan to Stevens and Scalia, June 24, 1988. Harry A. Blackmun Papers, Library of Congress.

28. Alan Pell Crawford, "Social Justice," *Dossier*, July 1990.

29. Rehnquist to Stevens, O'Connor, Scalia, Kennedy, and Powell, November 3, 1988. Harry A. Blackmun Papers, Library of Congress.

30. Rehnquist to Stevens, O'Connor, Kennedy, and Powell, November 14, 1988. Lewis F. Powell, Jr. Archive, Washington and Lee University.

31. Author interview with Antonin Scalia, February 9, 2009.

32. When asked about his reluctance to compromise, Scalia said in an interview with the author, "It's not that I was more rigid than Bill Brennan. It's that I had nothing to trade, nothing to deal with. If you're making it up . . . that's why Bill Brennan did . . . Bill Brennan could come and say, 'I'd like to do this new thing that had never occurred before. If the [justice] said, 'Oh, no, Bill, I can't do that.' Then he would say, 'Would you do this [instead]?' "

33. O'Connor agreed with Brennan's bottom-line vote against Johnson but disagreed with Brennan's rationale and wrote a concurring opinion that criticized Brennan's "expansive and ill-defined approach to voluntary affirmative action by public employers."

34. Scalia dissenting *Johnson v. Transportation Agency of Santa Clara County*, 480 U.S. 616 (1987).

35. Author interview with Antonin Scalia, May 1, 2008.

36. *Stanford v. Kentucky*, 492 U.S. 361 (1989); case was overruled in *Roper v. Simmons*, 543 U.S. 551 (2005).

37. *O'Connor v. Ortega*, 480 U.S. 709 (1987).

38. Scalia's opinion was joined in part by Justices O'Connor and Kennedy; only Chief Jus-

tice Rehnquist joined the opinion in its entirety; Justice Stevens filed an opinion concurring in the judgment.

39. Scalia opinion for the plurality, *Michael H. v. Gerald D.*, 491 U.S. 110 (1989).
40. Brennan dissenting, *Michael H. v. Gerald D.*, 491 U.S. 110 (1989).
41. *Cruzan v. Director, Missouri Department of Health*, 497 U.S. 261 (1990).
42. Blackmun notation on Scalia draft dissent, dated June 25, 1988, in *Morrison v. Olson*, No. 87-1279. Harry A. Blackmun Papers, Library of Congress.
43. Typically, dissenting opinions were not announced from the bench, but the justices undertook the attention-getting ritual of reading portions of a dissent aloud if they were particularly angered by a majority ruling and wanted to make sure their views did not get lost in the news of the day. Stevens and White had suggested to Scalia that he use *Morrison v. Olson* for his first dissent from the bench. Author interview with Justice Stevens, June 30, 2007.
44. *Morrison v. Olson*, 487 U.S. 684 (1988); regarding Scalia's reading from the bench, see Stuart Taylor, Jr., "High Court Rulings Hint Move to Right," *New York Times*, July 3, 1988.
45. *Mistretta v. United States*, 488 U.S. 361 (1989).
46. Charles Fried, "Manners Makyth Man: The Prose Style of Justice Scalia," *Harvard Journal of Law & Public Policy* 16 (1993): 529.
47. Erwin Chemerinsky, "The Jurisprudence of Justice Scalia: A Critical Appraisal," *University of Hawaii Law Review* 22 (2000): 385. For an overview of Scalia's rhetorical style, see also Yury Kapgan, "Of Golf and Ghouls: The Prose Style of Justice Antonin Scalia," *Journal of Legal Writing Institute* (2003): 72.
48. *Edwards v. Aguillard*, 482 U.S. 578 (1987).
49. Scalia, joined by Rehnquist, dissenting in *Edwards v. Aguillard*.
50. Scalia dissenting in *Lee v. Weisman*, 505 U.S. 577 (1992).
51. *Lemon v. Kurtzman*, 403 U.S. 602 (1971).
52. *Edwards v. Aguillard*, 482 U.S. 578 (1987).
53. Scalia concurring in *Lamb's Chapel v. Center Moriches Union Free School District*, 508 U.S. 384 (1993). "At least five sitting justices have criticized the *Lemon* formulation," Scalia told White in a memo dated May 17, 1993, explaining why he was writing a separate concurring statement. Harry A. Blackmun Papers, Library of Congress.
54. Justice Kennedy, May 4, 1993, note to the conference siding with Scalia. Souter, May 5, 1993, note siding with Stevens and, effectively, White. Blackmun to White, May 10, 1993: "I hope you will retain the paragraph and that you will not accede to the request of the Nino-Tony-Clarence trio. I agree with David's comments in his letter to you of May 1." Harry A. Blackmun Papers, Library of Congress.
55. Scalia's "ghoul in the night" concurring statement was signed by Thomas and endorsed in a separate statement by Kennedy.
56. Justice White in footnote 7 of *Lamb's Chapel v. Center Moriches Union Free School District*, 508 U.S. 384 (1993).
57. *Board of Education of Kiryas Joel Village School District v. Grumet*, 512 U.S. 687 (1994); Blackmun record of vote and discussion, April 1, 1994. Harry A. Blackmun Papers, Library of Congress.
58. Transcript, "Hearings Before the Committee on the Judiciary," August 5, 1986.
59. Scalia plurality opinion, *Employment Division, Department of Human Resources of Oregon v. Smith*, 494 U.S. 872 (1990).

60. Ibid.; O'Connor to Blackmun, April 17, 1990. Harry A. Blackmun Papers, Library of Congress.
61. Scalia speaking to ACLU annual conference, "Conversation About Civil Liberties with Supreme Court Justice Scalia," October 15, 2006, Marriott Wardman Park, Washington, D.C.
62. David G. Savage, "Intense, Feisty Scalia Gives High Court a Sharp Edge," *Los Angeles Times*, July 9, 1990.
63. Antonin Scalia, "Is Law Too Complicated for General Media to Cover?" *Chicago Daily Law Bulletin*, October 1, 1990. (Excerpt from August speech Scalia gave to the Los Angeles World Affairs Council and Pepperdine University School of Law.)
64. Author interview with Justice Scalia, February 18, 2009.
65. Jeffrey Rosen, "The Leader of the Opposition," *New Republic*, January 18, 1993.
66. Alex Kozinski, "My Pizza with Nino," *Cardozo Law Review* 12 (1991): 1583.
67. Justice Scalia concurring in part and dissenting in part, *Pennsylvania v. Union Gas Co.*, 491 U.S. 1 (1989).
68. Kozinski, "My Pizza with Nino," 1583.
69. Joan Biskupic, "Congress Keeps Eye on Justices as Court Watches Hill's Words," *Congressional Quarterly Weekly Report*, October 5, 1991; see also Joan Biskupic, "Scalia Sees No Justice in Trying to Judge Intent of Congress on a Law," *Washington Post*, May 11, 1993.
70. Joe Morgenstern, "Scalia the Terrible," *Playboy*, July 1, 1993.

8. DILEMMAS OF RACE
1. Supreme Court transcript, *McCleskey v. Kemp*, No. 84-6811.
2. Kenneth B. Noble, "High Court to Decide Whether Death Penalty Discriminates Against Blacks," *New York Times*, March 23, 1987.
3. Antonin Scalia, "The Disease as Cure: 'In Order to Get Beyond Racism We Must First Take Account of Race,' " *Washington University Law Quarterly* (1979): 147.
4. Views around the table based on notes by Powell and Blackmun in *McCleskey v. Kemp*, No. 84-6811. Lewis F. Powell, Jr. Archive, Washington and Lee University; Harry A. Blackmun Papers, Library of Congress.
5. Powell draft opinion November 13, 1986, *McCleskey v. Kemp*. Lewis F. Powell, Jr. Archive, Washington and Lee University.
6. Scalia, "Memorandum to the Conference," January 6, 1987. Lewis F. Powell, Jr. Archive, Washington and Lee University.
7. Author interview with Antonin Scalia, May 1, 2008. Dennis D. Dorin, a professor of political science at the University of North Carolina, wrote later of Scalia's sentiment: "Scalia's memo . . . suggested strongly that he was not willing to stop with Twentieth Century cases. He seemingly would go back to the roots of both American criminal justice and Equal Protection Clause doctrine to undermine even so established a case as *Strauder v. West Virginia*. Indeed, viewed in context, the Scalia Memorandum may well have championed a version of Equal Protection jurisprudence even to the philosophical right of Justice Henry Brown's in *Plessy v. Ferguson!*" Dennis D. Dorin, "Far Right of the Mainstream: Racism, Rights, and Remedies from the Perspective of Justice Antonin Scalia's *McCleskey* Memorandum," *Mercer Law Review* (1994): 1035.
8. McCleskey returned to the Supreme Court four years later in a final appeal, which was rejected. *McCleskey v. Zant*, 499 U.S. 467 (1991).

9. Antonin Scalia, "The Disease as Cure," 147.

10. Jeffries, *Justice Lewis F. Powell, Jr.*, 451–52.

11. *Batson v. Kentucky*, 476 U.S. 79 (1986).

12. Roger K. Lowe, "Convicted Murderer Loses Fight," *Columbus Dispatch*, October 18, 1994.

13. *Holland v. Illinois*, 493 U.S. 474 (1990).

14. *Snyder v. Louisiana*, 552 U.S. __ (2008).

15. Scalia and Clarence Thomas dissented in *Snyder v. Louisiana*, and Thomas wrote for the pair. The majority opinion by Samuel Alito scrutinized and rejected explanations offered by the prosecutor for striking blacks. The Court did not refer to the Simpson-related remarks, which Snyder's lawyer, Stephen Bright, contended showed that the prosecutor wanted an all-white jury before which he could compare Snyder's crime to Simpson's alleged offense.

16. Author interviews with Antonin Scalia, May 1, 2008, and February 18, 2009.

17. Supreme Court transcript, *Richmond v. J.A. Croson Co.*, No. 87-998.

18. Linda Greenhouse, "Court Bars a Plan Set Up to Provide Jobs to Minorities," *New York Times*, January 24, 1989.

19. Scalia concurring in *Richmond v. Croson*, 488 U.S. 469 (1989).

20. Marshall dissenting in *Richmond v. Croson*.

21. Ibid.

22. Antonin Scalia, "The Disease as Cure," 147.

23. Author interviews with Antonin Scalia, May 1, 2008, and February 18, 2009.

24. Ibid.

25. Klarman, *From Jim Crow to Civil Rights*, 450.

26. Randall L. Kennedy, "Civil Rights vs. Supreme Court: A New and Historic Battleground," *Los Angeles Times*, June 25, 1989.

27. Among the rulings Congress sought to reverse were *Wards Cove Packing Co. Inc. v. Atonio*, holding that in cases brought under Title VII of the 1964 Civil Rights Act, the burden was on the plaintiff to prove an employer had no business necessity for a practice with discriminatory effects; *Martin v. Wilks*, holding that non-parties to a court-approved affirmative action plan could challenge the plan as reverse discrimination, even years after it was adopted; *Lorance v. American Telephone and Telegraph Technologies*, ruling that seniority plans could not be challenged as discriminatory unless complaints were filed soon after the plans were adopted; *Patterson v. McLean Credit Union*, finding that an 1866 law forbidding discrimination in contracts applied only to hiring agreements, not on-the-job bias; *Jett v. Dallas Independent School District*, declaring that state and local officials could not be held liable for discrimination unless the alleged violation was part of an official policy. *Congressional Quarterly Almanac*, 1991.

28. *Wards Cove Packing Co. v. Atonio*, 490 U.S. 642 (1989); Joan Biskupic, "How an Era Ended in Civil Rights Law," *Washington Post*, May 24, 1993, detailing how the then newly opened files of Thurgood Marshall showed how Scalia pushed for a hard stance in the decision that made it easier for employers to fend off complaints about ostensibly neutral practices that had a disparate impact on minorities.

29. Joan Biskupic, "Provisions: Civil Rights Act of 1991," *Congressional Quarterly Weekly Report*, December 7, 1991.

30. "Bork's Path: Nomination, Rejection, Resignation," Associated Press, January 14, 1988.

31. Bronner, *Battle for Justice*, 314.

32. Linda Greenhouse, "Bork Is Back in Old Role of Intellectual Crusader," *New York Times*, January 17, 1988.

33. Joan Biskupic, "Bork, Uncorked: The Judge Holds the Supreme Court in Contempt," *Washington Post*, March 16, 1997.

34. Steven V. Roberts, "Ginsburg Withdraws Name as Supreme Court Nominee, Citing Marijuana 'Clamor,' " *New York Times*, November 8, 1987.

35. Facts of Brenda Patterson's claim drawn from briefs in *Patterson v. McLean Credit Union*, No. 87–107.

36. *Runyon v. McCrary*, 427 U.S. 160 (1976).

37. Blackmun notes from the justices' conference in *Patterson v. McLean Credit Union*, No. 87–107, October 14, 1988. Harry A. Blackmun Papers, Library of Congress.

38. Blackmun dissenting from April 26, 1988, order for reargument in *Patterson v. McLean Credit Union*.

39. Stevens dissenting from April 26, 1988, order for reargument in *Patterson v. McLean Credit Union*.

40. Kennedy to Rehnquist, White, O'Connor, and Scalia, April 8, 1988. Harry A. Blackmun Papers, Library of Congress.

41. See, for example, "Casting a Shadow Over Civil Rights," *New York Times* editorial, April 27, 1988.

42. Supreme Court transcript, *Patterson v. McLean Credit Union*, No. 87–107 reargument.

43. Brennan dissenting, *Patterson v. McLean Credit Union*, 491 U.S. 164 (1989).

44. For an extensive discussion of conservative clerks' influence on justices during the 1988–89 term, written by a former clerk to Justice Blackmun, see Edward Lazarus, *Closed Chambers: The First Eyewitness Account of the Epic Struggles Inside the Supreme Court* (New York: Random House, 1998).

45. For internal negotiations in *Patterson v. McLean Credit Union* based on papers of Thurgood Marshall, see Joan Biskupic, "How an Era Ended in Civil Rights Law," *Washington Post*, March 24, 1993.

46. Scalia joined O'Connor's opinion for the majority in *Metro Broadcasting v. Federal Communications Commission*, 497 U.S. 547 (1990), which said the ruling undercut *Richmond v. Croson*: "This departure marks a renewed toleration of racial classifications and a repudiation of our recent affirmation that the Constitution's equal protection guarantees extend equally to all citizens."

47. The 1982 amendments to the Voting Rights Act were intended to ensure that any voting practice that had the effect of discriminating against racial minorities was deemed unlawful, irrespective of the intention of local officials. The amendments responded to the Court's decision in *City of Mobile v. Bolden*, 446 U.S. 55 (1980); that decision had said the original Voting Rights Act covered intentional discrimination only.

48. *Chisom v. Roemer*, 501 U.S. 380 (1991).

49. Blackmun to the conference, May 21, 1991. Harry A. Blackmun Papers, Library of Congress.

50. "Tribute to Justice Antonin Scalia," by John C. Jeffries, Jr., *New York University Annual Survey of American Law* 62 (2006): 11.

51. *Johnson v. Texas*, 491 U.S. 397 (1989) and *United States v. Eichman*, 496 U.S. 310 (1990); Scalia joined Brennan's majority opinion in both cases.

52. See, for example, *Rust v. Sullivan*, 500 U.S. 173 (1991), and *Barnes v. Glen Theatre*, 501 U.S. 560 (1991).

53. During his Senate Judiciary Committee confirmation hearings, Souter had echoed some of Brennan's sentiment about personal liberty and dignity. Souter had told senators that his five years on a state trial court, before joining New Hampshire's top court, had left him with two lessons that he believed would help him as a justice. One lesson was that "at the end of our task some human being is going to be affected, some human life is going to be changed in some way by what we do." The second lesson he learned was that people's behavior would be influenced by Court rulings. "We had better use every power of our minds and our hearts and our beings to get those rulings right."

54. President George H. W. Bush press conference on the nomination of Clarence Thomas to the Supreme Court, July 1, 1991, Kennebunkport, Maine.

55. Ibid.

56. Thomas, *My Grandfather's Son*, 216.

57. "Clarence Thomas Wins Senate Confirmation," 1991 *Congressional Quarterly Alamanac*, 274–85.

58. Ibid.

59. Jay Sharbutt, "Far More People Watching Hearings Than Playoffs," Associated Press, October 13, 1991; Jane Gross, "The Thomas Nomination: Americans Riveted by Lesson in Civics," *New York Times*, October 12, 1991.

60. Thomas, *My Grandfather's Son*; see also Joan Biskupic, "Thomas Is Bolder, Confident—Outside Court," *USA Today*, January 31, 2001.

61. The eleven Democratic senators who voted to confirm Thomas were David L. Boren, Okla.; John B. Breaux, La.; Dennis DeConcini, Ariz.; Alan J. Dixon, Ill.; Jim Exon, Neb.; Wyche Fowler, Jr., Ga.; Ernest F. Hollings, S.C.; J. Bennett Johnston, La.; Sam Nunn, Ga.; Charles S. Robb, Va.; and Richard C. Shelby, Ala.

62. Powell to Scalia and wife, Maureen, December 10, 1991. Lewis F. Powell, Jr. Archive, Washington and Lee University.

63. Author interview with Clarence Thomas, June 24, 2009; Neil Lewis, "Justice Thomas Suggests Critics' Views Are Racist," *New York Times*, July 30, 1998.

64. Ann Hubbard to Blackmun. Harry A. Blackmun Papers, Library of Congress.

65. *Holder v. Hall*, 512 U.S. 874 (1994).

66. Stevens dissenting in *Holder v. Hall*.

67. *Adarand Constructors v. Peña*, 515 U.S. 200 (1995).

68. Ibid.

69. Thomas concurring in *Adarand Constructors v. Peña*.

70. Joan Biskupic, "Scalia, Thomas Stand Apart on the Right: Supreme Court Conservatives Challenge Majority's Views of the Law," *Washington Post*, June 24, 1994.

71. Michael A. Fletcher and Kevin Merida, "Jurist Embraces Image as Hard-Line Holdout," *Washington Post*, October 11, 2004; author interview with Clarence Thomas, June 24, 2009.

72. Author interviews with Antonin Scalia, May 1, 2008, and February 18, 2009.

73. Breyer writing for the majority in *Hunt v. Cromartie*, 532 U.S. 234 (2001).

74. *Grutter v. Bollinger*, 539 U.S. 306 (2003).

75. Scalia dissenting in *Grutter v. Bollinger*. Separately, Thomas penned a dissenting statement that began with an 1865 passage by Frederick Douglass that said in part, "What I ask for the Negro is not benevolence, not pity, not sympathy, but simply *justice*."

76. *Parents Involved in Community Schools v. Seattle School District No. 1*, 551 U.S. 701 (2007).

77. In a separate section of his opinion in *Parents Involved in Community Schools v. Seattle School District No. 1*, 551 U.S. 701 (2007), Roberts, joined by Scalia, Thomas, and Alito, but not Kennedy, broadly rejected school district efforts for "racial balance." He spurned arguments that such efforts are inclusive, calling them "exclusive" because they deny some parents their choice of school for a child. In his separate opinion, Kennedy said the door is still open to considering the racial makeup of schools broadly and not in a way that singles out individual students. Kennedy said that school administrators could, for example, pursue racial diversity by strategically considering where to build a school or where to allocate resources.

78. Michigan voters approved a proposition against affirmative action in education in November 2006. Tamar Lewin, "Michigan Rejects Affirmative Act, and Backers Sue," *New York Times*, November 9, 2006.

79. Stephen L. Carter, "Affirmative Distraction," *New York Times*, July 6, 2008.

80. Brisbin, *Justice Antonin Scalia and the Conservative Revival*, 180.

81. Author interview with Antonin Scalia, February 18, 2009.

9. PASSIONS OF HIS MIND

1. William J. Brennan, a Catholic, and William H. Rehnquist, a Lutheran, were memorialized at St. Matthew's Cathedral.

2. Author interviews with Eugene Scalia, June 8, 2007, and June 29, 2007.

3. Ibid.

4. Author interview with Antonin Scalia, January 28, 2008.

5. Author interview with Leonard Leo, January 2, 2007.

6. Author interview with Arthur Gajarsa, July 27, 2007.

7. Ibid.

8. Roger B. Taney, Edward D. White, Joseph McKenna, Pierce Butler, Frank Murphy, and William Brennan. (Sherman Minton, who was appointed in 1949, converted to Catholicism after he retired from the Court.)

9. Anthony Kennedy, Clarence Thomas, John Roberts, and Samuel Alito would in time serve with Scalia. The nomination of Sonia Sotomayor, also a Catholic, was confirmed by the Senate on August 6, 2009.

10. Lesley Stahl interview with Antonin Scalia on *60 Minutes*, April 27, 2008. (Catholic teaching forbids artificial contraception.)

11. Tim Russert interview with Antonin Scalia, May 2, 2008.

12. Stahl interview, *60 Minutes*, April 27, 2008.

13. Anthony DeStefano, "Priest Profile: Fr. Paul Scalia," *Priests for Life* 11, no. 2 (March/April 2001).

14. Penny Brown Roberts, "Scalia: Faithful Live for Christ; Supreme Court Justice Urges Christians to Live Fearlessly," *The Advocate*, January 23, 2005.

15. Barbara A. Perry wrote, for example, "In fact, most Catholics on the Court have exhibited an exaggerated degree of religious impartiality (as did President Kennedy in the White House)—perhaps, in part, as a defense mechanism against the charges of nativists and other anti-Catholic bigots." Barbara A. Perry, "The Life and Death of the 'Catholic Seat' on the United States Supreme Court," *Journal of Law and Politics* 6 (1989–90): 56.

16. Linda Greenhouse, "William Brennan, 91, Dies: Gave Court Liberal Vision," *New York Times*, July 25, 1997.

17. Author interview with Antonin Scalia, August 26, 2008.
18. Joan Biskupic, "Scalia Makes the Case for Christianity: Justice Proclaims Belief in Miracles," *Washington Post*, April 10, 1996.
19. Stuart Taylor, Jr., "Justice Scalia's Persecution Complex," *American Lawyer*, June 1997.
20. Michael Stokes Paulsen and Steffen N. Johnson, "Scalia's Sermonette," *Notre Dame Law Review* 72 (1997): 863.
21. Laurel J. Sweet, "Judicial Intemperance: Scalia Flips Message to Doubting Thomases," *Boston Herald*, March 27, 2006.
22. "Scalia Calls for Justice: Jurist Fires Back," *Boston Herald*, March 29, 2006.
23. "Here We Get the Last Word," *Boston Herald*, March 30, 2006.
24. Author interview with Antonin Scalia, February 9, 2009.
25. Robin Toner, "The Supreme Court's Catholic Majority," *New York Times* On the Record online column, April 25, 2007.
26. Author interview with Antonin Scalia, February 9, 2009.
27. The Pew Forum on Religion and Public Life, January 25, 2002. Transcript posted at http://pewforum.org/deathpenalty/resources/transcript3.php. Also author interview with Antonin Scalia, May 1, 2008.
28. George Kannar, "The Constitutional Catechism of Antonin Scalia," *Yale Law Journal* 99 (1990): 1297.
29. *Planned Parenthood of Southeastern Pennsylvania v. Casey*, 505 U.S. 833 (1992).
30. Author interview with Antonin Scalia, February 9, 2009.
31. Laura Sessions and Ann Devroy, "Bush Cites Abortion 'Tragedy' in Call to 67,000 Protestors," *Washington Post*, January 24, 1989.
32. Ethan Bronner, "Abortion: An American Divide: Church Activism Increases," *Boston Globe*, April 3, 1989.
33. Supreme Court transcript, *Webster v. Reproductive Health Services*, No. 88-605.
34. Blackmun notes at April 28, 1989, conference. Harry A. Blackmun Papers, Library of Congress.
35. Blackmun dissenting, *Webster v. Reproductive Health Services*, 492 U.S. 490 (1989).
36. *West Virginia State Board of Education v. Barnette*, 319 U.S. 624 (1943).
37. Powell to O'Connor, July 10, 1989. Lewis F. Powell, Jr. Archive, Washington and Lee University.
38. The Pew Forum on Religion and Public Life, January 25, 2002. Transcript posted at http://pewforum.org/deathpenalty/resources/transcript3.php.
39. See Perry, "The Life and Death of the 'Catholic Seat' on the United States Supreme Court," 56.
40. Author interview with Antonin Scalia, June 24, 2008.
41. First draft circulated by O'Connor, Kennedy, and Souter, June 3, 1992. Harry A. Blackmun Papers, Library of Congress.
42. Evans and Novak, "Professor Sways Justice Kennedy," *Chicago Sun-Times*, September 4, 1992.
43. Joan Biskupic, "Changing Faith: Protestants No Longer Rule the High Court," *Washington Post*, August 4, 1996.
44. *Stenberg v. Carhart*, 530 U.S. 914 (2000).
45. *Gonzales v. Carhart*, 550 U.S. 124 (2007).
46. http://uchicagolaw.typepad.com/faculty/2007/our_faithbased_.html, April 20, 2007; version reprinted in Geoffrey R. Stone, "Our Faith-Based Justices," *Chicago Tribune*, April 30, 2007.

47. See, for example, *Griswold v. Connecticut*, 381 U.S. 479 (1965).

48. Author interviews with Antonin Scalia, May 1, 2008, and February 9, 2009.

49. http://uchicagolaw.typepad.com/faculty/2007/our_faithbased_.html, April 20, 2007.

50. Robert Barnes, "Did Justices' Catholicism Play Part in Abortion Ruling?" *Washington Post*, April 30, 2007.

51. Robin Toner, "The Supreme Court's Catholic Majority," *New York Times* On the Record online column, April 25, 2007.

52. Author interview with Geoffrey Stone, April 23, 2009.

53. Scalia joined Rehnquist's opinion for the majority in *Zelman v. Simmons-Harris*, 536 U.S. 639 (2002), allowing public tuition aid in a "voucher" program for Ohio parents sending their children to private schools, including religious ones.

54. Kathleen Sullivan, "Justice Scalia and the Religion Clauses," *Hawaii Law Review* 22 (2000): 449.

55. *Locke v. Davey*, 540 U.S. 712 (2004), Rehnquist decision for the majority and Scalia dissenting.

56. By a separate 5–4 vote, the justices—including Scalia—allowed a six-foot Ten Commandments monument on the grounds of the Texas capitol, largely because the stone had been there for four decades.

57. Thomas B. Colby, "A Constitutional Hierarchy of Religions? Justice Scalia, the Ten Commandments, and the Future of the Establishment Clause," *Northwestern University Law Review* 100 (2006): 1097.

58. Author interview with Antonin Scalia, May 1, 2008.

59. Julia Vitullo-Martin, "Justice & Antonin Scalia," *Commonweal*, March 28, 2003.

60. Antonin Scalia, "Morality, Pragmatism, and the Legal Order," *Harvard Journal of Law and Public Policy* 9 (1986): 123.

61. Author interview with Antonin Scalia, January 28, 2008.

10. "A COUNTRY I DO NOT RECOGNIZE"

1. Timothy M. Phelps, "Supreme Test for Gay Rights," *Newsday*, October 11, 1995; John Brinkley, "Gays Gather at Supreme Court: Protesters Take Stand Against Amendment 2 as Justices Prepare to Hear Lawyers Argue For, Against," *Rocky Mountain News*, October 10, 1995.

2. Kris Newcomer, "Judges Often Out of Touch, Scalia Says: High Court Justice Says Social Problems Should Be Left Up to Legislators," *Rocky Mountain News*, September 7, 1995.

3. Justice O'Connor was in the majority in *Bowers v. Hardwick*, 478 U.S. 186 (1986), to uphold a Georgia ban on sodomy; Kennedy voted in *Beller v. Middendorf*, 632 F.2d 788 (9th Cir. 1980), to uphold a navy exclusion of homosexuals.

4. Joan Biskupic, "Gay Rights Case Closely Watched at High Court," *Washington Post*, October 10, 1995.

5. Murdoch and Price, *Courting Justice*, 466.

6. Supreme Court transcript, *Romer v. Evans*, No. 94-1039.

7. Richard L. Berke, "A Missing Issue in the Big Race," *New York Times*, October 13, 1996.

8. Among the places Scalia spoke or taught in 1996 were Rome, Vienna, and Malta. Financial Disclosure Report for Calendar Year 1996, Administrative Office of the U.S. Courts. See also Timothy M. Phelps, "Justices Like to Hit the Road: Trips to Exotic Places to Lecture, Earn Extra," *Newsday*, September 11, 1995.

9. Patrick Buchanan speech, Republican National Convention, August 17, 1992.
10. Joan Biskupic, "Court Strikes Down Colorado's Anti-Gay Amendment," *Washington Post*, May 21, 1996.
11. Scalia dissenting, *Romer v. Evans*, 517 U.S. 620 (1996).
12. Transcript of *The Lawyers Guild Show*, KPFK-FM Radio, Pacifica Foundation, June 13, 1996.
13. Scalia dissenting, *United States v. Virginia*, 518 U.S. 515 (1996); Rehnquist was in the majority; Thomas did not participate in the case, because he had a son who attended Virginia Military Institute.
14. Scalia dissenting, *Board of County Commissioners, Wabaunsee County, Kansas v. Umbehr*, 518 U.S. 668 (1996).
15. Author interview with Antonin Scalia, May 1, 2008.
16. Blackmun to Scalia, July 2, 1996. Harry A. Blackmun Papers, Library of Congress.
17. Scalia to Blackmun, July 2, 1996. Harry A. Blackmun Papers, Library of Congress.
18. Author interview with Antonin Scalia, May 1, 2008.
19. Joan Biskupic, "In Terms of Moral Indignation, Justice Scalia Is a Majority of One," *Washington Post*, June 30, 1996. See also Richard Carelli, "Supreme Court Justice Accentuates Traditional Values in Law," Associated Press, May 1, 2000, quoting Jay Sekulow of the American Center for Law and Justice, founded by the televangelist Pat Robertson: "I think it's important for [Scalia] to remind us that morality cannot be divorced from the law." Also quoting Erwin Chemerinsky, a University of Southern California law professor critical of Scalia's approach: "The irony is he professes that judges shouldn't be making moral judgments, and he as much as any justice in American history is all about articulating moral judgments."
20. Peter Huber introduction of Antonin Scalia at Wriston Lecture, Manhattan Institute for Policy Research. Transcript at www.manhattan-institute.org/html/wl1997.htm.
21. Joan Biskupic, "In Terms of Moral Indignation, Justice Scalia Is a Majority of One."
22. *National Endowment for the Arts v. Finley*, 524 U.S. 569 (1998); Joan Biskupic, " 'Decency' Can Be Weighed in Arts Agency's Funding," *Washington Post*, June 26, 1998.
23. Scalia concurring, *National Endowment for the Arts v. Finley*, 524 U.S. 569 (1998).
24. Supreme Court transcript, *Boy Scouts of America v. Dale*, No. 99-699.
25. *Boy Scouts of America v. Dale*, 530 U.S. 640 (2000); opinion for the Court written by Rehnquist and joined by O'Connor, Scalia, Kennedy, and Thomas.
26. See, for example, Joan Biskupic, "For Gays, Tolerance Translates to Rights: Legal Gains Reflect Shift in Attitudes," *Washington Post*, November 5, 1999; Joan Biskupic, "Court's Opinion on Gay Rights Reflects Trends," *USA Today*, July 18, 2003.
27. *Lawrence v. Texas*, 539 U.S. 558 (2003).
28. Joan Biskupic, "Decision Represents an Enormous Turn in the Law," *USA Today*, June 27, 2003.
29. O'Connor concurring, *Lawrence v. Texas*, 539 U.S. 558 (2003).
30. Scalia dissenting, *Lawrence v. Texas*, 539 U.S. 558 (2003).
31. *Goodridge v. Department of Public Health*, 798 N.E. 2d 941 (Mass. 2003).
32. Margaret Talbot, "Supreme Confidence: The Jurisprudence of Justice Antonin Scalia," *New Yorker*, March 28, 2005.
33. Maureen Dowd, "Nino's Opera Bouffe," *New York Times*, June 29, 2003.
34. James Taranto, "With Extreme Prejudice," www.opinionjournal.com/best/?id=110003692.

35. Bruce Ackerman, "High Court, High Stakes: On Morality, Regulation, and Privacy, the Right Seeks a Supreme Court Revolution," *The American Prospect*, 2005.

36. Joan Biskupic, "Gay Sex Ban Struck Down," *USA Today*, June 27, 2003; Biskupic, "Decision Represents an Enormous Turn in the Law."

37. Anne Gearan, "Scalia Ridicules Court's Gay Sex Ruling," Associated Press, October 24, 2003.

38. David Forte, "Illiberal Court: The United States Supreme Court Is Engaged in the Process of Undermining Democracy," *National Review*, July 29, 1996.

39. Jessica Garrison, Cara Mia DiMassa, and Richard C. Paddock, "Voters Approve Proposition 8 Banning Same-Sex Marriages," *Los Angeles Times*, November 5, 2008.

40. Stephen A. Newman, "Political Advocacy on the Supreme Court: The Damaging Rhetoric of Antonin Scalia," *New York Law School Law Review* 51 (2006–07).

41. Bork, ed., *A Country I Do Not Recognize*, xi.

11. *BUSH V. GORE*: NOT OVER IT

1. Antonin Scalia, "The Rule of Law as the Law of Rules," *University of Chicago Law Review* 56 (1989): 1175.

2. Scalia's 2001 Financial Disclosure Report for calendar year 2000 showed him earning for speeches and appearances: $5,000 from the University of Denver College of Law; $7,000 from Dickinson School of Law; $4,000 from the University of Idaho College of Law; and $5,000 from the University of Louisville School of Law.

3. "Dinner," features item, *The Times* (London), July 25, 2000.

4. David Johnson, "Audience Packs Room for Justice: Supreme Court Justice Antonin Scalia Gives Talk," *Lewiston Morning Tribune*, September 8, 2000.

5. Hannelore Sudermann, "Scalia Explains His Style: U.S. Supreme Court Justice Says He Sticks to the Original Intent of the U.S. Constitution," *Spokesman Review*, September 8, 2000.

6. Dan Balz, "Race Still Too Close to Call: Most Polls Show Bush Ahead, but Some Find Gore Gaining Ground," *Washington Post*, November 7, 2000; Chris Mondics, "Polls Predict a Drawn-Out Fight. A Very Late Night?" *Philadelphia Inquirer*, November 7, 2000.

7. Joan Biskupic, "Who's Next for the Court? Election May Decide Who Gets to Name up to 3 New Justices," *USA Today*, September 28, 2000; David G. Savage, "More Than Just the Oval Office at Stake; Supreme Court: The Next President's Appointments Could Shape the Outcome of Decisions for Decades," *Los Angeles Times*, October 2, 2000.

8. Jodi Enda, "Bush, Gore and Nation Wait as Historic Recount Begins," *Philadelphia Inquirer*, November 9, 2000.

9. Transcript of the *Today* show, NBC News, November 9, 2000.

10. Biskupic, *Sandra Day O'Connor*, 303.

11. Peter Nicholas and Ron Hutcheson, "As Partisans Protest Election in Florida, the Recount Continues," *Philadelphia Inquirer*, November 26, 2000.

12. Evan Thomas and Michael Isikoff, "War of the Weary: Chants and Chads: Riotous Politics and Human Stress Turn Florida into a Wild Circus," *Newsweek*, December 4, 2000.

13. *Gore v. Harris*, No. SC00-2431. December 8, 2000. The state supreme court, however, designated a lower court judge to oversee ballot disputes.

14. Scalia concurring statement to court order of December 9, 2000, stopping the recounts and ordering oral arguments in the case of *Bush v. Gore.*

15. Jack M. Balkin, "Bush v. Gore and the Boundary between Law and Politics," *Yale Law Journal* 110 (2001): 1707.

16. Bob Woodward and Charles Lane, "Scalia Takes a Leading Role in Case," *Washington Post,* December 11, 2000.

17. Stevens, dissenting from December 9, 2000, order to stop the Florida recounts and set oral arguments in *Bush v. Gore.*

18. Supreme Court transcript, *George W. Bush and Richard Cheney v. Albert Gore, Jr., et al.,* No. 00-949.

19. Boies, *Courting Justice,* 443.

20. Scalia dissenting, *United States v. Virginia,* 518 U.S. 515 (1996).

21. In the preceding two years, the Supreme Court had ruled that state governments could not be sued in federal courts for violations of federal law barring age discrimination or for infringing U.S. patent law. It had also struck down a federal law allowing rape victims to sue their attackers in federal court for money damages. *Kimel v. Florida Board of Regents,* 528 U.S. 62 (2000); *College Savings Bank v. Florida Prepaid Postsecondary Ed. Expense Fund,* 527 U.S. 666 (1999); and *United States v. Morrison,* 529 U.S. 598 (2000).

22. At the time, some Bush supporters pointed to the fact that Souter and Breyer also were troubled by the varying standards in ballot counting and termed the overall *Bush v. Gore* ruling 7–2. Scalia took the same tack in later years. But the key question in the case was the remedy—that is, whether to keep the recounts going. Souter and Breyer vigorously dissented on that question and said the recounts should continue.

23. Toobin, *Too Close to Call,* 266–67.

24. Breyer dissenting, *Bush v. Gore,* invoking the specter of the 1857 *Dred Scott v. Sandford* decision.

25. See Joan Biskupic, "The Rehnquist Court: They Want to Be Known as Jurists, Not Activists," *Washington Post,* January 9, 2000.

26. Michael Klarman, "Bush v. Gore Through the Lens of Constitutional History," *California Law Review* 89 (2001): 1721.

27. Garry Wills, "The Making of the President, 2000," *New York Times,* April 1, 2001.

28. Michael W. McConnell, "A Muddled Ruling," *Wall Street Journal,* December 14, 2000.

29. Transcript of Charlie Rose interview with Antonin Scalia, June 20, 2008.

30. Klarman, "Bush v. Gore Through the Lens of Constitutional History," 1721.

31. Mary McGrory, "Supreme Travesty of Justice," *Washington Post,* December 14, 2000; Richard K. Neumann, Jr., "Conflicts of Interest in *Bush v. Gore*: Did Some Justices Vote Illegally?" *Georgetown Journal of Legal Ethics* 16 (2007): 375. John Scalia, the justice's second son, began working in the firm's Tysons Corner (Virginia) office on January 10, 2001, according to a Greenberg Traurig press release.

32. See, for example, Robert L. Jackson, "Calls for Recusal of Thomas, Scalia Are Undue, Experts Say," *Los Angeles Times,* December 13, 2000.

33. Author interview with Antonin Scalia, June 24, 2008.

34. Author interview with Antonin Scalia, August 26, 2008.

35. Transcript of Lesley Stahl interview with Antonin Scalia, April 27, 2008.

36. Transcript of Brian Lamb interview with Antonin Scalia, May 4, 2008.

37. Richard L. Berke, "Examining the Vote: Who Won Florida? The Answer Emerges, but Surely Not the Final Word," *New York Times,* November 12, 2001.

38. Dennis Cauchon and Jim Drinkard, "Special Report: Florida Voter Errors Cost Gore the Election; Bush Still Prevails in Recount of All Disrupted Ballots, Using Two Most Common Standards," *USA Today*, May 11, 2001.

39. Author interview with John Paul Stevens, March 6, 2009.

40. Author interview with Antonin Scalia, August 26, 2008.

12. "QUACK, QUACK"

1. Chronology based on news reports at the time; Justice Scalia's March 18, 2004, memorandum; and author interviews.

2. "Justice's Ethics Questioned," *Newsday*, January 18, 2004.

3. Al Kamen, "Yuletide Greetings from Bush, Cheney Families," *Washington Post*, December 15, 2003.

4. "Cheney, Scalia Visit South La. for Duck Hunt," Associated Press, January 8, 2004; this account of the trip noted that Sheriff David Naquin said that Cheney and Scalia both shot their bag limits on the first full day of the hunt, three mallards and three teal.

5. David G. Savage, "Trip with Cheney Puts Ethics Spotlight on Scalia," *Los Angeles Times*, January 17, 2004.

6. Senators Patrick Leahy and Joseph Lieberman to Chief Justice William Rehnquist, January 22, 2004.

7. Rehnquist to Leahy, January 26, 2004; see also Rehnquist on recusals in *Laird v. Tatum*, 408 U.S. 1 (1972).

8. U.S. Reps. Henry A. Waxman and John Conyers, Jr., to Rehnquist, January 30, 2004.

9. Richard Carelli, "Court Issues Recusal Statement," Associated Press, November 1, 1993.

10. U.S. Code Title 28, Section 455.

11. Savage, "Trip with Cheney Puts Ethics Spotlight on Scalia." Follow-up account, David G. Savage and Richard A. Serrano, "Scalia Was Cheney Hunt Trip Guest: Ethics Concern Grows," *Los Angeles Times*, February 5, 2004.

12. Savage, "Trip with Cheney."

13. "High Court Duck Blind," *Washington Post*, January 28, 2004.

14. Matt Sedensky, "Ginsburg Sidesteps Questions on Colleague's Impartiality," Associated Press, February 10, 2004.

15. "Scalia Defends Cheney Trip," Associated Press, February 11, 2004.

16. Meg Scalia, "Scalia Boycott Is Insulting," letter to the editor, February 18, 2004.

17. Author interview with Antonin Scalia, August 26, 2008. He noted that in an incident more than a decade before the Amherst protest, when his daughter Mary was graduating from Bryn Mawr College, some students wore black armbands to the ceremony to protest Scalia's presence at the graduation event. "I was not a featured speaker," Scalia said. "I went there as one of the parents. You can imagine how it made Mary feel. She was so mad about it."

18. Author interview with Meg Scalia, March 29, 2009.

19. Among the headlines that demonstrated the opposition to Scalia's being on the Cheney case and how it drew puns: "If It Walks Like a Duck," *Chicago Tribune*, February 13, 2004; "Scalia Misfires in Cheney Case," *Cincinnati Enquirer*, February 13, 2004; and "Justice Scalia's Misjudgment," *New York Times*, January 25, 2004.

20. "Scalia and Caesar's Wife," *New York Post*, February 10, 2004.

21. Examples cited in request by Sierra Club that Scalia disqualify himself from the case, *Cheney v. United States District Court for the District of Columbia*, No. 03-475.

22. Alan Morrison previously had socialized and vacationed with Scalia. The Cheney case caused a chill in their relations.

23. Author interview with Leonard Leo, January 2, 2007.

24. Antonin Scalia, Memorandum, March 18, 2004, *Cheney v. United States District Court for the District of Columbia.*

25. Maureen Dowd, "Quid Pro Quack," *New York Times*, March 21, 2004.

26. Antonin Scalia, "Is Law Too Complicated for General Media to Cover?" *Chicago Daily Law Bulletin*, October 1, 1990. (Excerpt from speech Scalia gave to the Los Angeles World Affairs Council and Pepperdine University School of Law.)

27. Richard A. Serrano and David G. Savage, "Renewed Focus on Scalia Trip," *Los Angeles Times*, April 25, 2004. See earlier accounts, "Redistricting: The Partisan Games Continue . . . ," *Jackson Clarion-Ledger*, February 28, 2002; Thomas B. Edsall, "Supreme Court Rejects Redistricting Appeal: Democrats Accuse Judges, Justice Dept. of Favoritism in Mississippi Conflict," *Washington Post*, March 2, 2002.

28. Transcript of confirmation hearing on the nomination of Antonin Scalia to the U.S. Court of Appeals for the District of Columbia Circuit, Senate Judiciary Committee, August 4, 1982.

29. Benjamin Weiser and Al Kamen, "How Scalia Faced Ethics Issue: Though a Past Consultant, He Sat on AT&T Case," *Washington Post*, June 22, 1986.

30. "Reaction of Senator Patrick Leahy to Justice Antonin Scalia's Refusal to Recuse Himself from the Cheney Energy Task Force Case," March 18, 2004, statement issued to news media.

31. Don Van Natta, Jr., "Agency Files Suit for Cheney Papers on Energy Policy," *New York Times*, February 23, 2002. (The first lawsuit filed by the General Accounting Office was dismissed, leaving only the Sierra Club and Judicial Watch challenges.) President Bush's spokesman Ari Fleischer said that White House opposition to the document request reflected officials' desire to shore up executive branch prerogatives that Fleischer said had eroded in past decades. "It is about time for somebody in the administration, somebody in the executive branch to stop the slide, where presidential authority, constitutionally vested, has been yielded to Congress, since Watergate and Vietnam," Fleischer said. Bennett Roth and Karen Masterson, "The Fall of Enron: President Backs Refusal to Surrender Energy Files," *Houston Chronicle*, January 29, 2002.

32. Supreme Court transcript, *Cheney v. United States District Court for the District of Columbia*, No. 03-475.

33. *Cheney v. United States District Court for the District of Columbia*, 542 U.S. 367 (2004).

34. *In Re Cheney*, 406 F.3d 723 (D.C. Cir. 2005).

35. Stephanie Reitz, "Scalia Stands by Decision in Cheney Case," Associated Press Online, April 12, 2006.

36. Author interview with Antonin Scalia, August 26, 2008.

37. Author interview with Lenora Panaro, September 11, 2008.

38. Kiran Krishnamurthy, "Scalia: Religion Has Its Place: Justice Criticizes Ruling in Pledge Case," *Richmond Times Dispatch*, January 13, 2003; Gina Holland, "Scalia Discusses Church-State Separation," Associated Press, January 12, 2003.

39. Ibid.

40. A Department of Justice request for a rehearing was pending before the U.S. Court of Appeals for the Ninth Circuit at the time of Scalia's remarks. The Ninth Circuit

rejected the request on February 28, 2003. Federal officials then appealed to the Supreme Court.

41. App. No. 03-7, *Newdow v. United States*, suggestion for Recusal of Justice Scalia, September 5, 2003.

42. The former Scalia clerk Brian T. Fitzpatrick wrote years later that justices should be able to speak freely on issues of the day and that Scalia's pulling out of the Pledge of Allegiance case was a mistake. In an opinion piece for the *National Law Journal* in the context of Scalia's extracurricular remarks in later antiterrorism cases, Fitzpatrick referred to the pledge controversy: "Scalia's mistake was not making the remarks, but agreeing to recuse himself. There is nothing wrong with Supreme Court justices expressing their views on issues pending on the court's docket . . . Supreme Court justices are smart people with interesting things to say. We all stand to benefit when we are permitted to hear them." Brian T. Fitzpatrick, "Scalia's Mistake," *National Law Journal*, April 24, 2006.

43. *Elk Grove Unified School District v. Newdow*, 542 U.S. 1 (2004).

44. Amalie Young, "Scalia: Locals Should Decide on Law," Associated Press, February 10, 2002.

45. *Oregon v. Ashcroft*, 368 F.3d 1118 (9th Cir. 2004).

46. *Gonzales v. Oregon*, 546 U.S. 243 (2006), Scalia, joined by Chief Justice Roberts and Justice Thomas, in dissent.

47. The criticism Scalia faced on *Gonzales v. Oregon* was similar to complaints after the 2005 *Gonzales v. Raich*, which was raised during Scalia's November 2008 Federalist Society appearance (noted in Prologue). See, for example, Mark Moller, "What Was Scalia Thinking?" reasononline, June 14, 2005, www.reason.com/news/show/32933.html, noting that "what baffled many conservatives was the concurring opinion by one Antonin Scalia, who sided with big government against a sane interpretation of the Commerce Clause."

48. Author interview with Antonin Scalia, February 18, 2009.

49. Denise Grones and Melanie Rube said in depositions taken by the U.S. Marshals Service that they had been told they could go to the reception. "Hattiesburg Incident" report of U.S. Marshals Service, May 18, 2004, released December 12, 2007, posted at governmentattic.org.

50. Deposition of Melanie Rube, April 21, 2004, "Hattiesburg Incident" report of U.S. Marshals Service.

51. Deposition of Denise Grones, April 20, 2004, "Hattiesburg Incident" report of U.S. Marshals Service.

52. See, for example, Bob Herbert, "A Justice's Sense of Privilege," *New York Times*, April 12, 2004; "Overprotecting a Justice," *Chicago Tribune*, April 13, 2004; "What Was He Thinking?" *Indiana Lawyer*, April 21, 2004.

53. Barney Frank to Ashcroft, Rehnquist, Scalia, April 9, 2004.

54. Associated Press, "Supreme Court Justice Bans Media from Free Speech Event," March 19, 2003; Henry Weinstein, "Scalia Defends 'Immovable' Constitution," *Los Angeles Times*, January 24, 1997.

55. Scalia to Konz, April 9, 2004.

56. Scalia to Dalglish, April 9, 2004.

57. Deposition of Debra Sanderson, April 23, 2004, "Hattiesburg Incident" report of U.S. Marshals Service.

58. Stan Pottinger interview with Antonin Scalia, 2007, for *Beyond Politics* program. www.plumtv.com/videos/beyond-politics-justice-antonin-scalia/index.html.

59. Joe Conason, "So Who Put the Temper in Judicial Temperament," *New York Observer*, April 2, 2006.

60. Stan Pottinger interview with Antonin Scalia.

13. THE CENTER CHAIR

1. *Webster v. Reproductive Health Services*, 492 U.S. 490 (1989); *Lee v. Weisman*, 505 U.S. 577 (1992); *Romer v. Evans*, 517 U.S. 620 (1996).

2. Scalia dissenting, *Atkins v. Virginia*, 536 U.S. 304 (2002), joined by Rehnquist and Thomas.

3. Scalia dissenting, *Roper v. Simmons*, 543 U.S. 551 (2005), joined by Rehnquist and Thomas.

4. Author interviews with Ruth Bader Ginsburg, September 23, 2004, and John Paul Stevens, October 26, 2004.

5. Author interviews with John Paul Stevens, June 20, 2007, and March 6, 2009.

6. Supreme Court of the United States, Office of Public Information statement, October 25, 2004.

7. Chambers of Chief Justice Rehnquist, statement, November 1, 2004.

8. Jay Ambrose, "Time for Rehnquist to Resign," Scripps Howard News Service, December 16, 2004. The commentary distributed by Scripps Howard newspapers observed, "Rehnquist has served the court honorably and well, but there is no honor in clinging to a job that requires a healthy vigor he clearly lacks."

9. Rehnquist added four gold stripes to each of the sleeves of his black robe in 1995 after seeing a production of Gilbert and Sullivan's *Iolanthe*.

10. John A. Jenkins, "The Partisan," *New York Times Magazine*, March 3, 1985.

11. Staab, *The Political Thought of Justice Antonin Scalia*, 27.

12. *United States v. Dickerson*, 166 F.3d 667 (4th Cir. 1999).

13. *Dickerson v. United States*, 530 U.S. 428 (2000).

14. Together, Scalia and Thomas had dissented in the case of a Louisiana inmate who claimed that his constitutional rights had been violated when prison guards shackled and then punched him as a supervisor looked on. The beating left the inmate with a swollen face, loosened teeth, and a cracked dental plate. The Court ruled that the inmate's treatment violated the Eighth Amendment's prohibition of cruel and unusual punishment; Scalia and Thomas dissented, arguing that the Eighth Amendment was not violated by the "insignificant" harm the inmate suffered. *Hudson v. McMillian*, 503 U.S. 1 (1992). Scalia and Thomas also dissented from a 6–3 decision to ban the Alabama practice of chaining prisoners to outdoor "hitching posts" and abandoning them for hours without food, water, or a chance to use the bathroom. *Hope v. Pelzer*, 536 U.S. 730 (2002).

15. Steven Lubet, "A Liberal Case for Chief Justice Scalia," *Northwestern Observer Online*, January 3, 2005, www.northwestern.edu/observer/issues/2005/01/20/lubet.html.

16. Michael A. Fletcher, "Reid Says He Could Back Scalia for Chief Justice: Comments Anger Liberals and Thomas Supporters," *Washington Post*, December 7, 2004.

17. At the time of their appointments, O'Connor was 51, Scalia was 50, Kennedy was 51, Souter was 51, and Thomas was 43. Bork, who was rejected in 1987, was 60.

18. "Scalia Welcomes Speculation About His Future," Associated Press, February 6, 2005.
19. Dana Milbank, "Scalia Showing His Softer Side," *Washington Post*, March 15, 2005.
20. Margaret Talbot, "Supreme Confidence: The Jurisprudence of Justice Antonin Scalia," *New Yorker*, March 28, 2005.
21. Joan Biskupic, "No Shades of Gray for Scalia," *USA Today*, September 18, 2002.
22. Joan Biskupic, "High Court Justices Hold Rare Public Debate," *USA Today*, January 14, 2005; see also Federal News Service transcript, January 13, 2005.
23. Scalia appearance with Breyer and O'Connor, April 21, 2005, National Archives, Washington, D.C.
24. Warren Richey, "One Scenario: Chief Justice Scalia?" *Christian Science Monitor*, May 13, 2005.
25. Thomas Goldstein, "Further Thoughts on the Elevation Scenario—Justice Scalia," Supreme Court Nomination Blog, June 12, 2005, www.sctnomination.com/movable type/mt-tb.cgi/33.
26. *Almendarez-Torres v. United States*, 523 U.S. 224 (1998).
27. *Apprendi v. New Jersey*, 530 U.S. 466 (2000).
28. Ibid.
29. Author interview with Antonin Scalia, August 26, 2008.
30. Author interview with John Paul Stevens, March 6, 2009.
31. *Blakely v. Washington*, 542 U.S. 296 (2005).
32. Ibid.
33. *United States v. Booker*, 543 U.S. 220 (2005).
34. Author interview with Antonin Scalia, August 26, 2008.
35. *Maryland v. Craig*, 497 U.S. 836 (1990).
36. Scalia was joined in dissent by Justices Brennan, Marshall, and Stevens.
37. Facts drawn from *Crawford v. Washington*, 541 U.S. 36 (2004).
38. Ibid.
39. Author interview with Antonin Scalia, August 26, 2008.
40. Author interviews; Joan Biskupic, "With O'Connor Retiring, Focus Turns to Possible Successor," usatoday.com, July 1, 2005, www.usatoday.com/news/washington/2005-07 -01-oconnor-retirement_x.htm.
41. Joan Biskupic and Toni Locy, "Documents Offer Insights into Roberts' Work in '80s," *USA Today*, August 30, 2005; Joan Biskupic, "Roberts, Rehnquist Compel Comparisons," *USA Today*, September 7, 2005; Tom Brune, "Tilting the Balance of Power: Depending on Roberts' Ideological Views, His Confirmation as Chief Justice Could Alter Court's Makeup," *Newsday*, September 11, 2005.
42. Roberts argued seventeen times before the Supreme Court when he worked in the U.S. Solicitor General's Office during the first President Bush's administration; Roberts argued another twenty-two times before the Court while in private practice.
43. The Senate Judiciary Committee chairman Patrick J. Leahy, a Vermont Democrat, vowed to move quickly on Roberts's nomination and then was among the Democrats who voted for Roberts for chief justice.
44. Jon Stewart, *The Daily Show*. Noted in "Five Jokes," *Los Angeles Times*, July 24, 2005.
45. Author interview with Antonin Scalia, August 26, 2008.
46. Lorraine Woellert, "Why Not Scalia: The Pugnacious Darling of the Right Was Sidelined by the Political Calculus," *BusinessWeek*, September 19, 2005.

47. Senate roll call vote at www.senate.gov/legislative/LIS/roll_call_lists/roll_call_vote _cfm.cfm?congress=109&session=1&vote=00245.
48. Federalist Society annual dinner, Marriott Wardman Park, November 16, 2006.
49. Author interview with Samuel Alito, March 20, 2009. Alito said of the "Sc'Alito" nickname, "I was insulted by it, in the sense that I knew the only reason it was done was because of the fact that we were both Italians."
50. John Roberts appearance, Ronald Reagan Library, Simi Valley, California, March 8, 2006.
51. *Georgia v. Randolph*, 547 U.S. 103 (2006).
52. The decision reversed a lower court ruling that had barred Paul Gregory House from bringing a constitutional claim that his trial lawyer was ineffective. The Court majority, led by Kennedy, who had begun to take O'Connor's role as a swing vote, said that House qualified for an exception to the usual rule, based on his possible innocence. Kennedy emphasized that it was a close case but said that new evidence showing that semen found on the victim was her husband's, not that of House, other evidence, and testimony raised doubts about House's guilt.
53. *House v. Bell*, 547 U.S. 518 (2006).
54. *Gonzales v. Oregon*, 546 U.S. 243 (2006). Justice Thomas wrote a separate dissenting opinion as he signed on to Scalia's.
55. Herman Schwartz, "Legal Legacy," *Nation*, October 12, 2006.
56. See, for example, *Gonzales v. Carhart*, 550 U.S. 124 (2007); *Parents Involved in Community Schools v. Seattle School District No. 1*, 551 U.S. 701 (2007); *Frederick v. Morse*, 551 U.S. 393 (2007).
57. Joan Biskupic, "Roberts Steers Court Right Back to Reagan," *USA Today*, June 29, 2007.

14. SHOWMAN OF THE BENCH

1. Facts of case taken from the decision in *Humphries v. CBOCS West* by the U.S. Court of Appeals for the Seventh Circuit, 474 F.3d 387 (7th Cir. 2007); additional personal information about Humphries supplied by his lawyer, Cynthia Hyndman.
2. Another boss joined the Bradley restaurant the next year, and soon after that, one of Humphries's fellow black workers was fired. Humphries complained again to Cracker Barrel's district manager. The district manager said that Humphries should bring any grievance up with the new boss at the restaurant. Then a week later the district manager fired Humphries. (Chronology of personnel changes from brief filed by U.S. Justice Department, siding with Humphries.)
3. Section 1981 is the law that was at issue in *Patterson v. McLean Credit Union*, discussed at length in Chapter 8.
4. The Justice Department settled this lawsuit against the chain in 2004 with a consent degree that required Cracker Barrel to adopt and implement nondiscrimination policies. "Justice Department Settles Race Discrimination Lawsuit Against Cracker Barrel Restaurant Chain," U.S. Department of Justice Press Release, May 3, 2004. In 2006, as part of another case, Cracker Barrel agreed to pay $2 million for race and sexual harassment at three Illinois restaurants, in Bloomington, Mattoon, and Matteson. "Cracker Barrel to Pay $2 Million for Race and Sexual Harassment at Three Illinois Restaurants," U.S. Equal Employment Opportunity Commission Press Release, March 10, 2006.

5. *Humphries v. CBOCS West*, 474 F.3d 387 (7th Cir. 2007).

6. The question before the Seventh Circuit, and then the Supreme Court, was whether Section 1981, as interpreted in Supreme Court rulings (including the 1989 Patterson case) and then amended by the Civil Rights Act of 1991, applied to claims of retaliation. The Seventh Circuit held that it did.

7. Supreme Court transcript, *CBOCS v. Humphries*, No. 06-1431.

8. Judge Williams, a former prosecutor, was appointed by Ronald Reagan to a trial court and then by Bill Clinton to the appeals court; Judge Posner was appointed by Reagan.

9. Joan Biskupic, "Roberts, Scalia Strike Similar Chords on Court," *USA Today*, April 10, 2007.

10. Clement had been a law clerk to Justice Scalia.

11. "That's idiotic," from oral arguments in *McCreary County v. American Civil Liberties Union of Kentucky*, No. 03-1693; "Golly-woggle," from *Federal Communications Commission v. Fox Television Stations*, No. 07-582.

12. Wrightsman, *Oral Arguments Before the Supreme Court*, 90.

13. Author interview with Antonin Scalia, February 9, 2009.

14. Dahlia Lithwick, "Scalia Hogs the Ball," *Slate*, January 15, 2003; www.slate.com/id/2077031/.

15. Supreme Court transcript, *Nevada Department of Human Resources v. Hibbs*, No. 01-1368.

16. Author interview with Antonin Scalia, February 9, 2009.

17. Wrightsman, *Oral Arguments Before the Supreme Court*, 99.

18. Biskupic, "Roberts, Scalia Strike Similar Chords on Court."

19. Supreme Court transcript, *Schriro v. Landrigan*, No. 05-1575.

20. *Schriro v. Landrigan*, 550 U.S. 465 (2007).

21. Author interview with Antonin Scalia, February 9, 2009.

22. James J. Brudney and Corey Ditslear, "Liberal Justices' Reliance on Legislative History: Principle, Strategy, and the 'Scalia Effect,' " *Berkeley Journal of Employment and Labor Law* 29 (2008): 117–73.

23. Frederick, *Supreme Court and Appellate Advocacy*, 257–58.

24. Supreme Court transcript, *Arlington Central School District Board of Education v. Murphy*, No. 05-18.

25. "A Shot from Justice Scalia," editorial in *Washington Post*, May 2, 2000. See also Tony Mauro, "Court Declares Constitutional War on Congress," *Legal Intelligencer*, May 22, 2000.

26. Supreme Court transcript, *Crawford v. Metropolitan Government of Nashville and Davidson County, Tennessee*, No. 06-1595.

27. Supreme Court transcript, *Chandler v. Miller*, No. 96-126.

28. Supreme Court transcript, *Boumediene v. Bush*, No. 06-1195.

29. Supreme Court transcript, *Taylor v. Sturgell*, No. 07-371.

30. Supreme Court transcript, *Arthur Andersen v. United States*, No. 04-368.

31. Supreme Court transcript, *Owasso Independent School District No. I-011 v. Falvo*, No. 00-1073. The justices ruled that peer grading did not violate the Family Educational Rights and Privacy Act of 1974. *Owasso Independent School District No. I-011 v. Falvo*, 543 U.S. 426 (2002).

32. The Court jointly heard the case of Toledo-Flores with an appeal brought by Jose Antonio Lopez, a Mexican national who became a legal permanent resident in 1990 and was convicted in South Dakota of aiding and abetting possession of cocaine.

33. In the end, the Court dismissed the Toledo-Flores case as improvidently granted, with no other comment. Separately, in the companion case of Lopez, the Court ruled 8–1 that a foreign national living here legally should not be automatically deported if he is convicted of a low-level drug offense that would be a misdemeanor in federal law. *Toledo-Flores v. United States*, 549 U.S. 69 (2006); *Lopez v. Gonzales*, 549 U.S. 47 (2006).

34. The *Legal Times* Supreme Court correspondent Tony Mauro reported that Carlos Ortiz, former president of the Hispanic National Bar Association, said, when the "tequila" line was related to him, "Justice Scalia is supposed to be very smart, but anyone who is supposed to be so smart would not and should not say something that insensitive." Tony Mauro, "Scalia's 'Tequila' Remark Raises Eyebrows During Immigrants' Rights Argument," Law.com, October 4, 2006, www.law.com/jsp/article.jsp?id= 900005551433.

35. Dahlia Lithwick, "Tequila Mockingbird: Justice Scalia Opens the 2006 Term with a Bang," *Slate*, October 3, 2006, www.slate.com/id/2150905/nav/tap1.

36. Jerry Crimmins, "Justice Scalia Gives 'Em Slings and Errors in Speech," *Chicago Daily Law Bulletin*, September 17, 2008.

37. Author interview with Antonin Scalia, February 9, 2009.

38. Jay D. Wexler, "Laugh Track," *The Green Bag* 9, no. 1 (2005).

39. Adam Liptak, "So, A Guy Walks Up to the Bar, and Scalia Says . . . ," *New York Times*, December 31, 2005.

40. Wrightsman, *Oral Arguments Before the Supreme Court*, 91.

41. Supreme Court transcript, *Danforth v. Minnesota*, No. 06-8273.

42. Author interview with Ruth Bader Ginsburg, March 29, 2007.

43. Joan Biskupic, "Nothing Subtle About Scalia," *Washington Post*, February 18, 1997.

44. Supreme Court transcript, *Kansas v. Marsh*, No. 04-1170. (The case was being reargued, in April 2006, after Justice Alito had joined the Court.)

45. The Pew Forum on Religion and Public Life, January 25, 2002. Transcript posted at http://pewforum.org/deathpenalty/resources/transcript3.php.

46. See, for example, the dueling dissenting opinions of Justices O'Connor and Scalia in *Roper v. Simmons*, 543 U.S. 551 (2005).

47. Scalia and Roberts voted together more often than Scalia and Rehnquist had, just as Scalia and Alito were in sync on cases more than Scalia and O'Connor had been. In the first full term of Roberts and Alito on the bench, 2006–07, Scalia and Roberts agreed 89 percent in the nonunanimous cases; Scalia and Alito agreed 81 percent. SCOTUSblog End-of-Term statistics.

48. *CBOCS West v. Humphries*, 553 U.S. __ (2008).

49. *Nevada Department of Human Resources v. Hibbs*, 538 U.S. 721 (2003).

50. *Arlington Central School District Board of Education v. Murphy*, 548 U.S. 291 (2006).

51. In the consolidated cases of *Davis v. Washington* and *Hammon v. Indiana*, the Court ruled that a victim's emergency 911 call can be used at trial even if the victim does not testify, but if a victim recounts an incident to police at the scene after it has occurred, the account cannot be used at trial unless the victim is available for cross-examination. Scalia's opinion drew a line between statements made in emergencies, which would be permitted at trial, and those gathered by police after an incident has occurred "to establish or prove past events." *Davis v. Washington*, 547 U.S. 813 (2006).

15. POWER IN A TIME OF TERRORISM

1. Scalia had long enjoyed international travel. He visited several countries on the Sheldon Fellowship after graduating from Harvard Law School. As an assistant attorney general in the Ford administration he regularly volunteered for trips to foreign legal seminars, and as an appeals court judge he signed up for overseas trips sponsored by legal groups.

2. Scalia's March trip to Switzerland followed a January trip to Jerusalem for a legal conference. He would then travel to Sorrento, Italy, in July, to teach in a Hofstra University overseas program. Scalia also would travel to more than twenty domestic locales for conferences and lectures, according to his financial disclosure form for calendar year 2006.

3. For example, a CNN/*USA Today* Gallup Poll taken March 10–12, 2006, found that 60 percent of Americans polled said it was "not worth going to war in Iraq," 37 percent said it was worth going to war, and 3 percent were unsure. Two years earlier, in a poll taken March 26–28, 2004, only 41 percent said it was not worth it, 56 percent said it was, and 3 percent were unsure.

4. Michael Isikoff, "Supreme Court: Detainees' Rights—Scalia Speaks His Mind," *Newsweek* online, March 26, 2006, www.newsweek.com/id/45947. Published in *Newsweek*, April 3, 2006.

5. David H. Remes to Supreme Court clerk William K. Suter, March 27, 2006, in *Hamdan v. Rumsfeld*, No. 05-184.

6. John King interview with Dick Cheney, CNN, January 28, 2002.

7. Matthew Scalia, "On the Streets of Baghdad: A Soldier's Story About Building Democracy in Iraq, Neighborhood by Neighborhood," *Legal Times*, October 25, 2004.

8. Author interview with Antonin Scalia, February 9, 2009.

9. Ibid.

10. Marie Brenner, "Taking on Guantánamo," *Vanity Fair*, March 2007.

11. "Scalia's Ill-Chosen Words: Justice Crosses the Line—Again," *Philadelphia Inquirer*, March 31, 2006.

12. "The Over-the-Top Justice," *New York Times*, April 2, 2006.

13. *Republican Party of Minnesota v. White*, 536 U.S. 765 (2002).

14. Justice Department lawyers used the phrase as they urged the Supreme Court not to take up Hamdi's appeal. Brief in Opposition, *Hamdi v. Rumsfeld*, No. 03-6696. Government lawyers used similar arguments when the case was accepted for hearing.

15. *Hamdi v. Rumsfeld*, 542 U.S. 507 (2004). Signing O'Connor's opinion were Rehnquist, Kennedy, and Breyer. Justice Thomas separately provided a fifth vote for a majority, holding that the congressional Authorization for Use of Military Force allowed Hamdi's detention.

16. O'Connor opinion for the plurality, *Hamdi v. Rumsfeld*, 542 U.S. 507 (2004).

17. Richard H. Fallon, Jr., and Daniel J. Meltzer, "Habeas Corpus Jurisdiction, Substantive Rights, and the War on Terror," *Harvard Law Review* 120 (June 2007): 2029.

18. *Rasul v. Bush*, 542 U.S. 466 (2004).

19. Pfiffner, *Power Play*, 99. Pfiffner notes that the secretive drafting process excluded such Cabinet-level officials as Colin Powell and Condoleezza Rice.

20. Andrew Rudalevige, "The Contemporary Presidency: The Decline and Resurgence and Decline (and Resurgence?) of Congress: Charting a New Imperial Presidency," *Presidential Studies Quarterly* 36 (September 2006): 506.

21. Jane Mayer, "The Hidden Power: The Legal Mind Behind the White House's War on Terror," *New Yorker*, July 3, 2006; Scott Shane, David Johnston, and James Risen, "Secret U.S. Endorsement of Severe Interrogations," *New York Times*, October 4, 2007.

22. Ibid. See also "Cheney Reflects on Legacy: Defends Interrogation Policy," *NewsHour with Jim Lehrer*, January 14, 2009. www.pbs.org/newshour/bb/politics/jan-june09/Cheney _01-14.html.

23. David Cole, "Why the Court Said No," *New York Review of Books*, August 10, 2006.

24. Supreme Court transcript, *Hamdan v. Rumsfeld*, No. 05-184.

25. *Hamdan v. Rumsfeld*, 548 U.S. 557 (2006).

26. Scalia strongly expressed this view in a concurring opinion in *Kansas v. Marsh*, 548 U.S. 163 (2006), issued three days before the *Hamdan* decision. He criticized dissenting justices for considering international opinion on the death penalty and declared, "There exists in some parts of the world sanctimonious criticism of America's death penalty, as somehow unworthy of a civilized society. (I say sanctimonious, because most of the countries to which these finger-waggers belong had the death penalty themselves until recently—and indeed, many of them would still have it if the democratic will prevailed.)"

27. "A Supreme Court Conversation," *Slate*, June 30, 2006, www.slate.com/id/2144476.

28. Barton Gellman and Jo Becker, "The Unseen Path to Cruelty," *Washington Post*, June 25, 2007; William Glaberson, "Bin Laden's Former Driver Is Convicted in Split Verdict," *New York Times*, August 6, 2008.

29. "Cheney, Scalia Socialized While Supreme Court Decided Case," Associated Press, January 17, 2004 (noting that the *Star Democrat* of Easton, Maryland, and the *Daily Times* of Salisbury, Maryland, first reported on the Eastern Shore dinner of Scalia, Cheney, Rumsfeld). For further accounts of Scalia and Cheney socializing, see chapter 12.

30. Author interview with Antonin Scalia, February 18, 2009.

31. Colin Freeze, "What Would Jack Bauer Do?" *Globe and Mail*, June 16, 2007.

32. Author interview with Antonin Scalia, February 9, 2008.

33. Ibid.

34. Author interview with Antonin Scalia, February 18, 2009.

35. Mark Sherman, "Breyer Cites Israeli Court Decision Outlawing Torture," Associated Press, April 15, 2008.

36. *Boumediene v. Bush*, 533 U.S. ___ (2008).

37. After his return from Iraq, Major Matthew Scalia taught in the ROTC program at the University of Delaware.

38. Ronald Dworkin, "Why It Was a Great Victory," *New York Review of Books*, August 14, 2008.

39. Author interview with Antonin Scalia, February 18, 2009.

16. "YOU GET ONE SHOT"

1. Author interview with Antonin Scalia, June 24, 2008.

2. Author interview with Stephen Breyer, June 2, 2009.

3. Author interview with Antonin Scalia, February 18, 2009.

4. Clay Carey, "Scalia Champions Hunting and Conservation," *Tennessean*, February 26, 2006.

5. Author interview with Clarence Thomas, June 24, 2009.

6. Alito breaks from Scalia particularly on the use of legislative history in interpreting

statutes and, in the constitutional realm, on disputes over defendants' jury trial and confrontation rights.

7. Author interview with Samuel Alito, March 20, 2009.
8. Robert Levy, who was a senior fellow in constitutional studies and then became chairman of the Cato Institute, was at the center of the effort. The original lead plaintiff was Shelly Parker, which is why the case was known in early phases as *Parker v. District of Columbia*.
9. Transcript of *MacNeil-Lehrer NewsHour*, December 16, 1991.
10. *Parker v. District of Columbia*, 478 F.3d 370 (D.C. Cir. 2007).
11. *USA Today*/Gallup Poll February 2008; Joan Biskupic, "Do You Have a Legal Right to Own a Gun?" *USA Today*, February 27, 2008.
12. Author interview with Clarence Thomas, June 24, 2009.
13. *District of Columbia v. Heller*, 554 U.S. ___ (2008).
14. Stevens dissenting, *District of Columbia v. Heller*.
15. By June 2009, three of those lower court cases were on appeal to the U.S. Supreme Court, from disputes over weapons regulations in Illinois and New York. It appeared that the high Court could take up a case related to *Heller*'s implications in the near future.
16. Stevens dissenting, *District of Columbia v. Heller*.
17. Breyer dissenting, *District of Columbia v. Heller*.
18. Richard A. Posner, "In Defense of Looseness," *New Republic*, August 27, 2008.
19. Ibid.
20. J. Harvie Wilkinson III, "Of Guns, Abortions, and the Unraveling Rule of Law," *Virginia Law Review* 95 (2009): 254.
21. Author interview with Antonin Scalia, February 18, 2009.
22. Breyer, *Active Liberty*, 117.
23. Author interview with Samuel Alito, March 20, 2009.
24. Eisgruber, *The Next Justice*, 40–41.
25. Dawn Johnsen, "The Progressive Political Power of Balkin's 'Original Meaning,'" *Constitutional Commentary* 24 (2007): 417.
26. Edward Lazarus, "Four Myths About the Supreme Court," *Time*, June 8, 2009.
27. *Crawford v. Davis*, 541 U.S. 36 (2004); see detail of the case in chapter 13.
28. *Giles v. California*, 554 U.S. ___ (2008).
29. *Melendez-Diaz v. Massachusetts*, slip opinion No. 07-591, June 25, 2009.
30. Author interviews with Ruth Bader Ginsburg, March 29, 2007, and March 10, 2009.
31. *Baze v. Rees*, 553 U.S. ___ (2008). In the opinion for the majority, Roberts detailed the history of execution methods, including firing squads, gas chambers, and the electric chair. He noted that the court has never invalidated a state's chosen procedure for carrying out a death sentence. The chief justice said that prisoners would have to show that the method presented a "substantial" or "objectively intolerable" risk of harm to the prisoner.
32. Dissenting in *Baze v. Rees* were Justices Ginsburg and Souter. They said, "Kentucky's protocol lacks basic safeguards used by other states to confirm that an inmate is unconscious before injection of the second and third drugs."
33. Stevens concurring, *Baze v. Rees*.
34. Scalia concurring, *Baze v. Rees*.
35. Brian Haas, "U.S. Supreme Court Justice Shows Confidence, Combativeness at West Palm Beach Forum," *South Florida Sun-Sentinel*, February 4, 2009.
36. Author interview with Antonin Scalia, February 9, 2009.

37. Joan Biskupic, "Ginsburg: Court Needs Another Woman," *USA Today*, May 6, 2009. Ginsburg also recalled that as a young lawyer her voice often was ignored by male peers. "I don't know how many meetings I attended in the '60s and the '70s, where I would say something, and I thought it was a pretty good idea . . . Then somebody else would say exactly what I said. Then people would become alert to it, respond to it." She said that even after sixteen years as a justice, that still sometimes occurred. "It can happen even in the conferences in the court. When I will say something—and I don't think I'm a confused speaker—and it isn't until somebody else says it that everyone will focus on the point."

38. Joan Biskupic and Martha Moore, "From Humble Roots, a Court Nominee in Obama's Image," *USA Today*, May 27, 2009.

39. *Almanac of the Federal Judiciary 2009* 2 (Aspen Publishers): 23–25.

40. Joan Biskupic, "Sotomayor's 'Courtesy Calls' Not Photo Ops," *USA Today*, June 19, 2009.

41. Nina Totenberg, report on National Public Radio's *Morning Edition*, June 15, 2009.

42. "Double Standard: Funny How the Achievements on Sonia Sotomayor's Resume Suddenly Count for So Little," *Washington Post* editorial, June 2, 2009; Joe Conason, "Sotomayor Attacks Quick, Predictable," *Chicago Sun-Times*, June 1, 2009.

43. Author interview with Clarence Thomas, June 24, 2009.

44. Peter Baker, "Favorites of Left Don't Make Obama's Court List," *New York Times*, May 25, 2009.

45. Adam Liptak, "On the Bench and Off, the Eminently Quotable Justice Scalia," *New York Times*, May 12, 2009.

46. C-SPAN transcript of Steve Scully interview with President Obama, May 22, 2009, www.c-span.org/pdf/obamainterview.pdf.

47. Joan Biskupic, "Supreme Court Case with the Feel of a Best Seller," *USA Today*, February 17, 2009. The case began in 1997 when Massey canceled a contract Hugh Caperton's Harman Mining had to supply a plant in Pennsylvania. Caperton sued, alleging fraud, unlawful interference with his business dealings, and other grievances. A Boone County, West Virginia, jury sided with Caperton and Harman, and awarded a total of $50 million in compensatory and punitive damages.

48. Antonin Scalia, Memorandum, March 18, 2004, *Cheney v. United States District Court for the District of Columbia*.

49. Transcript in *Caperton v. A. T. Massey Coal Co.*, No. 08-22.

50. *Caperton v. A. T. Massey Coal Co.*, slip opinion No. 08-22.

51. Scalia dissenting, *Caperton v. A. T. Massey Coal Co.*

52. *Federal Communications Commission v. Fox Network*, slip opinion No. 07-582.

53. Brian Lamb interview with Antonin Scalia, C-SPAN, May 4, 2008.

54. Robb London, "At HLS, Scalia Offers Vigorous Defense of Originalism," *Harvard Law Today*, February 2007.

55. "Rep. Frank Calls Justice Scalia a 'Homophobe' in Interview," Associated Press, March 25, 2009.

56. Author interviews with Ruth Bader Ginsburg, March 29, 2007, and March 20, 2009; author interview with John Paul Stevens, March 6, 2009.

57. Author interview with Antonin Scalia, February 18, 2009.

58. Author interviews with Antonin Scalia, February 18, 2009, and July 22, 2009.

59. *Ricci v. DeStefano*, slip opinion Nos. 07-1428, 08-328.

60. The Supreme Court announced on June 29, 2009, that it would decide in the near future whether to uphold federal restrictions of corporate spending in elections, in the face of a First Amendment challenge in the case of *Citizens United v. Federal Election Commission*, No. 08-205.
61. Author interview with Stephen Breyer, June 2, 2009.
62. Author interview with Clarence Thomas, June 24, 2009.

SELECTED BIBLIOGRAPHY

ARCHIVES
Brooklyn College, Archives and Special Collections Division
Gerald R. Ford Library
George E. MacKinnon Papers, Minnesota Historical Society
Georgetown University Libraries, Special Collections and Archives
Harry A. Blackmun Papers, Library of Congress
J. Skelly Wright Papers, Library of Congress
Laurence H. Silberman Papers, Hoover Institution
Lewis F. Powell, Jr. Archives, Washington and Lee University
New Jersey Department of State, Division of Archives and Records Management
Ronald Reagan Library
Thurgood Marshall Papers, Library of Congress
Trentonian Room, Trenton Public Library
University of Chicago Law Library, Special Collections
William J. Brennan, Jr., Papers, Library of Congress

NEWSPAPERS, MAGAZINES, JOURNALS, AND PRESS AGENCIES
American Lawyer, American Prospect, Associated Press, *Boston Globe, Boston Herald, Chicago Daily Law Bulletin, Chicago Tribune, Christian Science Monitor, Commonweal, Congressional Quarterly Weekly Report, Economist, Harvard Law Record, Legal Times, Los Angeles Times, Nation, National Law Journal, National Journal, New Republic, New York Review of Books, National Review, New York Times, New Yorker, Newsweek, Philadelphia Inquirer, Regulation, Rocky Mountain News, Newsday, Slate, Trenton State Gazette, Wall Street Journal, Washington Monthly, Washington Post, USA Today*

LAW REVIEWS
Arkansas Law Review, California Law Review, Cardozo Law Review, University of Chicago Law Review, University of Cincinnati Law Review, Harvard Journal of Law & Public Policy, Harvard Law Review, University of Hawaii Law Review, Indiana Law Journal, Journal of Law

*and Politics, New York University Annual Survey of American Law, Notre Dame Law Review,
Stanford Law Review, Supreme Court Review, Virginia Law Review, Washington University
Law Quarterly, Yale Law Journal*

BOOKS

Barzini, Luigi. *The Italians: A Full-Length Portrait Featuring Their Manners and Morals.*
New York: Touchstone, 1996.

Biskupic, Joan. *Sandra Day O'Connor: How the First Woman on the Supreme Court Became
Its Most Influential Justice.* New York: HarperCollins, 2005.

Boies, David. *Courting Justice: From NY Yankees v. Major League Baseball to Bush v. Gore
1997–2000.* New York: Miramax, 2004.

Bork, Robert. *The Tempting of America.* New York: Free Press, 1997.

———, ed. *A Country I Do Not Recognize: The Liberal Assault on American Values.* Stanford, California: Hoover Press, 2005.

Breyer, Stephen. *Active Liberty: Interpreting Our Democratic Constitution.* New York: Alfred
A. Knopf, 2005.

Brisbin, Richard A., Jr. *Justice Antonin Scalia and the Conservative Revival.* Baltimore: Johns
Hopkins University Press, 1997.

Bronner, Ethan. *Battle for Justice.* New York: Union Square Press, 2007.

Buchanan, Patrick J. *Right from the Beginning.* New York: Little Brown, 1988.

Eisgruber, Christopher L. *The Next Justice: Repairing the Supreme Court Appointments
Process.* Princeton: Princeton University Press, 2007.

Fisher, Louis. *The Politics of Executive Privilege.* Durham, North Carolina: Carolina Academic Press, 2004.

Frederick, David C. *Supreme Court and Appellate Advocacy.* St. Paul: Thomson/West, 2003.

Greenburg, Jan Crawford. *Supreme Conflict: The Inside Struggle for Control of the United
States Supreme Court.* New York: Penguin Press, 2007.

Greenhouse, Linda. *Becoming Justice Blackmun: Harry Blackmun's Supreme Court Journey.*
New York: Times Books, 2005.

Hartmann, Robert T. *Palace Politics: An Inside Account of the Ford Years.* New York:
McGraw-Hill Book Company, 1980.

Horwitz, Morton J. *The Warren Court and the Pursuit of Justice.* New York: Hill and Wang,
1998.

Hutchinson, Dennis J. *The Man Who Once Was Whizzer White: Portrait of Justice Byron R.
White.* New York: The Free Press, 1998.

Irons, Peter. *Brennan vs. Rehnquist: The Battle for the Constitution.* New York: Alfred A.
Knopf, 1994.

Jeffries, John C., Jr. *Justice Lewis F. Powell, Jr. and the Era of Judicial Balance.* New York:
Scribner, 1994.

Karabel, Jerome. *The Chosen: The Hidden History of Admission and Exclusion at Harvard,
Yale, and Princeton.* New York: Houghton Mifflin, 2005.

Keck, Thomas M. *The Most Activist Supreme Court in History: The Road to Modern Judicial
Conservatism.* Chicago: University of Chicago Press, 2004.

Kennedy, David M. *Freedom from Fear: The American People in Depression and War, 1929–
1945.* New York: Oxford University Press, 1999.

Klarman, Michael J. *From Jim Crow to Civil Rights: The Supreme Court and the Struggle for
Racial Equality.* New York: Oxford University Press, 2004.

Mahler, Jonathan. *The Challenge: Hamdan v. Rumsfeld and the Fight over Presidential Power.* New York: Farrar, Straus and Giroux, 2008.

Mangione, Jerre, and Ben Morreale. *La Storia: Five Centuries of the Italian American Experience.* New York: Harper Perennial, 1993.

Mann, James. *Rise of the Vulcans: The History of Bush's War Cabinet.* New York: Viking, 2004.

Margulies, Joseph. *Guantánamo and the Abuse of Presidential Power.* New York: Simon & Schuster, 2006.

Meese, Edwin III. *With Reagan: The Inside Story.* Washington, D.C.: Regnery, 1992.

Murdoch, Joyce, and Deb Price. *Courting Justice: Gay Men and Lesbians v. the Supreme Court.* New York: Basic Books, 2001.

O'Neill, Jonathan. *Originalism in American Law and Politics: A Constitutional History.* Baltimore: Johns Hopkins University Press, 2005.

Pearlstine, Norman. *Off the Record: The Press, the Government, and the War over Anonymous Sources.* New York: Farrar, Straus and Giroux, 2007.

Perlstein, Rick. *Nixonland: The Rise of a President and the Fracturing of America.* New York: Scribner, 2008.

Pfiffner, James P. *Power Play: The Bush Presidency and the Constitution.* Washington, D.C.: Brookings Institution Press, 2008.

Regan, Donald T. *For the Record: From Wall Street to Washington.* New York: Harcourt, 1988.

Rossum, Ralph A. *Antonin Scalia's Jurisprudence: Text and Tradition.* Lawrence: University of Kansas Press, 2006.

Savage, Charlie. *Takeover: The Return of the Imperial Presidency and the Subversion of American Democracy.* New York: Little, Brown, 2007.

Savage, David G. *Turning Right: The Making of the Rehnquist Supreme Court.* New York: John Wiley, 1993.

Scalia, Antonin. *A Matter of Interpretation: Federal Courts and the Law.* Edited by Amy Gutmann. Princeton: Princeton University Press, 1997.

Scalia, Antonin, and Bryan A. Garner. *Making Your Case: The Art of Persuading Judges.* St. Paul: Thomson/West, 2008.

Schwartz, Herman. *Packing the Courts.* New York: Scribner, 1988.

Smith, William French. *Law and Justice in the Reagan Administration: The Memoir of an Attorney General.* Stanford, California: Hoover Press, 1991.

Specter, Arlen. *Passion for Truth: From Finding JFK's Single Bullet to Questioning Anita Hill to Impeaching Clinton.* New York: William Morrow, 2000.

Staab, James B. *The Political Thought of Justice Antonin Scalia: A Hamiltonian on the Supreme Court.* Lanham, Maryland: Rowman & Littlefield Publishing, 2006.

Sunstein, Cass R.. *A Constitution of Many Minds: Why the Founding Document Doesn't Mean What It Meant Before.* Princeton: Princeton University Press, 2009.

———. *Radicals in Robes: Why Extreme Right-Wing Courts Are Wrong for America.* New York: Basic Books, 2005.

Teles, Steven M. *The Rise of the Conservative Legal Movement.* Princeton: Princeton University Press, 2008.

Thomas, Clarence. *My Grandfather's Son: A Memoir.* New York: Harper, 2007.

Thomas, Evan. *The Man to See.* New York: Simon and Schuster, 1991.

Toobin, Jeffrey. *The Nine: Inside the Secret World of the Supreme Court.* New York: Doubleday, 2007.

————. *Too Close to Call: The Thirty-Six-Day Battle to Decide the 2000 Election.* New York: Random House, 2001.

Tushnet, Mark. *A Court Divided: The Rehnquist Court and the Future of Constitutional Law.* New York: W. W. Norton, 2005.

Wallison, Peter J. *Ronald Reagan: The Power of Conviction and the Success of His Presidency.* Boulder, Colorado: Westview Press, 2003.

Williams, Juan. *Thurgood Marshall: American Revolutionary.* New York: Random House, 1998.

Wittes, Benjamin. *Law and the Long War: The Future of Justice in the Age of Terror.* New York: Penguin, 2008.

Woodward, Bob, and Carl Bernstein. *The Final Days.* New York: Touchstone, 1987.

Wrightsman, Lawrence S. *Oral Arguments Before the Supreme Court: An Empirical Study.* New York: Oxford University Press, 2008.

ACKNOWLEDGMENTS

The genesis of this book traces back to a dinner in March 2006 hosted by the University of Virginia professor of government Henry Abraham, a longtime chronicler of justices and presidents. He and our companions persuaded me that the time was right for a comprehensive look at this singular justice who manages to inspire simultaneous admiration and wrath and whose influence continues to grow. I had been covering Antonin Scalia for nearly two decades, for *Congressional Quarterly*, *The Washington Post*, and *USA Today*, and my first in-depth interview with him was in 1990. In the years since that Charlottesville evening, I have tried to understand more deeply how Justice Scalia became such a force in America. The backbone of my research grew out of documents in judicial and presidential archives and more than a hundred interviews—a dozen with Justice Scalia. He was generous with his time and candor, and he encouraged colleagues, friends, and relatives to talk to me. For that, I am extremely grateful.

As my project progressed, numerous professional colleagues, friends, and family members were unstinting with their advice and encouragement. The words of appreciation that follow do not adequately express my gratitude to the people who sustained me—especially my husband and daughter—through this book project.

Five individuals must be singled out at the start because they offered the perfect complement of expertise and experience for a book about Justice Scalia. Richard Taranto, a Supreme Court and appellate litigator and a former Supreme Court law clerk, was a source of constant intellectual guidance and legal precision. It is difficult to overstate how much Richard contributed to this book—in time and wisdom, from start to finish. I sought out George Lardner, a former colleage from *The Washington Post*, for his knowledge about the Nixon and Ford years, but soon discovered that he had grown up in Queens not far from Scalia and attended a rival Jesuit high school (Regis). Throughout, George was generous with his expertise. Andrea Weiswasser brought her lawyer's sensibility and sharp literary eye to this project, and her constant enthusiasm was inspiring. Dennis Flannery, a former law clerk to Chief Justice Earl Warren, who coincidentally also grew up near Scalia and went to Regis, read the chapters with an instinct for the larger judicial history. Finally, Erwin Chemerinsky, dean of the law school at the University of California, Irvine, was always ready with advice and insights on the contemporary Court and how much Scalia has changed the terms of debate. These five friends read virtually everything, and some of them read everything twice. None of them, it should be emphasized, is responsible for any errors.

Several other thoughtful colleagues read portions of the manuscript and offered invaluable guidance, especially in the early, difficult drafting stage: Douglas D. Armstrong, Lou Cannon, Dick Carelli, Jim Drinkard, Alan Ehrenhalt, Pam Fessler, Dennis Hutchinson, Phyllis Richman, and David Savage. David, a reporter for the *Los Angeles Times*, is one of my most supportive colleagues in the Supreme Court press corps. Other journalists who went above and beyond with notes from their files and personal encouragement were Bob Barnes, Linda Greenhouse, Adam Liptak, Tony Mauro, Mark Sherman, Nina Totenberg, and Pete Williams. So much of their smart reporting informs this book. Justice Scalia has been the subject of countless profiles over the years. Two that stand out and remain relevant bear mentioning: Joe Morgenstern's, for *Playboy* in 1992, and Margaret Talbot's, for *The New Yorker* in 2005.

The Woodrow Wilson International Center for Scholars offered me an in-residence fellowship and a place for much of my research. I am grateful to the director, Lee Hamilton, and the deputy director, Michael Van Dusen, for their continued interest in my books on the Supreme Court. The Wilson Center provided me with a top-flight researcher, Edward Lawrence, who worked with me for several months at the Center and then rejoined me as a researcher in early 2009 as this project was racing toward its finish.

USA Today, which indulged lengthy leaves of absence for my biography of Justice Sandra Day O'Connor, generously allowed me two more leaves to work on this book. I am indebted to the editor John Hillkirk, his predecessor Ken Paulson, the managing editor for news, Carol Stevens, and the legal affairs editor, Rachel Smolkin. Many colleagues at *USA Today* have been encouraging throughout this project: at the top of the list is the Washington bureau chief, Susan Page, and the reporters Kevin Johnson, Kathy Kiely, and Alan Levin.

At the Supreme Court, Public Information Officer Kathy Arberg and her deputy, Patricia McCabe Estrada, were swift in running down information and helping to arrange interviews. The Court photographer Steve Petteway was diligent throughout in digging out photographs from Justice Scalia's life.

Most important at the Court, the access provided by Justice Scalia, and his blunt honesty, made this book. He; his wife, Maureen; and the children I contacted were similarly generous with their time and patient with my requests. Justice Scalia's administrative assistant, Angela Frank, was a tireless sleuth in helping to track down elusive facts and resolve discrepancies in earlier published reports. My appreciation to Angela knows no bounds. A special note of thanks is due Justice Scalia's aunt Lenora Panaro, who opened her home and spilled out her memories. One of the most satisfying aspects of my research involved taking the train up to Trenton to hear stories from the dynamic woman fondly known in the Scalia family as "the Babe."

I have been guided in my approach to Justice Scalia by the late literary biographer Leon Edel's challenge to be "cold as ice in appraisal yet warm and human and understanding." Justice Scalia can be a polarizing figure who inspires strong reactions. I have worked hard to be both fair to him and true to the readers of this book.

My editor at Farrar, Straus and Giroux is the incomparable Sarah Crichton. Sarah understood where I wanted to go with this project and helped me get there with her intelligent touch and innate sense of storytelling. She also was a hell of a lot of fun. Cailey Hall, Sarah's editorial assistant, helped keep the project on schedule, connecting me and Sarah at crunch times and across travel itineraries and time zones. Cailey's successor, Daniel Piepenbring, did the same in the last days of production. I could not be happier with the Sarah Crichton Books imprint. My agent,

Gail Ross, and her deputy, Howard Yoon, shaped the book proposal in 2006 and connected me with Sarah and FSG, which has made all the difference.

Finally, my very large, far-flung family, especially my parents, Vince and Mary Jane Biskupic, were encouraging throughout. My father, a lawyer, voracious reader, and man of many interests, sent a stream of news clippings from legal and other periodicals. In the Racing Form, he discovered a horse named Scalia and was certain a connection must exist between the justice and this horse, whose sire was named Holy Bull. Justice Scalia had never heard of the horse and doubted any link. But the Lexington, Kentucky, breeder told me he chose the name as a tribute to the likeminded justice after the ruling in *Bush v. Gore*. I decided that little discovery—tracing to my pony-playing father who died as this book was nearing completion—would simply have to make these pages, even if at the end.

All the way through this project, the most sustaining influences have been my husband, Clay Lewis, and our daughter, Elizabeth. They put up with much more than the piles of papers, stacks of books, clutter of recordings, manila folders, and three-ring binders that took over spare bedrooms, the dining room, and, near the end, ate the whole house. They cheerfully indulged all my deadlines and distractions. Their enthusiasm fueled this project. They are my first readers.

INDEX

A NOTE ABOUT THE AUTHOR

Joan Biskupic has covered the Supreme Court since 1989 and currently writes for *USA Today*. Previously the Supreme Court reporter for *The Washington Post*, she is a frequent panelist on PBS's *Washington Week*. Biskupic earned her law degree from Georgetown University Law Center. She is also the author of *Sandra Day O'Connor: How the First Woman on the Supreme Court Became Its Most Influential Justice* and several legal reference books, including a *Congressional Quarterly* two-volume encyclopedia on the Supreme Court. She lives in Washington, D.C., with her husband and daughter.

HAMPSTEAD PUBLIC LIBRARY